GRAHAM BONNET
The Story Behind The Shades

Steve Wright

Graham on tour in Japan 2015.

FOREWORD

The first time I met Graham Bonnet was February 1979, in the dungeon of financier Bernie Cornfeld's Chateau in the Haute Savoie in France. Rainbow were recording an album there using the Red Bus mobile, as you do, and the cellar was where Ritchie Blackmore had set up his Marshalls and where the 2 Leslie Cabinets for the Hammond Organ resided. Graham had just flown in from the UK to audition and was brought down by tour manager Colin Hart to say hello.

Rainbow had been recording for about five weeks with a variety of singers who'd come and gone with astonishing regularity – no-one stayed long enough to imprint their musicality on the nascent album it has to be said, just long enough to acquire a posthumous nickname such as '*S.A.S*', '*The Waiter*', '*Nice Guy*' and '*Mr. Trucker*'. Graham, with his short hair, nervous manner, and quizzical stare looked the least likely of the lot to succeed, and the thought occurred that it wouldn't be long before the name 'James Dean' was added to the roll of dishonour. Nevertheless in our first conversation it became clear he had absolutely no idea who Ritchie was, or Deep Purple, or Rainbow for that matter, which was enormously heartening.

We went to the keyboards and briefly ran through 'Mistreated'. He took a cassette and went upstairs for an hour to recover from his journey, and learn the song. The band then convened in the minstrel hall, where the equipment was set up, and Graham came down to join us, looking as though he was being lead to the scaffold. After brief pleasantries we kicked into the intro of the song - dat Dah, dat Dah, dat Dah, Dah Dah, and like an earthquake, completely out of the blue, with astonishing impact, in came Graham singing "I've been mis –" - Ritchie looked up stunned, Cozy's face became wreathed in a huge smile, Roger Glover stopped playing and yours truly nearly fell off the organ stool. With three syllables Graham had got the job! The song ground to a halt in confusion with the singist (as he refers to himself) looking slightly non-plussed. All I could think to say was "Do you want to try it again with a microphone?!"

Try it again we did, then we jammed on Elvis Presley's 'Trouble' and Carole King's 'Will You Love Me Tomorrow', both to devastating effect. Our prayers were answered, so to speak, and Graham joined the band that afternoon. The rest, as they say, is history, with a series of peerless vocal performances added to tracks such as 'SYBG', 'All Night Long', 'Love's No Friend', 'Lost in Hollywood' and 'Eyes Of The World', setting the seal on the 'Down to Earth' album, which became a worldwide hit.

The year long tour that followed cemented deep friendships between Graham, Cozy, Colin Hart and myself that, with one sad exception, survive to this day. There are some wonderful memories. Of getting a taxi with Graham to a shopping mall in Tokyo, being followed by 40 taxis full of girl fans, and of the two of us having to run for our lives through the arcade, chased by the screaming teenage throng. Straight into a taxi at the other end and back to the hotel empty handed. Some amazing gigs, including the Spectrum in Philadelphia, the Forum in LA, two nights at the Budokan in Tokyo and, with singles and album riding high in the charts, two nights at London's Wembley Arena, the first ending in a spectacular riot.

Graham and Don : *photographed backstage by Colin Hart, on the Rainbow U.K. tour. The two young lads are Steve and Paul Mann (now an orchestra conductor.)*

The most memorable show (which turned out to be Graham and Cozy's last with Rainbow) was the headline spot at the first Donington festival on Aug 16th 1980. Ozzy Osbourne, who was watching from the wings, subsequently told me it was the greatest performance by a singer he had ever seen.

Graham is a strange mixture of fragility and steadfastness, naivety and wisdom, and he can go from being a bottomless pit of despair to the funniest man on the planet. Walking down some foreign street looking for somewhere to eat, we'd end up convulsed with laughter, clinging to lampposts as he regaled us with impressions of the people he'd met whilst working as a butcher in Skegness, or with fantasy monologues about those with whom he was strangely obsessed, such as 'Play-in-a-Day' guitarist Bert Weedon, or puppeteer Harry Corbett and Sooty.

The extraordinary range of his voice matches the range of experience in his life. He has plumbed depths and risen to heights few can match. Through it all he has remained the same person, the lad from Skeggy, utterly loyal to his friends and family, and still blessed with a voice and a genius that rise deep from within an untrammelled soul.

I am proud to know him. This is his story. Enjoy!

Don Airey

INTRODUCTION

Probably like many readers of this book, I first became a fan of Graham Bonnet after hearing him singing with Rainbow, specifically their first hit 'Since You Been Gone', in the Autumn of 1979. Within a few weeks I'd obtained his 1977 debut solo album during one of my record buying trips to Manchester. Before long I managed to build up a modest collection of Graham's early recordings and had made a start on gathering cuttings and articles. I found his pre-Rainbow career especially interesting, discovering his hits from the late Sixties and the success in Australasia in the Seventies.

In 1991 I found myself with a bit of spare time due to a strike at the company (where I still work). I'd been thinking about writing Graham's biography and started work, but before long I changed my mind and decided to do what many fans did back then and began a self-published fanzine, 'Under The Bonnet'. Sold through adverts in the music papers and rock magazines, Issue One came out in May that year, followed by fourteen more through until the end of 1994.

I sent Issue One to David Kassner, head of President Records, who was behind the most recent two Forcefield albums Graham had sung on. David kindly sent me Graham's new solo album, 'Here Comes The Night' and phoned me one evening. After we had talked for a few minutes, he said: *"I have someone here who wants a word with you."* It was none other than Graham Bonnet! I didn't believe him at first and we had a good laugh, talked about his new album and other things. Graham was in the UK rehearsing for the performances of Eddie Hardin's 'Wind In The Willows'. I arranged to meet him over the weekend of June 8th/9th for an interview for my fanzine. We got on extremely well and he seemed surprised that I knew so much about his career. I was invited to the rehearsals and I'll never forget the power in his voice when he let rip. Since that first meeting we kept in touch by letter and then email. Graham also put me in touch with his Dad, Lou, and I spent many hours with him as he told me all about the bands Graham had played with in and around his home town of Skegness. Fascinated by all this I made more trips to Skegness, interviewing people Graham had worked with and writing these up for my fanzine. Lou saw that I was serious about the research and told me I could stay at his house whenever I wanted.

I got to know Kenny Bray, who lived close by. He had grown up with Graham and was also a drummer like me, so I knew he was as at least as mad as I was! He told me so many funny stories I ended up creating a column in my fanzine titled 'Kenny's Corner'. Sadly, Kenny is no longer with us and neither is Lou. Trevor Gordon who I interviewed in London in December 1991, Peter Tomlinson or Roger Sleath who I emailed on a regular basis have also all passed on.

I also got to know John and Julie Tuplin, along with their daughter Donna, very well, as they ran a family print business on Drummond Road, Media House Printers. Due to all the cuttings Lou came up with, I spent a lot of time there on the photocopier each visit (and they then offered to print the fanzine.) Sadly, their business later went under and they even lost their beautiful home. I hope they have managed to come back from this because they were such a wonderful family and always made me very welcome.

On another occasion during June 1993, I was told that ex-Graham Bonnet Set bass player, John Davenport, had taken his own life. Shocked is an understatement as I'd been trying to track him down for quite a while for a chat.

Fast forward to 2007. Graham was touring the UK with the Taz Taylor Band. I'd known promoter Mark Wheatley for quite a while as he had been booking Graham's UK tours since 2001 and he asked me if I wanted to do the merchandise stall, which I did and it was fun! During the tour Graham asked me if I was still going to do the book. I'd mentioned the idea on numerous occasions over the years but still not found time to plan it out.

Finally towards the end of 2009 I started to work on it with purpose, gathering material researched for the fanzine, interviewing more musicians, producers and fans. The aim was an in-depth story of Graham's life, the bands and musicians he's played with, the solo projects and day to day life of a rock singer as told to me both by the people involved as well as Graham, who I've spoken to more times than I can remember.

In 2010 I rekindled my friendship with drummer Steve Hardy (who worked with Graham in his formative bands). I'd interviewed Steve in London during June 1993 and we talked so long I ended up having to borrow a cassette off him because my two C90s just weren't enough for all the information and funny stories he was coming up with. As he made me my first cup of tea, he could see from the look on my face that it wasn't strong enough. Three teabags later he got it right and we still laugh about this today.

Later in March 2014 I met Bob Turner (ex-Graham Bonnet Set keyboard player) again for the first time in just over 20 years. I had first interviewed Bob in the Firbeck Hotel and what amazed me was he seemed to know everyone and helped me track down many ex-members. He now lives in Spain but came over to London for Graham's gig at The Garage on March 19th 2014. Steve Hardy also made it and after the show Graham met up with them, the first time the three ex-Graham Bonnet Set members had been together since they played at the Revolution Club in London in early 1968.

In July 2014 I completed the circle by returning to Skegness to meet up with Graham, his partner Beth-Ami, and Steve Hardy who hadn't really socialised with Graham since 1968. It was so funny listening and watching them chat to each other. I felt as if I'd gone back in time to the mid-60s!

So yes, it has been a long time getting this together and something of a labour of love, but I hope you enjoy the read and discover a few things you didn't know about Graham. I wouldn't like to think how much time and money I've spent on records, memorabilia and travel to Skegness, London and other places during my research, but it has been well worth it; I've met some amazing people and made some great friends. It has also been rewarding to help people rekindle old friendships where they might not have met up again otherwise.

I also really appreciate everyone's contributions. If you see anything that needs to be corrected, please do not hesitate to contact me via the publisher. At the end of the day I am just a fan and I've written this for every fan of Graham Bonnet, as well as for his family.

Lastly, I would like to dedicate this book to : Lou Bonnett, Tony Bonnett, Kenny Bray, Trevor Gordon, Howard Kehl, Roger Sleath and Peter Tomlinson.

Steve Wright

CONTENTS

	Foreword by Don Airey	2
	Introduction	3
	Acknowledgements	4
1	Starcarr Lane	5
2	Night Of The Shooting Star	19
3	Too Young To Die, Too Drunk To Live	33
4	Desert Diamond	51
5	Skyfire	65
6	Breaking The Heart Of The City	73
7	Island In The Sun	81
8	God Blessed Video	93
9	Undercover	101
10	Dangerous Games	109
11	It's My Life	119
12	Will You Be Home Tonight	129
13	Jet To Jet	139
14	Wire And Wood	147
15	Discography	157
	Appendix 1 - Concert Diary	161
	Appendix 2 - About The Songs	170
	Appendix 3 - Sixties Set Lists	173
	Credits / Bibliography	174
	Easy On The Eye Books	176

Blackthorne • *San Diego, June 30th 1992*

ACKNOWLEDGEMENTS

Graham Bonnet – 'ey up! Thank you for all the great stories and you're still as daft as ever! Keep the show going my friend and don't stop … keep rockin'!

Boz and Lyn Boorer and family – For nearly three decades your home has been my 'second home' and the backbone for a large part of the research I've put in to this book. Your kindness, generosity and warmth is very rare in this world. You are true genuine friends.

Steve Hardy – For over two decades your never ending stories are truly amazing and told here. Thank you for supporting my book in such a big way. It has been wonderful having you on board.

Giles Lavery – Your help to make this book a great offering speaks volumes about the person you are. Your continuous supply of discoveries never ceases to amaze me. Blackthorne and out!

Simon Robinson and Easy On The Eye Books – I couldn't have done this without you. I thank you greatly for believing in my project and for all your hard work and ideas. It's been a long journey, but worth it.

Andy Skiller – Your time and patience for the smallest queries has always been appreciated. Thank you for being my personal proof reader.

Dave Thompson – You and your many music books have been a huge inspiration to me ever since I got to know you nearly three decades ago. Here is my offering.

Special thanks to: *Keeley Bonnet, Vicky Bonnett, Daffy, Sue Hedley, Andrew Môn Hughes, Howard Kehl RIP, Dirk Krause, Rob McKenzie, Philip Madden and his family, Trond Nicolaisen, Mario Parga, Michael Richards, John Tucker* and *Masaya Uchimura*.

Thanks to *Christine Acred, Kenny Bray's family, Andy Bolton, Jo Bonnet, Vin Conserva, Dr. Peter Cooper, Jamie Crompton, Roy Davies, Rich Davenport, Ian Doughty, Liz Hay, David Kassner, Anssi Korkiakoski, Peter Ljungberg, Diane Lusk, Chris McLaughlin, Bruce Mee, Gary Mitchell, Emili Muraki, Peter Nikolic, Stephen Oates, Karl Radcliffe, Jay Schellon, Arvinder Singh, Victoria Sleath, Marko Syrjälä, Ginny Twist, Shaun Waddington, Tom Wallace, Reinhard Wenesch, Mark Wheatley, Markus Winterhalter and Gina Zamparelli.* And not forgetting *Wetherspoons, Hadfields* for the sandwiches and all the staff at *Swiftprint* in Huddersfield.

I would like to thank everyone I've spoken to and the ones who spoke to my friends for me. Their words are now published here: *Don Airey, John Aizlewood, Lou Bonnett, Kenny Bray RIP, Daffy, John Eden, Ray Fenwick, Peter Foldy, Andy DiGelsomina, Trevor Gordon RIP, Steve Hardy, Beth-Ami Heavenstone, Iain Ashley Hersey, Chris Impellitteri (by Rob McKenzie), J21, Natasha Lea Jones, Kaplan Kaye (thanks to Gina Zamparelli), Dirk Krause, Bob Kulick (thanks to Ken Tighe), Justin Lack, Martin Motnik (thanks to Dirk Krause), Micky Moody (thanks to Rich Davenport), Tony Nicholl, Trond Nicolaisen, Mario Parga, Rob Pippan (by Howard Kehl RIP), Ainhoa Prieto, Bob Richards, Noel Robinson, Roger Sleath RIP, Victy Silva, Taz Taylor, Sean Timms, Peter Tomlinson RIP, Bob Turner, Joe Lynn Turner (thanks to Lisa Walker & Gina Zamparelli), Kevin Valentine (thanks to Masaya Uchimura), Alan Vickers, Robin Walker, Mike Wells, Mandy Wheatcroft, Doogie White (thanks to Rob McKenzie), Pip Williams, Chuck Wright (thanks to Gina Zamparelli)* and *John Zak (thanks to Gina Zamparelli).*

Thanks also to *Russ Ballard* and *Tony Carey* (both thanks to *Rob McKenzie*), *Roger Ferris* (thanks to *Victy Silva*), *Donal Gallagher* (thanks to *Rob McKenzie*), *Colin Hart* (thanks to *Simon Robinson*) *Anssi Korkiakoski, Giles Lavery, Peter Ljungberg, Simon Locatelli, Diane Lusk, Rob McKenzie, Neil Murray* (thanks to *Rob McKenzie*), *John Otway & Dave Storey* (both thanks to *Andy Skiller*), *Conrado Pesinato,* and *Mark Zonder* (thanks to *Giles Lavery*) who all gave me quotes.

The quotes by *Cozy Powell* and *Roger Glover* are from the Deep Purple Appreciation Society magazine *Darker Than Blue / Stargazer*. Thanks to *Giles Lavery, Philip Madden, Junko Ogawara, Rick Oswald, John Tucker* and *Masaya Uchimura* who all recalled gigs.

CHAPTER 1
Starcarr Lane (1947 – 1966)

Featuring: Young Graham, The Skyliners, The Peter Tomlinson Band, The Jimmy Aldred Band, The Jan Ramsden Band, The Missing Links, The Blueset, The Bluesect and The Bluesecte

Striking a happy note . . .

Skegness, a seasonally busy seaside resort on the far east of Lincolnshire's coastline, has few claims to fame. Search 'famous people from...' and you know they're struggling when the top hits are a holiday camp developer actually born in South Africa and a rotund fisherman who exists only as an advertising campaign.

But then Skegness was a very small fishing village until the rapid development of the railways brought it within reach of a number of industrialised cities in the mid-1870s. Drawn by the wide sandy beaches and mild climate, a small tourist industry existed in the days of horse-drawn transport, but with investment from the Earl of Scarborough (who owned much of the land in the area) a full blown holiday resort quickly developed. A pier followed, and the arrival of the first Butlin's holiday camp (that South African I mentioned) set the seal on the town's tourist industry, which eclipsed that of other coastal towns in the area like Chapel St. Leonards and Mablethorpe.

The railway also provided the town with its other 'famous person', the Jolly Fisherman with his "It's So Bracing" tourist slogan. First appearing on posters in 1908 he marked the opening of a direct line to London, thus ensuring an even larger influx of visitors until well into the sixties, when cheap Spanish air-holidays with guaranteed sunshine began to lure Brits abroad.

If famous Skegness people are in short supply, rarely is the town mentioned in documentaries about the blitz either - yet the town received over fifty visits from enemy bombers during World War Two, with civilian deaths and property damage resulting from secondary raids on what had become an important naval facility.

It was in the middle of all this that Louis Bonnett and his new bride Irene (Rene to everyone) found themselves in 1940 for the birth of their first son Anthony on January 28th. Louis - or Lou as he was always known - was a native of Tealby, in nearby Scunthorpe, and had married Rene in 1938. Rene had been born in London but her father had been advised to move to the coast for the air, so the family moved to Skegness when she was quite young.

Dependent as it had been on tourism, Skegness Council found themselves with a major clear up task after the War, rebulding and regenerating. Louis Bonnett, his war-time home guard duties over, was one of the team, working for the Council on the seafront to restore parks and flower-beds as the town picked itself up and hastily prepared to welcome visitors again.

Lou and Rene moved into their first house in Grove Road (where Tony was born) then to Lancaster Avenue. It was here that their second child Graham was born two days before Christmas on December 23rd 1947. Needing more room, they moved into a modest brick built semi-detached two bedroomed 1930s house at 26 Albany Road on the western side of the town, far enough from the centre that they wouldn't be bothered with tourists during the season, but just a short walk into town for work or shopping.

The immediate post-War years were not easy for anyone, with austerity still the order of the day, but Skegness was quick to gear up for business, and Butlins reopened as early as 1946. The Bonnetts got on with life with Rene working at the Imperial Café and later Nelson's jewellers. She was by all accounts a good singer and took part in local talent competitions, one of which was recorded direct to disc, with Rene contributing a version of '*Where Are You*' to the one-off acetate pressing, though looking after two young children didn't leave her much opportunity to persue this as a career.

Even so music was still important to both parents and through records and the radio the children listened to a varied selection, as Graham recalls: "*My Mum was more interested in music changes back then. She liked Rosemary Clooney, Teresa Brewer, Kay Star and Patsy Cline. My Dad hated all the Frank Sinatra kind of singers and my Mum too.*" Nor was this just a passing phase; both Mum and Dad kept up to date with changes in popular music as their children grew. "*They both loved the new music, rock and roll and artists like Bill Haley, Chuck Berry and Little Richard. Both were well away from your Glenn Miller types that most people back then were listening to.*" When the beat boom began, they were quick to pick up on The Beatles and other sixties groups.

This early and continued exposure to music would clearly have an influence on Graham, but for the time being he and his brother were discovering the joys of pet ownership.

Graham's parents bought a couple of tortoises for their sons and 4 year old Graham named them both, calling his Joey and Tony's tortoise Bill, after their Granddad, William (Bill) Bonnett. "*Granddad called all his animals Bill. Plus, these creatures are cheap and low maintenance!*" It was also a good choice for a pet as Graham developed an allergy to cat fur in later years (Joey didn't last the winter, but Bill lived on until 2013.)

With TV still in its infancy, the local cinema was as popular as ever and Graham was allowed to go once he was old enough. One of the first films he remembers seeing was the Walt Disney animation Peter Pan which reached the local flea-pit in 1953. Education also beckoned and Graham attended the Cavendish Road Infants School (where his teacher was Marjorie Sleath, mother of Roger, who would play with Graham in the not too distant future). Graham and Tony shared the back bedroom on Albany Road and it must have been pretty obvious to his brother that Graham was very interested in music, because at the age of seven he bought him

Family photographs : *Above: Rene and Lou on their wedding day in 1938, and with young Tony. Below: Graham and his parents on their bikes ("We'd just been to see the showing times for the Disney movie Peter Pan. You can see the poster in front of the cinema."). Tony and his young brother Graham.*

a plastic ukulele as a present. His Mum and Dad continued to bring home interesting pop records and Graham heard *'The Rudder And The Rock'* by David Whitfield which they had liked. Whitfield was in fact closer to light opera than popular music. The song was a B-side to *'My September Love'*, which made the UK charts at No. 3 in April 1956. Graham liked the song better than the A side and for ages afterwards, whether out with his parents or playing with his friends, he was forever singing the track. The A side also eventually got through to him: *"I still sing 'My September Love' sometimes while I am walking around. It reminds me of my childhood and my Mum and Dad. I am a very sentimental person and the song takes me back to those feelings I had at the time. I liked the B-side because it was heavier I guess!"*

From infant school, Graham moved up to the Junior County School, and found that singing came naturally and quite easily to him. One morning in class assembly while everyone was singing a hymn, Graham suddenly began singing in harmony, so loudly that everyone could hear him. His astonished teacher congratulated him, but asked him to do it a little more quietly in future. Even at this early age, he was listening to artists such as Mario Lanza and walking around the family home singing with a naturally powerful voice, much to the amusement of his parents.

The Scout movement was still huge in Britain in the fifties, and like many of his friends, Graham joined the St. Clement's 5th Skegness Wolf Cub Pack. How well he did at his badges isn't known, but it didn't take him long to show off his vocal prowess as his father recalls: *"He sang 'You Ain't My Sunshine' when he wasn't all that old, about seven, and also sang 'Good Companions' at a Cub concert at the age of eight. When he was in the Cubs, he had a very good ear for music."* At the Cub's parent's evening on Friday March 20th 1959 Graham sang a powerful version of *'Diana'*. How can we be so certain of the date? The local press turned up to report on the event and were so impressed they published a photograph of Graham in full voice at the microphone. He was eleven years old. His Dad remembered the event: *"I think when he sang 'Diana', that was the last time he sang for the cubs. During the song, Graham turned to the pianist and looked at him, because he was playing for himself. He wasn't a pianist for that kind of thing, he was a pub pianist. Graham went down well."* The young singer was also now the proud owner of a proper acoustic guitar, though he struggled with the tuning, and like every other schoolkid in the country, had to master the recorder. Graham was also able to sing at church hall functions from time to time.

Once the tuning had been mastered the world was his oyster, as pointed out by Diane Lusk (nee Grunnill) who is a relative of Graham's and attended the same infants and junior school as him. *"We used to ride the school bus to the County Junior School and Graham would get on with his guitar and serenade the whole bus of kids. He did a wonderful rendition of Elvis songs and the one I always liked was 'Good Luck Charm'. He even had the Elvis curled lip too! I always remember him being a bit of a joker at school, but he always took his music seriously. He never seemed bigheaded and he could have been with his powerhouse voice. Graham was pretty much liked at school and friends liked*

Cub Scouts : *Graham belted out the big 1957 Paul Anka hit 'Diana' during a parent evening for the local Cubs troop in 1959. He had debuted at the same event a few years before.*

Albany Road: *Graham posing with his guitar on Albany Road in Skegness aged 11. Note the baseball boots, every kids' dream footwear back then.*

his singing. He was popular for sure and a good looking guy at a young age. We were both in the same talent competition one year at the Embassy Theatre, 1962 I think it was, I sang a Helen Shapiro number and he sang an Elvis song. We both have music running through our blood. He came first and I came second. Not bad for kids!"

As her children grew a little older, Graham's mother was able to dust off the sheet music a little, singing at the local Butlin's holiday resort in nearby Ingoldmells, on the Northern edge of Skegness. *"My mother had always wanted to be a singer, but never really made it, and I think it was my mother more than anyone who got me started. I'd always been into music and my heroes were people like Buddy Holly, and Elvis. I thought Paul Anka was great. I used to stand in front of the mirror miming 'Diana' when that came out."*

"We had to make our own entertainment in those days" is such a cliché but no less true for that. Christmas time was always fun in the Bonnett household as they used to have numerous sing-a-longs, with family members playing various instruments. *"My Mum would sing,"* says Graham, *"and one of my uncles would play the trumpet and another uncle would play the accordion. So we always had a good time."*

The fifties were still a time of early academic segregation and failing his Eleven Plus exam meant that Graham's next school would be Morris Secondary rather than the more academic Skegness Grammar. But it offered opportunities for Graham and one of the very first things he did there was to make a ukulele in his woodwork class. Sport was also important and on one occasion, during a kickabout football match, he scored a goal past his school friend, twelve-year-old Ray Clemence (who went on to play professionally as goalkeeper for Liverpool and England.) Graham was also beginning to become good at art, and spent quite a bit of his time at school sketching on his schoolbooks, as well as writing out words to songs he was making up during the lessons. He was also starting to attract the girls.

His good looks and wit seemed to charm the opposite sex but quickly got him into trouble. When a teacher caught him with an older girl on the sports field he was hauled before the headmaster ... and immediately expelled. Graham was just twelve and his girlfriend, Janet, was fifteen. *"We hung out together all the time,"* remembers Graham, who had just joined the school orchestra. *"Her friend became attached a little to my cousin Trevor."* Trevor's parents had left for Australia in the mid 1950s from Blackpool but had returned to Skegness for a short while. *"We all used to go down to the park every day and meet the girls down by the swings."*

Because it was the only Secondary school in the area, the school had to have him back but he lost his place in the school orchestra. *"Everything I did after that was wrong. They wouldn't even allow me to bring my guitar to school, because it always attracted the girls."*

Still just twelve Graham decided to enter a local talent competition, Discovery Time, which took place at the Embassy Ballroom on the Grand Parade in Skegness during June. To his amazement, he won and went on to appear in the grand final at a later date. He didn't progress any further, but the experience was invaluable.

Graham and his brother Tony didn't get away from Skegness often, their only real holiday would be a week spent at their Grandfather's place near Brigg in Lincolnshire, which they enjoyed. He had a smallholding where he reared pigs and chickens and also grew vegetables.

Outside school, all Graham really wanted to do was play his guitar, and there was talk about him attending an open audition in Skegness for a band called Alan Caldwell's Texans, who were in Skegness playing at the Butlins Holiday Camp for the summer season in 1960. He was to be disappointed. *"I never auditioned for them, because I was too young to play. For some reason you had to be 15 years old to perform in front of an adult audience."*

The Texans later changed their name to Rory Storm and the Hurricanes, and their drummer was one Richard Starkey, better known later as Ringo Starr.

Back at school in 1961 Graham was allowed into the orchestra once more, one of two guitarists in the Morris School Band. They provided the music for the newly formed art group's songs at shows in the local

---

LOCAL TALENT TOPS POLL
In " Discovery Time " contest

A 13-YEAR-OLD Skegness boy, of 26, Albany Road, gained first place in the second edition of " Discovery Time " at the Embassy on Thursday evening. He was Graham Bonnett, who sang "The Story Of My Love" and "Young Love."

Baptist Hall. Pianist in the band was Derrick Dutton, who was head of Morris School's music department. *"I was part of the school orchestra along with my cousin, Trevor. We both played guitar. I remember performing the show Oklahoma as a local production at a church. I used the guitar my Mum and Dad had bought me for Christmas a few years earlier. Derrick Dutton was my favourite piano player."*

Graham also became a big fan of the latest vocal sensation Helen Shapiro whose unusually deep voice was very similar to his. She was not much more than a year older than Graham, yet during a space of twelve months between March 1961 and February 1962 she scored two UK top 3 hits, two No. 1s, and had The Beatles supporting her on tour. Graham would spend a lot of time learning the lyrics and singing along to her songs.

During June 1961, Graham decided to have another go at the Discovery Time talent competition and once again he came first, this time singing the Conway Twitty song *'The Story Of My Love'* and *'Young Love'* by Tab Hunter. He faced strong competition from twenty-two other heat winners during the final and despite not winning with his rendition of the recent Cliff Richard hit *'A Girl Like You'* (accompanying himself on the guitar) got a lot of attention. These competitions were encouraged by his parents, who in November that year bought him an electric guitar and amplifier, which cost 42 guineas, quite a sum at the time. Keen to get more experience, the same year he auditioned for a local beat group called Take 4 which featured bassist Roger Sleath, his old teacher's son, but again age counted against him. Even so the local newspaper was starting to follow this young talent and early in 1962 interviewed him, describing him as a 'beat singer'. He wasn't shy about expressing his opinions either.

As well as Helen Shapiro, Adam Faith was proving to be an inspiration but on the whole Graham felt frustrated by many of the singers he heard, telling the reporter he felt there was a 'lack of originality' among most of them. He also explained that he rarely bought records. Instead, after his nightly practise session, he used to tune into Radio Luxembourg. Any song that had something special about it, he would make a note of and then work out the chords in his bedroom, adding it to his repertoire. With a bit of luck, he would pick up some of the lyrics as well. By not listening too closely to the songs, Graham claimed he wouldn't be too easily influenced by another singer's style. *"Whatever I sing,"* he said, *"it will be just me."*

It wasn't any surprise that his number one fans were his Mum and Dad, but they had only heard him sing in public once. Graham, who never suffers from stage fright, explained why: *"I could get up and sing in front of thousands of people, but if I knew Mum and Dad were among them, it would put me right off!"*

During Carnival Week in Skegness, Graham made an appearance at Cyril Catlyn's Party Night at the Embassy and was listed in the adverts for the show (along with his guitar). This was the town's premier venue and six acts appeared. Graham went down so well the enthusiastic audience demanded an encore. Following his excellent performance, Cyril Catlyn asked the fourteen-year-old to appear on his weekly 'Talent Time' show, which took place on a Monday evening at the Derbyshire Miners Welfare Club in Skegness. Once again, Graham went down very well and Cyril was quick to praise him in a report of the show in the local paper: *"I was very pleased with Graham tonight. This was his first solo spot before a large audience and he took it in his stride like an old trooper. The boy has got a lot of talent and should go a long way."* Graham had covered four big pop ballads, *'Blue Moon'*, *'Bachelor Boy'*, *'Lonesome Me'* and *'It's All Over Now'*. Inspired by all this, just before Christmas 1962 Graham wrote to the BBC asking if he could audition for them, but nothing ever came of it.

Saxophonist Alan Vickers who would later work with Graham was at the 'Talent Time' debut: *"It was a variety show and he was still at school. The compere introduced Graham and said he was from Skegness, and all the girls started screaming. I was thinking good grief! Graham came on stage on his own and sang. You could tell straight away he had charisma, but I was just thinking 'this is someone from Skegness!'"*

The venue became a regular Monday evening gig for Graham for a time as his Dad recalled: *"If he was accompanied by an organist and drummer, and the organist wasn't in the right key, he'd soon stop them!"* Graham had also now picked up on girl groups like The Crystals and The Ronettes and was interested in their vocal approach to material.

In 1963 Graham joined a local jazz trio or quartet (depending on the booking), The Skyliners. The bandleader was keyboard player Peter Tomlinson. Graham played guitar and sang, with the much older Bill Gardner on drums and Alan Vickers on alto sax, or occasionally tenor sax and clarinet. It was Graham's first proper band experience.

Peter remembers him

Local beat singer fourteen-year-old Graham Bonnett with the guitar his mother bought him. (Photo: Wrate's Press.)

Graham believes in a guitar and originality

Work and play : *Left: Graham posing with his guitar for the local paper, and Above: with staff at the North Shore Hotel.*

joining: *"One of the band members mentioned this young boy who was still at school. So, through his Mum and Dad, who I knew at the time, I approached him. I also knew his brother. Graham said that he was interested in getting experience so I used to pick him up after school and basically run through some songs, ones that he wanted to do. I tried to help him. It might not sound a lot, but he was still at school and I had to fit him in when I could in those days. A few weeks went by, and we started taking him on jobs. But the prime job he did with us was The Parade Hotel in the summer, which was on the promenade and run by Des Holdsworth. We used to play there a lot and Graham used to come with us on a regular basis. When the winter came along we still did gigs there, as well as other hotels like The Bell in Burgh le March. We also played village halls like the ones in Friskney, Wainfleet and Benington. Back then they used to have three or four piece bands every Friday or Saturday night. So, if I'd got a three piece booked in, he used to come with us. I'd give him some money, buy him a few drinks and he was quite happy to get the experience. Later on, he came and got paid. I can't remember how much, but it was acceptable to him. Even in those days he certainly had something."*

Never having really enjoyed his time at secondary school, Graham was happy to be able to leave that Easter aged fifteen. Band mate-to-be Roger Sleath remembers Graham telling him about one grim day at school: *"When he was in his last year at secondary school he used to take his guitar in. One of the teachers there – some sadist – caned him on both hands for 'showing off'! He couldn't play for days. I think his Mum went in and complained."*

School over, it had never really dawned on Graham to get a job, even though he had been quite good at English and felt he might do something connected with journalism. All he ever really thought about was performing. At least with Skegness being a seaside town, there were always plenty of casual jobs available and Graham ended up working at the North Shore Hotel. Lou remembers: *"He went waiting-on. He did the washing up and all sorts of different things like stoking the boiler. Then at night he would play with Pete Tomlinson in The Skyliners, and would sometimes sing."* Graham adds: *"I was originally going to be a waiter at The Parade Hotel but, they moved me to The North Shore Hotel on my very first day. One day while I was coming out of the kitchen with some tomato soup, one bowl in each hand and one balanced on my arm, I accidentally spilt the bowl on my arm over a gentleman sat at a table in a very expensive suit. It went all down his back. He wanted me instantly sacked and even threatened to sue the hotel. I got banished to working in the kitchen, stoking the boiler … I even helped dig what is the car park now. We buried stuff from inside the hotel when they were refurbishing it. It will still be there!"* Graham settled at the hotel for quite a while, but was forced to call it a day when he was suddenly taken ill. *"I just passed out and they thought I had a brain tumour. I had to have my head x-rayed. There was nothing wrong, but I really thought I was going to die."* Eventually Graham was diagnosed with epilepsy and doctors were able to get this under control with medication.

Graham was able to resume his guitar duties in The Skyliners as Peter recalls: *"In those days there were far more places to play. We could do up to five gigs a week in the winter, and more in the summer. If we did two gigs it was a bad week! With us, Graham learned dance band stuff - quicksteps, waltz's and foxtrots - which I don't think he liked playing very much, but he did it."* Graham confirms this, but then how many young teenagers do like the music of their parent's era? But he realised they had to do it to get work and it stood him in good stead. *"Graham lived just over the back from my bungalow and he used to come here quite often, complete with equipment; he had his guitar, amplifier and speaker. Graham did the top pop songs of the time with us. Typical songs that I call small dance band stuff, pop stuff, which is what I wanted him to do and is what the crowd wanted him to do as well, so it worked both ways. During the instrumentals he'd strum and play his part. His reading was quite good, although he hadn't done much of it. That was the hard bit for him. As for his vocals, that was the easy bit. It came naturally to him! We used to rehearse at The Parade Hotel during the day sometimes. Des (the owner) wouldn't say anything. We also rehearsed at my bungalow, because I have a piano there. When we were doing a song, we used to use the old fashioned orchestrations. Graham learned quickly, because the guitar parts are only chord symbols. He soon learned how to play those and they came easy to him. Sometimes we would get to a job early. Graham knew his own songs and if we couldn't rehearse, he'd pick the other songs up as we went along, ad-lib here and there. You could tell if there were any fluff notes, but Graham was intelligent enough to know that if he couldn't get through a passage to just leave it out! Around Christmas 1963 we changed our name to The Peter Tomlinson Band, but that wasn't my idea. We were at The Parade Hotel. Graham was on the payroll then. Christmas gigs incorporated five nights. It was a good spell from Christmas Eve night right through."*

Power trio : *Right: The Skyliners warming up; Bill Gardiner (drums), Graham (guitar) and Peter Tomlinson (keyboards) photographed towards the end of 1963.*

During his time with Peter Tomlinson, an opening came up with the Joe Loss Orchestra: *"Someone put my name forward for it. I think it was either Pete Tomlinson or my Uncle Ray. But again, I didn't audition, because I was too young to play in front of an adult audience."*

Around Spring 1964 Graham left the band as Peter explained: *"Graham stayed with us for around one year to eighteen months. He did two winters and at least one summer season with us, before leaving and moving on to play with lads who were more his own age in The Missing Links. He definitely learned a lot from his time with us."*

Graham certainly had. Clearly the material was not of his choosing, but this kind of graft tightened up his playing, as well as giving him an experience of life as a semi-professional musician. Looking back now he says: *"We did all the songs you could imagine. 'Take Five', 'San Francisco', 'Go Away Little Girl', Sinatra tunes, Tony Bennett, etc. and all the awful pop tunes that were around at the time, but no Beatles. It was all Mum's and Dad's type songs. It was horrible. Lots of instrumentals, Joe Loss type things and jazz stuff."*

For now, Graham kicked about a bit trying to find an opening with a pop or beat group. To keep his hand in he played a one-off at Butlins with a Skegness seven-piece dance outfit called the Jimmy Aldred Band, and also sat in with another local outfit The Jan Ramsden Band once or twice. His chance for something more modern came with The Missing Links. Their story began a little earlier when in 1962 eighteen-year-old bassist Roger Sleath had started teacher training at Kesteven College of Education at Stoke Rochford, near Grantham. He formed his own group, The Pioneers, but it wasn't too long before he began to dislike the songs they were playing, so he resigned in 1964. Back home in Skegness Roger decided to give it another go: *"I started to form a new group and found a young drummer called Mick Parker, a guitarist called Noel Robinson and a singer called Keith 'Second-Hand' Smalley. Mick was a drummer because basically his Dad, who was a jeweller, had bought him a set of drums. We called the group The Missing Links and it was pretty rough!"*

Guitarist Noel Robinson was already trying to get his own band going when Roger Sleath turned up. *"He contacted the band I was playing with. He came and met us at a vicarage where we were rehearsing and immediately sacked the lead guitarist!"* Roger confirms the meeting: *"The vicarage was in Wainfleet, which was about four miles from Skegness. My parents had a big house (at 2 Albany Road) with a double garage that had loft space accessed by a wooden ladder. We used that as our practice venue. Then one day, Graham, who lived a few doors away, just turned up to see if he could join in. He had been playing with a six or seven piece dance band. He wasn't happy with the repertoire of fox-trots, waltzes and popular ballads of the time. As soon as he joined in, it was immediately obvious that his singing voice and guitar playing was streets ahead of anyone else's in the band. So Keith Smalley was immediately sacked."*

Noel remembers the garage loft only too well: *"We used to have to climb up into the loft above the garage. Depending where you were stood, you sometimes had to play with your head facing down, because of the beams in the roof!"* The band also discovered that their amplifiers were picking up the Dick Van Dyke Show more times than not...

Chirpy cockneys aside, the band were very excited to have Graham on board, and as for Keith 'Second-Hand' Smalley, he didn't even manage a single gig with The Missing Links. Noel had seen Graham before: *"Roger said he had heard of this Graham Bonnett character and that is how I came to be introduced to Graham. I had seen him previously, because he used to play in a dance band called The Peter Tomlinson Band. I think I also saw him at a grammar school Christmas party. Graham was doing 'Twist and Shout'. The rest of the material was waltzes, and then Graham would do his little bit. But I think it was good training for him though, that sort of style. He must have learned a lot of good chords that he wouldn't do normally in the standard bands."*

Graham's strong vocals, and his experience of playing both lead and rhythm guitar, instantly gave The Missing Links an extra level of professionalism and also opened new doors. Graham's ability was far ahead of Mick's and Noel's as they had only been playing for about eighteen months and were teaching themselves. As the band started to put their set together, Noel and Roger began to add harmonies to various songs to support Graham's vocals and fill out the sound. The band started to build up a good collection of songs and everyone was happy how things were progressing. Roger says: *"Now we had a really good sound, with Graham's voice and guitar work carrying us along."* Mick's father Fred (nicknamed Fes) took on the roll of manager while Roger, who was now twenty years old, acquired the nickname 'Granddad'. Being four years older than the others he also took control of band duties. Arranging a band rehearsal though wasn't as easy as it might seem, because he was at Kesteven College during the week. So, they used to rehearse on a Friday evening when he got back home for the weekend. Mick and Noel were both still at Skegness Grammar School, while Graham was now working full time at Dewhurst's butchers in Lumley Road, Skegness (which he disliked a lot!).

Missing Links filled the loft with a 'gear' sound

The Missing Links in the middle of yet another madcap stunt. Left to right they are: Roger Sleath, Noel Robinson, Mick Parker and Graham Bonnett. (Photo: Norman Beckett).

As he had at school, Graham tempered his work routine with boredom relieving pranks. Kenny Bray worked alongside him: *"I was about fourteen years old. My brother worked there as well and when he left Graham and I started to become very good friends. One day, there were all these boxes of tomatoes outside the shop and Graham had this idea about who could throw the best. So, we used to see if we could hit Woolworth's shop from outside Dewhurst's! It was quite a fair way off, but we were throwing these tomatoes and they were landing in the crowd in front of Woolworth's."*

"There were two outside toilets in the yard. One particular day, the manager, Nobby, went to the toilet. So, I said to Graham 'I'm going to the toilet,' because I'd an idea of the trick he might play. So I went out but then ran upstairs out of the way. Graham thought I was sat in the toilet having a fag so he got this mop and metal bucket, which was full of water, and then hung the mop over the top of the toilet door and proceeded to shake it! The manager was shouting everything you could imagine and I was upstairs laughing!"

Graham's ultimate cure for work blues was playing though, and The Missing Links made their debut at the Chatta Box Coffee Bar on High Street in Skegness. From there they started playing youth clubs, coffee bars and social clubs, anything suitable within a 20 mile radius. Their main influences were The Rolling Stones, The Merseybeats, and Chuck Berry. In fact Noel reckoned he looked like a Rolling Stone and Mick like a Beatle: *"We played chart material of the time like The Beatles, Chuck Berry, and that sort of thing. Anything that people knew and that got in to the Top 10 really. Graham would work the song out on a Friday night and we would play it on the Saturday. The Beatles had come on the scene and they were quite big. So we took a fancy to wearing Beatle suits, the ones which had those collarless jackets."* Graham remembers some of the other material they covered: *"We played 'I'm A Hog For You Baby' and 'Johnny B. Goode', plus songs by The Animals, and lots of Top 30 songs."*

A local reporter was tipped off about the group and visited the garage loft where they rehearsed one day in July 1964. They ran through a version of the Rolling Stones' *'Walking The Dog'* (described in the paper as 'a real swinger'), and *'Juliet'* that had been recorded by The Four Pennies. The reporter described Graham as having a slightly husky, but melodious voice, and that he came over extremely well. Noel recalls: *"Mick's Dad (Fes) was our 'so called' manager. The reason being, he was the only one with a telephone and a car. So he also took us to gigs! At the gigs, Fes used to walk up and down, and mess around with the PA system. So if someone from behind the bar happened to say 'they're a bit loud tonight', he'd be the one who would go and turn it down. But, then, Graham would just turn his mic or his guitar back up! If we were playing a medium sized venue, Graham wouldn't really need a microphone, because his voice was that strong. Fes used to think he really was someone. But he did have transport and a telephone, which were two very important things!"*

Having only just moved to Skegness, Steve Hardy saw Graham for the first time: *"He was playing in a coffee bar called Brief Encounter, which was in the High Street in Skegness (fish & chip alley). He was with The Missing Links. I was impressed by everything he did. He seemed to be working himself to death. He was doing rhythm, lead, vocals, the lot! I was sat right next to the stage. I had already been studying piano for years and so that night I saw that Graham was no ordinary guitarist as I recognised that many of the chords he was playing were full 'jazz' inversions and not the basic stuff that other guitarists were doing. It was only a small coffee bar, but I was really impressed by what Graham was doing. So from there on, this is what really drew me to find out more about him. I started to check him out, because there was nobody else around with that quality in Skegness, or around that area. I would say that he was my first major influence."*

Noel recalls the show routine: *"The band did quite a few gigs. The caravan sites all had social clubs. Plus, there was the village halls and youth clubs. We'd rent the hall and put a dance on. There were also coffee bars we'd play. You'd never get paid anything. You'd be able to have two cokes at the end of the night! There was never any money in it. I think when we were working properly we got about £10 - £12 a night. We also did some pubs as well like the Sea View in Skegness, which we did on Sunday lunchtimes. It was mainly local places we played."*

Graham also expected a certain respect from the band as Noel recalls: *"I remember one thing that I wasn't very happy about, and that was if Graham broke a string, he used to borrow my guitar. Then I would have to repair his. We used to argue about it. He did keep the show going though, and he was a far better guitarist, so I suppose it was the way to do it. I certainly moaned about it a few times. We couldn't afford spare guitars or anything like that."*

With a number of gigs under their belt, the band started to notice issues in the drum department, as Roger recollects: *"We were having a lot of problems with Mick's drumming ability. He couldn't play any fast numbers. He tired easily and slowed everything down, which drove Graham crazy. I remember playing 'Johnny B. Goode', and it slowed down to walking pace! We had to keep him on though, because his Dad used to run us about in his car and also got us most of our gigs."*

It wasn't too long before Roger was driving which helepd. *"My Mum bought me an estate car, a Morris 1000 Traveller."* This gave them two vehicles to get to and from gigs. Sixteen year old Graham thought he would give driving a go as well. So, with his parents' approval he started having lessons. This nearly came to a sticky end when he shot through a red light to avoid a crash, then ended when he borrowed his Dad's Mini. *"I took the learner plates off the mini and drove the car without my Dad's knowledge. He caught me as I was parking the car. So he took it away from me!"*

 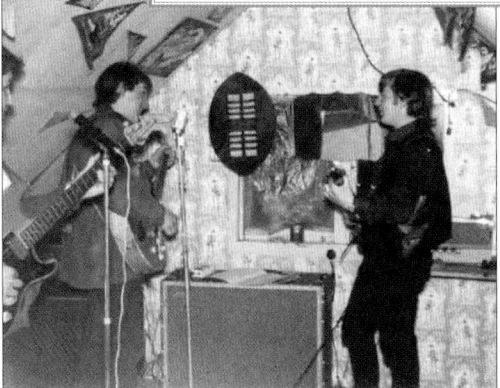 

In the loft : The Missing Links rehearsing in their garage loft 'studio', Graham on the left, Noel on the right and Roger with his back to the camera. The garage still stands but has yet to be honoured with a blue plaque.

In May 1965 the news that Alan Price had left The Animals was quite a big deal. When he formed The Alan Price Set it launched a brief trend for bands to add 'Set' to their own name. This coincided with Graham and Roger talking about a change of name for their band. Since Graham was getting in to blues music in a huge way they wanted something with the word 'Blue' in it. *"After much deliberation, we changed our name to The Blueset, which was all one word,"* explained Roger. He arranged for some business cards to be printed, but when they were collected, the word Blueset was printed as 'The Blue Set', along with the helpful description 'Rhythm & Blues' and Fred Parker's phone number.

Shortly after the name change, Noel decided to leave as he wasn't too keen on the blues direction they were now going in. *"After about twelve months I left and went back to the vicarage in Wainfleet. I rehearsed there with a band called The King Bees. Steve Hardy was the drummer. We played a few coffee bars and places. Then the lead guitarist had a motorbike accident and broke his leg. I then broke my arm, so we were out of action for a while."* Steve Hardy had moved to Skegness from Mansfield and had as we've seen caught Graham live already. The King Bees was his first group.

In the meantime The Blueset, who were now a three-piece, were getting totally fed up with drummer Mick Parker. They needed someone who could handle what they wanted to do. Graham: *"Someone told me about Steve Hardy. It could have been Noel as they played together in The King Bees."* Graham checked him out as Roger recalls: *"Graham discovered Steve Hardy and I seem to remember Graham turning up at my place with him one day. He told me what a good drummer he was. Steve was a young lad and still at school. We gave him an audition and he was really good. So we gave him the job and sacked Mick, much to the anger of his Dad!"*

Steve remembers the subterfuge: *"I went for this audition, which was in the loft over a garage next to where Roger lived. Mick Parker was still actually a member of the band at the time, but all this happened behind his back. I just played a few songs with them and they liked what I did better. So that was how I got in with them. I think Roger would have told Mick Parker that he was no longer in the band, because it wasn't Graham's sort of thing."*

As soon as Mick was ousted, not surprisingly his Dad stopped managing them. The Blueset gigs were mainly arranged from now on by Roger (nicknamed 'Tubbs') as the others were still shy about touting for bookings when they got to a club. Steve: *"I would say to Graham, 'you go and ask him.' And he would say, 'no, you go and ask him.' Neither of us wanted to do it and we would end up arguing who was going to approach the guy for a gig! Graham was worse than me. Sometimes we'd be sat there all night, and in the end, we would just leave! Nine out of ten times Graham and I would chicken out of it."*

Part of Graham's change of musical direction was down to a growing musical maturity. Steve again: *"I think Graham wanted to change his playing to a more blues style because he was at an age where he wanted to show that he could progress, and he got a lot of encouragement from me. We used to meet every day and bounce ideas around and sort things out. We got feedback from each other. He probably didn't get that before in his other groups too much. He was probably more on his own when he came to saying what was good and what was bad. It was like when I first saw Graham, I thought this lad is going to go places. But as I got to know him, we became good mates. I saw potential in him to do even more than he was already doing, so I was quite happy to become a drummer for him. We played the Ex-Servicemen's Club in Skegness as well as at a lot of places on the front like Hildred's Hotel, and at the Sea View Hotel, which was like a folky meeting place, with a blues edge to it. That was the time when we used to get all these old trogs and mods in. All the scooters were parked outside the front. I would say that we were the sound-around for Skegness at that time. People would come up to us and say 'your repertoire is so different; you do some really good stuff'. It was all way-out, but it was done well. It wasn't any old thing. Graham knew the riffs and he used to be able to fill in and improvise as well. Sometimes it was*

Hitting the road : Playing The Imperial Cafe in early Summer 1965 (l-r Roger, Graham and Steve) as The Blueset.

a bit hard as there were only three of us."

The Blueset started to spread their wings a little with gigs further afield and, with Roger studying in Grantham, he started to get the band booked in there. The gigs were great, but for drummer Steve Hardy the travelling got him down: *"We did Stoke Rochford Hall a lot, because that was where Roger was studying. The Blueset played all over the place. Sometimes we used to tie the drums to the roof rack on the top of Roger's car! We didn't have a van at this point, although we did get one eventually. Roger used to insist in taking his girlfriend, Janet. That would mean that I'd be in a confined space of about two square feet! Janet would be in the front, with Graham, and I was in the back with the gear. So I was squashed up in this really small space going to places like Grantham!"* Roger admits it was a bit cramped: *"My then girlfriend (later my first wife) Janet came with us on several gigs, probably to keep an eye on me! She usually sat with Graham in the front passenger seat. They were both very slim and if Graham sat right over to the left against the door, there was just enough room for Janet to sit next to him – I think she put a cushion over the hand brake! Steve was squashed in to the back along with the drums, amps and guitars."*

Recollections of the band's shows still remain with them. Steve remembers one night Roger broke a bass string: *"He tied it together with a pair of pliers! It used to annoy Graham. He broke it in such a place that if he wanted to play a note, he would have to play it higher in another position!"* Roger pleads forgetfulness: *"It was the D string on my bass that had snapped between the machine head and the nut. It lasted for weeks until I remembered to buy some new strings!"*

Steve feels there were differences over their sound too: *"We always wanted a nice fat solid bass sound, but we never had it with Roger."* Roger explains that he was hamstrung: *"There was very little in the way of affordable bass amplification in 1965 so we were very limited."*

"If Graham used to start doing something a bit fancy," Steve points out, *"Roger used to get a bit annoyed, because the crowd were all watching Graham. So he used to start playing high on his bass to show everyone that he could also do it and to stop Graham stealing the limelight. Graham used to look round at me as if to say 'where has the bass gone?' The drums would sound very tinny without the bass foundation going with the bass drum."*

Despite these niggles The Blueset enjoyed playing many local gigs, as Roger says: *"In the summer we were really busy in Skegness with regular bookings at the Hildred's Hotel, the Sea View Hotel, the Beachcomber Bar, the Chatta Box coffee bar, the Derbyshire Miner's Holiday Centre, the British Legion Centre, as well as many others."*

Steve also recalls attempting to add a fuzz box to their gear: *"I tried to make one for Graham from a diagram which I had seen in the magazine Practical Wireless. This was just using an OC71 transistor and a diode joined together inside a matchbox! It never worked, I remember first bringing it along to the Sea View Hotel to try it out. I gave up trying after that!"*

On one occasion in the summer of 1965 at the Hildred's Hotel Roger recalls a harmonica player asking if he could join them on stage for a jam: *"He played blues harmonica with a group in Leicester, The Junco Partners. He said his name was Mick Grainger and he played a few numbers with us that night. He also turned up at our next gig ... and asked to join the group! It seemed a good idea at the time and he became our fourth member for a while. Mick was a shadowy figure and was two or three years older than me even. He stayed on in Skegness in a squalid room, living on gig money and handouts."*

With the addition of a fourth member, the band decided to buy a van (much to the delight of Steve), which Roger remembers: *"Mick used to share the driving when we were gigging and he was always cold. I remember him hunched over the wheel with a cigarette dangling out of his mouth coughing and grumbling, 'it's fucking freezing cold here, fucking freezing. I'm fucking frozen!' Mick did have contacts in Nottingham though and was able to get us some gigs at the Dungeon Club there, which was a rock club in the basement of an old lace mill in the city centre. He was a real wild card and used to borrow stuff and then sell it! I had an expensive black leather flying jacket, which I lent him one night as he had no overcoat and it was freezing. I never saw it again..."* Graham experienced the same thing: *"He stole my parka!"*

The van also doubled up as a passion wagon on a couple of occasions as Roger remembers, much to his amusement: *"Mick used the van one night to entertain a young lady, one of many actually, and he parked it with the wheels perilously close to the edge of a drainage ditch. His vigorous actions in the back of the van caused the van to tip over sideways into the dyke. He had to pay a farmer to come and tow him out with a tractor! The side of the van was badly stoved in."* The band repaired it themselves later. *"We all laid on our backs inside with our feet against the bodywork and kicked it back in to shape! We found out later that he had no driving licence, and had never taken a driving test!"*

Some of the older audiences didn't take too kindly to the blues music the band was now pumping out, and thought it was far too loud as Steve recalls: *"On one occasion we had to do a gig acoustically. It was a really old place out in Lincolnshire. I had to use brushes! We had to turn everything right down. We'd only played a few numbers and we could see these all these old dears on the back row pulling their faces!"*

Despite the odd mis-matched crowd, The Blueset got plenty of bookings according to Roger: *"We gradually progressed further with gigs at Boston's 10-20 Club, the Art College in Lincoln, Peterborough's Girls' College, my old college Stoke Rochford Hall several times, plus various pubs and village community halls."* Steve also worried a little about the strain Graham was under: *"Sometimes when we were on stage, Graham's nose would bleed, and this was because of his singing! His veins used to stick right out – even his teeth had veins! We used to play 'Reelin' And Rockin', 'Anthony Boy' and 'Johnny B. Goode' by Chuck Berry. 'Goodbye My*

Teenage daydreams : *Above: proudly wearing his college scarf in 1964. "That is in the mod days. Everyone wore them for riding the scooter."*

Below: Graham outside his house with his Gibson.

Love' by The Searchers, 'Fever' by Peggy Lee and 'Up A Lazy River', which was a 30s number and a lot of artists had done it. Rog also sang 'Boys', which The Beatles had covered."

The band also did some Bob Dylan material, as Steve remembers: *"We did 'Mr. Tambourine Man'. Whenever we were out in the streets in Skeggy, invariably we'd hear groups of girls singing this song, but thanks to The Byrds' version the harmony was stronger than the main tune and we got a bit obsessive about telling them that the version they were singing was different to the original main vocal on Dylan's, which went 'down' where as The Byrds' version went 'up'. I also seem to remember us doing 'Blowin' In The Wind'. 'Mr. Tambourine Man' was also a good chat up line as it gave us a chance to speak to the birds! I think we did try 'Mighty Quinn' as well."*

After gigging in Nottinghamshire one night, Roger remembers being stopped by the Police: *"We were returning home in our Thames van at about 1:30 in the morning. In those days it was very dark out in the Lincolnshire countryside; there were no streetlights and very few houses and this was a rainy, moonless night. We were travelling over the fens somewhere near Billinghay on the A193 when we saw a tiny red light up ahead. As we got closer we could see a single figure dressed in a dark cap standing in the middle of the road. It was a young policeman waving his police lamp so I slowed to a stop and wound the window down. The constable came up and announced 'I am commandeering this vehicle – there have been reports of a burglary at the Rectory and I need to get there.' We shoved his bike in the back of the van, he climbed in next to Graham and we set off through the pouring rain – straight off the main road and deep into the middle of nowhere along a maze of narrow roads with deep drainage ditches on either side. We eventually arrived at a huge spooky old house surrounded by trees, miles from anywhere – the Rectory. The policeman climbed out and said he was going inside to investigate. At this point the general consensus was that we should dump his bike and bugger off quickly in case there were any armed robbers inside, but, as I pointed out, we had no idea where we were. Nobody fancied the idea of going in to look for him and time dragged slowly by with no sign of him. Finally, after about 25 minutes the policeman reappeared. 'False alarm,' he said, 'the vicar made me a cup of tea. Can you take me back to the main road?' So we did!"*

Mr. Tambourine Man : colour photo : The Blueset at Hildred's Hotel, August 1965. Mono photo : Roger says: "This is at the Sea View Hotel Long Bar with the open book with the words to 'Mr. Tambourine Man' - I think. Graham had a really good memory for lyrics and it was only really long numbers like 'Mr. Tambourine Man' he needed an aide memoire."

The majority of the bands on the circuit were just covering top 30 songs, or old time rock 'n' roll, but with The Blueset playing a combination of blues standards and more obscure tracks, they stood out from the crowd. Steve explains: *"We were doing songs by Blind Blake and Ledbetter Leadbelly. The audiences seemed to like it. Nobody was doing this underground blues. Everyone was doing rock 'n' roll and chart stuff. I used to do a drum solo in the middle of a Blind Blake number called 'Too Tight'. Graham used to start by explaining the lyrics and putting a chord behind it. It was about this man who bought a suit, and when he went out in the rain, it shrunk when it got wet! I liked that song. We used to speed it up at the end on purpose. I remember we were doing it one night and my drums fell over. I felt such a prat!"*

They also used to perform a version of The Rolling Stones' cover *'High Heeled Sneakers'*. Roger remembers: *"Graham used to sing 'Take off your red dress baby, because we're staying in tonight' as the first couple of lines to the song. The correct lyrics were 'Put on your red dress baby, because we're going out tonight'! We got some blues lyrics from the local library and we used to listen to Radio Caroline; it came in clear on the Lincolnshire coast and so did Radio London. The American Forces Network played some blues as well. We also did 'St. Louis Blues' and 'Kansas City Blues'"* Graham remembers: *"You name one and we did it! All the old blues tunes, like 'Walking The Dog' and 'Bring It On Home To Me'. We did blues tunes from the 30s. Lots of blues songs that no one had heard of from old vintage blues records we listened to."*

Steve adds: *"I don't know where all the songs came from. I think Graham used to come up with them. Some of the songs were probably from the twenties or thirties, like 'Black Girl' by Leadbelly. On one of our handout cards, we put blues/folk. So I suppose it was half a dozen of one and six of the other - I guess it was like folky-blues, which is what Leadbelly was. He was the forerunner of the blues, with songs like 'Goodnight Irene'. We used to get songs like that and do them up a bit."*

They had yet to do any original material but that almost changed one evening according to Steve: *"When we were playing at the Sea View Hotel on one occasion, this bloke came up to us who had a wooden leg. He said 'I've got a great song here lads.' The words were 'come on Sue, hit me, hit me, hit me Sue, hit me, oh yeah. I love you and you love me, oh yeah.' All this was written down on a piece of paper. Graham and I were humouring him a bit! We did it in a twelve-bar style. This guy thought it was*

great before Graham had even started singing it! He was saying 'that's it, that's it - better than The Beatles that is!' We had to pull him up the ladder to get him on stage, and we had to keep him straight, because of his wooden leg; we couldn't stop laughing! We always seemed to attract these types of characters. They would either attach themselves to Graham or me."

Graham was still working at Dewhurst's and keeping Kenny Bray amused with his antics. *"One of Graham's tricks was bending his legs as he was working behind the counter so all the customers thought he was going down some stairs! A customer would say to Graham 'can I have a pound of sausage?', and Graham would reply 'yeah, we're a bit short up here; I'll just go and see if there is any more in the cellar.' Then he would start walking along behind the counter and bending his legs and the customers automatically thought he was going down some stairs in to the cellar! I also remember going to see Graham play at The Bamboo coffee bar in Wainfleet. It was Bonfire Night and I'd bought a lot of fireworks for my brothers and sisters. At dinnertime, Graham and I were in the storeroom and he said 'what's in the bag?' So I said 'fireworks.' Graham said 'shall we set some off?' So I said, 'okay' because there was a big yard at the back. But Graham decided he wanted to set the fireworks off there and then. He got them out of the bag and set them off in the storeroom we were in! The place was full of smoke. I mean it was everywhere! The place was made out of wood as well!"*

Roger also remembers hearing stories from Graham's stint as a butcher, reminiscent of an episode of Open All Hours. *"The manager was a big bloke called 'Nobby' Clark. Graham's least favourite job was delivering orders on the shop bike, which was one of those with a small front wheel and a big frame above it to hold the basket. Some of the meat orders for the hotels required two or three trips each. So he could regularly be seen riding round town wearing a blue and white striped butcher's smock and apron. I used to drive up behind him and hoot! When he got bored in the shop, which was most of the time, and whilst Nobby was in the back, he used to attach a pork sausage to the front of his trousers and cavort around until Nobby caught him and clipped him round the ear!"*

While the band generally got on well with each other, one thing that was always in the back of their minds was just why Mick had left his Leicester based band and moved across to Skegness. Roger says: *"I sometimes called Mick Grainger 'Lone Grainger'! I'd just started teaching in Alford and two CID officers came in to school to interview me. Apparently, one of the members of The Blueset (Mick) had allegedly been dealing in drugs; amphetamines apparently. Needless to say my headmaster, Mr. Smith, was not overjoyed to have the police in his school interviewing his new probationary teacher!"*

At the end of 1965 with Christmas only a few days away, Steve and Graham were chatting about various things, when Graham's birthday came in to the conversation. *"I remember Graham saying to me, 'I'm eighteen tomorrow.' And he had this funny look on his face. I said, 'Graham, you got a funny look on your face.' And he was looking at me like a zombie and just said, 'eighteen tomorrow' Then every so often afterwards I would say, 'eighteen tomorrow.' He would know exactly what I meant as we found things like this very funny."* Another of Graham's opening conversational gambits was *"As I was saying to the vicar in bed this morning..."*

Mick Grainger's time in the band also came to an end around the same time, as his naferious activities grew. Roger explains: *"He stayed with us until Christmas then disappeared one day, taking our van with him! I think several people were after him. He had also pinched, of all things, his landlady's kettle! The van was later found abandoned near Boston, having run out of petrol. Mick had been using the kettle as a toilet! The landlady actually asked for it back. We never saw him again."*

To mark the New Year, The Blueset changed their name to The Bluesect. According to Roger: *"This was because Graham thought it sounded vaguely French!"* Graham says: *"It was another popular thing to do by other bands and we just followed a trend."* Once again, the band got some business cards printed and

Hitting the road • *Above: The Blueset with Mick Grainger on harmonica at the Hildred's Hotel in Summer of 1965, and outside the venue (l-r Steve, Roger, Mick and Graham).*

as before, the printer split Bluesect into two words. This time prospective bookers were advised they played 'Rhythm / Blues / Folk', and given Roger's Mum's phone number to book them. Never happy with their name split into two, this was soon amended when another set of cards was printed and included the 'Folk - Blues', along with the same phone number.

For a short while guitarist Noel Robinson returned. Roger says: *"Noel turned up at my house one afternoon. It didn't last very long as there was only room for three in my car, so poor Noel got the sack! To be quite honest, with Graham's powerful lead and rhythm guitar, it made virtually no difference."* And it was better to split modest gig fees three ways rather than four. Steve recalls: *"I can't remember too much about Noel rejoining. I don't think it was for a long time. I do remember Noel's arm when he was playing guitar though. It seemed to be going faster than everyone else's. It was like a pneumatic drill! He seemed to be playing twice as fast as everyone else. He used to have this little leather jacket on and his arm was going so fast. I've heard of down strokes, but this was ridiculous!"* Even Noel admits he was largely redundant: *"They realised* they could manage without the second guitar. The rhythm guitar, which The Shadows had introduced years earlier, was becoming a thing of the past."

The band did however acquire a roadie, as Roger explains: *"His name was Brian and he was an electrician in his late thirties or early forties who lived on his own in a seaside bungalow further up the coast. He worked in Herrick Watson's electrical store opposite Dewhurst's where Graham worked and they knew each other. Brian started coming to some of our gigs and helping us set up. One of the big problems in those days was the non standard variety of power sockets in different venues."* Both Graham and Roger experienced close shaves with live connections and explosions due to poor wiring. *"Brain made us an adaptor unit with several 13 amp connections and a very large variety of plugs on the supply end. Eventually he came with us to every gig. He drove the van, carried the gear and bought drinks – an all round nice guy. He didn't want paying, but one thing he did really crave was to be allowed to sing just one number occasionally. His favourite was 'Pretty Flamingo' which he sang in the 'club mode', full of garbled phrases and tremolos. It was so bad that Steve was usually reduced to helpless laughter and had to stop drumming! It was nice though to have someone to help load the van and not have to drive home after a heavy gig."*

Steve Hardy always liked to keep an eye on the local scene and loved nothing more than to check out the opposition when The Bluesect wasn't playing. The band were also hooked on the brass sound which was becoming increasingly popular and were thinking about trying someone out. Steve says: *"I was horrified one day to learn that The Chosen Four were to play at the Embassy ... and they had brass. This was a major challenge to us. Graham and I were obsessed with brass and hammond organs, etc, and to hear that they had a trumpeter was horrific."* Happily when Steve went to check them out live, the opposition's much vaunted brass debut proved to be just one song, *'Midnight Hour'* by Wilson Pickett. *"It was horrendous. He was bloody useless and sounded like a strangulated cat and that was it. He only played on that one song and he bloody murdered it. I couldn't wait for the morning to tell Graham."*

The Bluesect made their move not long after and added saxophonist Alan Vickers to the line-up, who had played with Graham in The Peter Tomlinson Band. Roger recalls: *"Graham brought him along for an audition one evening and we signed

On the beach Summer 1965 • *Roger (in the photo on the left) says: "We were being American marines landing on the beach in Vietnam - just being daft!" Graham adds: "The water was freezing. After this photo was taken, and we'd got back to Roger's house, the guys pulled me down and took my wet jeans off and threw them into a tree. So that was a struggle to get them down off the tree. I wasn't happy!" Right: Steve and Graham on the promenade. Below : The Blueset at the Ex-Servicemen's Club, Skegness, Autumn 1965.*

him up straight away. The addition of a sax player in such numbers as 'Midnight Hour' and 'I Feel Good' made a huge difference and completely changed the sound of the group." No sooner had Alan joined and they'd done a handful of gigs as a quintet, than Noel decided for a second time that this wasn't for him and quit. He gave up music for good. To mark the change of direction the band got a fourth set of business cards printed and decided to add an 'e' to the end of their name, now spelling it the Bluesecte. This time the cards said 'Soul / Blues'.

As well as band name changes, around the spring of 1966, Graham dropped the second 't' from his surname. *"I thought it looked more show-biz and more posh. I was very influenced by the media, Top Of The Pops and stuff like that. I also thought it would be fun to be mistaken (in name only) for Graham Bonney who had a record in the charts in 1966 called 'Supergirl'. I guess it was a way to impress the girls and my peers!"*

Graham also started to write his own songs. Steve says: *"We played 'Rare Specimen' during this period, which Graham wrote. He didn't write a lot of songs, but I always liked it. It was one of the key numbers in our set. We always used to do it. We'd also do some jazz things, mainly because Graham could play the chords. There were a lot of ninths and thirteenths, etc. A lot of rock guitarists couldn't play these chords, but Graham could. So we built up quite a repertoire around the fact that Graham could do this. Graham played a semi-acoustic, rather than a plank. He used to call Telecasters 'planks'. I guess it rubbed off on me!"*

Another song the band did which Graham wrote included the line 'High heeled shoes and a sweater, I'd like to know that girl better'. Graham remembers the song: *"It was called 'Just To Get Her' and the opening line was 'Bell bottomed jeans and a sweater'."* Roger adds: *"Gradually, we developed a large repertoire of numbers, around one hundred - many from the late 1950s and anything new we liked from the Top 10. In those days you could buy sheet music for each new song that came out. Graham once turned up on his scooter one night with 'Pretty Flamingo' by Manfred Mann rolled up and tucked in his top pocket."*

It was also around this time that Graham heard 'Pet Sounds' by The Beach Boys, released in May. Graham really liked Brian Wilson's song writing on this album and their vocal harmonies started to have a big effect on him.

As did another Sixties icon, the scooter, which Steve remembers well: *"Graham got a Lambretta motor scooter and he said to me, 'how do you work this thing?' But I wasn't old enough to drive it! So, we went off on Warth Lane, which is a long lane in Skegness, and I showed him how to drive it, because I knew a little bit about engines. I got it going and revving up and then we just took off on it. It was a bit hair-raising but after that we got used to it. I used to sit behind him, even though he hadn't passed his test."* With the scooter he and Graham could get to see a few bigger bands. *"We used to go to the Glyderdrome in Boston. We saw Otis Redding there, as well as Chris Farlowe & The Thunderbirds, Dusty Springfield and Alan Bown. On one occasion we set off on the scooter to go to Boston during the winter and it was really icy on the roads. As we were travelling around we used to sing 'Day Tripper' and other songs and harmonise together. Anyway, the 'we found out' part of 'Day Tripper' became 'we fell off', because as we were travelling along, and singing the song, we fell off at exactly that point! The scooter just went from under us. We always sang 'we fell off' from then onwards!"*

Good as they were, The Bluesecte came to an end around late 1966, the familiar conflicts of work and careers to blame, with Roger wanting to carry on teaching, Steve and Graham wanting to move on, as Steve recalls: *"Roger was a fully qualified teacher now and he was older than us, so it was obvious he was going to leave at some point. We wanted to carry on and go to London. We were always on about it. We were fanatics and we weren't bothered about school, jobs or anything. He was a good bass player but he used to follow what Graham was playing. In a three-piece band you need to anchor things down more."* Looking back, Roger agrees but points out that he had little choice: *"I had to follow Graham – he was both lead guitar and lead vocalist. Often when he went off on one his guitar solo improvisations, I would watch the chord shapes he was making and follow him on the bass."*

Roger remembers the split came about for several reasons: *"I'd become a classroom teacher and playing in a band was frowned upon somewhat in those days. Plus, it was very tiring. I'd got married and, being three or four years older than the others, I felt increasingly uncomfortable in the group. Graham wanted to go professional and I had a career to follow. I vaguely remember the band had an opportunity to tour Europe and I didn't want to go. But the real reason for the break up was that Graham was a musical genius and we were just average – he'd outgrown us. Plus, Graham is an outstanding guitarist in his own right – we often forget this. His idiosyncratic finger work and the way he uses his thumb as a 5th digit always amazed me. He could play any riff you care to mention and sing at the same time! His twenty minute solos with feedback and raw metal sound back in the 60s used to stop the show, people would gather round open-mouthed."*

"Steve and I wanted to do something different," agrees Graham. They didn't have to look very far. Steve had stood in with The Chosen Four for one gig at the Pig & Whistle in Butlins Holiday Camp when their drummer couldn't make it.

When Graham and Steve started mulling over the names of musicians for their next band, they kept coming back to Bob Turner and Robin Walker from The Chosen Four. Since Steve already knew them a little, he went to take another look at them: *"I went on a scouting mission to the Embassy Club. After watching them, I thought that organ player Bob Turner and bass player Robin 'Podge' Waker would make a better group with Graham and me. So, with Roger going teaching, Graham thought it was a good idea. It all came together nicely. I think we just approached Bob and Robin and put it too them."*

Graham's take on it? *"They had better amps!"*

In the mirror • *The Graham Bonnet Set at an early photo shoot - L-r : Bob Turner, Graham Bonnet, Robin Walker, Steve Hardy and Alan Vickers.*

CHAPTER 2
Night Of The Shooting Star (1966 - 1969)

Featuring: The Graham Bonnet Set and the Marbles

Caught With A Girl On The Rugby Pitch...

Better amps aside, Graham and Steve Hardy might have been thinking that organist Bob Turner and bass guitarist Robin Walker would be perfect for their next band project, but what they didn't know was that Bob and Robin had designs on them.

The Chosen Four had lost their drummer shortly after Steve had seen them at the Embassy Club and once Bob and Robin got wind of The Bluesecte splitting up, the first thing they thought of was to team up with Graham and Steve. It was left to Bob to meet up with Graham and sound him out about these plans. Getting a positive response, a get-together was then arranged at a local coffee bar in Skegness. Bob says: *"Both bands had broken up. Various things happened, girlfriends and that sort of thing. We were all having a drink in a coffee bar at the time and just said 'why don't we join forces?'"* Alan Vickers was still around and joined on an ad hoc basis.

Rehearsals were arranged in Bob Turner's garage and the only real question was which songs should they learn. Bob recalls: *"We started rehearsing at Chapel St. Leonards. I was the only one driving at the time, so I used to collect the lads and all the gear. We used to rehearse in my Dad's garage for a while."* Graham was quite happy to do material by The Chosen Four, but they were keen to do Graham's material as Robin admits: *"There was a bit of a conflict at first as to whose songs we were going to learn. We won in the end, because Graham's stuff was better than ours - ours was a bit teeny-boppy!"* By agreement (and possibly as he was the best known of the group) the band decided they would go out as The Graham Bonnet Set (or The Graham Bonnet Sect as Graham sometimes used to call it). All this happened quickly and once more it was down to the local jobbing printer for a new set of business cards. This time they had Graham's address on, along with Bob's phone number.

There were only a couple of weeks or so between The Bluesecte finishing and The Graham Bonnet Set starting to gig. They took up where their previous bands had left off, hitting the local venues in the run up to Christmas 1966. Bob: *"The first bookings were in Skegness, mainly at The Parade Hotel. We worked for a chap called Des Holdsworth. He gave us a few bookings to get us started. We just took Friday and Saturday night work mainly, whenever we could get it. Skegness council used to provide us with gigs at the Festival Pavilion, which was quite a new place at the time. Plus the Embassy Club."* Robin also remembers the early Graham Bonnet Set shows: *"We played at The Blue Anchor in Ingoldmells; doing songs by The Beatles, The Rolling Stones, The Troggs and 'My Girl' by The Temptations, as well as many others."*

Alan Vickers normally stuck to doing just the local gigs, but did travel further with the band occasionally as Steve recalls: *"He was like a part time player. We did gigs with him at The Derbyshire Miners Welfare Club, the Embassy Club and upstairs at The Parade Hotel, etc. in Skegness."* Alan himself recalls some of the shows, often with good reason: *"We did weddings and social events. I also remember doing a gig in Peterborough with them and we did some RAF bases. We used to do the Sea View Hotel in Skegness, and it was rare if we used to get through a whole night. It was around the end of the mods and rockers era. When we were on stage, Graham used to stand on one of those round bar tables in front of the stage with his microphone stand on another. Then, about half way through the night, a fight would start. It was like the old cowboy movies, with the tables flying about."* The band normally stuck it out until inevitably someone would knock over the table with Graham's microphone stand on. Alan adds: *"Graham would step back on to the stage and it would all disintegrate. Then we would pack up and go home! We used to do lunchtime gigs as well, we'd never complete those gigs either as there were even fights then."* Graham's friend Kenny Bray remembers the rucks: *"One night there was a massive punch up that more or less finished the place. There were chairs and bottles flying here, there and everywhere. You name it, and it was flying."* It wasn't just the Sea View either, fights would sometimes break out in other pubs while the band was playing, as Steve recalls: *"We'd just stand there and carry on playing. There used to be a bloke in one of the pubs called George. He was from Nottingham and was a bit of a rough neck. He'd always end up scrapping. I used to stand in front of my drums thinking 'don't break them up' while the fight was going on."* The band themselves were even slung out of the Embassy Club on one occasion, although not for fighting, but for having women in the dressing room!

With the New Year and a new start for the band, they decided to get some publicity photographs taken by their friend, John Gladwin. This photo shoot started out in front of Bob Turner's house and progressed down to the seafront as Graham recalls: *"The beach idea was all of us thinking about something different to do for a photo instead of the usual guys standing in a line. It was cold and wet that day and the sand stuck to my jeans. It was the thing back then to do photos in unusual settings as The Beatles did, industrial type backgrounds, etc."*

John Gladwin had his own photo studio, which was basically a shed in his garden in Skegness, but he was also a bit of a music buff as Steve remembers: *"Graham and I in particular used to have conversations with him about bands and groups he was into. He'd come up with all these strange sounding names of groups and say things like, 'hey Hardy, have you heard of Little Anthony and the Imperials'. I'd usually reply, 'no, never heard of 'em'. Whereupon he'd say something like, 'what? Never heard of Little Anthony and the Imperials, where y'been? They're fucking brilliant,' emphasising the word 'brilliant', which was one of his buzzwords. I'd probably have been going on about The Beatles or somebody else I really liked at the time but they weren't 'progressive' enough for him. He was a sort of John Peel of the time. We'd usually end up arguing the toss and I'd wind him up by going over the top. Of course, Graham and I would generally lark about pretending to be him, as we always did with 'characters'."*

Graham and Steve were now becoming very good mates and spending a lot of time together. *"When Graham and I were out on a winter's night, he would*

Against a wall • *The Graham Bonnet Set - L-r : Alan Vickers, Graham Bonnet, Robin Walker, Steve Hardy and Bob Turner.*

sometimes sing his guts out on the seafront because there was no one around. We would do harmonies and things. If there ever happened to be somebody around, you could see them looking round, wondering where it was all coming from! You could hear Graham all along the seafront, because he had such a powerful voice."

The band secured a one-off gig as support to Cliff Bennett and The Rebel Rousers who had taken their version of The Beatles' 'Got To Get You Into My Life' almost to the top of the UK charts the year before. Robin recalls the event: *"We were in a marquee. We were using some good gear, but we could have done with some louder speakers, because it is dead in a marquee. While Cliff was having a break, we played 'Got To Get You Into My Life' which was in our repertoire at that time. Then these heads started to appear round the curtains; it was Cliff and The Rebel Rousers seeing what was going on. They took it in good humour!"* Lou remembers the band covering another Beatles song: *"They played at The Butterfly Club in Skegness and Graham had to sing 'Please Please Me' seven or eight times to satisfy them! He could sing anything."* Another song the band covered was Tom Jones' version of 'Green Green Grass Of Home', which was No. 1 in the UK charts over Christmas 1966. The Graham Bonnet Set decided to put it straight in to the set. Graham says: *"I used to sing it regularly. It had been a big hit and everyone kept requesting it. I had the 'Green Green Grass Of Home' coming out of my ears!"*

Steve remembers that certain songs worked better in some places than others: *"Around this time we were doing stuff by the Spencer Davis Group like 'Keep On Running', 'I'm A Man' and 'Somebody Help Me'. Also, The Animals' 'Don't Let Me Be Misunderstood'. These songs used to go down very well in the Boston Copper Kettle Club where we'd built up quite a following. Particular pubs and clubs seemed to like certain sets of songs and we'd often write down the list of songs to do in the van on the way, sometimes running through the harmonies on ones which were still new to us. We also did 'Happy Together' by The Turtles, 'Sweet Soul Music' by Arthur Conley, 'Out Of Time' by Chris Farlowe and 'Working In A Coal Mine' by Lee Dorsey amongst others.*

When we did more MOR clubs we'd do stuff like 'Green Green Grass Of Home' and The Beatles' 'When I'm Sixty Four' and 'Lucy In The Sky With Diamonds', which was another good number that went down well wherever we played. I remember doing it at a club called the Penny Farthing in Leicester. The only problem with that place was there was no stage, so we were actually playing on the floor. My drums used to slide all over the place so I tied them to my drum stool as I couldn't screw my stop-block in to the parquet wood floor..."

During the spring, the band was approached by an agent, as Bob recalls: *"My father, who was a local accountant, had a client called Harry Segal. Harry was a local entrepreneur. He used to put shows on at the arcade and theatres. He happened to come and see us one night. I think we were doing a dinner dance at The Imperial in Skegness. Harry said 'who do you work for?' We told him we got our own bookings and Harry replied by saying 'how would you like to work for me? I've got a lot of contacts in the business'."* The band went over to his office in Winthorpe for a chat and were told 'get some photos done of yourselves and a write-up.' Harry soon began to find them work further afield.

"We also started working through different agencies. Harry would split the commission with whomever we were working through. This was new to us. All of a sudden we were a band on the road," says Bob. On the road certainly, but still striving to hold down day-jobs as well. Bob was an apprentice bricklayer, Steve was working at a printers, Robin was a TV engineer, Alan was an apprentice painter and decorator for his father and Graham was still working at Dewhurst's, where his anarchic sense of fun still impressed his fellow workers; Graham's mate Kenny Bray recalls the mayhem: *"When Nobby, the manager, went out for his dinner break, Graham would lie on this chopping block at the back of Dewhurst's and go to sleep! He was gigging so much with his band at the time and always felt tired. I used to tie him down with butcher's string, and shave his legs, or draw matchstick men on them. Then when the manager came back, Graham couldn't get up. Nobby would say 'what are you*

> **Out and about** • *The Graham Bonnet Set photographed in Skegness for some publicity material, starting out at keyboard player Bob Turner's garage, then down to the beach.*

doing there?' and Graham would say 'well, er…'"

There was also something of a Robin Hood spirit to some of Graham's antics. "When the old women, who couldn't afford much, came in to Dewhurst's," recalls Kenny, "Graham used to give them a lot more and say 'this is on Jimmy Dewhurst!' Lord Vesty he used to call him after the Vesty family who owned the chain. At Christmas time he used to give the old ladies turkeys as well, and he would say, 'this one is on Lord Vesty!' On one occasion a person came in and asked for two sausages. So Graham said 'why what's up?' The person replied by saying 'it's all I can afford.' So Graham would say 'here, have the full tray!' There he was, wrapping them all up!" Dewhurst's closed down in the late 1980s, clearly never having quite got over the generosity of Messers Bonnet and Bray.

Graham had been getting to know a girl called Ewa Widås (pronounced Eva) for a while. She was from Gothenburg in Sweden and was working in Skegness as an au-pair. With Ewa's time in Skegness nearly at an end, she started planning to return home. Steve wanted to visit the country: "I'd always had a picture in my mind about the place. I was set to go on my own prior to the band going. I mentioned it to the others and they said 'we'll come along.' Ewa came over with us and helped us with the language and things. She even let us stay in a relative's cottage."

Bob also recalls the trip: "She knew somebody in the world of radio and said we could stay in her father's holiday bungalow, which was just outside Gothenburg." There was even the mention of a possible radio session. So Ewa and the band, minus Robin (who didn't want to leave his girlfriend) set off from Skegness in June for six days in Gothenburg in their van.

Coincidentally on the ferry over were two members of another Skegness group who were doing quite well in Scandinavia as Bob remembers: "The band was called Sandy Martin & The Red Squares, who used to be known as The Seminoles. They were doing ever so well and we wished we could imitate them. We went to see them as they were appearing in Gothenburg. They did a hell of a show! We'd only seen them round Skegness but they had really polished their act up. They were a terrific band."

In fact Scandinavia was a busy destination for many British beat bands who could often get short tours there simply on the strength of being from the UK. True to her word, through an old boyfriend who ran the place, Ewa arranged a visit to Gothenburg's radio station where the band recorded some songs, even though the only gear they had with them was Graham's guitar. Steve says: "I'll always remember that particular studio in Sweden. It wasn't quite finished and smelt of Norwegian wood! I think the guy in the recording studio was just happy to have an English group in there. The main song we recorded was the Beach Boys version of 'When I Kissed Her', which we did as a four part harmony and without instruments, or perhaps just a guitar. I think the other song was the Beatles' version of 'Devil In Her Heart', which also leant itself to harmonies."

Bob adds: "We met these two guys who were sound engineers, and one of the chaps was obviously the director of the radio station. Whether anything came of it on their radio station, I'm not sure. If we had taken the equipment, or could have had equipment brought in to the studio, we could have done them a show." Another reason for the studio visit was to see if they could do some demos as Graham remembers: "We went to see if we could get a Swedish deal by putting down tracks, but only I had a guitar. So it was me alone. It didn't come to anything. We did a recording of 'Release Me' which Engelbert Humperdinck had taken to the top of the UK charts in January."

If this was an opportunity missed, the band did get a bit of a taste for the rock life. Steve says: "We did go to see The Who, but you really needed a pair of binoculars to see them properly!" The band also went to a gig by The Hep Stars, which Steve enjoyed: "They were a top group in Sweden at the time. Benny Andersson, later of Abba, was in the group. Then all of a sudden this gentleman came up to us and asked

21

us if we were in a group. He then took us to the front of the queue and gave us the best seats in the house! Jimi Hendrix was staying in one of the hotels while we were there. We saw Sammy Davis Jr. The people of Sweden were really nice to us."

They also got to see a British band called Sounds In Steel, a calypso outfit whose only claim to fame was playing the steel drums on The Hollies hit single 'Carrie-Anne'.

While the band and Graham were enjoying their break, Dewhurst's were down one butcher's assistant, as Graham had neglected to ask for the time off, relying on his shopmate Kenny Bray to make something up: *"I knew that he had gone, but I made up all these lies every time they asked me something. Nobby would say: 'well if he isn't here on Monday, he's finished. I bet he's having a lie in.'"* They even sent Kenny out looking for their errant worker. *"I just went round to Lou's and René's and had a cup of tea with them."*

After getting back from Gothenburg, Graham decided not to return to Dewhurst's; whether they would have had him back is probably open to question! As far as he was concerned Sweden had shown him the way and he was now a professional musician. The Graham Bonnet Set had now got a new rehearsal venue at the local YMCA (although saxophonist Alan Vickers never rehearsed with them there). They went straight back on the road and began stretching their wings. Bob remembers them gigging in Lincoln, Horncastle, Louth, Wisbech in Cambridgeshire as well as several appearances at events for various Town Halls and Skegness Council. They even got as far as Sheffield, *"We played at Firth Park WMC and Dial House, which we played on several occasions as we always went down very well. This was as well as Nottingham, Mansfield and Chesterfield."*

Travelling in the van was still a bit of a gamble as Bob recalls only too well: *"It used to break down on the A1. It always seemed to happen as the van was very unreliable. It was pieced together with elastic, glue and everything! That's how we kept it going. We couldn't afford a decent van."*

Bob also remembers that they had all been inspired by the success of Sandy Martin & The Red Squares in Scandinavia. For a time in 1966, mainly in Denmark, they were the biggest band over there (and are still working there) and he wanted to emulate this. Graham thought he knew how to push things forward, by bringing his cousin Trevor Gordon into the band. This had been in the back of his mind for quite a while. He knew Trevor was an excellent musician and could certainly help to take the band to the next level. Graham wrote to him in Australia asking him to come back to England and join his group. As Bob says: *"Graham thought he would be a big asset to the band."*

Banner Productions in Nottingham had picked up on the band's growing professionalism and began getting them work in the Midlands. Impressed with the feedback from the venues they suggested that The Graham Bonnet Set do some recording for them. Steve says: *"We recorded a couple of songs, 'A Love Like Yours', which Ike & Tina Turner had recorded [issued as a single in 1966] and 'Devil In Her Heart' which The Beatles covered."* It had first been released by the all girl group The Donays in 1962 and Bob remembers the session: *"We went to these recording studios in Nottingham and they were impressed; we got a lot of work out of it. They were going to make a disc of our recordings but somewhere along the line copyright came in to it and it couldn't be done. Phil Banner did his best and wanted to release a record, but at least he got us a lot of work around Derby and Mansfield, because he was a big name around there."*

Steve remembers life on the road with The Graham Bonnet Set: *"We played at the Golden Diamond in Sutton in Ashfield [which Graham would return to perform at much later, in 2007] quite a few times and always went down very well. Each time we always stayed with my sister, Norma. We also played at a pub in Newark and another venue was The Scales - I think it was in Doncaster and obviously we had to stay overnight. My uncle Jim who lived there, knew this guy so it was perfect, or so we thought. The guy's wife had died about six months earlier, yet her stuff was still all over the house. We actually thought she was still alive, because there were all these slippers everywhere. It was very eerie. Also the bed felt damp as it hadn't been used for ages. Graham and I were sharing a double bed in this room and he said to me 'is your bum wet?' I said 'yeah it is'. He said 'I'm wet through.' Anyway, we switched the light off and put our heads down. Sometime later I remember jumping out of bed in horror and shouting at Graham to look towards the bottom of the bed. Staring back at us from the dressing table in front of the bed was a ghoulish iridescent green crucifix about a foot high. It was one of those tacky luminous ones that light up in the dark and scare you to bloody death. It was like something out of The Exorcist. That did it. We couldn't sleep at all. We managed*

Above • Concert poster 1967. Below : Ewa Widås next to the group's van.

to make it through to the crack of dawn by laughing and joking about it all before leaving as fast as we could - sod the breakfast."

"Again in Yorkshire," Steve recalls, "we were doing a gig and a so-called American promoter came up to us and asked us if we wanted to play some RAF bases abroad." They were immediately suspicious when broad Yorkshire kept sneaking into his American drawl.

As the summer of '67 was coming to an end Graham and Steve read in the music press about the Bee Gees' guitarist and drummer being told by the Home Office that they must leave the country because they were Australians who had travelled to England on a visa. So Graham wrote to Barry Gibb on the off-chance. Steve says: "We thought we would go for their jobs. It was just an idea and I thought we had a good chance. I told Graham to put it in the letter that he was Trevor Gordon's cousin (Trevor had recorded with the Bee Gees), just to see if it would rub off." Fans protested and eventually the Prime Minister got involved, the musicians got their immigration documents and Graham's scheme fell at the first hurdle.

He was soon cheered up by another letter, this one from his cousin saying he would like to join the band. The timing was just right for Trevor, who had already been thinking about returning to England. Graham was really excited, and when he told his fellow band mates the news it forced a decision on whether the band should turn professional or not. This wasn't a problem for Graham, Bob Turner or Steve Hardy, but it was for Alan Vickers and Robin Walker. Robin recalls the split: "I left the band when they went professional. I knew I wasn't a good bass player, and I didn't think I would make it on the professional scene. It was just a dream. I also thought I should be a bit more responsible because of my commitments to my family."

Steve confirms this: "Robin lost interest when he started going out with this girl - he was more interested in settling down so he left and we got John Davenport in. John lived in Mablethorpe, which is actually quite a way from Skegness. I think Bob Turner knew about him. Again though, we never had that solid bass sound, we just couldn't achieve it for some reason. We did have it a bit with Robin, but we were obsessed about trying to get this foundation stone. John had all the equipment and had just bought a speaker called a Selmar Goliath, it was a great big thing. He was always on about his woofers and tweeters but nothing ever seemed to work right. Later on he bought some Marshall equipment. We went down to Bletchley to pick it up but when we got it home we found that there was something wrong with it and we just couldn't get it to sound right. While we were down in Bletchley some of Jimi Hendrix's road crew were there. They had one of Jimi's broken guitars from the previous night's gig so we asked them if we could have it and they gave it to us. I think John ended up with it."

The sound might not have been perfect but the new bassist fitted in and they continued to gig as a four piece, working hard as Bob remembers: "We'd all packed our jobs in and we'd been out on the road doing it for a living for a few months, going out for a week at a time and kipping in the van. We were playing nightclubs like Clouds in Derby, Talk Of The Midlands in Nottingham, Motown in Grimsby and others in Doncaster. This was as well as still performing on the pub and club circuit."

During October, Trevor Gordon arrived after a four week trip from Australia to England by sea, with Bob going to meet him at the docks: "My girlfriend and I drove down to Southampton. We had a brief description of him from Graham and we held a sign up with his name on and brought him back to Skegness."

Trevor Gordon Grunnill had been born in Blackpool in May 1948. His family emigrated to Sydney, Australia in 1955, but he kept in touch and met up with Graham again in 1960 when he returned to England for a year or so. "I then went back to Australia and got involved in the music business over there." In fact he was spotted singing at a concert on the ship over by an Australian musician who fixed him up with a television audition in Sydney, which lead to a TV appearance on the Johnny O'Keefe Show, a top rated programme there. Trevor was still at school but his performing career progressed quite quickly. The TV debut lead to Trevor getting his own children's TV show with ABC (Australian Broadcasting Corporation) and

Out and about • *The Graham Bonnet Set four-piece line-up with new bassist John Davenport under Skegness pier and in the promenade gardens.*

doing cabaret. Johnny O'Keefe then talked Festival Records in to promoting a batch of new artists and this included Trevor who now had his own slot on Johnny's TV show. His debut single for Leedon Records, 'Going To Church On Sunday', was released in May 1964.

Trevor's career had coincided with the emergence of three young brothers on the music scene, the Bee Gees. They too had emigrated to Australia from England with their parents and being on the same label as Trevor became very friendly with them. They backed him on a couple of singles, and he played guitar on some of theirs, while they also did some live shows together.

Trevor's best friend, Peter Foldy says: *"The Bee Gees and Trevor were working at the Royal Easter Show in Sydney. They did a sideshow in a tent. It was a rock and roll sideshow, with a guy who stood outside saying, 'step right up, step right up, live from television, it's the Bee Gees with Trevor Gordon and The Dolly Sisters', who were Bee Gees' sister Lesley Gibb and one of her friends. They were the go-go dancers. The guys would do about twenty shows a day. Half hour shows I think."*

In 1966 Trevor returned to England to record some material for Pye Records and two singles were later released here (and also in Australia and America). He got a bit of work as a session singer in The Cotton Singers on the Billy Cotton Band Show and saw Graham when he could. *"We did a bit of playing. When I returned with my parents to Australia at the end of the year, I missed swinging London. Then in 1967, Graham wrote to me and said, 'why don't you come over to England and join my group?' And that is what I did. I was 19 years old."*

Lou says: *"Trevor came and lived with us. He was a great influence on Graham, who had always said 'he's a damn good musician.'"* There was talk around the time that Trevor arrived that The Graham Bonnet Set might change their name to Bonar Law. Graham says: *"I thought of it, because my brother had a friend with that name, and I thought it was unusual. It sounded tough, I suppose. Bonar Law had been a prime minister of England way back in 1922 and that is where the name came from."* The idea was dropped, but not forgotten.

Trevor was quickly rehearsed on second guitar and backing vocals, and as a result Graham felt the band was stronger than ever, and well equipped to handle whatever the future had to offer. It didn't take Trevor long to learn their set: *"I wasn't required to do very much. Graham sang all the lead vocals. I just sang harmonies and played a bit of guitar."* In fact Trevor wasn't sure what he was doing there. *"The band would have been quite good without me in fact. I wasn't necessary at all!"* Steve agrees that Trevor's sound didn't add a great deal *"but he did play a different style of guitar to Graham."* Trevor used to record rehearsals so he could take them away and listen to them and decide what needed to be improved. *"We rehearsed in an unheated donkey shed in the middle of winter. It was freezing. I had my tape recorder and recorded a couple of my own songs with Graham singing."*

Soon Trevor was in at the deep end, facing the tough crowds of the North-east working men's club scene. Steve remembers the travelling: *"We used to go to Newcastle, South Shields and places up that way. Often on the way to gigs we would have our stock in trade numbers to run through to pass the time while driving. The Beatles 'If I Fell' was lovely to put harmonies too, plus 'Devil In Her Heart'. There was a harmony we used to put in at the end of the chorus, the last 'ahs' over the words, 'she's an angel sent to me…', which never worked. I later listened to The Beatles' version and they stopped short of doing this, no doubt realising that it didn't work."* Trevor does remember them playing 'Baby I Love You' by The Ronettes as part of their set, and they also did another song by The Ronettes which provided a full three-part harmony in the background with Graham on lead vocals, 'Be My Baby'.

There were vague promises of a German tour, but it never materialised. The group kept at it however as Steve recalls: *"We always felt that something was just around the corner. We never got down over anything. To be honest, I can't remember having a bad night because we used to enjoy it so much. The acoustics at some of the places we played were appalling. The places would have really high ceilings and the sound would go everywhere. We couldn't hear ourselves on stage because we didn't have any monitors. Everything used to go through one amplifier. If you couldn't hear it, hard luck! You would sometimes hear the sound five minutes later. The guitars and drums would bounce back at you."*

The band had progressed to staying in digs now instead of the van, as Bob remembers: *"In the North-east where we did a lot of work for Bobby Brown (a promoter) we used to stop in Sunderland. It was a proper place for theatrical acts and bands. You got your breakfast at 1:00 pm, and your lunch at 6:00 pm. Then you would go out and do your gig at the club. You would probably return about midnight and there would be a proper evening meal for you if you wanted it. Nobody got up before midday. The lady who ran the place was called Mrs. Downy. She would never take lorry drivers or anyone like that. There would be jugglers, singers, and special acts all stopping there. You all used to get round the table. The teatime session was the best; you would be asking people, 'how have you gone on?' And they would possibly reply 'great, yeah. Done a bomb mate. How have you gone on?' 'Never going to that place again - died a death!' It went round, how you had gone on and where you had been. 'Watch that Concert Secretary at that club, he's a sod!' We used to swap a lot of stories like that, and we met a lot of nice people."*

Even so it was clear that The Graham Bonnet Set needed to step up a gear if they were going to progress further and, apart from the North-east circuit, they didn't actually do many shows with Trevor who already had ambitions of his own for the band. He decided that they wouldn't really make it based in Skegness, and suggested they think about going down to London, which made some of the band a bit nervous as Bob recalls: *"We thought, London! My God! He said 'don't worry, I know people there.' And he did."*

Trevor says: *"It probably was my idea, but Graham was just as keen."* It was something of a leap of faith, giving up their local connections and contacts, but the band were in agreement and they travelled to London in January 1968, settling in rented accommodation in Wembley Park. Trevor says: *"We didn't get any work for quite a number of weeks. We were on the verge of selling microphones to pay for the rent. All of us were getting quite fed up."* The band did the rounds of the agencies, and eventually this paid off as Bob remembers: *"We went to Brian Morrison and then Harvey Block. Brain Morrison was okay. He said: 'I'll give you a few gigs to try. There will not be a lot in it for you until we've heard you and seen what you are like.' Harvey Block asked 'who have you worked for before?' So we said 'Banner Productions in Nottingham.' Straight away he got his secretary to phone Phil and ask him all about us - all this happened while we were sat in his office!"* Harvey Block Associates had been formed by Derek Block and his partner Dru Harvey. They were already handling some big names and to be taken on there was quite a step up.

It was a pivotal moment in Graham's career, and things began to move quickly. The Harvey Block Agency got the band two gigs one February weekend at the Revolution Club which Bob remembers well: *"It just stands out in my mind, because it was such a plush place. We did a weekend there for nothing. It was like an audition. It was probably Derek Block who put us in there. He said 'if you go down well, there will be people in the audience that will see you and approach you for work. But they will go through us and we will let you know.' And, sure enough, as soon as we had come off stage we were in the dressing room and that is what happened. This French bloke called Françoise de Luville came up to us. Everyone seemed to know him. He said 'I'm going to bring some people to see you tomorrow night.' He did as well! He said 'I want you in France and I want you to work for me.'"*

The Revolution Club was a really hip venue, used by the fashion industry to show new collections, and by many people in the record industry to showcase and check out new bands. Steve also remembers the gig: *"We went down a bomb. By this time the band were a bit more commercial. We were doing sixties standards with some classics thrown in, but it was the way we did them. Graham used to give the songs a bit more personality and feeling. Far more than a lot of average bands did. We would lend ourselves to any style really and make the songs more exciting for us to play. One*

Out and about • *The Graham Bonnet Set's expanded line-up with Trevor, photographed on an abandoned farm near Skegness.*

song I personally liked at the time was Brenton Wood's 'Gimme Little Sign', which we did at the Revolution Club. I used to do the high falsetto over Graham's lead vocals. Of course we used to do things like 'Whiter Shade Of Pale' and a few Beatles numbers like 'Eight Days A Week' and 'Day Tripper'. We had all these people wanting to talk to us. There was Chas Chandler, Françoise de Luville and Ossie Byrne, who was the Bee Gees string arranger."

On the second night, manager Robert Stigwood was in the club and he recognised Trevor Gordon as having been in some home movies the Bee Gees had made. After the band had done their slot, Robert, Ossie Byrne and Trevor had a chat. The following day Barry Gibb, who hadn't known Trevor was in England, phoned him up at their flat. *"Barry just wanted me. He didn't know about the rest of the band, or Graham. I told him about Graham, saying you must hear him, he's fantastic. So he said 'yes, all right. Bring him along then.' And when they heard him, they were really knocked out!"*

Bob remembers the excitement at these developments: *"Trevor had got the address of Polydor Records, who the Bee Gees were signed to. All this was a dream to us. I mean we knew someone who knew them! They had just had a few hit singles and were big stars. So, sure enough, we drove round in the old group van to Brook Street, in the West End, which is where Robert Stigwood's office was. Barry and Robin Gibb were also there."* Trevor and Graham went in to chat but perhaps unsurprisingly Robert Stigwood laid it on the line and made it quite plain he didn't want the band, he was only interested in signing them. Trevor and Graham auditioned on some Beach Boys and Stevie Wonder songs with acoustic guitars.

They went away to think about Stigwood's suggestion, but before long Françoise de Luville got in touch again, now saying he wanted to sign the band. It turned out he did work for Robert Stigwood but wanted to try and beat him to the deal as Bob quickly grasped: *"Françoise had Robert Stigwood's accountant with him. The two of them wanted to start their own agency and were looking for new bands. Françoise started doing his best to sign us up by himself."*

The Graham Bonnet Set all ended up journeying back to Skegness with Françoise, along with a contract. Bob remembers: *"We travelled through the night in his Rolls Royce, driven by his chauffeur. We arrived in Skegness and Chapel St. Leonards much to the amazement of several people, because we were riding around in a Rolls Royce. They thought we'd hit the big time!"*

In fact the band were too young to sign any contract, and would need their parents' signatures, which was quickly refused (and in the case of Trevor would have been very difficult because his parents were in Australia). Graham remembers the fuss: *"He tried to get my Mum and Dad to sign it, but they didn't."*

Françoise's subterfuge was eventually brought to the notice of Stigwood by Barry Gibb. Françoise was saying that he had spotted the band first. Bob says: *"About one week later Françoise phoned up and said 'look, we definitely want you. There is months of work in France.'"*

Once Robert Stigwood explained that he was still interested in Trevor and Graham they headed back down to London, and Steve Hardy decided to tag along too. Bob says: *"Graham was trying his best to convince Robert Stigwood that he should keep the band, but he just wasn't interested. He said 'I told them that we had been together for quite a while and that I wanted them with me.' Robert Stigwood said, 'no. You either come with me now and we do what we can, or you might as well walk out of the door.' We kept in touch with them down in London for a while and said to Graham 'do the sensible thing mate. You've got a chance here so take it.' And that is exactly what he did."* The Graham Bonnet Set was over.

Having made the decision to go with Stigwood, Trevor and Graham were instantly put on a retainer. Trevor says: *"They gave us about £15 a week each, which was just enough to pay the rent and buy some food. We went through a few periods where we didn't have any money. We had to walk miles and miles to pick up our retainer from where we lived in Harrow, near Wembley Park, to the West End of London."*

Robert Stigwood was born in Australia, but emigrated to the UK in 1955 and learnt a lot of his trade working with producer Joe Meek, before setting up on his own. Signing Cream and then the Bee Gees he had a reputation as a ruthless and tough operator and by the end of the Sixties was one of the most important music industry names in the country after a tie-up with Brian Epstein's NEMS agency. It's hard to know exactly what his vision was for Graham and Trevor, it may have been as much to help promote the Bee Gees song catalogue and earn producer royalties as to establish the pair as a new act.

Steve Hardy stayed on with Trevor and Graham. He was also put on a retainer, because he was helping out with various jobs and doing harmonies on some songs. He recalls: *"When we were living in Wembley Park Maurice Gibb used to come round in a wig! We also went round to Barry Gibb's house as well. Plus, I met Robert Stigwood too. After a while, Gibson Kemp was put with us to try and sort something out. I was sure all they were interested in was Graham. Up to that point, I always considered myself to be part of everything with me being on a retainer."*

Around mid-March Trevor and Graham entered IBC studios to record a song the Bee Gees had written for them and Trevor's voice in particular. The session line-up was pretty impressive, with Barry Gibb on guitar, Maurice Gibb on bass and piano and their band members Vince Melourney on guitar and Colin Peterson on drums. This line-up played on all the Bee Gees penned songs that the duo would go on to record, though Trevor and Graham both played guitar on a few and Graham even played bass guitar on a couple as well, with various session musicians for whatever else was needed.

Early rehearsals took the form of jam sessions, doing Stevie Wonder and Beach Boys songs. Graham says: *"Trevor originally sang 'By The Light Of The Burning Candle'. He sang the vocal and then said to Barry Gibb 'I think Graham should sing this.' So, it became a different song, because we've got completely different voices, Trevor's is very sweet and soft."* Trevor adds: *"I told them no, Graham is going to sing this. It's ridiculous. Get Graham to do the lead vocal on it. Barry Gibb didn't really know Graham's vocal capabilities, as he had only heard him sing on a couple of occasions, and one of those were at the audition."* This early unissued version of the song still remains in the vaults under the title 'Burning Candles'. Once Barry had heard Graham's range, he changed his thinking.

As soon as the Bee Gees UK tour was over in early May they turned their attention back to Trevor and Graham. Graham now laid down a vocal for 'By The Light Of The Burning Candle' at IBC, with Trevor and Steve Hardy providing harmonies. Steve was also around for the recording and the mixing of the song: *"We were slightly out of tune, my guess is that it probably had something to do with concert pitch. So, when they added the orchestra, it was decided that as it was a B-side, and as they couldn't really retune the orchestra, they would speed up the track slightly, taking it up a semitone or thereabouts, until it matched the key. When you hear 'By The Light Of The Burning Candle', Graham's voice to me sounds something like Jerry Lewis in parts. To hear it at its correct speed on vinyl you can rest a finger gently on the edge of the record, without disturbing the mechanism too much of course, which slows it down very slightly, a semitone, and you'll hear its original recording speed. Incidentally, this session was arranged by Bill Shepherd and I remember giving a hand helping a couple of men carry in a harp that was used. I hadn't realised how big they really were until then!"*

Graham took three weeks off after the recording to allow his voice to get back in to tip-top condition. By then Barry had come up with another song and Graham started singing 'la-la-la' over the basic tune, which was in a country music style. Recalling Barry writing the lyrics, Steve Hardy says: *"I saw him write the lyrics out on a piece of card. It was torn from something like a fag packet, or off a carton. We were at IBC studios; Barry wrote down the lyrics very quickly as if he'd been thinking about the title and words beforehand and wanted to get them down."* Lyrics developed and the song became 'Only One Woman', starting life as quite a fast song. Robin wanted to call the song 'Picture', but from what Graham can remember, Barry wasn't having any of it. *"Robin thought it was more sort of mysterious and not as obvious as the line I kept repeating, but Barry insisted it was mostly his tune anyway, except for the high notes which were Trevor's idea."* The 3/4 time signature always worried Graham, but when the song took on a slower tempo it became more soulful. In the studio, it started to take shape when Trevor suggested that Graham sing the melody high, instead of low.

'Only One Woman' developed into a very strong ballad, which definitely suited Graham's more powerful voice and range. Recording then began with Barry and Maurice Gibb, along with Robert Stigwood, handling the production.

With everyone concerned happy with the way things were progressing, they spent time trying to come up with a name for the duo. Robin Gibb wanted Peanuts, Robert Stigwood suggested The Gravy Train, while Trevor and Graham resurrected their rejected band name Bonar Law. Graham says: *"We thought Bonar Law was good. It sounds very positive and forward sounding, like a statement. Then Barry came up with the name Marbles. God knows why or where that came from in his head!"*

Steve remembers Graham's obsession with the name of the old Prime Minister. *"The first time I heard Graham actually mention the name was when we lived on Brook Avenue in Wembley Park. Graham did a pencil sketch drawing of him once and from then on thought it would be a good name for a band. Graham was very good at drawing and sketching."* It was, though, Barry Gibb's suggestion of the Marbles which eventually won out.

Steve was trying his very best to keep in with the progress but realised there wasn't much chance of a permanent position with the Marbles. *"I held on for a while. In those days there was a big gap between the recording of something and getting it released. Naturally I was upset at not being included, especially after I'd had a little taste of things. I also played drums on one of Graham's songs, 'Rare Specimen', which was from our days in The Bluesecte. We recorded that at Marquee studios, though drummers were ten-a-penny."*

Eventually Robert Stigwood drew a contract up for Trevor and Graham and also signed the duo to Polydor Records in the UK as he had financial connections with them. The five-year contract came into effect on June 1st 1968, with Louis Bonnett signing as a guardian for Graham. The contract was fairly typical of the time, and offered get-out clauses for both sides. The Marbles were entitled to terminate the contract at any time after twelve calendar months if their gross revenue was under £2,000 in the proceeding twelve months, while the Robert Stigwood Organisation was entitled to terminate if the Marbles refused to carry out their obligations under the contract. RSO would take 30% of the gross revenue which Graham and Trevor received from their activities in the entertainment industry in all countries except America (where it rose to 40%!).

With two finished songs in the can, it became apparent that 'Only One Woman' was the obvious choice as the lead track on what was to become their debut single, especially with such a powerful vocal delivery. The single was released on July 31st with Record Retailer commenting: *"Two boys, discovered by the Bee Gees, and one of them has an amazingly high-pitched voice of considerable power. This is a sturdy slow-paced ballad and there's an American soul intensity about it, even from the piano at the back."* The New Musical Express commented that it was *"notable for the powerfully gripping performance from the lead singer."*

Barry Gibb wrote a weekly column for Fabulous 208 magazine and told readers about his new discovery: *"The Marbles are different. They are two blokes who are destined to become super-stars in pop music. There was this boy, Trevor Gordon, someone who I knew five years ago. And there was his cousin, Graham, working in a group at the Revolution Club in London. Trevor told us how Graham had the most unusual voice. Unusual? It's ridiculous. His voice is as high as the Empire States Building. And talk about powerful – why, he has to stand about seven feet away from the microphone otherwise he damages the mechanism. Yet off-stage he's an incredibly quiet sort of guy. You'd never believe this voice could come out of someone like that."*

Barry also mentioned Robert Stigwood first hearing Graham sing: *"He just sat there in the flat and Graham let rip. It took him about thirty seconds to appreciate that the two boys together were really going to set the scene alight."* Barry was obviously very excited about the Marbles and told the New Musical Express: *"Graham Bonnet has the most powerful voice I have ever heard. I am complementing him when I say he is a freak, that he has a freak voice. He doesn't need a microphone."* When Graham spoke to Tony Wilson of Record Mirror he said: *"I sing from my stomach not my throat.*

Barry Gibb kept saying, 'go back, go back.'"

Despite this praise and a large advert for the single on the front cover of the New Musical Express' August 10th issue, it took a while for the single to start moving. Slowly various radio stations began to pick up on the song, and the duo started to make a few TV appearances, debuting on the Mike Mansfield directed (and Brighton based) Southern ITV show Time For Blackburn on August 31st, hosted by DJ Tony Blackburn. This started the ball rolling and Graham recalls they did both tracks on the show: *"Mike Mansfield thought 'By The Light Of The Burning Candle' should have been the A-side. He loved it so much."*

The single finally entered the charts on September 25th at No. 48 and the Marbles made their Top Of The Pops debut on October 3rd (repeated on the 31st), appearing again on the show on October 17th. By October 30th 'Only One Woman' peaked at No. 5 and spent twelve weeks in the charts in total. They also appeared on one of the main entertainment programmes of the time, the Simon Dee Show. This resulted in a phone call from none other than Paul McCartney, wanting to know more about them, who had produced the single and who their management was.

With 'Only One Woman' a hit in the UK, Polydor Records were given the green light to release the record in Australasia, Europe, Japan, Scandinavia, South Africa and various South American countries. No country was off limits and even Lebanon, Malaysia, Singapore and Turkey got in on the act. Robert Stigwood was also able to negotiate a deal in North America for the duo via the Polydor subsidiary label Atlantic Records, who placed the Marbles on their Cotillion Records imprint. All this for a record the duo had actually thought wasn't going to make it, as Graham told New Musical Express: *"At one point, we really thought it had had it, but when it started getting the plays and TV it started selling."*

"Having a hit like this with our first record has really caught us unawares," Trevor admitted to Record Mirror during October. *"We haven't even got any decent equipment together yet. We've started working on an album, but the Bee Gees have leant us most of the equipment for that until we buy our own. We've written quite a few songs, but there are four so far that we'll definitely be using. We don't write together, strangely enough. We sit in different rooms and write numbers and then get together on them after they're written."*

Graham also told Record Mirror: *"We haven't a lot of work lined up yet. It's mostly television at the moment. As soon as we get ourselves together, and get the new equipment, we'll start to make some personal appearances – but we don't really want to do cabaret or ballrooms. I don't think it'd suit our style particularly. I think we'll just try and do concerts and that sort of thing."* Graham also answered questions about his unique voice: *"It's just my natural voice. I think it's noticeable because most singers sing from their throats and rely on the microphones a lot. I sing from down in my stomach – so it's a lot stronger."*

Suddenly the Marbles were told they'd been added to the German leg of the Bee Gees' forthcoming European Tour in November. The duo had been waiting for something like this to come along and it seemed to be the perfect platform to launch themselves on the live front. Yet for reasons which were never explained, and despite appearing on posters, they were taken off the bill before the tour began (ironically the Bee Gees themselves had to pull-out half way through the tour due to illness.)

Instead the duo were booked on a four-date tour of Ireland starting on October 31st, performing in ballrooms - which they had already said they didn't want to do. They needed a backing band and Bluesology fitted the bill. Reg Dwight had just left them to pursue a solo career as Elton John, and had been replaced by Jimmy Horowitz. The Marbles squeezed in a few rehearsals, planning to properly rehearse once they were in Ireland.

Graham spoke to journalists about the tour: *"I hope people don't associate us too much with the Bee Gees, though we appreciate their help in starting us off, of course. I*

> ***Also available on Polydor is the debut disc by Marbles, titled "Only One Woman," written and produced by the Gibb brothers. And there's no mistaking the Bee Gees' influence in this dramatic rhythmic ballad, notable for the powerfully gripping performance of the lead singer. Gorgeous backing, too.

The Marbles • An early publicity photograph of the duo, Graham (left) and Trevor.

wouldn't like to think that we're making it because of them. I'd like to feel that we have done it on our own merits. I suppose we'll be doing old fashioned numbers - they tell us they dig Orbison there, so we'll do things of his as well as Elvis things. We just sing songs and make music. I hate being pigeon-holed and classified. What we want to do is get to the stage of influencing people with our music. The sort of thing we like to do on stage is Little Richard and things like that, but not all raving, beaty ballads. Neil Sedaka is another one, his things still sound great."

The Marbles got as far as the rehearsals but Graham suddenly got a virus through contracting Mao flu and the tour was cancelled. They had to make do with just a few public appearances at which as Graham later reported: *"The kids went mad. They grabbed at us."* Their retainer also enabled the pair move to a cheap flat on Cromwell Road, in Kensington. *"David Bowie lived near us and we would see him at the post office,"* recalls Graham. Rock and roll...

Trevor also played down the Bees Gees connections: *"The Bee Gees have helped us in a way I suppose, but we don't want to become known as another Bee Gees group. We want to use our own material on the next single. We want to develop our own sound."*

This distancing began to have repercussions as the Bee Gees felt the pair were ungrateful to people who had got them their break. For now though Trevor and Graham were planning to audition musicians for their permanent backing band as they wanted the right people on board for when they made their eventual debut.

Trevor told Melody Maker they were looking for *"piano, bass, drums, tenor and baritone saxes and two trumpets."*

Irrespective of the media attention and the success, Graham was far from satisfied with the record. Chatting to a reporter at Melody Maker he tried to articulate his concern: *"The next single will be in 4/4 time. 'Woman' is in 3/4 time and no one can dance to it, unlike Joe Cocker's hit. Also we'd like the next single to be a lot more developed, with more happening. This one was done literally in five minutes and it's not really what we wanted. In fact it's a bit boring."*

Despite this on November 6th the Marbles appeared on the Granada TV show Hats Off performing the single, and both singers also acquired personal managers; Trevor had Robert Masters, while Graham had David Oddie. One reporter was curious to know why the Marbles were a duo and not a band. Graham explained that it wasn't their idea: *"We wanted to have a group. It was Robert Stigwood's idea to have a duo, because it would be something different, and Barry Gibb wanted someone to sing his songs."*

Barry could no longer contain his annoyance at these interviews and responded in the New Musical Express: *"I got them started in the same way Robert Stigwood opened the doors for us. We were friends at school. But as soon as they get a hit they turn around and criticise me in the papers. It is very sad what you learn about human nature in this business."*

Despite this friction (which really their managers should have jumped on right away), 'Only One Woman' was picking up in Europe. Trevor and Graham were invited to appear on a TV show in Paris on November 18th when the song reached the French Top 20. They came back to the UK as Stigwood's guests for Cream's final farewell concert at the Royal Albert Hall in London on the 26th, supported by another of his signings, Taste, featuring Rory Gallagher. Graham says: *"Trevor and I knew Don, Rory's brother. Both of us went to the after show party. I fell asleep on the couch! Don would come and pick us up or we would meet him at the Café Des Artistes. It was a cool place and had nice girls!"*

The Marbles then dashed back to France for more TV work. The single was now a world wide hit, going Top 10 in Austria, Belgium, Germany, Holland, Ireland, Norway and Switzerland. In New Zealand the song went to No. 1 but curiously in Australia,

despite Trevor having lived there and the Bee Gee connections, it only managed to reach No. 23. In Italy and Canada it just crept in to the Top 50.

Which just left the big one, America. Robert Stigwood put together one of his biggest promotion campaigns to date, authorising a massive £50,000 advertising and promotion campaign to launch the single. His reward for all this was a meagre Top 50 placing. A two week promotional tour there during December was pulled, as was a trip to Bermuda for the duo's Christmas holiday.

Back home the Marbles graced the cover of Fabulous 208 magazine but were still far from happy about being labelled a duo - though quite what else people could call them was never quite explained. *"The Everly Brothers, The Righteous Brothers and Simon and Garfunkel are the only great duos. Most British duos tend to sing together in close harmony. I think we've got a different sound, because between us we have a range of about three and a half octaves,"* Trevor explained.

After an extremely busy six weeks, thoughts now turned to the follow-up single. The second week of December found the Marbles back in the studio with Barry Gibb at the helm. The Gibb brothers and Robert Stigwood were all helping out with the production, the accompaniment and the recording sessions were again directed by Bill Shepherd. Even though the Marbles and Barry had said things publicly that they now regretted, Barry was still prepared to work with Trevor and Graham who, incidentally, had just got over a bout of laryngitis (this scare prompted their management to insure Graham's throat and hands, along with Trevor's too.) For the session they worked their way through three new Bee Gees songs, of which one was to be their follow-up single, 'The Walls Fell Down'. 'Love You' became the B-side and featured Trevor on lead vocals, and he also fronted the third (unissued for the time) song 'Little Boy'.

With Graham's birthday approaching, he found out that Maurice Gibb's birthday was the day before. He was two years younger than Graham. Never really needing an excuse, they both went out and celebrated in style. At the end of the year, the Marbles were voted the 7th best new group of 1968 in the New Musical Express poll, a tremendous achievement.

The New Year saw 'Only One Woman' reaching No.1 in South Africa during January and there was a lot of talk about the album, which Graham told Melody Maker would be stripped down: *"It'll be just the two of us backed by guitars and strings on a few tracks."* Work on this had to be fitted in around another very busy schedule. They appeared in a French TV spectacular from January 3rd to 5th, followed by a Bremen TV slot, then on the 10th two days recording at IBC studios, and back to Paris on the 12th for three more days of television work, during which they performed 'By The Light Of The Burning Candle' to give them a break from doing their hit all the time. It was followed by another German TV show on the 26th, '4-3-2-1', plus visits to Belgium, Holland and Spain. The tiring schedule was sometimes lightened by days off, one of which happened to be in Germany.

"After a day at a TV studio taping a music show", recalls Graham, *"Trevor and I decided to go out to a club with our manager for a drink and some relaxation. We were told to go to this place by the TV station, because they loved our record there and played it all the time, so we would be given a great reception. We arrived outside the club and to our surprise through the open door we could hear, being played very loudly, our song. We walked up to the guy at the door all smiles and thinking 'hey that's our record playing what perfect timing for a perfect entrance!' The guy looked at us and said 'halt!' Trevor and I said 'what?' 'I'm sorry, you can't come in', said the guy. 'Why?' we said. 'Your hair is too long' the guy replied. 'But that's our song you're playing inside' we said. 'Well I know but it is 7 o'clock!' said the guy. We looked at each other and said '7 o'clock?' The guy then said 'yes, there is no long hair allowed after 6 o'clock.' Dumbfounded, we burst into tears of laughter and disbelief then went elsewhere for*

The Marbles • Previous page : photographer Barry Plummer was sent to cover a story about how the pair were big stars but broke and living in a cold London flat!

30

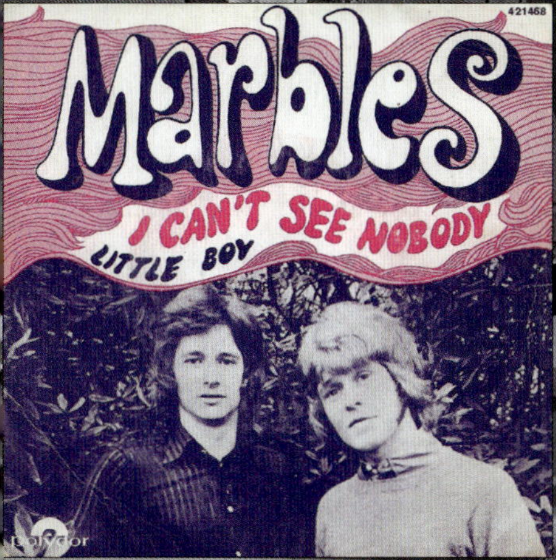

the night!"

The Marbles did more work for their album in early February, this time under the watchful eyes of Jimmy Horowitz (who had now left Bluesology) and Bill Shepherd, recording 'Elizabeth Johnson'. They planned the album to include four songs written by the boys, four from the Bee Gees and four standards. 'The Walls Fell Down' was released on February 21st and the rift between the duo and Barry had been sorted out as Trevor explained to the press: *"We are back with the Bee Gees and very happy about it too."* A slow song, it received some rave previews in the music press: *"superbly well presented – powerfully handled by the duo, it's sung with spirit, soul and controlled emotion,"* said the New Musical Express. Melody Maker went with *"a superb sound from Trevor Gordon and the powerful chords of Graham Bonnet,"* and Record Mirror was also very positive: *"near breathtaking emotion in the vocal harmonies."*

Despite this universal acclaim, the single did only moderately well in the charts. Even with airplay on Radio 1 and Radio Luxembourg, and an appearance on Top Of The Pops on April 3rd. the single stalled at No. 28.

The Marbles went over to Germany for promotional work at the end of March, including a live slot at the Polydor Records annual convention in Berlin on March 22nd (which was televised) and 'The Walls Fell Down' was far more successful in Europe, peaking in Holland at No. 3 during April for example. This prompted a rare promotional film for the song, which saw the pair miming while walking through a building dressed in suits, shirts and ties, Graham with a Gibson SG, and Trevor on a Gibson acoustic. Recalling the occasion, Graham says: *"I think it was filmed in an office block or a school. I seem to remember saying to Trevor 'what the fuck are we doing in this place singing this dramatic love song?', because it did not fit! I wore a three-piece*

suit influenced by the Bee Gees." The band also filmed a 60 minute TV spectacular for Belgium television.

Back in Britain though the pair were still trying to get their elusive band off the ground. There was talk of them taking on a permanent backing group, The Trifle, a soul group, for dates in Europe. Three girls were to be flown in from America to provide vocal backing. It never happened. Meanwhile Trevor and Graham moved in to a new flat, which previously belonged to Maurice Gibb, who had moved out to live with Lulu.

Finally on April 13th came their UK live debut, albeit as part of the Daily Express Record Star Show, a charity event which was held at London's Empire Pool at Wembley. A star studded event, the importance of the occasion for the pair was rather lost amidst the general razzmatazz. Plans for a short Scottish tour were now worked out, and rehearsals with a backing band had taken place, with warm-up shows at the Batley Variety Club and at the Stockton Fiesta during May. Even so, the lack of a serious UK tour was now becoming something of an embarrassment.

Instead, a third single was now recorded. Once again both sides were written by the Bee Gees while Barry took full control of the production duties. 'I Can't See Nobody' featured another very strong vocal performance by Graham and as before Trevor took the lead vocals on the B-side, 'Little Boy', a leftover from their last studio trip.

It was released in America on May 27th and also in Europe (where No. 23 in Holland was the best placing), Japan, Scandinavia and South America, but not in the UK. This puzzled fans here (including those who had joined the newly formed Official Marbles Fan Club), and prompted a press statement from RSO saying that *"we are still looking for a suitable song to release as a single here. The two are writing a lot at the moment, and it could be one of their own compositions which is chosen."*

Poorly organised and promoted live shows in West Germany in June with an unknown backing band didn't give the duo much confidence in their situation either. Graham recalls the tour, in particular a show in Munich which went very wrong. *"We lost all the sound. It was terrible. Everything blew up! The band wasn't very good. They were just a bunch of session guys thrown together to do these few gigs. There was no heart in it. It was purely mechanical and we didn't get very good audiences. Nothing was promoted properly. We always played in little lousy places. It was very depressing. It was like, what the hell is going on? We've had a hit single and nobody cares about us."*

Away from the Marbles, Graham was now dating actress and singer Adrienne Posta, who had herself released half a dozen singles on Decca under her original name of Adrienne Poster. They met at the Speakeasy Club in London after Adrienne purposely bumped into Graham! *"I'd seen him before and the only reason I went was because I thought he might be down there. I made sure I bumped into him,"* she told Fabulous 208, who went to town reporting the pair's romance for their mainly female readership, and the fact that she had dropped her previous boyfriend as a result. *"It's ever so cruel I know, but I just couldn't be without Graham. I can't imagine life without him now."* Graham was also roped in for a quote: *"She's interesting to talk to, she's lovely and she's nice. She measures up to my ideal type of girl."* Such was the press interest in the Marbles that features like this abounded about the pair. They later made the front cover of Fabulous 208 as a star couple.

Trevor and Graham returned to Skegness as special guests during July when DJ Alan Freeman fronted a Radio 1 Club live broadcast from Butlins Holiday Camp in Ingoldmells. These roadshows were a feature of summer for several years, and a crowd of over 2,000 turned up at the Princess Ballroom. The Marbles were introduced to the spectators but were not able to perform live. Instead Alan Freeman played 'I Can't See Nobody' even though Polydor had no plans to release it here.

Back in London the Marbles returned for a show at The Revolution Club, which at least kept their name in the press. Talking to Rob McKenzie of Fireworks, Donal Gallagher remembers the show: *"I had time on my hands and the Marbles were doing a gig. They didn't haven't any roadcrew and I was asked to help out by Robert Stigwood's people. I didn't quite realise they had a string quartet and I got a bollocking from the conductor because I didn't have any music stands for them!"*

Apart from this and more TV work across Europe (some of it with David Bowie, who was re-promoting 'Space Oddity'), the Marbles were clearly being sidelined by their management and were understandably far from happy. RSO showed no interest in them becoming a proper group, there was still no sign of a new single and their album was still in limbo.

The album was actually ready as far as the record company was concerned. Press reports had originally been given January 1969 as a release date, then in April RSO said it would be ready *"in five weeks time"*, with all twelve tracks recorded and the duo looking forward to it being released during the late summer. Sadly, though, it wasn't to be. This lack of commitment had a corrosive effect on the pair and eventually in early October it was announced to the press that they were splitting up to follow separate careers and would also record separately. Barry Gibb would be taking complete control of Graham's future recordings and his first solo record would be on the on the new Bee Gees label in mid-November. Barry told the New Musical Express that he had high hopes for Graham: *"I predict he will become one of the best known solo names on the pop scene."*

As for Trevor, his immediate future was less well mapped out, but it was suggested that he would be working with Maurice Gibb, who had written some songs for him. Trevor feels the Marbles had reached some sort of parting of the ways musically: *"We were doing different kinds of music. Graham was very dramatic and powerful. I was into more gentle lyrical stuff. I was interested in writing and arranging, Graham was interested in performing and I think that was the big difference. I could see that if I had stayed with Graham as a duo, it wouldn't have been successful really. He needed to be a soloist. That's what I always felt."* Looking back, Graham felt that his voice had matured a lot since their early days and agrees that the split was for the best: *"The act just didn't work out on stage. My voice was too strong and often overshadowed Trev's. Plus, our musical tastes were very different."*

CHAPTER 3
Too Young To Die, Too Drunk To Live (1969 – 1978)

Featuring: Graham's solo career, Southern Comfort, Trevor Gordon, Adrienne Posta, Ronnie Harwood Band, Victy Silva, Snow Goose and the Alpha Omega Project

Down under and right on top

Following the Marbles' split a solo career beckoned, but the path to Graham's first LP was tortuous indeed. He started to record material with Barry and Maurice Gibb on hand. Trevor also got involved: *"Graham started to do an album and I did some arrangements, but it never got finished. I think there was a problem with the material actually. He did bits of mine and bits of his, along with a few standards. Perhaps Graham was going through a period of not being sure about what material he wanted to do at that time."* Graham recalls doing *"a load of good demos with Maurice Gibb and Trevor. When I had inspiration! I remember one of them was called 'Somebody Left Me'. We recorded at Marquee studios and Trident in London."*

The press were naturally interested and suggested the finished record would be on sale before the end of 1969 but the sessions began to peter out. It was clear to both Trevor and Graham that they were now going in different musical directions, even though they were still helping each other out on sessions. And although they were both very happy to have parted company with the Robert Stigwood Organisation, towards the end of the year and into 1970 Robert started to show a renewed interest in Graham and put pressure on him to go along with his plans. Graham was having none of it.

Stigwood stopped paying the rent on Trevor's flat, and Graham realised he would also find himself on the street if he didn't go along with the idea. *"Robert Stigwood wanted to make me into this Tom Jones creature. He had this thing about me doing Tom Jones type songs. Cabaret, you know? It was an awful time. I said 'I've had enough. I don't want to do that. I don't want to sing Tin Pan Alley songs.' I was then evicted from my apartment and it was terrible. I remember this ladder coming up against the window and I was there with my girlfriend in bed, and we said 'what the hell is that?' Then we heard some banging and I said 'Oh my god, they are going to evict us!' We were really scared, so we called up a guy called Billy Gaff, because he had some kind of knowledge about the law. He sorted a few things out that enabled us to stay there for a little longer."*

Billy would become Graham's manager later on, but for now Graham went to live in Albert Terrace, near Primrose Hill and Regents Park. What was a miserable time for Graham and Adrienne was cheered by the purchase of an Old English sheepdog puppy that they called Sachi, after Shirley MacLaine's daughter, Stephanie Sachiko Parker. *"It's Japanese. She had made a movie in Japan called 'My Geisha', and that is how Ade came across the name."*

The situation calmed down and as he took stock in early 1970, Graham settled on the idea of continuing as a solo artist. However, without the Gibb connections he struggled to get people interested and realised it wasn't going to be as easy as he had imagined. The doors he presumed would open for him because of the big hit he'd had with 'Only One Woman' stayed firmly shut and this came as a shock. Graham even considered becoming a singer on the Butlin's Holiday Camp circuit, but eventually decided against it.

It was a good job Adrienne's career was still relatively flourishing, and she was happy to help and support Graham through the slack period. She had done two films the previous year, All The Way Up and Spring And Port Wine, and more were in the pipeline.

Ludicrously, as the duo were no longer around to promote it, Polydor Records released a fourth Marbles single during March, a revival of Neil Sedaka's 'Breaking Up Is Hard To Do' with Gibson Kemp handling the production duties, possibly to try and recoup some of their investment. Looking back on the recording, Graham says: *"It was maybe the fastest recording I ever did with Trevor. We were done in about 30 minutes. The harmonies and the whole thing! It was a song Trevor and I had sung when we were kids."*

This time the single did come out in the UK, backed with the A-side Polydor had refused to issue here the year before, 'I Can't See Nobody'. Other territories went with one of three different B-sides. The record had virtually no promotion in the UK whatsoever and didn't trouble the charts.

The New Musical Express suggested that the release had something to do with a new American version by Lenny Welch, while Record Retailer reckoned that *"this one is strong enough to give them a farewell seller."* Bob Dawbarn in the Melody Maker was less convinced; *"It's a rotten song, and the treatment sounds like just anybody."* Polydor then belatedly sneaked out the long lost Marbles album in Germany, simply titled 'The Marbles', presumably while the name was still remembered by some pop fans. And even now, the album turned out not to be the finished article.

33

Just over half of the songs had already seen the light of day (depending on which country you lived in), and the remainder of the material had never been completely finished despite sitting around for over a year. Trevor and Graham had three compositions on the album, 'Daytime' and 'Elizabeth Johnson' written by Trevor and 'Little Laughing Girl' by Graham. More than 20 years later, Trevor said of the release: *"It wasn't a proper album… just bits and pieces they put together."* One track still remains unreleased to this day and Graham remembers: *"We did a song by The Everly Brothers called 'Let It Be Me'. We did it very high, very very high in fact. The highest note in it was the high G above top C. It was too high!"*

Graham's plan to be allowed to design the sleeve had also been forgotten, and a publicity photo was used instead. Curiously the album wasn't released in Australia or New Zealand despite 'Only One Woman' being such a big hit there, but it did come out in America during July, and a little later in Canada, Norway, South Africa and Spain but not in the UK. New Zealand decided to do their own thing, issuing four of the tracks as an EP of 'Bee Gees Hits'.

Adrienne was soon involved in two more films - Percy and Up Pompeii - but while Billy Gaff was doing what he could to help his new signing get on his feet, Graham was basically just watching the world go by: *"I had a lot of time doing nothing. Nobody wanted to know me, for whatever reason. I was a has-been before I had been anything! It was an awful time. I went through a lot of depression about it. I would walk around all night, because I didn't know what was wrong. I knew I could sing, but I couldn't understand why no-one wanted to know me. Adrienne would come and sit with me in the middle of the night. I'd just sit there in a dark room. It was horrible."*

Trevor was having more luck; Polydor Records had kept him on as a singer-songwriter and decided to fund a solo album. The budget was insufficient and nobody was very happy with the end result but Graham did get to sing and play on it. Of the eleven songs recorded, two of them had been done before by the Marbles, 'Elizabeth Johnson' and 'Daytime'. Called 'Alphabet', the album was released during July 1970 in the UK (along with a single 'Spend All The Money' b/w 'Daytime') and a little later in Germany (where the single was backed with 'Wounded Soldiers'). Trevor says: *"I wasn't happy with the album, or with my voice. It was done on a very low budget. I hated it. It cost £1,500, which is nothing. I was trying to be too ambitious. I wrote all the arrangements and I had session musicians in to play them. We were on a strict time limit. You know, it has to be done and if it wasn't good enough, it will have to do. It was a right mess."*

The New Musical Express was remarkably upbeat about the end product, *"it is always a bit of a risk putting out an LP by a solo singer who hasn't had a hit in his own right but in this case it seems to be justified by the content, even though it won't be a massive seller."* They were correct. Polydor continued to persevere for a while longer but Trevor's second album was never completed and, sadly, that was the end of his professional career as a musician.

As Trevor was bowing out, things started to move for Graham, who with Adrienne had now moved to Highgate in North London. He found himself doing the vocals for a handful of TV adverts - jingles for beer, aftershave for Gillette, Ski Yoghurt and one for Ritz Crackers which was sung to a Charles Chaplin tune. *"The money was very good and you always got a little cheque every time they were shown on TV. It just kept me afloat, but luckily my girlfriend was working and she kept saying 'don't worry, something will happen. We will get through this.' I honestly didn't know what to do."* It didn't help that Marbles tracks were still being pushed out as singles, or added to hit collections, as Graham didn't earn anything from these re-issues.

His next gig came via another Lincolnshire boy, Iain Matthews, who had gone down to London during 1966 and eventually formed Fairport Convention before recording his debut solo album, Matthews' 'Southern Comfort', in 1969. A band was then formed and during September 1970 they achieved a No. 1 hit single in the UK, 'Woodstock'. During the last week of November however Iain Matthews quit and Graham found himself rehearsing the bass lines for the band's set and attempting the odd backing vocal here and there. He says: *"The band happened to be living in the same building as me and asked me one day to play with them as Iain Matthews had left. Just the right place at the right time kind of thing!"*

Southern Comfort played a handful of gigs with Graham in and around London during early 1971: *"I found it very hard to play bass and sing at the same time. So I hardly sang anything, just 'oohs' and 'ahs'. I never recorded anything with them, we just played live. Their manager thought I was nuts and too much of a lunatic!"* Graham wanted to turn the laid back outfit into more of a rock 'n' roll band but it didn't happen and he soon parted company with

In London • *This, the photo on the next page top, and chapter header were taken in July 1971.*

them and went back to twiddling his thumbs. Apart from a house move to Quadrangle Court off the Edgware Road, to say he was bored would have been an understatement and depression was slowly setting in again.

Just down the road, a trio of musicians and session players began recording at Phillips studios in Stanhope Place, near Marble Arch, London in July 1970. Roy Wood, Bev Bevan and Jeff Lynne from The Move had been working on some new musical ideas for about a year, songs that featured cellos and violins.

It was a slow process, but along the way they became unhappy with the bass work of Rick Price. Graham's name came up and this certainly lifted him as he went over to Philips studios for a chat. Sadly, he thought they needed a singer and wasn't aware they wanted him to play bass as well. *"When I went along to see Roy and Jeff they played me all this classical-come-rock stuff and I remember sitting there thinking how fabulous it was. They said to me 'can you play bass and sing?' I replied 'No.' Jeff said 'we need you to do all the vocals and play bass.' So I said 'no, I just can't do it.' It is something I just can't do, because I start singing the bass line. I can play guitar and sing though. But I loved the stuff they played me."*

Back home, the news that he wouldn't be joining actually seemed to go down well with Adrienne. She wasn't keen on him getting involved in a band at all, let alone going on tour. She was worried that Graham would attract more attention than her. Graham remembers: *"She would become very jealous in case I got some kind of admiration from girls, and certainly didn't want me to go out on the road. She wanted me in her pocket, and to be in the house all the time. I hadn't done anything for a long time and suddenly when this came along, she didn't want me to do it. She wanted to work and have me at home."* He was offered other auditions, including one with Hawkwind surprisingly, but didn't attend, so it was back to square one. As for Jeff Lynne and the boys, the project became the first ELO album released in December; they redid the bass lines themselves.

Early in 1972 a friend mentioned the name of Chris Brough to Graham and, after a meeting he started helping Graham and eventually became his manager for a short while. At the same time Roy Wood's manager got in touch with a song Roy thought would work for Graham. 'Whisper In The Night' had been written for ELO's debut album so Chris set about finding a record label for him. RCA Records agreed a one-off deal for the UK.

Along the way Graham managed to meet his childhood hero, Helen Shapiro. Looking back in 2012, he remembered the encounter with great affection: *"Adrienne was friends with Helen and I met her at Earls Court. Adrienne and I were promoting something. Helen was there with her brother, so I said 'hello' and we talked for a few minutes. Talk about suddenly being like a little kid! I was so in love with her. When I was at Morris Secondary School in Skegness all the girls hated her. I told Helen she was my biggest influence in the way I sing and that when I was 14 we sounded much the same. The voice timbre was so similar, although I developed my*

Long hair • *another early photo, May 1972.*

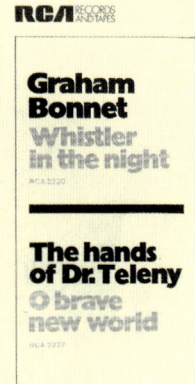

own singing style eventually. I was in awe of her when I met her… and still am! I sang higher than Helen and Lulu commented on that years later, saying her highest note was an A where as mine was a D back then. It was my cousin's fault, because he changed the melody in 'Only One Woman' when we recorded it and put the high note in there. So I got lumbered as the guy with the 'high voice' tag! And this has been the way most of my recordings have been since. That high part has to be there. The 'Only One Woman' original tune was the same as the first line of the chorus all the way through. So Trevor said to Barry: 'I think the melody should go up on the second line of the song'. Barry didn't know that I could get up there. So it became a trade mark."

Around spring, Graham was booked into a studio to start recording 'Whisper In The Night' but really struggled. He hadn't done any recording for over two years and had lost confidence in himself and his ability. On top of his depression, he was suffering from red-light-syndrome, and dried as soon as the studio light went on. "I remember the singer Ayshea coming into the studio and saying 'don't worry it will be all right. You'll be okay. You've got it, just have confidence in yourself.' So I asked if I could come in tomorrow and do it again. I did, and it was a little better. It was never my favourite song. It wasn't me. In fact I thought it was terrible. Roy Wood liked it!"

They now needed a B-side. Graham suggested a song which he had written back in Skegness with The Bluesecte called 'Rare Specimen'. The recording went very well and Graham played guitar and bass on it too, along with session musicians (who had played on all of 'Whisper In The Night'). Graham was far happier with 'Rare Specimen' than the A-side, it certainly had far more life and charisma about it than the slow ballad. It also showed off Graham's personality and sense of humour. Chris Brough handled the production for both the songs and Nick Harrison was in charge of conducting and handling the arrangements.

'Whisper In The Night' was released on June 9th (although promo copies said the 2nd) and RCA added it to their regular half-page 'new releases' advert in Melody Maker the week before, where it had to compete against both Elvis Presley and an inept proof-reader who re-titled it 'Whistler In The Night'! Neither Elvis nor Graham stood much of a chance amidst the glam rock scene which was dominating the charts, and fellow RCA act The Sweet seemed to dictate the label's mindset. As such they didn't really have a clue what to do with Graham's single and he was far from impressed: "I remember being pissed off as the single did nothing and it wasn't promoted by the record company. There was just a small little advert with the wrong title, which amused my friends and me at the time. At least it got a bit of a laugh out of a non-event." Such was the disappointment surrounding the event that Graham soon split from Chris Brough. With Adrienne being a friend of singer Lulu, her manager Marion Massey was introduced to Graham and she agreed to manage him.

Through this connection he was invited to appear on Lulu's TV show

It's Lulu, Not to Mention Dudley Moore. The show's producer, Stewart Morris, was at Lulu's house and heard the Marbles' album. He knew he had to have him on the show and told the Skegness Standard: "He's too good a talent to miss and I think he could be as big as Tom Jones." Typically, rather than plug his own single, Graham instead chose to cover a track from Neil Sedaka's new album, 'Emergence', called 'I'm A Song (Sing Me)', which certainly suited Graham's range and vocal power. He was backed on the show by The Young Generation, which was broadcast on August 19th.

Everything suddenly got put on hold when Graham suffered his first epileptic seizure and had to be rushed in to London's Whittington Hospital where he was put in a ward for the terminally ill because there weren't any other beds available. Discharged, Graham found himself sought out by the manager of Stealers Wheel. The Scottish folk-rock band's self-titled album had been very successful but lead singer and co-founder Gerry Rafferty suddenly left. They also needed a replacement for their bassist player. Who you gonna call as the catchphrase would later have it...

Graham said he was interested and was sent a copy of their album but in the end he didn't really feel the music was his kind of thing. Once again the Bee Gee connection kicked in. A couple of years earlier, Maurice Gibb (Mo) and Lulu's brother Bill Lawrie (By) had formed a production company, Moby Productions. As they all knew each other it was a natural progression for Graham to start recording with them around late spring 1973. Graham had already decided that he wanted to record a Neil Sedaka song. "All of his comeback stuff was great, such a young voice. I was thinking of recording a song from his new album, which I loved," he recalls. "So Maurice and I recorded 'Trying To Say Goodbye'."

As this was going on, Graham actually got to meet Neil: "We saw him play at the Royal Albert Hall and the Talk Of The Town with our friends Maureen Lipman and Jack Rosenthal. We had to educate Jack who Neil Sedaka was! They used to stay with Ade and me when they came to London as they lived in Manchester."

Maurice knew Neil and invited him along to listen in on the session before the Albert Hall show. It was all Graham needed! "I was singing and he opened the door. This little face looked round and said 'hello'! Neil hung around while I did the vocal and was very impressed. He was giving me the thumbs up when I did the takes."

Graham was very impressed that he would bother but admits it made him extremely nervous. "I changed one note in the melody of his song on the words 'Maybe a song', because I didn't listen closely enough to the notes he sang and I was also nervous about him being there. Graham Preskett was doing the

Lulu, not to mention our Graham

THE BONNETT family of Skegness will be glued to their television on Saturday when singer Graham Bonnet — he's dropped the second "t" of his family's surname since going professional — appears on the Lulu show.

arrangements and as soon as Neil and wife Leba walked in, he said, 'oh, that's it. Graham is going to be terrible now. Session over!' He knows my biggest downfall for crappy singing is my nerves and my own insecurity of not being good enough, which remains with me today. I fear being bad and it affects my voice. Vocal tension. It is my worse enemy and pisses me off as I know in the back of my mind I can do it. Yet it takes me over and I get people saying 'what's wrong with you? You were fine earlier'. It's a question of mind over matter. I still haven't got a handle on that yet after all these years."

Coincidentally Adrienne bumped in to Neil Sedaka a little later on. *"Ade saw Neil outside the BBC one afternoon. It was about one week after we had finished the recording. She ran up to him and introduced herself and mentioned that I was her boyfriend. He said, 'you must be very proud of your boyfriend.' That was very nice of him and I think he liked my version of his tune."*

Casting around for a suitable B-side, Graham settled on the Bee Gees song 'Castles In The Air', from their unreleased 1973 album 'A Kick In The Head Is Worth Eight In The Pants'. Session musicians once again played on the song which left Graham free to concentrate on his vocal performance.

With the single in the can, Marion negotiated a one-off deal with RCA Records. Whether they remembered his previous offering on their label is anyone's guess, but once again one wonders why they bothered. Issued on June 29th (though promos said June 15th), there was absolutely no promotion for the record, even though Graham had delivered a very passable vocal with a lot of personality. Nobody at RCA showed the slightest interest. They didn't even organise any promotional photographs.

After this failure, Graham decided to part from manager Marion Massey: *"She didn't quite know how to market me."* He was quickly introduced to Hazel Malone and she took over the reins. Her son, Cavan also helped out, but it was easier said than done. *"I liked them both,"* recalls Graham. *"Hazel and Cavan were sort of together on my management or maybe that should be mismanagement. The two of them were heavy drinkers and with me added to the mix that was fatal."*

By now glam rock had almost totally taken over the UK pop charts and Graham started to ask himself where did all this leave him. Over the summer he was offered a part in a London West End musical called Pippin, a big Broadway hit, but he turned it down: *"It was my nerves of doing something that other people could do better."* Manfred Mann vocalist Paul Jones got the part.

While Graham was struggling to find his feet, Adrienne's career continued to blossom. She was busy on the film front with a film sequel, Percy's Progress, and in-between the filming schedule she was now herself working with Maurice Gibb and Bill Lawrie at Moby Productions cutting another Neil Sedaka song 'Love Will Keep Us Together', which Graham played bass and guitar on.

Ex-actor and entertainer Kaplan Kaye (son of comedian Davy Kaye) was the head of A & R at DJM Records (the label founded by Dick James in 1969.) He had known Adrienne since his own acting days, and signed her for a one-off single which he also produced. Adrienne suggested recording 'Dog Song', which Graham had written but put on the back-burner: *"it was about our dog. She always liked it!"*

Graham was asked along to the studio with Adrienne to play the song on his guitar for Kaplan. Kaplan knew him from the Marbles, and liked 'Dog Song'. He suggested it should be the A-side of what would be Adrienne's first single since 1966. As for Sachi, the dog which inspired the song, she had been chosen by the Dulux paint company to front their advertising campaign, becoming (as he was quick to admit) more famous than Graham.

For the 'Dog Song' session Graham played acoustic guitar and bass, and then returned later to record some backing vocals. Arranger Graham Preskett had come on board and given the song a 1930s twist, with some very nice textured bass playing from Graham, good piano and a couple of clarinet solos from the session musicians involved. Adrienne turned to Neil Sedaka's 1972 album 'Solitaire' and chose 'Express Yourself' for the B-side, with Graham once again supplying acoustic guitar and bass.

'Dog Song' was released on November 23rd (promos say the 16th). DJM were probably hoping for a bit of a novelty hit with the Christmas market but promotion was limited to a half page advert in the trade magazine Music Week. Melody Maker suggested Adrienne *"sounds a trifle squeaky on this bouncy, showbiz tune."* But if the single did little for Adrienne, Graham's input hadn't gone unnoticed by Kaplan. Realising the singer was unsigned, he snapped him up for DJM before the year was out. The recording and publishing deal was reported to come with a £75,000 advance, and they were really keen to have Graham record an album. It was the best news he had heard in a while. Elton John was the label's biggest act, and served as a good benchmark for Graham. But there were still disagreements over direction. *"I remember Dick James saying 'we'll make him a singing John Voight', but he didn't mean him at all, he meant James Dean. Then he said 'can you act?' and I said 'no'!"*

Since DJM were diversifying into movies with the acquisition of Diverton Films, they decided to green-light a comedy film, Three For All, about a local band that suddenly gets booked to tour Spain, with resultant girlfriend troubles and a No. 1 hit single.

Adrienne got the lead role, with Graham chosen to play Kook, the singer in the band Billy Beethoven. A supporting cast – pretty much a who's who of Seventies British Film talent - was put together which included Edward Woodward, Diana Dors, Arthur Mullard and many more. Showaddywaddy appeared as themselves and Graham's band included Robert Lindsay (Tom – drummer), Paul Nicholas (Gary – bass guitarist), Christopher Neil (Ricky – guitarist) and Richard Beckinsale (Jet Bone – Manager).

Graham and Adrienne couldn't escape their newsworthy celebrity couple status either. 1974 had hardly got under way when they got a call to do a photo shoot modelling their hair for a top London hairstylist Ricci Burns, followed by a fashion show.

Having steadily built up a batch of songs over the last twelve months, Graham spent most of January and February in the DJM and Marquee studios recording for his album. Kaplan's team included engineer John Eden and arranger Graham Preskett. John remembers the first time he came across Graham: *"I was assisting Kaplan on many of his sessions. He was involved in bringing artists to the label. One of the artists that he came in to the studio with was this incredible singer. I'd never heard anybody with the power and range."* Kaplan brought in a bunch of top session musicians: Chris Ray on guitar, Frank McDonald on bass guitar, Barry DeSouza on drums, Mike Moran on piano, Mel Collins on saxophone and clarinet and Roy Marlow on accordian. Graham Preskett did the string arrangements and Graham played acoustic guitar. The songs took in a variety of different styles, and would give Graham an opportunity to show the record company his true vocal capabilities. As well as laying down his lead vocals, being the perfectionist that he is, Graham also handled all the backing vocals as he knew exactly how he wanted them to blend in.

One of the first songs Graham recalls them doing was a new version of 'Dog Song'. *"I never really expected it to reach the studio! We completely re-recorded the whole song."* Then there was the country-pop 'Private Eye' which saw Graham's sense of humour creep in as he did a Goon-type voice on the word 'Careful' after the chorus. *"I'm playing with my Adam's apple to create that effect"*, he says. *"The song is about a guy who wants to know if his girl is faithful and puts a private eye out there to watch her."* It ends with 'shoo-be-do-wah' type backing vocals which were to be a feature of the album.

The 1930s' style 'Back Row In The Stalls' features Adrienne while 'Mamma Mine' sees Graham really let rip vocally on a stomping bluesy-rocker where saxophonist Mel Collins took all the solos. Graham says: *"This is just about a guy who is confused about whether or not his girlfriend feels the same way for him as he does for her. It is a simple love song, but a shouter! Very Slade like."*

The slow, laid back 'Saturday's Over' is full of emotion with a potential stadium anthem atmosphere. Graham also added some wonderful backing vocals to the song which was inspired by family memories: *"This is about my brother, Tony, at the age of 18 when he had to marry his pregnant girlfriend, Gill. That was the Fifties and pregnant girls had to marry back then…"*

The punchy 'Don't Drink The Water', full of memorable backing vocals from start to finish, is the shortest song of them all, clocking in at just over two minutes. The title says it all, when you are abroad drink water from the bottle, not the tap!

'She May Be Not Much To Look At (But She's Certainly Got A Heart)' is based around a reggae rhythm as Graham recalls: *"This one is about a girl who isn't that good looking, but pursues guys including the storyteller and is an easy lay, but you had better tell her she's beautiful, or she will maybe kill you."*

The more middle of the road '(Untitled) Here Comes The Rain' starts off quite slowly, but picks up the pace while the rocker, 'Ghost Writer In My Eye' shows Graham's husky and gravely vocals off to perfection.

A poppier 'What's This 'Ere Then?' features a slow verse and an upbeat chorus, both vocally and musically. *"The backing vocals are what I always wanted*

Celebrity couple •
Graham and Adrianne, hair style modelling January 1974, and showing off her engagement ring for the press at Heathrow, March 1974.

… to be a Beach Boy! Brian Wilson is simply the greatest songwriter. It's the same with The Beatles. They do all genres of music and that is what REAL musicians do." Originally pulling ideas for the song from how he felt after the Marbles had split, Graham completed the lyrics when he and Adrianne moved to a townhouse in Quadrangle Court, off Edgware Road, around late spring 1973. *"This is about my sarcastic view of my own personality. It is me when nothing at all was happening for me in my music career. Walking in Regents Park in the snow, wondering what was to become of me as everything seemed a waste of time. I made a snowman to befriend as I didn't have any friends. It seemed my career was over. I had no title. I was questioned in the studio and was asked, 'What's this one here then?'"*

'We're Free' looked back lyrically to Graham's carefree teenage gigging days, with a tasty guitar solo from Chris Ray. Graham had also penned the beautiful ballad 'Ade's Song' inspired by difficulties in his relationship with Adrianne, for which he blamed himself. *"It is when she started seeing leading men behind my back. I thought it was all my fault and didn't give her all she needed. So I began to do the same. Then she stopped when I left her and begged me to come back to her."*

'Dreams (Out In The Forest)' starts out with Graham's voice screaming away before dropping down to a half-tempo verse, which doubles up in the chorus, and lyrically sees him wondering what other people might be dreaming about.

The very last song to be laid down was the jazzy multi-tempo 'Relaxae', with Graham introducing all the band members and studio technicians featured on the songs. Graham says: *"It's a club type thing and a goodnight from the band with introductions to the players. It was a joke title that Kaplan gave it."*

Graham occasionally reworked some of the music: *"I played acoustic guitar, but we used other bass players sometimes, because when we put the whole band down it saved time. Later I added a couple of bass lines after the vocals were done. Mostly we had someone else playing bass though. I also recall Rick Wakeman was on one track, along with Phillip Goodhand-Tait. Those sessions were great fun, and it was exciting to be recording for the first time my own compositions. We had some great people playing on the record."*

Kaplan was also involved on the both sides of the studio window: *"I played a bit of percussion and vibes on one track. I have great memories of working with Graham; his vocal harmony work was and still is amazing."* Graham recorded more than enough songs for his album and was very happy with them as they sounded

Ade weds at last

THEY'RE married at last... Cockney charmer Adrienne Posta, 25, and her very good friend, songwriter Graham Bonnet, 26.

The couple have lived together happily for several years without ever finding the time to wed. Until yesterday.

They were pictured after being married quietly at Haringey Civic Centre in North London. So quietly that even Ade's mum, Mrs. Minnie Posta, wasn't there, although she made it to the West End reception later.

Actress Ade was determined to become a real Easter Bonnet, so to speak. She rejected a million-dollar contract for an American television comedy series until the producers guaranteed that she could have time off to marry.

professional and covered a wide variety of styles, though happily he resisted Cavan Malone's attempts to try and turn him into the new Frank Sinatra: *"Cavan didn't have a clue! He was a Frank Sinatra fan and always pulled me up on my phrasing in songs saying, 'no, it's not like Frank!'"*

With the album in the can, Graham moved on to cut another one-off session: *"I was broke and needed some money. I remember working with an in-house writer called George Alexander who had been in Grapefruit, John and Yoko's discoveries. The song was called 'Heely Heely' and the vocal on the track was done in one night. Very fast for me! It's a great title. It was like a Motown type song The Supremes would do. It was a mandrax induced night. Two guys wrote it and booked me. I also remember another song in a one-off session with them called 'Jet Silver Bird'."*

George and his friend had written the tracks and thought Graham's vocals would suit perfectly. They were taped but nobody knows if they ever came out or remain in the can. George incidentally was one of the three Young brothers, two of whom later formed AC/DC.

Over in America, the producers of a new TV show called Lampoon now wanted Adrienne to head the cast, but when they approached her with a $1,000,000 contract she told them she wanted time off during the recording to get married in April; otherwise, forget it! The producers agreed and Graham flew out with her on March 15th for the duration of the filming with British press photographers snapping their departure for the papers. With Hazel Malone travelling with them, it was also a good excuse for Adrienne to show off her diamond and ruby engagement ring. Graham says: *"It cost quite a bit of dough for back then, a few thousand I think, maybe £2,000!"* For the trip Graham wore an incredibly jazzy jacket. He adds: *"It was the groovy things people in the biz wore in London. The jacket had a grey background and pastel colours, green, pink and orange. Something like that! It was sort of hippy looking in a strange non-hippy way. It was my first trip to America and I did not want to return to grey old England! Lampoon featured Harry Secombe, Desi Arnaz Jr and Toni Basil with her dancers, The Lockers, as well as others. Harry called Desi 'Dozy' and the pot was certainly being passed around by Desi. It was a very drunk, but fun time. The whole thing was recorded but then the magazine of the same name threatened to sue. It was never aired, which was a real let down."*

Back on home soil on April 13th, Easter Saturday, Graham married his girlfriend of nearly five years at Haringey Civic Centre in North London. It was certainly one of the major celebrity events of the year, with reporters and photographers waiting to get a glimpse of the newlyweds. Graham and Adrienne didn't disappoint, dressed for the occasion in medieval outfits. The newly weds didn't go on honeymoon because, as Graham put it: *"We were broke!"*

Graham now returned to the solo album, which he had titled 'Back Row In The Stalls', and cover shoots were arranged: *"Some photographs were taken on the roof of the office. I also remember a studio shoot taking place with Ade."* DJM had chosen four of Graham's songs to feature in the soundtrack for the upcoming film. Shooting was due to start in July in Brighton before moving to London for a week. Just prior to the filming Graham suffered a serious throat problem that affected his voice. *"I had lymph nodes on my vocal cords while I was recording the songs for the film and I had to stop talking for one month and use medication. I had to heat some liquid over a burner type thing they gave me and inhale it before each song. I could hardly talk. It was horrible. The doctor also gave me some white pills, which I think were cocaine based, although I'm not sure; they got me through the sessions! On the very first day I had to do my scene there were about 300 on the set as the director asked everyone to be quiet. He asked me if I was ready and I said 'yes'. The moment the cameras started I farted! Everyone on the set collapsed with laughter, but I just went bright red!"*

During a break in filming in London's Leicester Square, Graham went to

ADRIENNE POSTA & GRAHAM BONNET

A case of one ZIP! too many

the Golden Egg greasy spoon café with Adrienne and some of the cast. Two girls who were working on the set walked past the café and one unzipped her trousers for a laugh. Graham decided the only gentlemanly thing to do was stand up and do the same, sticking his thumb out through his fly for added effect! However, as he did so, a secretary happened to walk by and took offence at the gesture which she assumed was aimed at her. She reported the incident and also claimed Graham had flashed her, which saw the police soon on the scene. Adrienne went crazy at this over-reaction and was nearly arrested herself. At the police station Graham's solicitor advised him to plead guilty in order to get the incident out of the way as quickly as possible.

The following day for a laugh Graham decided to go jogging totally naked and ended up at Camden Lock. Unbelievably, no-one reported him until a policewoman eventually stopped him and, seeing he was a little drunk, took pity on him and leant him some money to get a taxi home.

On August 6th Graham and Adrienne flew out to Malaga in Spain with the rest of the cast to shoot more scenes for Three For All, including sequences with the band playing 'Dreams (Out In The Forest)' and 'We're Free' where Graham even got to play the piano. He then had to return to London to appear at Bow Street magistrates' court for the alleged flashing incident. His solicitor said: *"Mr. Bonnet has never been in trouble before. When one of the girls unzipped, he was tempted, in some kind of retaliation, to do the same. It was meant as a joke – perhaps a stupid and tasteless one."* Graham was fined £30.

With the film coming, DJM decided to release two songs from Graham's album, 'Back Row In The Stalls' b/w 'Ghost Writer In My Eye' on October 4th. Bizarrely they did no promotion on it at all, and no reviews appeared so nobody even knew it was available, which was a shame because it was a well-written and well-sung song about trips to the cinema on a Saturday morning when you were a child. The edited B-side was more of a rocker, and enabled Graham to flex his vocal cords a little more. DJM had really missed a trick here as male solo singers were enjoying a lot of popularity at the time. George McCrae, Carl Douglas, John Denver, Ken Boothe and David Essex all reached the top of the UK charts over the next few months. Instead, with the single stiffing, DJM suddenly decided to shelve the album. This came as a real blow. *"They just weren't interested in me. It got a little bit nasty and they wanted more than I could give,"* Graham says. The fact that the movie would give Bonnet's profile a real boost and help promote an album seemed to pass them by.

The cancellation had a far bigger effect on him than people realised at the time. Happily for the newly-weds, Adrienne's film career kept them afloat, albeit she was capable of doing more than Carry On Behind and Adventures Of A Taxi Driver.

1975 began with Graham again wondering what the future held. He now only had the four songs on the soundtrack LP by way of a new release, and they were under the fictional group name Billy Beethoven. DJM showed no interest whatsoever in releasing any of the songs from his embargoed album although songs like 'Private Eye', 'Ade's Song' or 'She May Be Not Much To Look At (But She's Certainly Got A Heart)' would have been potential hits.

Three For All was finally finished and all of Graham's performances made the final cut with '(Untitled) Here Comes The Rain' and 'Dreams (Out In The Forest)' also heard during the film. Everyone at Dejmus and DJM Records were now concentrating on the release of the film and the soundtrack with a £100,000 TV campaign to promote them both. Unusually DJM even offered the LP to dealers on a sale-or-return basis.

Just before the premiere, two singles were released as a taster for the soundtrack, including 'Dreams (Out In The Forest)' b/w 'We're Free' by Billy Beethoven (alias Graham and co.) on May 9th. Both singles amazingly made it to the offices of Melody Maker who were quite upbeat: *"Mr. Beethoven coming over very intense and over emotional as if he was auditioning for a part in 'Tommy'."*

The film premiered in Brighton three weeks later. Graham and all the cast were in attendance, and the movie then had a staggered release, eventually reaching London where it opened on June 22nd in over seventy cinemas. But despite the huge promotional campaign the film was a total flop at the cinemas, and seemed to come from another era to many viewers. Music Week suggested that *"the overall impression of the film is that it is a throw-back to those features of the early sixties – enjoyable while they last, but instantly disposable afterwards."*

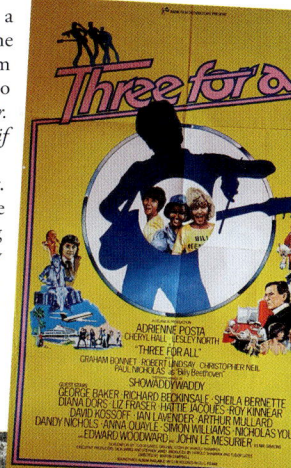

Cardigan man! • *April 1975.*

The soundtrack album featured eighteen songs, and Graham was seen on the front cover playing his guitar with a drumstick, albeit in silhouette. Music Week were as puzzled by the album as they had been by the film (*"not very inspiring listening"*).

Although the movie flopped a few people saw potential in Graham and some offers did come his way, including the lead in a James Dean biopic. He recalls: *"It fell through for some reason, I'm not really sure why. I even had scripts given to me, but nothing came to fruition. I also had two scripts sent to me from the Hemdale Film Corporation, which was actor David Hemmings' company."*

So once again while Adrienne kept busy, set to appear in a new Laugh-In TV series playing the part that Goldie Hawn made famous in the late Sixties, Graham was really down. He parted company with his manager Hazel Malone, and then her son, Cavan. The final blow came as his marriage fell apart.

"Adrienne and I lived together very happily for six years. We got married in 1974 and it was a disaster. It was a dreadful mistake. We just let it drift. It was a last attempt to save the relationship I suppose but by that time, if I'm honest, Adrienne had had enough," he told The Sun in 1981.

In October Graham moved out of their north London house. To get away from London he returned to Skegness to be with his parents, taking Sachi with him. His health had really suffered. His confidence was at an all time low, his weight dropped to just seven-and-a-half stone and he had serious depression. *"The doctors told me that if I didn't start responding to treatment and putting on weight, I had only a few months to live. I did try to keep going. I used to go round local bands in pubs and see if I could work with them. I even went down to Butlins in Skegness to try and get a job as a Redcoat, anything."*

Graham spent just over three months in Skegness recuperating and trying to get his life back to some sort of normality. He was on social security for the first time since a teenager. This was a very hard and difficult period emotionally, physically and mentally but with the help of his parents, Graham started to gradually pull back.

It was a telegram from David Oddie (who used to work for the Robert Stigwood Organisation as a booker) that got him back on track: *"David was the person that got me into the music scene again. He got in touch with me and said 'what the hell are you doing there? Come and see me.' He thought I was wasting my time just waiting around and doing nothing in Skegness. He was managing Micky Moody and Rory Gallagher as well."* David offered to take on Graham and see what he could do career-wise. Talking to Rob McKenzie of Fireworks, Donal Gallagher adds: *"David Oddie had remembered Graham and signed him up and got him to come down to London. He had a very James Dean persona at that time."*

So Graham moved back down to London during January 1976, taking Sachi with him, and settled in a shared flat in Cricklewood. David Oddie quickly secured a deal for him with Quarry Productions, with Andy

Graham and Sachi, the Dulux dog, August 1976.

Heath (now a publisher) and Stuart Taylor (a producer) whom Graham had known from the Marbles days supporting him financially.

Straight away David introduced him to singer, songwriter and guitarist Ronnie Harwood (also signed to Quarry Productions) who had his own trio, the Ronnie Harwood Band, singing lead vocals and playing guitar, with Alan Jarman on bass and backing vocals and Mike Wells on drums and backing vocals. The trio gigged regularly around London doing the pub and club circuit and after watching the band on a couple of occasions Graham was invited to help out. Mike Wells says: *"It wasn't too long before Graham joined us at local venues as a guest artist singing a few songs."*

Graham was actually enjoying himself for the first time in ages and he was soon offered a place in the band. *"It was decided that Graham would replace Alan Jarman on bass,"* recalls Mike. *"We used to play the Old Spotted Dog in Neasden; we would frequently go to Chinese and Indian restaurants after the gigs. All we talked about was music and song-writing. Graham had a great sense of humour, he was very laid back and we laughed a lot. Graham and Ronnie really hit it off. They would spend hours writing songs, although it never really came to much. Graham contributed a couple of lines to Ronnie's 'Rocking Rolling Man'."* The song was later recorded by Jerry Williams and Ronnie Angel.

"I was only in the band for about one month or so," recalls Graham. *"We mostly did covers with maybe two or three originals in the set."* Mike adds: *"Our main set consisted of a few Chuck Berry songs like 'Little Queenie', 'Roll Over Beethoven', 'Around & Around' and 'Johnny B Goode'. Graham would always do his Marbles hit 'Only One Woman', plus some of his self-penned songs of that era. Graham and I would duet on 'Long Tall Sally' and 'The Girl Can't Help It'. He and Ronnie would also do some harmonies on a couple of Neil Sedaka songs too. We always did a variety of Ronnie's songs as well, along with an Elvis medley which included 'All Shook Up', 'Don't Be Cruel', 'Teddy Bear' and 'Hound Dog'. Some of the more easy listening songs we did were 'By The Time I Get To Phoenix' by Glen Campbell, the Charles Aznavour song 'Dance In The Old Fashioned Way' and 'Don't Take Your Love To Town' by Kenny Rogers. Plus, we always included a Beatles three-part harmony set."*

Ronnie also had a daytime business, which enabled Graham to earn a few more bob. Mike says: *"Ronnie also had a TV aerial rigging business and Graham loved to go out with him. So no fear of heights back then! Plus, on another occasion Graham and Ronnie took to fence-repairing after a spectacular gale!"*

Producer Stuart Taylor also looked after the musical interests of a singer-songwriter called Victy Silva, a female singer who had toured with and recorded backing vocals for Kiki Dee, Nazareth, Mick Ronson and The Sensational Alex Harvey Band. In March, Andy Heath and Stuart Taylor mentioned to Victy that they thought Graham's voice would suit her songs. She says: *"They arranged for him to demo some of them at Advision studios, which gave us 'Such A Shame'. The song is about a teacher I had who had lost his wife and he kept drifting off in lessons. That is the 'numb and dumb and blank behind the eyes' bit. That section Gray always called 'Norman-doorman'!"*

Victy was an excellent songwriter and this session also produced the ballad 'Loving Touch'. Her voice blends well with Graham's and they produced some strong harmonies. During April they teamed up a couple more times to do demos, with Graham singing a song called 'Prayer', which Victy had written.

Everyone was keen to help Graham get back on his feet and Victy recalls that they auditioned for TV commercials together as well. *"I remember that we were both at a voice casting at Olympic studios for a Kellogg's advert or something, which of course Gray didn't want to do, but everyone was trying to help him earn some money."*

Their relationship also developed outside the music business and they started dating. In August Graham moved into Victy's house in South-East London but only a few days later Victy was wondering just what she had let herself in for. They found themselves in a pub where Graham got drunk and became belligerent. *"I saw another side to him,"* she says. A little later, the two had an argument. *"He opened the window, which was on the main road, and threw out his plate, food and all, to a resounding crash below."*

They continued to work together, both laying down vocals for RCA Records' album of Paul Gallico's 'Snow Goose' in August, but on a different occasions. Spike Milligan had co-written one of the songs, 'Walking By The Sea', and suggested that it would sound far better if Graham sang it without the words. So Graham ended up singing 'la-la-la-la' to the music and was chuffed to meet one of his childhood heroes.

But while on the surface Graham seemed to be on the mend he was still having mental and physical health problems. Victy says: *"I seemed to spend most of my time trying to get him home in one piece without him starting a fight with someone. He nearly got arrested by deciding to have a pee in full sight of the Camberwell Road in broad daylight! He would push and see how far you would let him go. Beer was his 'comfort'. He couldn't afford spirits!"*

The couple decided that a trip back to Skegness might help, and they arrived on August 31st. Victy says: *"We stayed with Lou and Rene. Lou told us the story about turning on the seaside lights and them saying 'Skegness is so bra' instead of bracing as only the first three letters lit up!"*

Graham and Victy went to see his long-time friend Kenny Bray perform with his band. Kenny says: *"I was doing a gig with my band at the Benvenute Hotel in Chapel St. Leonards. During the gig Graham got up on stage and played bass on some numbers, and Victy played the piano. The stage was rocking. It was a night to remember alright!"*

Back in London through one of Victy's friends, Eric Roberts, who hosted cabaret evenings at Maunkberry's nightclub on Jermyn Street, she and Graham got offered three gigs at the venue from September 21st to 23rd. The shows had already been booked when Graham was asked if he wanted to go on tour with Telly Savalas, but the dates clashed. They worked out a shared eight-song set list, with Victy on vocals and Graham on bass guitar and vocals. The rest of the band consisted of Hugh Burns on guitar, Graham Preskett on piano and a drummer no one can remember. The large poster advertised 'Miss Victy [in large letters] and Graham Bonnet [in small letters] in cabaret', admission £1.00, and featured recent photos taken by Terry O'Neill.

"I'm amazed that it came together so quick," Victy says today. *"On one of the gigs he accidentally hit me on the head with a wild guitar swing and I spent the rest of the set with blood pouring out of my head! One night Graham walked off stage during the gig. Don't know why. Actually he never needed a 'why'! The last night was the best though when Gray hadn't been drinking."*

Graham recalls the appearance: *"I remember a few gay guys trying to pick me up! And that Françoise de Luville was there. He came up to me and complimented my voice. Even though we had a chat he didn't recognise* me from when he'd tried to sign The Graham Bonnet Set in 1968."

Victy points out: *"Our set was mostly covers with two of my songs and one of Gray's called 'Relaxae'. There was also 'I Can Hear The Music', 'The Hungry Years' and 'A Love Like Yours'". I also did a Sondheim song called 'Another Hundred People' which has a fearsome piano part. I don't think my pinkies were ever up to playing that!"* The venue asked them back but Graham decided not to repeat the experience.

During October they moved to a flat in Southfields, but Graham was still battling his depression. He was drinking heavily, or spending all day in front of the TV. *"I'd turn the TV set on as soon as I woke up and watch anything, all the kids' shows, the school programmes, the cartoons, and then turn to the BBC later for documentaries, which I loved."* Victy remembers the problems. *"His 'so called' friends used to take him out for a drink and deliver him back pissed. They took him to parties and the like without me. I got the feeling people like David Oddie thought I was trying to muscle in on Grays' what? Fame? Potential? Talent? Yet I was the one the one earning money, doing jingles, etc!"*

Victy bore the brunt of the depression. *"I was so desperate to please him and yet trying so hard not to let him damage himself at the same time. So I'd hide some pills. He would then go ballistic and call me a thief. On one occasion Graham tried to take the dog for a walk with no clothes on! There was one time when he insisted we went to the pub three times in one day. Another time he had an epileptic fit in the back of a taxi bringing us home. He either hadn't taken his medication, or had drunk too much and then took it. Once he got very upset, and started saying 'I feel James Dean is with me all the time.' He was certainly going through it."*

While this was going on, Quarry Productions had been talking about Graham recording an album. They wanted someone who could handle the production but who was also right for Graham. When Pip Williams' name came up he seemed to tick all the boxes. Pip agreed and brought his right-hand man, John Eden, who knew Graham from his DJM days, to engineer the session. It all seemed a perfect fit. Pip Williams was only a few months older than Graham and had become one of the most sort-after session guitarists of the early Seventies before moving over to the production side of the business. Pip had first come across Graham while he was with the Marbles and recalls: *"I'd never forgotten that voice."*

There was still the question of material, as Pip points out: *"No song choices had been made when I came on board. We sat round - Graham, David and me - and threw ideas into the pot. I also had a couple of songs I'd written with a writing partner, Peter Hutchins, 'Soul Seeker' and 'Heroes On My Picture Wall'. I phoned publisher colleagues and asked if they had anything suitable, which is how things like 'Goodnight and Goodmorning' came along."*

With the trio bouncing ideas around, the Gerry Goffin/Carole King song 'Will You Love Me Tomorrow?' was high on Graham's list, because it was and still is one of his all time favourite songs. Another which Graham had always liked was 'Danny', written by Fred Wise and Ben Weisman. He first heard Cliff Richard's version at school and he used to sing it at various school concerts. *"The songs were ones I liked from when I was younger and the others were chosen from a lot of demos that people sent me."* 'Sunday 16', written by John Kongos was also chosen, because Graham knew he could really flex his vocal cords on it, along with the Al Green classic, 'Tired Of Been Alone'.

Graham also asked Victy if she had any songs for him but was unable to contribute much himself. He had done very little songwriting because of his health problems and his drinking. He had one song half-written, appropriately called 'Wino Song', and Victy helped him to finish it off. She says: *"I wrote the 'and do I see myself here, beside a hatful of beer in time. With lady luck by my side, a rhythm queen on the slide together on a bench we'll sing in harmony'. Hatful of beer - get it? Bonnet!"* Graham had got his idea from seeing the many drunks in Hyde Park where he used to walk his dog.

Three more songs had been put forward to Pip and Graham which had been previously recorded at Abbey Road and Morgan studios in London. These were 'It Ain't Easy', written by Ron Davies with the version being arranged by Graham Preskett. The song, however, had been previously covered by many artists including David Bowie. The other two were versions of 'You've Lost That Lovin' Feeling' that The Righteous Brothers made famous in the mid-Sixties and 'Do What You Gotta Do' which Nina Simone recorded in 1958. The band which played on these three tracks was Micky Moody (guitar), Colin Gibson (bass guitar), Terry Popple (drums), Kenny Craddock (piano) and Graham Preskett (acoustic guitar). These three songs were added to Graham's list, and he could do new vocals over them.

Although they had planned to use the Marquee studio, come December it was full and so Graham was booked into Manor studios in Oxford instead for three weeks, as John Eden recalls: *"I had worked at the Manor with Ronnie Leahy from Stone The Crows. I knew the studio and liked it."* John was paid for the session as a freelance engineer by Quarry Productions. *"The Manor was a perfect set-up. It was a residential studio. It had everything that you could imagine. A great team of girls who cooked breakfast for us and the chef came in and made snacks for us in the afternoon and an amazing meal that we sat down to every night and then went back to work again. It was an ideal place to make music."*

The nucleus of musicians on the session were Micky Moody (lead & rhythm guitar, acoustic & slide guitar), Dave Markee (bass guitar) and Mike Giles (drums), although Pip actually played on quite a lot: *"I did the lion's share of the guitar work on the album. Micky was part of the band that had played on the rhythm tracks and I had done all of the guitar overdubs, including the slide solo and voice box guitar on '…… Baby Blue', and the electric mandolin on '…… Baby Blue' and 'Goodnight and Goodmorning'."* Pip even played synthesisers on the album, although Tony Hymas was brought in to add some extra keyboards. Quarry stable mate and future Whitesnake guitarist Micky Moody also knew Graham from the Marbles. *"David Oddie was aware of my activities at the time, especially with David Coverdale and Bob Young, and wanted me to connect with Graham too."*

While cover versions dominated the material, the melodies and arrangements were completely changed from the originals. Pip says: *"Obviously, with such classic songs, we weren't just going to copy them verbatim. Graham was given free rein to interpret them how he felt best."*

In the studio, Graham would strum his acoustic guitar every now and then. One day he was playing the Bob Dylan song 'It's All Over Now Baby Blue' and Pip immediately wanted to record it. The song had always been a favourite of Graham's, but to give it a bit more of a lift they moved it up a key to F from E.

Looking back, Micky recalls: *"I don't think I was there for more than one week. Dave Markee was on bass and we got on well together, appreciated each other's musicianship and enjoyed a spliff! Pip Williams was also a renowned studio guitarist and I'm sure he could have played anything that I did on the sessions, but was happy to have me there. Mike Giles had that very English sense of humour and I enjoyed the vibe in the studio. Keyboard player Tony Hymas appeared around this time; he was also witty in that dry style and a great player to boot!"*

John says: *"It was Pip's call to bring in these players. I knew these guys and of course they were on the session circuit and playing on different albums at the time. Mike was a very seasoned drummer and so was Dave."*

Three additional musicians were brought in; Frank Riccotti (percussion), Peter Zorn (alto sax) and Graham's drinking buddy, Graham Preskett (violin). John recalls: *"Graham Preskett was known to us all and he was a great fiddle player and an amazing arranger. A really great guy. So, there wasn't really any question when there was some fiddle parts to do, he was the man."*

Even though Graham did some backing vocals, it was also decided to bring in some female singers. Jackie Sullivan, Joy Yates and Stevie Lange were the vocal backing group Bardot, as Pip explains: *"They'd done a couple of other backing vocal gigs for me and were amazing."*

It seemed very strange that Victy wasn't used as a backing singer, but Graham didn't want her involved. She says: *"He insisted, despite two of the backing singers being the two girls I regularly worked with. He also said he didn't want me to come to the Manor and didn't even want the dog there! Chauvinism doesn't even begin to cover it. While I was there Graham's voice packed up before he could sing my song 'Such A Shame'. So he sang 'Rock Island Line' instead."* Graham already knew the song from when he played it in The Bluesecte during the mid Sixties.

With ten new songs recorded, plus the three previously recorded backing tracks which Graham had added his vocals to, ten songs were selected for the album and one for a B-side. The album was later remixed at Marquee studios in London where a little re-recording was also carried out. Graham also did a low key gig around this period in London with Micky Moody and Graham Preskett at Brown's Club, but all details are now forgotten.

But even though Graham had finished recording, all wasn't well between him and manager David Oddie. David was far from happy with Graham's drinking and the amount of pills he was taking. On January 30th he even threatened to sack Graham and send him back to Skegness.

Graham and Victy decided to take a break there anyway before she started rehearsing for a tour of Belgium with Charles Aznavour. Graham was far from happy about her going on tour, but someone had to bring the money home. In the end Victy got food poisoning and when she returned home joined Graham in becoming a vegetarian.

From the end of 1976 and into 1977, Victy had been recording the vocals on a song for a project called Lords Of The Universe, written by Cat Stevens' brother, David Gordon. Graham also recorded a song for it called 'I Who Am I' but David Essex was brought in to redo it, possibly because the project leaders wanted someone with a bigger name. The project was later re-titled 'Alpha Omega' and released in 1979.

By now Victy had bought Graham a Kawasaki 250 motorbike. She says: *"He couldn't even get it out of the car park! Well, it was on a very steep hill. After managing to start it and whilst trying to get it up the steep hill out of the car park, he fell off! I don't remember it actually going anywhere, to be honest. We somehow convinced the shop to take it back. I have to say that buying him that bike was a bit of an error of judgment on my part. He was tired of being tied to cabs and the No. 39 bus. I thought it might make him sober up!"*

David Oddie had been talking to various record companies about Graham's album and by early spring Quarry Productions signed him to Polydor Records' subsidiary label Ring O'Records, begun by Ringo Starr in 1975. Largely dormant for a time Ring O were looking to reactivate the label.

Talking to Rob McKenzie of Fireworks, Donal Gallagher remembers them looking for a deal: *"David was trying to get him signed with labels such as Charisma. We were having a beer at The Ship in Wardour Street where the bands and people from the film industry used to drink. I think Graham was getting quite frustrated and felt that Quarry weren't doing enough for him. At the time though, everything was about groups and the Marquee; maybe his image was a little bit too clean-cut. I thought Graham had one of the most underrated voices. He should have had a lot more attention along the lines of Rod Stewart."*

Terry Condon, Polydor A & R manager, was appointed as Ring O's managing director and Graham Bonnet was the first new signing, with 'It's All Over Now Baby Blue' with the non-album 'Heroes On My Picture Wall' on the B-side; his debut release for new label, and their first since teaming up with Polydor. They also agreed that 'Danny' would be the follow-up and in order to create some publicity two promotion videos were filmed.

It had now been over two years since Graham's last release and the music scene had changed out of all recognition. Punk rock had arrived towards the end of 1976 and by the time Graham's new single was released on May 27th 1977 was dominating much of the music (and indeed national) press. But contrary to revisionist pop music history, there was still a strong market for other types of pop and rock.

Ring O did their job well and the Bob Dylan cover was well received; Record Mirror described it as *"a pretty competent version."* Melody Maker said, *"if you want to give a good guy a break and you do fancy his case, you wouldn't be disappointed."* 'It's All Over Now Baby Blue' got a tremendous amount of airplay, and made the Radio 1 playlist, but failed to dent the national charts. Mind you, Tony Blackburn didn't help as Graham says: *"I remember him playing it on the radio one morning and he said, 'yes, that was Graham Bonnet with 'It's All Over Now Baby Blue'. It certainly is.' He obviously didn't think it was up to much!"*

As this was going on, Graham was offered the lead in a new musical called 'Dean', based on the life of actor James Dean. The show was due to begin in London's West End in August. Some four years earlier, Graham had been offered the chance to make his West End debut, but said no because of his nerves. This time he simply turned it down flat. *"I really think it's about time people left the James Dean thing alone. I'd never heard anything of him until my ex-wife [they had begun divorce proceedings in April], Adrienne Posta, told me how much I resembled him!"* he told Mates Magazine in November 1977.

Looking back on the situation recently, Graham says: *"I didn't think I*

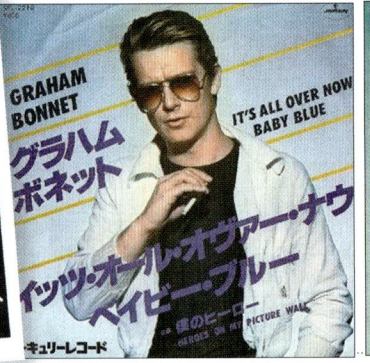

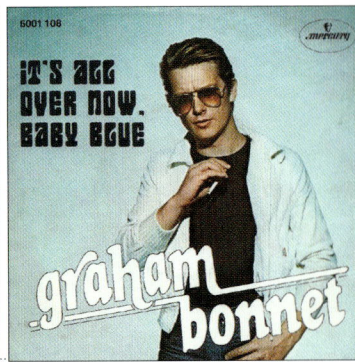

could do it. I'd never done a stage musical before. I would do it now, as I have become used to being on stage, and showing off!" The Dean connection returned a couple of years later when Graham was approached about another proposed biopic, which fell through.

By mid-June Victy and Graham had moved back to her place in Camberwell. Graham was still drinking heavily, and it got worse, as Victy recalls: *"Graham got drunk every day. He saw things and got angry. On one occasion I thought he was going to collapse in the street again."*

Despite the lack of sales in the UK, Quarry secured deals across Europe and behind the scenes the promotion team at Ring O had been preparing an even bigger campaign for Graham's next single and his debut album. 200 press kits

were compiled which included the album, single, biography, photograph, poster and details of their advertising plan. 'Danny' was released on August 12th backed by 'Rock Island Line' and the UK was deluged with 500 wall posters while record stores got sleeves, posters and window streamers. It hardly mattered as no one seemed to be paying attention. As the New Musical Express commented in its review *"if at first you don't succeed, try, try, etc. Poor old G. B.'s been at it for so long my heart bleeds, but the goofs just keep on coming."*

The record did even worse than its predecessor, and radio plays were far and few between. However, everyone still seemed optimistic about the release of the album on September 5th, simply titled 'Graham Bonnet', an idea his manager David Oddie came up with. *"Original eh?"* was Graham's comment. It has to be said that the packaging was superb, something the New Musical Express commented on. In fact it impressed them far more than album. *"Bonnet blasts his way through a selection of classic songs and on each one proves himself lacking in any kind of sensitivity or subtlety. His own songwriting, showcased in 'Wino Song', is a little better."*

Record Mirror got near the root of the problem: *"Sure the guy can sing, right up high he goes. But two sides of cover versions ain't gonna impress anybody. 'Will You Love Me Tomorrow', 'Tired Of Being Alone' and 'Rock Island Line' are all done very well, but surely Bonnet could have contributed more than the one original. A shame, because Bonnet has an undoubted talent. Instead of plumping for a safe bet, he should have taken a gamble. He needs to."*

Ring O'Records kept up the momentum with half-page adverts in the big music papers for the week dated September 7th and more fly-postering, but it failed to generate any significant interest.

Yet if the UK remained largely indifferent, elsewhere there were signs of life. 'It's All Over Now Baby Blue' (which had been released in Japan and throughout Europe by Mercury Records though copies on Ring O' Records from Holland also surfaced) was becoming popular in Ireland, while in Germany they wanted Graham to make some personal appearances. On October 15th he appeared there on the TV show Disco and sang live to a backing track and the song went on to become a big success. 'It's All Over Now Baby Blue' was also released in Guatemala and in nearby Mexico in 1978.

In Australia 'It's All Over Now Baby Blue' was powering its way up the charts and after five weeks was at No. 3. It also peaked at the same position in New Zealand. This lifted sales of the album, which in Australia reached No. 7 and in New Zealand No. 11. Mercury

Records quickly arranged a two-week promotional tour over there for November. On November 1st Graham and David, having stopped off in America to see to a few business details, arrived in Sydney, with Mercury releasing 'Danny' b/w 'Wino Song' to coincide with the visit.

Graham did a solid week of media and radio interviews there, before moving on to Melbourne for three days, where he was the guest compere on the ABC TV music programme Countdown. *"I was scared to death. I'd never done anything like it before and as I didn't know the groups, I had to read their names from a script!"* He was also presented with his first ever gold disc for 'It's All Over Now Baby Blue'.

The record company held a 'welcome to Australia' barbeque on the banks of the Yarra River, but hadn't bothered to learn that Graham was a vegetarian. *"I ate all the lettuce and tomatoes,"* he told Byron Smith of Juke magazine. *"I just remember drinking a lot of beer on that particular day and falling asleep under a tree with a dog!"*

Talking to The Sun, Graham admitted: *"I would have preferred to have had a hit in Britain first. 'It's All Over Now Baby Blue' was at one stage the most played single on air, but it only got in to the lower end of the charts. I'm willing to live anywhere I have a hit and Australia is a nice country!"* He told the Adelaide reporters: *"It's weird. I've come half-way round the world and suddenly all these people recognise me! But I'm grateful it's happened. I've enjoyed myself here. I've never drunk so much beer in my life! In England, if you're not a punk rocker you've had it!"*

Behind the scenes, David Oddie was trying to negotiate a tour of Australia and New Zealand for May with the Paul Dainty Corporation, but in the end it never happened. Graham was talking about his follow-up album, to be cut in December. *"My girlfriend writes songs too – in fact she has four songs on the next album. I don't write songs because I am too lazy!"*

By the time he moved on to New Zealand around the middle of the month, the album had also achieved gold status in Australia (and went silver in New Zealand). Graham had made a lot of friends with his good nature, quick wit and obvious talent but the schedule was beginning to take its toll and he was taken to hospital suffering from fatigue.

'Danny' didn't do as well as its predecessor, only reaching No. 79, while back in the UK Ring O, seemingly gluttons for punishment, issued a third single, an edit of 'Goodnight and Goodmorning' (which also came out in Holland.) It disappeared without trace.

When Graham arrived back in England he broke up with Victy. He had met a lady called Jo Eime in

Adelaide and was expecting her to fly over. He moved into Pip Williams' place for the time being. Pip recalls: *"Graham needed a calm place to be at the time and Appletree Cottage was a lovely little house. I remember I had an account at the local wine store, which got used quite a bit!"*

Graham had also been listening to quite a lot of songs with a view to assembling his next album. He settled on thirteen to record, these being: 'Won't You Join Me', 'Pyramid' and 'Only You Can Lift Me,' by South African songwriter John Kongos, 'I'll Be Your Baby Tonight' by Bob Dylan, the little known Bee Gees song 'Warm Ride', 'Is There A Way To Sing The Blues' by Ray McRiner, 'Can't Complain' by John Otway, 'Givin' Up My Worryin'' by Francis Rossi and Bernard Frost (Graham liked this song straight away. With Status Quo sharing the same management, they used to bump into each other at the offices quite often. The original version appeared on Quo's 'If You Can't Stand The Heat' album), 'Stand Still Stella' and 'Cold Lady' by Pip Williams. Pip says: *"These two were played at song selection meetings and obviously enough people thought they were suitable, though to be honest, I'm not mad on 'Stand Still Stella' these days! But it's always good to have your songs there."* 'Such A Shame' by Victy Silva, and Graham's '10/12 Observation' and 'High School Angel', for which Graham had written the music and Peter Hutchins the lyrics, completed the selection.

Sessions were due to start on December 5th at Marquee studios in London with Pip Williams and John Eden. Quarry also wanted another hit single in Australia (and clearly Graham was not against the idea!), and a possible song emerged as Graham recalls: *"Robin Gibb had a rough idea for the 'Warm Ride' song and Barry finished it off. It was a very short demo that Robin made and it came to my management - I think David Oddie got that together."* The Bee Gees had in fact written 'Warm Ride' during the Saturday Night Fever sessions and offered it to Roger Daltrey, who turned it down.

Another set of excellent musicians was assembled. The only survivor from the previous session was bassist Dave Markee, Micky Moody having now joined Whitesnake full-time. He recalls: *"I was asked to play on the album, but my Whitesnake commitments prevented it. We were actually rehearsing to go on tour at the time of the recording."* Les Davison played rhythm guitar, with Pip playing all the lead guitar and acoustic guitar parts, as well as well playing mandolin and electric sitar. Mick Underwood came in on drums, with Lance Dixon on keyboards, Frank Ricotti on percussion, Cliff Hardie on tambourine and Jim Cuomo playing the alto and tenor saxophone solos that were required. The cream of the UK backing singers was again used, the three women from Bardot along with Barry St. John and Liza Strike. Graham also contributed to the backing vocals.

John explains how drummer Mick Underwood came to be part of the session: *"Pip and I had been working with Mick Underwood in a band called Strapps that Pip was producing, and that's really how that relationship came about, but I do believe that Pip and Mick had known each other from other bands over the previous years. He did a good job."*

After Graham had been in Marquee studios a few days he played Pip a song he had written, which became '10/12 Observation'. Graham says: *"I'm interested in mysteries, flying saucers, the Loch Ness monster and other things like that. That is what the song is really about. It's just about fantasies. Pip made up the title. I was wondering what I could call the song and he said 'the date is the 10th of the 12th, it's an observation. What you've done here is you've wrote down stuff you've looked at and thought about.' So that is how we ended up with '10/12...'"*

Deciding how to proceed with 'Warm Ride' wasn't immediately obvious because the song was in sections on the demo. Graham kept the bits he liked and dropped the rest. Barry and Maurice came by the studio, but when Robin heard the finished version later he apparently wasn't very keen on it.

After the work finished at Marquee studios, some additional recording was done at Startling studios in Ascot, which engineer John Eden remembers well for a number of reasons: *"It was John and Yoko's old house and John's studio, the room where they did 'Imagine', and the piano was there. We did a number of vocals and overdubs down there."* Graham also recalls the good vibes, *"It was a magical time there and great to see the place. To live there for a week or two was amazing! There was a full size T. Rex. Plus Yoko's art work too!"*

Pip too remembers the studio well: *"It was in the house that Ringo had bought from John Lennon. Startling was a lovely place to be, though to be honest, there were better studios around technically and John Eden did a great job with the equipment available to us. One day, Graham and I were having a stroll around the grounds and wandered into a barn. Up on a raised floor in the barn was an old Ludwig drum kit covered in dust and stuff, but with the logo 'The Beatles' on the front skin. That kind of freaked us out a bit."*

He explains how Graham worked on the album: *"Graham used to give 110% every take and this led to problems occasionally. For instance, I'd prepare a studio budget, based on how long we thought the lead vocals would take to record, only for Graham to give it everything and then the voice would need a couple of days rest, before he was match fit again. For live performances, this is not a problem, but when recording an album, one can hear the difference from track to track. I remember he used to get pretty tired after an energetic session."*

Towards the end of December, 'Rock Island Line' b/w 'Soul Seeker' was released in Australia, while New Zealand got 'Goodnight And Goodmorning' b/w 'Wino Song' in January.

'Warm Ride' b/w '10/12 Observation' had been earmarked as the first single, and towards the end of January both were mixed. The title of the album, 'No Bad Habits', came from Micky Moody, as Graham recalls: *"It was his joke. I didn't snort cocaine, or do any heavy drugs. Micky's comment, when the other guys were putting in their drug orders, was 'well Graham has no bad habits'! Drinking was looked upon as being a good habit back then. It was the norm."*

Graham's new girlfriend Jo had arrived and the couple moved in to a flat in Earls Court. *"It was horrible. It was just two rooms and rats!"* In the spring they decided it was time to start looking for a new place to live, and moved in to an apartment in Maida Vale. His divorce from Adrienne also came through.

After a photo shoot, Ring O' Records once again set about their promotional push during February for 'Warm Ride' with 12" white label pressings and a batch of 7" promo copies featuring a short version and a long version of the song, lasting well over six minutes with a wonderful guitar solo by Pip Williams.

Outside the UK Mercury Records agreed to fund three promotional videos at the Rainbow theatre in London on March 6th, the day before the official release of 'Warm Ride' in 7" and 12" long version formats. The other two songs selected for release later in the year were 'Can't Complain' and 'Only You Can Lift Me'. Micky Moody was brought in for the filming, even though he hadn't appeared on the album. *"It made the videos look more like a live thing with two guitar players,"* says Graham and with Micky doing well in Whitesnake, it certainly added a bit more bite to things as Micky recalls: *"I can only assume that the guitarist from the album was unavailable for the video. I was miming to someone else's guitar. During a break I went to the pub across the road*

48

with Dave Markee. When we came out we were stopped and searched by the then notorious SPG [the rather controversial Special Patrol Group of the Metropolitan Police Force] as the pub was known for drug dealers! I'm pleased to say that they wasted their time." As indeed were Ring O. There were no reviews and they forgot to place any press adverts, relying on button badges suggesting 'I Want A Warm Ride'!

Despite this Pip Williams and John Eden went back in to Marquee studios to mix the rest of the songs for the album and stayed there until March 13th. Looking back today on Graham's albums, Pip is still very proud of them: *"I got the job of producing Quo after they heard the first album I'd done with Graham! I'm still pretty pleased with both of them, but specifically the first. It would have been nice to have spent more time sourcing unusual material and allowing Graham to write more, but I think the choice of covers was good; it was representative of the time."*

The video line-up, l-r : Dave Markee, Micky Moody, Graham, Pip Williams, Mick Underwood and Lance Dixon.

Since 'Warm Ride' wasn't creating any interest the song was re-mixed. The hi-hats were brought up and it was given more of a disco feel, and then issued as a promotional one-sided 12" single. What Ring O'Records did with these is anyone's guess, although this time there was a little bit of publicity stating it was 'another disco smash written by the Bee Gees'.

The single similarly failed to make much impact abroad (even in Zimbabwe where it was issued by Philips!), which came as a big blow to Mercury, until it came out in Australia and New Zealand - where yet again it charted at 2 and 6 respectively. Plans were made for another promotional tour of the two countries later in the year.

In September Ring O'Records suddenly closed down and became a production company. Graham was without a UK label but things were going very well down under. His second visit to Australia towards the end of October ran along much the same lines as before, with 'No Bad Habits' released to tie in. He did eight TV appearances across New Zealand and once more David Oddie was trying to organise a tour for early next year but again nothing ever came of this, despite the fact that the album went gold, reaching No. 6 in the Australian LP charts. 'No Bad Habits' was also released in Holland but with 'Warm Ride' omitted.

An edit of 'Only You Can Lift Me' followed in Australasia but didn't sell well. The B-side began back in Advision studios in March 1976 and was written by Victy Silva. The wonderful 'Such A Shame' only ever appeared on this pressing. The track wasn't necessarily recorded as a B-side as John Eden points out: *"I think we started out doing tracks just to see how they turn out sometimes and that's really what happened there."*

'Can't Complain', the song written by John Otway, was issued in Europe on Mercury, but sadly this didn't sell very well either. When Graham was listening to songs for the album, John Otway had just charted with 'Really Free'. John says: *"'Can't Complain' was one of three songs I wrote about this girl called Lisa that I had a crush on. I was very impressed when I was contacted by Graham - not many people want to cover my songs! I think the link was my publisher, Brian Morrison, who was also the Gibbs' brothers' publisher at the time. I had just signed with him and he wanted me to publish more songs. Everyone used to hang out at the Warrington Pub in Maida Vale. It was a trendy area and I was trendy for a while so I lived there! Graham met me there and we had a chat. I thought he had an amazing voice."*

Graham, who co-wrote the B-side 'High School Angel' also recalls the meeting: *"He lived in Maida Vale too, just down the street, not far from my place. He wanted to go busking in the street, he said, one day in the pub, but I chickened out as I wasn't drunk enough!"*

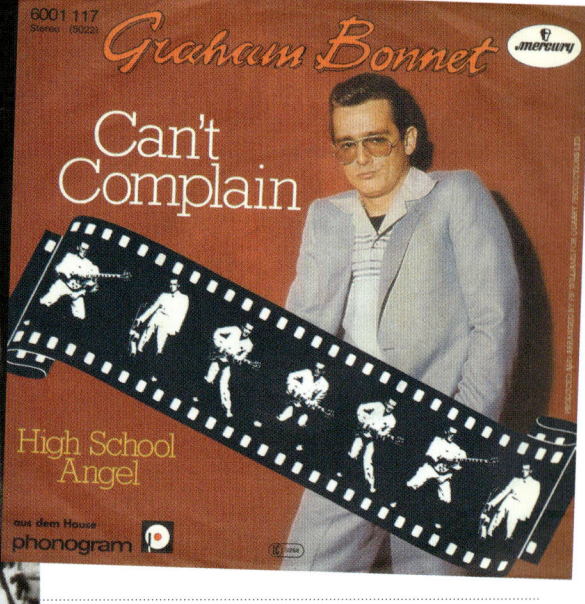

Graham during the filming of the Mercury Records promotional videos.

CHAPTER 4
Desert Diamond (1979 – 1980)

Featuring: Rainbow

Lost in the danger zone

> RAINBOW have asked me to help them find a replacement lead singer for Ronnie Dio who quit the band last year.
> The heavy metal giants desperately need to find one before their Spring tour, and they are already a month behind in recording their forthcoming album.
> If you think your voice can match Ritchie Blackmore's guitar playing phone 839 3527—and become a star.

As 1979 began, Graham was still basking in the Australasia success of 'No Bad Habits'. It had taken quite a while to re-establish himself after the Marbles and even though success was 12,000 miles away, it really didn't matter to him. Back home, Graham was still doing the occasional TV commercial in London and the thought of a third solo album hadn't even crossed his mind.

But his reputation was growing and people were still trying to coax him into joining their bands. Brian Connolly had left The Sweet in February and Graham's name was top of their list. Pip Williams, who played guitar on many hits by the band, is thought to have suggested him. Graham was flattered as always: *"It was not my thing. I just didn't fancy it and didn't audition for them. It was nice of them to ask me though."* His next offer came from a perhaps even more unlikely direction.

Graham had until now been largely involved in the singer / songwriter genre, working with session players, recording some original material as well as lots of covers. So when word reached him that one of the world's top hard rock bands was interested in having a chat, Graham was nonplussed; he had very little knowledge of this type of music, and certainly knew nothing of the already convoluted history of Rainbow.

Formed in 1975, and with three studio albums to their name already, Rainbow had been formed by former Deep Purple guitarist Ritchie Blackmore. They had quickly achieved huge success across Europe and Japan but the heavy costs of touring a rock band on this scale could not be sustained without making it in America, where the band was just a little too heavy and uncompromising for some audiences, and certainly for radio play.

With bassists and keyboard players coming and going, the core of the band was Ritchie on guitar; singer Ronnie James Dio and drummer Cozy Powell who had ousted Rainbow's first drummer before the group even began touring. Ritchie and Ronnie wrote the lion's share of the material but by 1978 unresolved issues over equal recognition for the singer's input, and the fact that the band were still seen as Ritchie's rather than a more democratic outfit, began to grow.

Wanting, indeed needing, to move in a more commercial direction, Ritchie recruited another former Deep Purple musician Roger Glover in the role of a writer and producer. He and Ritchie had worked well together in the past, while Roger was fast making a name for himself as a successful producer, someone who could give Rainbow a more radio-friendly edge. It was a bit of a departure for Ritchie, who had worked with Martin Birch as a producer since 1971. As they began recording their fourth album at the end of 1978, Ronnie realised he was not enjoying it any more. He felt (and time would prove him right) that he had built up enough of a following and reputation to do something on his own and before the year was over it was agreed that he would leave Rainbow.

Ronnie's departure was made public in January 1979, although Graham hadn't been following the story and had little idea of how it would affect the rest of his own career.

Rainbow's next few months were something of a rock soap opera. Cozy suggested recruiting the services of keyboard player Don Airey, who he knew from his pre-Rainbow band Hammer. Don took some persuading but eventually joined in December 1978. Bass player Clive Chaman had also been brought on board and the quartet started working on material at Ritchie's home in Connecticut over a three-week spell, but it proved largely fruitless. Clive went, Strife bassist Gordon Rowley replaced him, but only lasted one day...

Down to a trio again, they spent the Christmas period back in England. More rehearsals took place, this time with ex-Pretty Things bassist Jack Green, who Ritchie had brought along. In the meantime, he also approached former Deep Purple vocalist Ian Gillan and tried to get him to join. Ian declined and threw Ritchie a curveball by suggesting instead that the guitarist join his own group. Nothing came of this horse-trading although Ritchie did make music paper headlines by turning up unannounced at one of the Gillan band shows in London over the holiday season for a jam.

It is a mark of the standing of the players concerned that this was again a big story in the music press. Ritchie returned to Connecticut in January, and having auditioned former Trapeze singer Pete Goalby over the phone, Ritchie's manager invited him over for four days of rehearsals and the band asked him to join as their new singer.

Ritchie reasoned that Rainbow could now crack on and the band reconvened at the Chateau Pelly de Cornfeld in the south of France for more rehearsals during early 1979. Recording began (and they even did a version of 'Since You Been Gone') but it wasn't long before Pete and Ritchie began to argue. It was left to Roger Glover to inform Pete that his six week stint in Rainbow was over. Things were not working out for Jack Green either, who couldn't get into the music. Ritchie did try to keep him, but Jack departed. Chris Glen of the Sensational Alex Harvey Band auditioned next, but the chemistry wasn't there.

They decided to have a break from trying out

> **LEAD VOCALIST**
>
> Required for
>
> **MAJOR ROCK BAND**
>
> TEL: 01 839 3527

bass players and put all their efforts into settling on a singer. The fact that the Maison Rouge mobile studio was costing $2,000 a day probably focused minds. A veritable rock A-Z of rock singers took part. Each would be flown into Geneva and driven to the Chateau by the band's road manager Colin Hart. Roger Glover stood in on bass for the auditions (though still seemingly not wanting to go on tour again, given the illnesses and pressure he'd gone through in his final Deep Purple days.) Many vocalists came and went including Marc Storace (later of Krokus), ex-Geordie frontman Brian Johnson, and Kenny Driscoll from Lone Star. There were so many others that in later years nobody could be sure if they auditioned or were simply names on a list, like Chris Thompson from Manfred Mann's Earth Band who may have made the trip and Roger Ferris of No Dice who had previously written songs for Smokie, Racey and the Arrows was also asked to audition. Talking to Victy Silva, Roger Ferris says: *"I had a call from Cozy Powell, who asked if I would fly out to Geneva and sing a few tracks with Rainbow, but I declined as we were about to record our second album. In hindsight I should have done it as our album was no way as good as the first!"*

With the atmosphere getting a little fraught, to try and lighten the mood, Cozy would play his 'guess the single' game with everyone. He always carried a batch of cassettes with him and for a laugh he would play a very short snippet of one of the songs to his bandmates who had to work out what the band or record was. One evening he just happened to play a few bars of 'Only One Woman' by the Marbles, which sparked a conversation about the singer and what had ever happened to him. At first, Don Airey was under the impression they were talking about Graham Bonney, as he says: *"I thought he was the guy who sang 'Supergirl!'."* Which is exactly why in 1966 Graham had dropped the second 't' from his surname to avoid the same mistake.

They all had vague recollections of a youthful, good-looking, long-haired singer, and Roger Glover was quickly given the job of tracking Graham down via someone he thought had done a session with him just over one year earlier. After a few phone calls Roger was put in touch with guitarist Micky Moody, still with Whitesnake. He shared the same management, Quarry Productions and put Roger onto David Oddie, Graham's manager. David then called to ask Graham what he felt about going to France for the audition.

Graham was more than happy to continue with his life in London: *"I actually didn't know who Rainbow was or even what kind of music they played."* David suggested that there was nothing to lose going for the audition and, if everything went well, it could be a good career move. So he went out and bought some Rainbow albums for Graham so he could hear what the band sounded like. When he listened to them it was a bit of a shock. The music was totally different to anything Graham could have ever imagined and very unlike what he was doing. However, he agreed to attend the audition and was told to learn the Deep Purple song 'Mistreated'. As he'd never heard that either it was back to the record shop for his manager, as Graham says: *"David then went out to buy the album which featured that song as I needed it for my audition piece."*

During February, with Rainbow paying for his flight and accommodation, Graham set off to Geneva. He followed a by now well-worn path, with Colin Hart meeting him at the airport and driving him to the Chateau Pelly de Cornfeld across the French border. Colin remembers almost missing him at the airport, as he was checking arrivals for a rock singer, and Graham didn't fit his idea at all. In the end Graham recognised Colin as a likely rock roadie and introduced himself. Graham recalls: *"I went alone and stayed one night. 'Mistreated' was my audition song, I didn't learn any Rainbow songs."* Despite this seeming drawback, as soon as Graham started to sing the others knew they had found their next front man, as Don Airey remembers: *"We all looked up, it was so extraordinary, but nobody said anything."* As well as not knowing who Rainbow were, Graham was totally unaware that, during the first line of the song, he had blown the minds of all the musicians he was auditioning for. Apparently Ritchie's look said it all after Graham had sung the first three syllables - 'I've been Mis …'

Rainbow, after listening to around fifty potential candidates, must have been hugely relieved. They went through the song again and Graham was offered the gig. Even so he was in two minds about what to do: *"I went back to London to think about it, because I wasn't sure if I liked this music. I was into a completely different thing. Not that it wasn't great, but it wasn't really what I had done before."* In turn Rainbow had been taken aback by Graham's image but felt the voice was the thing, the rest could be worked on. Little did they know.

In London, Graham had a long conversation about his musical future and the pros and cons of joining Rainbow with David Oddie. *"When I spoke to my manager, I said I don't think I fit. He said 'yes you will.'"* David eventually convinced Graham that it was a good move, and he accepted the position. It was reported at the time that Graham was paid between £6,000 and £10,000 for joining, although he says of this: *"If I was, I never saw a penny of it!"*

Chatting later to Sounds in July 1979 about how Rainbow had found Graham, Ritchie gave his view on events: *"He sang with the Marbles, an incredible singer. When I heard ['Only One Woman'] in '69 I couldn't believe the vocal. He's a great singer and I think people will be very pleased with him. He's very dynamic… You have to watch the guy because he's a virtuoso as a vocalist, he's just not a poser stereotype kind of hand on hips and all that nonsense you know, he can sing and there's very few of them around. That's why it took us so long to get this thing going, because I wouldn't settle for a second best singer. Nobody could hit the high notes… he's got a three octave range, which is amazing."* Roger Glover told the same music paper in March 1980: *"A singer to measure up to Rainbow's requirements was very hard to come by. We auditioned many singers, some really good ones, but they weren't quite right. Ritchie's always been an idealist and perfectionist. We listed all the requirements a singer should have and I think there were twenty-eight of them. You're never gonna get anybody who supplies all that. I think what Ritchie wants is a guy like himself who can sing, which he'll never find 'cos there's only one Ritchie, like there's only one of everybody else. However, Graham fitted most of the billing, the main thing being that he had a good voice. He's also a good front man for the band plus he's got a fresh image."*

Rainbow might have found their singer, but were still faced with the problem of finding a permanent bass player. Graham, who hadn't even got his feet under the table yet, suggested Roger Glover. *"I said to Roger, 'how come you aren't going to play bass live?' He said, 'well no one has asked me!' So I said, well I will. And that was just the way it went down. Not thinking that my suggestion would carry any weight!"* Don Airey also had a quiet word with Ritchie, and the decision was made. Roger now had to come up with the lyrics and a basic melody, because the band didn't have anything to go with the arrangements for the songs they had already written and recorded. To try and help lighten his load, Roger offered Graham the opportunity to do some of the writing. Not having written material like this before, rather than have a go, Graham declined. This surprised Roger and also threw Ritchie, because they had always been used to singers putting their stamp on the songs. In fact Graham was actually quite nervous about submitting lyrics. It was a totally different musical genre to what he had been used to and he was worried that his lyrics wouldn't be right. He also felt a little intimidated by the change of musical direction; it being the first time Graham had ever been involved in a band set-up of this magnitude. Graham had of course written before, and in hindsight with some encouragement his work would undoubtedly have fitted in.

For now though the pressure was put back on Roger, who soon got some ideas worked up, as Graham recalls: *"There were no vocal guides for the album, until Roger came up with them as we went along with the recordings."* Although not known as a singer, Roger could carry a tune (and had sung a lot with his first professional band Episode Six). Actually getting his own vocals down on tape was not as easy as Graham had thought it might be. Using Roger's guide vocals, Graham attempted to get to grips with a couple of songs, but didn't yet feel at ease in the environment he was in, specifically trying to work in an old chateau in the middle of winter, something else he'd never been asked to do before: *"It was after a few days. My vocal attempts were terrible in very uncomfortable surroundings. It was a cold and depressing place. Plus, because of my depression, my voice was very average. I felt really down and just … strange. It was the place. It was like a haunted house! We tried to record my voice all over the castle, trying to find a room that sounded acoustically good for vocals. There really wasn't anywhere. It was all very uncomfortable and there was an echo that would go on for years! So, I ended up saying to Roger 'I can't do it, mate.'"*

Explaining himself later, he elaborated: *"I hate being stuck in the middle of nowhere with nothing to do when, if it's not a good day, in a real studio you can at least go out into the street and you see other people instead of just the people you are working with. I remember Roger Glover put me in the dining room or whatever it was and we tried to do a vocal in this room, it just didn't work. We had no songs as such, just grasping at straws and it really needed to be done in the office so to speak instead of the middle of the countryside. I can't explain it; I just love to be in a proper work area."* Eventually it was decided that he could fly over to America and finish the vocals off in a proper studio, Kingdom Sound in Long Island. Once there Graham began to relax, and staying in a proper hotel also helped. *"As soon as we went into a studio then it started to happen,"* Graham recalls. Blackmore, who had a real aversion to 'proper studios', was perplexed, unable to understand why anyone would not be able to work in an old castle.

One of Roger's contributions to the overall direction of the band was to bring a more earthy element to some of the lyrics. *"It lacked sex - as sex is the most potent form of excitement, I tried to introduce it into the music!"* Roger told a reporter at the time. He had also tried different approaches to most of the tracks, as Graham was to find out. *"One tune would be written probably four different ways, with four sets of lyrics, and we would pick the best parts and put it all together."*

By the time they quit France, nine backing tracks had been recorded altogether. With the exception of their cover of ex-Argent guitarist Russ Ballard's 'Since You Been Gone', as they had no finished lyrics the other eight songs were all given working titles: 'Stone' ('Bad Girl'), 'The Steamer' ('Lost In Hollywood'), 'Bluesing' ('Love's No Friend'), 'Mars' ('Eyes Of The World'), 'The Plod' ('Makin' Love'), 'New York' ('Danger Zone'), 'Once More With Feeling' ('All Night Long') and 'Sparks Don't Mean A Fire' ('No Time To Lose'). Along the way, 'Bluesing' was changed to 'Ain't A Lot Of Love In The Heart Of Me'. The band members put their parts down very quickly and Cozy even used to travel back to England when he wasn't required. Graham says: *"The backing tracks were more or less completed in France. The main body of the tracks were. Then guitar overdubs and vocals were done in the States, with solos from Ritchie, and I added all the vocals."*

Persuading the band to record 'Since You Been Gone' was easier said than done for Roger. Getting Cozy Powell to sit behind his drum kit for it took a lot of coercion. He never liked the song and thought it was far too 'poppy' for the band. If the stories are to be believed, Cozy only agreed to do a maximum of two takes as he explained later: *"I said you must be kidding, no way is this a Rainbow track. It wasn't that I didn't like the song, I didn't like it for Rainbow."*

The idea for the cover of 'Since You Been Gone' had come from manager

Rainbow • *One of the first photographs of the new line-up; l-r Blackmore, Glover, Airey, Powell and Bonnet.*

Bruce Payne because he knew it was 'hit single' material. The Russ Ballard penned track had originally featured on his 1976 album 'Winning'. As well as being picked up by Clout, American band Head East had also covered it in 1978, reaching No. 46 on the US Billboard chart. Bruce was sure that Rainbow could do the song justice in their own way. It would also serve as a vehicle to help get Rainbow on to the radio, which was critical in America. Ritchie was already open to commercial ideas, and even a big admirer of Abba's music. Bruce won the guitarist over by playing him Clout's version of the track, and was pleased when Ritchie too saw the potential. When the rest of the band were told that Ritchie had decided to do a song he'd heard via an all-girl band from South Africa, they were surprised to say the least. But Ritchie wanted chart success again and saw the song as the perfect vehicle to achieve this. Convincing the others wasn't easy but they all agreed to give it a go. They also listened to Russ Ballard's original version, which was even 'poppier' than Clout's. They set about changing the song to give it more of a rock feel and it was recorded very quickly. It was actually the final song recorded for the album, because the others hoped Ritchie and Bruce would forget about it! With the basic track complete, once Graham's lead vocals were added along with his backing vocals, handclaps and tambourines in a bid to try and create a radio friendly sound, the finished product was a record tailor-made for the American charts.

Graham seemed to be accepted and says he always got on very well with Ritchie. Of course they had their moments, like everyone does in band situations, but there was nothing too serious and a good bond developed between them. Ritchie pointed out to Graham that Foreigner's Lou Gramm was the main competition, probably not realising that Graham likely didn't have a clue who Lou Gramm was either!

Graham always had the feeling that Ritchie was basically a shy person, who liked to keep himself to himself, which he respected. Even when the band was recording in France, according to Graham, Ritchie would wander off with his girlfriend now and then as he didn't like hanging about with the band too much. As for Roger, he too was very private and quiet according to Graham and was having personal issues of his own at the time. As a result Graham never really got to know him that well. Plus, he was extremely busy writing the lyrics, recording the bass and producing, a huge job for anyone to undertake. But Graham quickly got to like and enjoy the company of Don and Cozy.

Once ensconced at Kingdom Sound studios in Syosset, Long Island, Roger started writing yet more lyrics. What Graham probably didn't realise was, this was also the first time Roger had been called upon to write an entire album. He'd contributed to Deep Purple, but nearly all the lyrics had been Ian Gillan's responsibility. Had he known this, Graham might have been persuaded to do get more involved. As it is he did contribute here and there but was never credited.

Ritchie was on hand to add the guitar overdubs and Graham recalls he would go into the studio and record three or four different solos in no time at all and then Roger would pull them together creating the perfect composite. Given the protracted nature of the recording, some of the songs were re-recorded and some demos exist with early versions of lyrics and also different melodies. There was no set pattern as to how Graham recorded his vocals, as he says: *"I did things different every time. If my voice was in good shape for lead, I'd do that. Or on tired days I'd start with back-up vocals. It varied."*

It was here that the songs were given their final titles. Graham was told exactly what to do with regards to the arrangements of where the verses and choruses came in, and he was happy with that. However, he did stamp his own authority on the melodies, as he says: *"All the words were done at Kingdom Sound studios. The melodies in the songs were the parts that were mine. Roger gave me a rough idea and then I would do my own thing on some of the songs. Sometimes though, Roger had an idea that we kept."* In the end, Ritchie picked out what he thought were the best lines and melodies and pieced everything together.

One thing that Graham found very strange was how the band had gone about writing their songs, because they did the arrangement before the song was written. Graham was always used to doing it the other way round. Also, he found that the music came first, followed by the vocals and then the guitar solo. When Graham had written songs during his solo career, he completed the song in one go, incorporating the words and melody. So all this too was very new to him.

If 'Since You Been Gone' was regarded as their likely hit, the album had another which ran a close second, 'All Night Long'. The origins of the song lay in The Rolling Stones song 'Out Of Time', which Ritchie played to Graham one evening on his acoustic guitar. He asked him if he could build a melody around it, showing him a basic chord progression. Back in June 1966 Chris Farlowe had covered 'Out Of Time' (which first appeared on The Rolling Stones album 'Aftermath') and had taken it to No. 1, with Mick Jagger producing and also singing backing vocals on it. It had clearly been at the back of Ritchie's mind for a few years. With a melody from Graham, Ritchie himself proposed an idea for the lyrics, which Roger then brought together and Graham also helped on the arrangement of 'All Night Long'. *"The tune was partially mine. I was a fool and didn't say 'wait a minute, I wrote that.'"* Don Airey was similarly left out as Graham adds: *"He wrote a lot of the arrangements and was never given credit for it."* Cozy Powell later agreed that Graham's contribution was significant. *"He wrote most of 'All Night Long', they aren't the most inspired lyrics but it was a hit!"* The basic idea was very simple, as most of the best rock songs are, based on making eye contact with a girl in the audience, and deciding she was worth meeting afterwards. It did come in for some criticism at the time, though Roger tried to explain it was tongue-in-cheek.

As for 'Lost In Hollywood', Ritchie simply asked Graham if he would sing the song as Little Richard would do it. Graham did his best on what would be for many Rainbow fans one of the album's highlights.

With the recording and mixing complete, the Graham Bonnet fronted line-up of Rainbow began to knock it up a gear. The album title had been around since before Graham had joined, 'Down To Earth' coming from a suggestion of Ritchie's. Having heard the rough mixes, Polydor, who had signed Rainbow back in 1975, decided on two songs for singles, 'Since You Been Gone' and 'All Night Long', though it would have been a surprise if they'd chosen otherwise. Promotional videos were filmed for both and a big promotion campaign for the album was begun. This being a top flight signing, Polydor went to town with a big press campaign using full-page adverts, some in full colour. Posters and displays for the stores were also a priority. While Graham had seen advertising for some of his solo albums, it was nothing like on this scale. To appeal to fans and collectors, and in line with the multi-format gimmicks of the era, the first 10,000 copies of the album were pressed in clear vinyl. On July 28th 'Down To Earth' was unleashed on the British public and the fans didn't disappoint, snapping up 120,000 copies during the first week. The album was simultaneously released worldwide.

The inner sleeve for the album featured individual photographs of the band members, which included two vintage ones of Graham from his Terry O'Neill shoot three years before. Eventually a proper publicity shoot for the new line-up was arranged.

The album entered the UK charts on August 18th at No. 11 and two weeks later on September 1st, it peaked at No. 6. 'Down To Earth' spent over two months in the charts, becoming Rainbow's biggest-selling album to date, and indeed it marked a peak for the band commercially, which must have given Ritchie confidence that he was making the right move. Rainbow had managed to successfully bring together elements of AOR with a more European rock core. The band was actually very well positioned to capitalise on a rock sound which would dominate American charts for the next decade or more.

While the band's direction and sound had been given a makeover, Rainbow made a real effort to bridge the gap between their old sound and the new. A couple of the songs on the new album followed in the tradition of a more epic Rainbow sound of old. 'Eyes Of The World' clearly took inspiration from 'Stargazer' and 'Gates Of Babylon'. Geoff Barton in Sounds likened 'Danger Zone' to 'Gates Of Babylon', the Eastern-sounding track from the previous album, while after listening to 'No Time To Lose', Steve Gett from the Melody Maker clearly felt the new singer was more than up to the task: *"Graham Bonnet's vocal cords are ideally suited to the music."* He also understood what the band were trying to achieve: *"Rainbow have made a concerted effort towards survival in the rock world."* Geoff Barton was also quite supportive: *"Don't despair AOR-haters, contrary to previous reports Rainbow haven't done a Foreigner and mustered an all-out assault on US drive-time radio."* He agreed with what Cozy had told him a few weeks earlier that this was the strongest line-up yet. He wasn't yet won over by Graham's vocals but did see possibilities: *"While he's got a hell of a lot more range and variation to his cords than Dio, to my ears on this album he tries a trifle too hard, his shouts 'n' screams resulting from a conscious effort on his part."* He had to admit admiration for 'Love's No Friend' though, saying: *"Heavy metal blues in the finest 'Mistreated' tradition. Bonnet's vocals send shivers up the spine."*

Record Mirror was far from complimentary but even they found room to praise the single; *"I have to admit they do it rather well and it's the obvious choice for a single, showing the lighter shade to the band."*

Polydor had planned the single carefully. Assuming initial album sales would go to Rainbow fans, they held back the single for a month. 'Since You Been Gone' b/w 'Bad Girl' was released on August 31st in the UK in a limited edition picture sleeve. A non-album track, 'Bad Girl' (often mis-spelt 'Bad Girls' in adverts and even on some labels) was of interest to fans, and helped initial sales as well. The A-side was issued in most countries, though some didn't get the original B-side.

The music papers had a field day, with Sounds commenting, *"the unchallenged heavy metal cult of the world decide to have a pop hit."* The New Musical Express was shocked, to say the least, describing it as *"sensitive heavy metal."* Melody Maker just called it *"a turgid and perfunctory dollop of noise"*, and bizarrely said the song seemed to be *"jinxed"*.

They had of course missed the point. What Rainbow had done was turn 'Since You Been Gone' into a powerful blast of commercial pop/rock, and this gave Ritchie Blackmore his first return to the UK single Top 20 since 'Fireball' back in 1971. The band was now rubbing shoulders with the likes of Michael Jackson, Blondie, The Police and Kate Bush amongst others. 'Since You Been Gone' went straight in at No. 33 on September 15th and Top Of The Pops showed the promotional video (incredibly Rainbow's first ever UK TV appearance) the week after. By October 6th, the single had peaked at No. 6 and it stayed in the charts for a total of ten weeks. Such was the demand Polydor had to press extra copies of the single in their French plant.

In Australia, Graham's solo success certainly came in to play and helped 'Down To Earth' reach No. 27. In New Zealand they added a sticker saying 'featuring New Lead Singer, Graham Bonnet'.

Perhaps the important question for the band though was how did it play in America. Ironically given how much they had geared the music to that market, their plans didn't go as expected. The single reached No. 57 (despite a huge amount of airplay), whilst the album peaked at No. 66. Still, that was a lot of albums sold, and to back this up Rainbow decided to go for a live debut of the new line-up there.

As regards preparing for the tour Graham recalls: *"We did rehearsals in Hampstead, Long Island. Cozy, Don, Roger and I all stayed in the Holiday Inn there. Rehearsals were in the afternoons, for two hours. Ritchie always told me 'just sing the verses a bit and the chorus; don't sing everything so as not to blow out your voice in rehearsals'."* When it came to choosing which songs to play, Graham was told he would have to learn some of Rainbow's older material for the live shows.

Not yet a major draw, in America they initially went out as support to Blue Oyster Cult during September and

Rainbow LP and tour

RAINBOW release their new album on August 3 on Polydor called 'Down To Earth'. It's the first since the group underwent substantial personnel changes earlier this year.

Only Ritchie Blackmore and Cozy Powell remain from the previous line-up. They're joined by Graham Bonney vocals, Don Airey keyboards and Roger Glover bass.

A limited edition of the album, which was produced by Roger Glover, is being pressed in clear vinyl.

October. In fact Rainbow had already swallowed their pride there the year before, playing shows as support to REO Speedwagon. It was an interesting decision to support BOC, and it did take some of the pressure off the new line-up of Rainbow. It also meant that they would be fully prepared for the European shows which were to follow.

Rainbow's opening show was at the Coliseum in New Haven, Connecticut on September 18th and Graham admits he was very nervous. It had been over two years since he had done a gig and that was an exceptionally low key affair; indeed since the days of the Marbles he'd only done just over a dozen or so in total. Added to which, he'd never done anything on the scale of fronting a band like Rainbow, or a tour of this magnitude. It was a huge task. And although he wasn't about to change, Graham was also worried how the heavy rock fans would react to his short hair and laid-back stage gear of white jackets and brightly patterned shirts. Inevitably there was a bit of shouting for Ronnie (it must be appreciated that particularly in America rock news travelled slowly, so some may not even have been aware of the changes), but he won them over and many in the crowd were singing along so had clearly got the new album. Given the shortened set-time, the group opened with 'Eyes Of The World', 'Love's No Friend', 'Somewhere Over The Rainbow', 'All Night Long', 'Lost In Hollywood' and 'Long Live Rock 'n' Roll'.

Away from the shows, Ritchie was known for elaborate practical jokes to stave off the boredom of touring but the rest of the band were quite protective of Graham since he was the newcomer, as he told Juke magazine: *"Cozy Powell supposedly said to Ritchie 'now don't you pull any of your practical jokes on Graham, otherwise he'll clear off!'"*

Melody Maker flew Steve Gett out for the show at the Memorial Auditorium in Utica on September 28th to file a report for fans in the UK. Chatting to the band members he found Roger Glover enthusiastic about touring again after so long off the road, and Graham Bonnet also keen to be playing live. *"British fans must be eager to learn how the current band compares with past line-ups. Those who are planning to catch them on the British dates won't be disappointed. But the most striking aspect of the new act is definitely the vocal performance of Graham Bonnet. He has an incredible range and leaves his predecessor, Ronnie James Dio, way behind. The Utica audience was knocked out with Rainbow."*

In the main Rainbow found fans to be equally enthusiastic for both groups on the bill, giving them a good reception. Steve Gett added his thoughts on their show in Philadelphia the following night in front of a crowd of 15,000: *"The cheering reaches a deafening crescendo until at last Rainbow hit the stage. Ritchie launches into the opening chords of 'Eyes Of The World'. Cozy Powell is hammering away fiercely behind his drum kit, with keyboard player Don Airey and bassist Roger Glover joining the attack. Within seconds new vocalist Graham Bonnet emerges in suave jacket and shades to let out the opening lines of the song. Then comes 'All Night Long' during which even Ritchie stands back to marvel at the singer's incredible vocal range. Graham reaches some tremendous notes and the effect he creates with the song is spine chilling. Rainbow closed their main set with 'Lost In Hollywood'. Inevitably they are summoned for an encore and return with an aggressive rendition of 'Long Live Rock 'n' Roll."*

Steve asked Ritchie about their new singer: *"It drove us all mad. I didn't know there are so many non-singers around. We had some nice guys turn up, but none of them really moved us – until Graham came along. I remember in about '68, when Deep Purple had just started, hearing Graham's voice on 'Only One Woman' and thinking at the time 'how on earth could we compete against that?' We had a good singer, but not of that calibre. Then in about '73, I started asking people what happened to that guy in the Marbles, but I was told he had lost his voice – no doubt by all these so-called singers!"*

In total, with just a couple of cancellations, Rainbow did around twenty-five shows on the tour which ran through until the end of October 1979. There was certainly a momentum built up during the tour, so much so that a long European tour during November and December was cancelled in favour of continuing the American tour, but this time as headliners.

The change around gave them two weeks off, and Rainbow were able to rehearse 'Man On the Silver Mountain', which was instantly included in the set, along with 'Since You Been Gone', although it took a few shows before it was introduced, and even then it was dropped occasionally. Both songs helped to expand the set, which now ran as follows - 'Eyes Of The World', 'Love's No Friend', 'Since You Been Gone' 'Somewhere Over The Rainbow', 'All Night Long', 'Lost In Hollywood' (including solos and 'Beethoven's Ninth'), 'Man On The Silver Mountain' (with 'Lazy' often used as the introduction), 'Blues', and 'Long Live Rock 'n' Roll'. 'Kill The King' was included towards the end of the tour as an instrumental.

The first six shows of the new tour were all in California, the opening night being at the Civic Auditorium in Santa Cruz on November 6th. Sylvie Simmons, Sound's magazine's West Coast correspondent, caught the band's appearance at Warners Theater in Fresno on November 13th and was impressed. *"Graham Bonnet, looking like Rob Halford in a Moss Bros ad, hits notes that must have surprised even perfectionist Ritchie. [He] was definitely quite a find, his voice and appearance adding a new dimension to Rainbow."*

The band worked their way across America to the East Coast, a total run of around 25 shows which concluded at The Palace Theater in Albany on December 9th. But while Graham was handling it all fairly well, Cozy Powell was becoming increasingly fed up with the new

Rainbow • *American tour in 1979.*

material. *"Ritchie and I fell out over a number of points, and I thought it best to leave,"* was how he summed it up later. He also added that he had *"not joined Rainbow to be in a pop band"*.

Cozy told the management and his fellow band mates of his decision. It was agreed that he would stay with the band until the end of the Japanese tour in May 1980, though his leaving wasn't announced in the press for some months. It would give them enough time to look for a replacement.

Ritchie generally travelled to the gigs apart from the band and crew, sometimes on a plane with the rest of the band on the tour bus. *"Ritchie travels separately – basically because he doesn't really enjoy going on school outings!"* explained Roger. Graham would sometimes get a bit fed up of the long trips between shows as Don Airey recalls: *"He didn't like touring overmuch, always saying he needed a holiday. I'd point out to him that we were in great hotels, the sun was often shinning and he should get out more."* At the venues each member would have their own personal dressing room and Ritchie used to invite Graham in for a chat and a drink quite regularly before a gig, but none of the other members.

Graham got his holiday over Christmas and after a well deserved break Rainbow were soon back on the road as they started the long awaited Scandinavia and European tour on January 17th 1980 in Gothenburg at the Scandinavium, with a rehearsal the day before. Needless to say Rainbow retained their headline status in what had always been their biggest market. 'Catch The Rainbow', as well as 'Will You Love Me Tomorrow?' had now been added to their set list, thanks in part to Don: *"It was Graham, Roger and my warm-up number in the dressing room shower with most of the crew joining in!"* It is also known that Ritchie was fond of Graham's version of the song. The guitarist also included 'Beethoven's Ninth' during the Stockholm gig and it was resurrected later during the tour, while 'Makin' Love' made a very rare appearance for the Grenoble show. The bands set list was now: 'Eyes Of The World', 'Love's No Friend', 'Since You Been Gone', 'Somewhere Over The Rainbow', 'All Night Long', 'Catch The Rainbow', 'Lost In Hollywood' (including solos and 'Beethoven's Ninth'), 'Man On The Silver Mountain' (again with 'Lazy' often used as part of the introduction), 'Blues', 'Will You Love Me Tomorrow?' and 'Long Live Rock 'n' Roll' (including 'Kill The King').

While in Denmark, the band visited Sweet Silence studios in Copenhagen on January 19th and recorded an instrumental called 'Weiss Heim', which would become the B-side to 'All Night Long'. Released on February 1st worldwide, the A-side had been beefed up with a remix, with Cozy's drum sound certainly benefiting. Limited edition picture sleeves were again the order of the day and these varied depending on which country you lived in. With the accompanying video (which was tweaked with live footage in some versions) it would have been a huge surprise if it hadn't been another massive hit. The moment the band comes in after Ritchie's opening guitar riff it is hard not to be sucked in to the rock solid groove. The record entered the UK charts on February 16th at No. 37 and four weeks later it was in the No. 5 position, staying in the charts for nine weeks in total. In America though (where 'Danger Zone' was on the B-side) the single stopped just short of the Top 100, an incredible flop and one which must surely reflect more on the state of the promotion there than the disc itself.

The tour itself was intense, running through into early March, but apart from a severe dose of flu which caused Roger Glover to collapse after the show at the Sporthalle in Cologne (and the following night's cancellation while he recovered), there were no other major incidents. Apart, that is, from the mysterious fire which set light to a suitcase full of Graham's stage shirts on one dark night...

Rainbow's new line-up finally made their UK debut on February 19th at Newcastle City Hall opening a 14 date tour (a fifteenth show at Bristol was cancelled). Fans were keen to see the band again, as this was the first time they had played in the UK since November 1977. The opening two gigs at Newcastle sold out in four hours - without the internet.

across the back of his head." Graham could feel the vibe. "I walked on. Ritchie took one look at me and stormed off stage. He played the whole night behind the stack!" Graham may have been exaggerating about the last bit when he spoke to Chris Collingwood of Metal CD, but repercussions were to follow as Graham recalls: "He called a meeting the next day with the whole band and told me it was an insult to him that I'd had my hair cut!" Colin Hart remembers getting lectured by Blackmore for allowing it to happen and Cozy was unable to contain himself with laughter. The subject of hair (the thinning thereof) had become a bit of a sore point with the guitarist around this period, so maybe he felt Graham was poking fun somehow. Needless to say the rest of the group couldn't care less; it was Graham's voice that was the most important thing.

The opening two nights at Newcastle brought reporters up from London and the overall reaction was very positive. As the shows were sold out there were kids outside hoping to find a way in and Graham dedicated a song to them and pointed out the exit signs to the journalists who were taking up space. Hugh Fielder of Sounds was one: "*There's vocalist Graham Bonnet, looking positively suave in heavy metal terms with slicked back hair, dark glasses and a white suit. He's left most of the stock HM vocalist clichés for the so-called 'New Wave heavy metal bands' (ho ho). Instead he goes for the straightforward approach and relies on his powerful but pitch-perfect voice to make its impact. And despite the fact that his throat has 'turned yellow', as he admitted shortly before the gig, the impact is very impressive. If Rainbow are to expand their following – which even Ritchie would probably admit is the name of the game – then they should start capitalising on Bonnet's arrival because he transforms the emphasis from the past to the future.*"

Record Mirror's Malcolm Dome also enjoyed the "*almost-bluesy 'Love's No Friend Of Mine' [sic], with Graham Bonnet's intensely emotional vocals sounding more effective live than on the album cut.*" There is perhaps little doubt that the album would have really benefited from being recorded after a few months of touring, rather than having been done 'cold'. As for people in the audience, Graham won over many of them, and comments that he had a lot more stage presence must have not only pleased him but also proved that his 'look' was absolutely no issue for most people.

Rainbow arrived in London on February 29th for the first of two big back to back shows at the Wembley Arena. As fans had shelled out £4.50 for tickets the last they'd expected to see was a riot.

Rainbow-fan Philip Madden was at the show: "*After a three-year gap there was a great sense of expectation. Rainbow was riding high in the singles chart. There was also excitement at the prospect of Roger Glover and Ritchie Blackmore playing together on stage for the first time since the break-up of Deep Purple. I loved Bonnet's voice. It really suited the new 'commercial' vibe of the band and he had such a great range to his voice and it sounded different on all the tracks. I really liked his 'James Dean' image which was totally different to the vocalists in other heavy rock bands. When Rainbow hit the stage with 'Eyes Of The World' I remember Graham being dressed in red trousers and a smart cream jacket with shades looking really cool. I really enjoyed the concert and was amazed at how powerful and strong Bonnet's voice was. He transformed the image of the band and gave it style.*"

But trouble was brewing. Graham's hair style had been the subject of conversation for a while now, but it didn't bother him. He just took it in his stride and got it cut as and when. Ritchie however was determined it would be grown longer. Ritchie later went into elaborate detail about how, on the day of the band's UK debut in Newcastle, with everyone thinking Graham was in his dressing room, and with road manager Colin Hart outside to keep an eye on him, Graham sneaked out of the window and went off to the barbers. Graham's recollection is far less melodramatic, he says he was out for a walk and simply decided to get a trim.

Graham agrees Ritchie was the one seemingly obsessed with his hair, but suggests much of the story was the guitarist's fantasy, although he does agree he gave Ritchie the shock of his life, because he didn't find out until he saw Graham stride onto the stage. "*We went on and I was looking at the back of his head with this military-style cut. I was that close to taking my guitar off and just going 'whack'*

But while most of the fans were likewise appreciative of the show, Blackmore was in a miserable mood and clipped his own playing to bring the set in at around 70 minutes, then refused to come out for an encore. He later 'explained' that he had felt that the London audience was 'not appreciative enough'. Philip accepted that the show was over. *"When the house lights came on we made a departure. I remember as we left there were hordes of fans staying put and booing. It was not until the following day that I discovered that there had been a riot, arrests and damage caused. Disgruntled fans refused to leave and ended up ripping out seats and throwing them on to the stage."*

The cost of damage at the Wembley Arena came to a total of around £10,000, with 500 seats and other fittings broken and even fire extinguishers had been thrown at the stage. Police arrested ten fans, three of who were under seventeen. Sounds' correspondents maintained that the crowd reaction on Friday night was everything the band could have hoped for and thought Blackmore was just being a pain. He also took it out on support band Samson, who later turned up for the show in Leicester and were told they were no longer required. Their manager said: *"We were given no reason for this. Graham Bonnet had even given us a round of applause during our Wembley set on Friday."* It seems as if Ritchie had found out they'd been supporting Gillan recently and this sealed their fate.

'All Night Long' though was riding high in the UK charts during the tour and the UK leg ended on March 8th at the Rainbow Theatre in London, a much more intimate venue than Wembley. Graham's parents were able to attend some of the gigs and Ritchie got to know Graham's Dad, Lou, very well. Graham recalls: *"Ritchie was very friendly towards my family; he liked chatting to my Dad."*

A decision had been made to drop 'Will You Love Me Tomorrow?' for the tour of the UK even though it had been played previously in Scandinavia and Europe. The set list for the tour was 'Eyes Of The World', 'Love's No Friend', 'Since You Been Gone', 'Over The Rainbow', 'Man On The Silver Mountain', 'Catch The Rainbow', 'Lost In Hollywood' (including solos and 'Beethoven's Ninth'), 'All Night Long', 'Blues' and 'Long Live Rock 'n' Roll' (including 'Kill The King' at most shows).

Overall the tour seemed to go well, though as Rainbow had been massively popular in the UK from day one, it was perhaps more difficult for fans of four years' standing to come to terms with the change of singer. Ronnie had after all been a part of Rainbow longer than Ian Gillan had fronted Deep Purple. But on the whole Graham appeared to be handling it all very well. Touts even turned up with boxes full of his old solo album to try to offload some outside some shows. Ritchie however was still carping and went off to catch a Gillan show at the Rainbow theatre, and make another attempt to get the singer to join, but was again unsuccessful.

With a two-month break before the six-date Japanese section of the world tour, Graham and his girlfriend Jo took the opportunity to up sticks and move to New York, something they had been thinking about for over a year. Graham explains their decision: *"We moved there because Ritchie lived there and so we could get out of England too. I had wanted to move way before Rainbow and this was my opportunity. Jo couldn't stand it there either, the rubbish wages and the lousy weather. We had a fully furnished house. A musician called Harry Frank was going to Florida and we rented it for a while before moving to Los Angeles. It was cold in New York though and it is a very rush-around kind of place."*

On arrival in Japan, rumours instantly started to spread that Cozy Powell was leaving the band, probably something to do with him signing his autograph 'Cozy Powell ex-Rainbow'! It would only be a matter of time before the story was out, though Cozy reasoned that they kept it quiet as they weren't sure he really was going to quit.

Graham too was causing the Japanese to ask a few questions, because the

Rainbow • *UK tour 1979.*

girls there liked their rock singers to look the part. He stuck to his guns, even when his stage clothes mysteriously disappeared mid-tour, and refused to change his image. One magazine even organised a Graham Bonnet lookalike competition. Despite a bit of reaction against the album due to what some saw as a lack of guitar, the tour had sold well enough, with three nights at Tokyo's famous Budokan Hall starting on May 8th, followed by three consecutive nights at Osaka's Festival Hall. A final fourth show which would have seen them return to Tokyo was dropped.

During the tour it was reported that 'Will You Love Me Tomorrow?', which had been brought back in to the set from the second Tokyo show was going to be their next single. According to Japanese Graham Bonnet fan Masaya Uchimura: *"It seems the band cut a version of the song before one of the shows in Tokyo. Roger and Graham spoke to a Japanese*

reporter from 'Viva Rock' and said that three shows in Japan had been recorded, and 'Will You Love Me Tomorrow?' was done during their sound-check." The rough demo and the live recordings were for a follow-up to the band's live album 'On-Stage' later that year. These recordings, though, never progressed any further and still remain locked in a vault.

The Japanese shows were a huge success and Graham had won over many fans, so much so that a fanzine titled, 'Only One Singer', was started. Cozy Powell also got to plug his new solo album 'Over The Top' with a drum seminar.

Rainbow now had another three month break and returned to America. Ritchie and others tried to talk Cozy out of leaving but his mind was made up. They had to start looking seriously for a new drummer. Graham can't remember being at any auditions, so it is likely the other three did them without him. A decision was made that ex-Samantha skin beater Bobby Rondinelli (who was also on the short-list for Kiss at the time) was the right choice for the band.

Rainbow reconvened towards the end of July to concentrate on rehearsing a set for the Monsters Of Rock festival at Castle Donington on August 16th. Ritchie decided that they would bring 'Stargazer' back into the set, one of the bands' most revered tracks. To make the trip worthwhile, three warm-up dates in Scandinavia were also booked, starting in Aarhus, Denmark on August 8th, then Malmö in Sweden and back to Denmark to play Aalborg. ('Will You Love Me Tomorrow?' was dropped for the Scandinavian shows but brought back for Castle Donington). These dates were largely in response to the successful shows there earlier in the year and showed the band had lost none of their popularity. Ritchie promised some set surprises for the rain-soaked open-air Malmö show; what the audience didn't really expect was to see all the group disappear during Don Airey's solo, and not return due to the bad weather.

By now everyone knew Cozy was doing his last shows with Rainbow (the rumours were confirmed officially a week ahead of the festival) and the atmosphere within the band changed. It affected Graham who had actually been thinking about leaving Rainbow himself for quite a while. The nearer the date of the final show got, the more the idea of him also leaving seemed the right thing to do. For the show at Castle Donington, the band was booked into a hotel in Leicester, arriving on Thursday the 14th. Being a large festival, the next day was devoted to stage and sound-checks, and to make sure all the planned effects were working. There was a huge buzz about what the band might have in store and Graham, interviewed for ATV, said he was thinking about riding a moped from the back of the stage to the front. This really would have been so typically Graham. It's a shame it didn't happen. One can only imagine Ritchie's reaction…

Estimates still range from the expected 35,000 to over 70,000 people attending what turned out to be the inaugural Monsters Of Rock festival, which went so well that it became a regular fixture on the British rock calendar, and which on the day also featured Judas Priest, Scorpions, April Wine, Saxon, Riot and Touch.

The festival was largely the brainchild of Paul Loasby, who worked for Harvey Goldsmith, one of the main UK music promoters. They had handled all Rainbow's UK tours to date. Loasby was about to branch out on his own, and wanted to develop his idea of a day long rock and metal event. He spoke to Rainbow's manager Bruce Payne and suggested Rainbow could headline. He then had a meeting with Maurice Jones, who owned Midland Concert Promotions and was also a partner in the company that ran the Donington Park Race Circuit. Maurice in turn spoke to his co-partner Tom Wheatcroft and eventually they agreed to back the idea. They got it all together in just three and a half months.

Tom Wheatcroft's daughter Mandy was on hand to watch, and recalls that during the testing for Cozy's spectacularly over-the-top pyrotechnics, he blew the PA system apart causing £20,000 of damage. Cozy was apparently zipping around the place getting up to mischief, which Mandy seemed to get the blame for: *"Maurice caught up with me, and everywhere something had gone wrong, I seemed to be there! So I got a massive lecture and a bollocking, but Cozy took the blame and each time he'd get Graham to tell Maurice that I had been with him all the time. Poor Graham didn't have a clue what mischief we had been up to! Cozy just said, 'Mandy was with you at that time, wasn't she, Graham?' And a puzzled Graham just looked totally confused and said, 'err…..yeah!' Both Cozy and Graham made such a big impression which has never left me."*

Cozy's feelings were mixed as it was his last show. *"I was determined to go out with a bang. There was a lot of tension in the air when we took to the stage and it was every man for himself."*

Rainbow's entire set was recorded for a projected double live album and a limited number of white label copies were even pressed up. The whole gig also was filmed by Greenback films and Graham remembers going to a screening of this. The film was offered to the BBC who decided to take a shortened version, and they aired around 30 minutes, greatly edited and with the running order totally out of sequence. In the end Polydor issued a single album featuring tracks by all the bands at the show (aside from Judas Priest), with Rainbow contributing 'Stargazer' and 'All Night Long'.

Philip Madden was at Donington and says: *"As for Graham it appeared that he was still integral to the bands image and commercial success, reinforced in my opinion by witnessing his spectacular vocal performance during 'Will You Love Me Tomorrow?'. The Donington show, on that beautiful sunny day, would turn out to be a fitting climax for that short-lived line-up fronted by Bonnet."*

New drummer Bobby Rondinelli had been invited over to watch Rainbow in action at the show and Ozzy Osbourne was also there. He spoke to Don Airey afterwards and told him that it was the greatest performance he had seen by a rock singer.

Graham's entire family were also in the audience, and afterwards it was time to say goodbye to Cozy Powell back at the hotel. Graham and just about everyone else stayed up until about 6:00am chatting, but he found it very hard to say goodbye to Cozy, because he and Don Airey had become such great friends with the drummer. They had even travelled to gigs together with Cozy. Graham knew

it had been a very special day. In the programme which marked the thirtieth anniversary of the event (which is today known as Download) Graham said it was a career high and a great experience.

For the moment Graham kept his future plans to himself and no sooner had he returned to Los Angeles after the gig, than he was back on a plane and heading for Sweet Silence studios in Copenhagen where rehearsals and the recording of the next Rainbow album were due to take place.

Ritchie brought quite a few song ideas to the table and there was another Russ Ballard song in the offing, 'I Surrender'. Given his uncertainty about staying with Rainbow, Graham admits he had really struggled to come up with any ideas at all and what he did offer was far from earth-shattering. As a result the rest of the band didn't take any of it too seriously. *"Don and I played something [to Ritchie] one day. He said, 'no I don't like that.' It was very unproductive."*

Curiously for a group which had gelled well on stage, as far as the others were concerned, they never had the feeling that Graham was totally committed to the band, or felt 100% comfortable. As a result, even during the 'Down To Earth' tour they kept their ears open for possible singers should Graham decide to leave, and so one day when Don and Cozy were travelling through New Jersey, they made a mental note of a band called Fandango when they heard them on the radio. Their singer, Joe Linquito, had made their ears prick up. They later went to check the band out live.

As the recording sessions continued, along with 'I Surrender' and 'Magic' (which was written by Brian Moran), various original compositions and riffs were being bounced around and developed in the studio, mainly by Ritchie, Roger and Don. It was also down to Roger to come up with lyrics for the songs once again. Since joining Rainbow, Ritchie seems to have formed the impression that Graham wasn't too bothered about music in general, lacked motivation, and didn't appear to have many interests outside the band either, apart from walking his dog. Graham did backing vocal work on a version of 'I Surrender' (although Don Airey thought Graham had done a lead vocal as well) and also provided the melody for what became 'Spotlight Kid'. He recorded a very early version of 'No Release' with different lyrics too.

Ritchie continued to play his jokes on various people as Graham told Record Mirror: *"One of his favourite tricks was setting up new roadies with transvestites; some of them look so much like women that the only way you can find out for sure is by feeling the bulge in their knickers. Ritchie introduced a really nice looking transvestite to a new roadie. The two of them eventually went off together to a hotel room and the roadie came down later and said: 'Hey, I really enjoyed that. I've never tried anything like that before and I want to do it again.'"*

As far as real work went though the sessions ground on. Colin Hart was witness to the mood. *"The atmosphere was heavy as if everyone had no energy or spark. In my opinion it was because Cozy was gone and it felt like the band was incomplete."* As time went on, Graham realised he wasn't happy with the situation, and never really settled to the idea of having to start all over again with new drummer Bobby Rondinelli. He also felt there was a lack of interest in general. He describes his time there as: *"Quite a few weeks of not very productive days, which were very depressing and boring."* Things eventually came to a point where the recordings couldn't progress and Graham returned to Los Angeles during early September. Shortly afterwards, Graham was voted the tenth best male singer in the Sounds Top Male Singers Poll. While Graham was back in America, Ritchie discussed the situation. It was pretty obvious that Graham wasn't interested and they needed to sort the situation out. As usual it was down to their hard-nosed manager to make the call. Bruce Payne rang, asked him to return to the band, and as a way of getting the situation going, suggested Graham could just do the material he felt comfortable with, and the band would bring in another singer to do the songs he didn't like. If this was a genuine offer it seems a very strange one and as far as Graham was concerned it was clearly a non-starter. It may well have been designed to force Graham's hand, and so he quit. David Oddie, Graham's manager, was far from impressed. When reality did kick in for Graham and he realised he was now out of one of the biggest rock bands in the world he said: *"It was a time of panic!"*

Talking to Sounds magazine in early 1981, Graham said of his departure from Rainbow: *"It had to come about that I leave, I couldn't contribute anything to the band anymore. There were lots of ideas flying around from Ritchie, but nothing I could add to. My mind was completely empty about what to do with Rainbow. After Cozy left it went downhill for me in a lot of ways; we were losing roadies and then missing having a happy chap like Cozy around, the atmosphere of the whole band went downhill. Ultimately why I left was because there was nothing there, nothing that interested me. And that's why Cozy left. From what we rehearsed of the 'Difficult To Cure' album, the only song that I thought was half decent was 'I Surrender', which wasn't even written by Rainbow. It is a great song, although I don't think it is particularly well done. I thought the Russ Ballard original had a lot more bollocks than the Rainbow version. It sounds very thin to me, there's no guts. I think I could have done it better."*

Apart from finding it hard to get on with bassist Roger Glover, there seemed to be a lot of posing going on, which didn't impress Graham. He also felt the band was becoming very mechanical and the atmosphere within the set-up became quite vindictive at times. Looking back today though, Graham wishes he had stayed around for at least one more Rainbow album. Talking to Steve Gett of Melody Maker just after leaving the band he said: *"Being in that band meant a hell of a lot to me."*

There are always two sides to everything but being in a band, it is generally accepted that the singer comes up with the lyrics. Graham had written before and composed full songs but not for a rock band. At the end of the day Graham had come from a different world when he joined Rainbow. In his world he'd mostly worked on covers or songs written by other people and then did the album with a producer. Sometimes Graham never even saw the session musicians who had done the backing tracks. In Rainbow though, he was working with a full time band who basically expected him to live, breath, eat and sleep the music 24/7 rather than as a 9 to 5 job.

Graham had in fact already begun to feel he'd like to try another solo album. *"I had it on my mind that maybe I could do something by myself at this point, that was it. I left. I wasn't fired, I left."*

As for Rainbow, Don Airey remembered that road trip in New Jersey and Joe (Linquito) Lynn Turner quickly joined the band. Some stories suggest that they wiped Graham's vocals as they went through the material at Sweet Silence studio. Joe says not: *"I never heard Graham's vocals. The band was respectful of that. I was given a few songs to sing my lyrics and melodies and that's all, no Graham vocal tracks."*

The news media often loves to assess politicians after their first one hundred days in office. Graham had managed in the region of one hundred gigs fronting Rainbow.

Bonnet the latest to quit Rainbow

RAINBOW vocalist Graham Bonnet has left the band, according to American sources. The reasons for his departure aren't clear and attempts to contact his manager in London this week were unsuccessful, but he is believed to have recorded songs for a solo album which will be released next year.

Work and play • *photographs from Colin Hart's collection, taken by him on tour with Rainbow; signing autographs in Japan, shopping with Cozy, enjoying a shandy with Colin and in Copenhagen with Cozy and Don. All courtesy Colin Hart.*

CHAPTER 5
Skyfire (1980 – 1981)

Featuring: Graham's solo career

Graham rocks the charts

By the time fans were reading in the press from late November 1980 onwards that Graham had left Rainbow, he had already recorded a new solo single. A decision had been made with his manager, David Oddie, to resurrect his solo career and he presented Graham with a batch of demos to listen to, which he did on his travels. He says: *"A lot of writers just came along who were friends of his or someone in the offices at Quarry Productions. We had demos all the time. Bryan Adams was one writer I remember, before he became well-known doing his own thing. I listened to them in the Waldorf Hotel in New York on my way to Miami and then Australia. It was one way of breaking up that terrible long journey!"*

One song in particular really stood out from the others. 'Night Games' had been written by Ed Hamilton, whom David Oddie had signed to Quarry Productions as a song-writer a little earlier. *"Ed was a friend of a friend"*, Graham recalls. *"He is just one of those guys who sends singers demos."* The version on the demo was more or less how it ended up being recorded, apart from the last line of the chorus, which was in French: *"The 'Night Games' demo had everything on there. I just changed a bit of the French he put in it, French for 'games of the night'. I thought it sounded a bit phoney."*

Given his increased profile, Graham was quickly signed by Phonogram. Even so, before committing to an album, they would only agree to fund a one-off single. David Oddie and Graham originally wanted Pip Williams to produce the 'Night Games' session, since he had worked with Graham previously, but on this occasion Pip was tied up so David approached John Eden since he had engineered the earlier sessions. John brought on board a very competent set of musicians, which included the Whitesnake duo of guitarist Micky Moody and bassist Neil Murray. Cozy Powell, who had just joined MSG, and keyboard player Andy Bown joined the crew. The session included the Bob Young and Micky Moody penned song 'Out On The Water', owned by Quarry Publishing.

Graham flew in from Australia and stayed at his manager's place throughout the 'Night Games' session. John Eden recalls the set-up: *"It was all part of the Quarry empire at the time really, with Graham and Status Quo both being managed by them. That is just how it ended up."*

The session began towards the end of September, as John Eden recalls: *"'Night Games' and 'Out On The Water' we did at Red Bus studios, off Edgware Road. It was the same console in there (well, one generation later) as was in Marquee studios and I liked it. Plus, it was a good live room. On 'Night Games' we did all the tracking there. I had Cozy set up right on the very far back wall in a live area that had marble floor and glass walls, so I was able to put some good ambient mics up there."*

Micky Moody also recalls the session: *"Most of my stuff was recorded at Red Bus. I also did some overdubs there including the guitar solo on 'Night Games'."* Bassist Neil Murray spoke to Rob McKenzie of Fireworks about the session. *"I just did one day in the studio on September 26th 1980 with Graham, Cozy Powell, Micky Moody and Andy Bown. I played on 'Night Games' and 'Out On The Water', but the bass sound I was using with Whitesnake at that time wasn't right for what they were after, so another bassist replaced what I played on 'Night Games'. In my diary it says I didn't play very well, so I'm not surprised! I was used to making up my own, rather busy, moving bass lines at that time, with a sound that worked for that style, but for Graham's songs a more standard bass sound and style were needed. It's still a blow to the ego when you get replaced, particularly on a hit single!"*

The replacement was Gary Twigg. John Eden says: *"We did end up replacing Neil's part when we did overdubs down at Francis Rossi's place. I'd worked with Gary before in 1976 and he came in to replace the bass on 'Night Games'."* Graham saw the wisdom of the move: *"I saw Gary with Barbara Dickson when she did the 'John, Paul, George, Ringo & Bert' musical in a West End theatre. He was very good and because she became well-known later, he was sort of a name as well."*

Having completed the recording, the mix was done at Marquee studios. As soon as the A&R people at Phonogram heard 'Night Games' they immediately knew they had a hit single on their hands. A promotional video was quickly shot at London's Rainbow theatre. Graham performed with Cozy Powell, Micky Moody, Gary Twigg and Jon Lord (even though Jon had not appeared on the single sessions). Additional film of Graham walking around the streets late at night was then cut in: *"It was filmed all around London, the Covent Garden area and the theatre district. It was a very funny day!"* To add to the storyline (such as it was), as Graham is walking around he stops outside the Peppermint Club and notices an advertising poster for himself and his backing band, The Hooligans, a name which Cozy Powell came up with. Shortly after filming Graham returned to Los Angeles.

Meanwhile, Polydor Records, after passing on the release of a Rainbow live double album, issued their compilation album from the Castle Donington festival, and 'Monsters Of Rock' was released on October 10th in the UK.

Word was spreading fast in the music business that Graham had now left Rainbow and Black Sabbath's management didn't waste any time contacting him. They had parted with Ozzy Osbourne the previous year and were still looking for a replacement. Grateful for the interest, nevertheless Graham asked his manager to tell them he wasn't interested. Looking back on the situation now he says: *"I didn't think I would fit that type of thing. I didn't think they were the greatest band in the world anyway. Then Ronnie comes along and does two albums with them that are very successful and turned the band around. I was probably stupid not to."*

Phonogram had decided to get Christmas out of the way and push the debut single early in the New Year, and assigned it to their heavy rock label Vertigo.

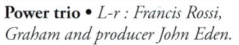
Power trio • *L-r: Francis Rossi, Graham and producer John Eden.*

During February 1981, adverts hit the press suggesting 'You don't know what you're missing till you've played Night Games'. 'Night Games' b/w 'Out On The Water' was released on February 27th in the UK in a colourful picture sleeve, which featured photographs of Graham on the front cover from his Rainbow days to help it on its way. The song was in fact very much in the vein of the two Rainbow hits Graham had fronted and further suggests that the former were silly not to try and hang on to him longer.

Unusually however there was no album in the wings, as John Eden explains: *"Obviously like all record companies they're wanting to test the ground. It was always 'you're going to do a single first and we'll see what happens, and hopefully we'll end up doing an album'. The single was delivered and pressed and went out to radio. It just happened so fast. It wasn't a song that had to be worked for weeks and weeks and weeks to radio. It was very instant in that sense."* Talking to Robin Smith of Record Mirror about the single, Graham said: *"The single sounds quite like Rainbow. But obviously I have to do something which the kids can identify with. I'd be a fool to make a complete change from the Rainbow style."*

With the song getting a tremendous amount of airplay, it entered the UK charts at No. 69 on March 21st. Two weeks later it was No. 26 and then another two weeks after that it reached its highest position, No. 6, on April 18th. It stayed in the Top Ten for two more weeks, dropping slowly to No. 57 on May 30th, before bowing out after spending a very respectable eleven weeks in the UK charts.

As well as showing the promotional video, once he had returned to the UK, the BBC offered Graham (along with his Hooligans) a live slot on Top Of The Pops on March 26th. Only Cozy and Gary from the session could make it so the band was completed with London based American guitarist Issac Guillory and keyboard player Ian Lynn.

'Night Games' was also released in Australasia, Japan, parts of South America and throughout Europe, mostly in the same picture sleeve as in the UK. The Japanese (who changed the cover photo into a striking black, white and red image) also issued a cut with a slightly longer ending. With Japanese imports beginning to become very collectable amongst fans worldwide, copies were sold in specialist UK shops such as Flyover Records in London. In Japan, the title was slightly altered to *"'Kodoku no Night Games' which literally means 'solitary night games'"* according to Masaya Uchimura. The Portuguese, however, used a photo from Graham's 1976 photo shoot with Terry O'Neill on their release.

The moment 'Night Games' started knocking on the door of the UK singles charts, Phonogram immediately wanted a follow-up single and also agreed to fund an album. Cozy Powell and Micky Moody were quick to make themselves available. Jon Lord was also invited but couldn't commit to playing on the entire album, but did join the session that included 'Bad Days Are Gone' and 'Don't Stand In The Open'. John Eden recalls: *"I would have loved it if Jon had stayed and we could have got him. We asked, but he just couldn't do it."* Micky Moody confirms Jon's involvement (which has been the subject of much speculation over the years) on just the one session: *"I'm pretty sure that's all he did. It was more like a cameo – a good name to get on the album sleeve. Although he was in the video for 'Night Games', he didn't play on it."*

With an album to do, Graham started to listen to more songs, as well as suggesting a few to cover. John Eden says: *"What was needed was to sell an album on the basis of this. What should have happened in the true sense was that we had an album first and all ready to go, and we were selling the album at the same time as we were selling the single. However, that wasn't the case this time, so we then had to find the material and there were some songs around, but we didn't have all the songs ready to do a complete album. We started to do things in batches when we rearranged and found the songs."*

Thanks to the huge success of 'Night Games' the UK press were eager to interview Graham and find out what the future held as well as why he had left Rainbow. He explained to Sounds in April: *"Basically I left because I was very bored with the music, and because of inner politics. Girlfriends coming in and saying what the band should be doing, saying 'isn't Graham singing that well' or 'isn't Graham singing that badly'. They were taking it a bit too seriously. They were being so deep and the music itself wasn't that deep. There was a lot of posing going on within the band and if I did my Butlin's Holiday Camp routine one night I'd get told off for doing it; if I went out there and enjoyed myself with the audience I'd get a bollocking - 'it's not heavy metal, man'. Okay sometimes I overdid it a bit but that was nerves, because I had this feeling of insecurity all the time. I have to admit that it did me a lot of good."*

"Today though I feel like a new man, I've blown the cobwebs out of my system.

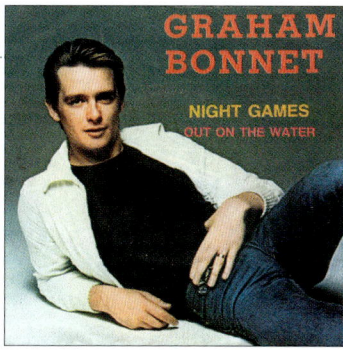

Graham is a Night Games winner!

By NINA MYSKOW
The pop writer ALL the stars talk to

JUST four years ago, Graham Bonnet was a living skeleton. The British rock singer whose single, Night Games (Vertigo), has shot up to No. 6 in our charts, was down to 7st 12lb.

His marriage was in ruins, his career non-existent and his life in danger. Bonnet, 35, told me from his home in Los Angeles : " The doctors told me that if I didn't start responding to treatment and putting on weight, I had only a few months to live.

GRAHAM BONNET . . . Left Rainbow and found gold

I'm breathing again", he told Robin Smith of Record Mirror. Speaking to Steve Gett of Melody Maker, Graham added: *"The material I'm working on at the moment is very much in the same vein as the songs I sang in Rainbow like 'Since You Been Gone' and 'All Night Long'. Basically it's retaining the commercial element - I believe I've got to stick to this format. I can hardly wander into other areas and try something completely different because it simply wouldn't work."* As regards what he thought of the UK, he said: *"I do find it rather boring here. I like the buzz in the States and there's much more music to chose from. In England I can't see that much going on except for stupid records like 'Shaddup You Face'."* To get a break from all the press, April also saw Graham visit his parents in Skegness.

While the album preparation was going on, Graham was asked to record the vocals for a Levi jeans advert that Bob Young and Micky Moody had written, which was simply called 'Levi's'. *"It was just a three-hour session or so"*, Graham remembers. With the advert being screened a lot during late March and April, it got people talking and asking the question if it was Graham singing. With quite a lot of interest Bob and Micky decided to cut a single. Graham though turned down the offer to sing on it, saying later that he thought it *"a bit daft!"* so it was left to The Young & Moody Band (Bob and Micky, with Cozy Powell) to do the honours, with Ed Hamilton providing the vocals.

Three more songs had been chosen for Graham's album and Phonogram were itching for a follow-up single. Recording once again took place at Red Bus studios. First up was 'I'm A Lover', which Cozy Powell really liked. The song was written by David Kerr-Clemenson and Andy Locke (who had both played in a band called Merlin Q, and then went on to join Edison Lighthouse). The other two songs were the Paul Bliss penned 'That's The Way That It Is' and 'Liar', which was written by Russ Ballard and had been chosen as the next single. By now the album even had a working title, 'Dangerous Line-Up'.

Graham wasn't always in the studio when the backing tracks were being recorded as John Eden recalls: *"He was there for when we were putting basics down and we were putting a guide down, plus putting the tracks together. He was off doing other things and going back to Los Angeles. He had to go back there many times and there was Rainbow stuff going on at the time, I seem to remember. So, it was entirely his option to be there or not be there. I loved Graham being around. For me, it was also about getting hold of people."* Since bass player Gary Twigg was unavailable for the recording of 'That's The Way That It Is', ex-Frankie Miller and Joe Cocker bassist Chrissie Stewart was drafted in.

Soon after Graham had begun recording the vocals for the three songs, he had to fly back to Los Angeles. His Mum and Dad were due at the family home for about five weeks, the big talking point being Graham's marriage to his Australian fiancée Jo Eime, which had been arranged almost a year before and was taking place in London during May.

John Eden recalls the issues raised by the break: *"There was a period where Graham went back to California, and he was wanting me to go over there and certainly we had talks with the label at the time. David did try to suggest that they send me over there, but they wouldn't agree to that. So, in the end I went on my own steam and took a holiday. I'd never been to Los Angeles before and I stayed in the Beverly Hills Hilton. It was way out of my pocket-book really! Then I called Graham, and he and Jo came down and then I'd started to look for a studio. I found this studio called Skyline Recording which was very reasonably priced, it was about $55.00 an hour and compared to some of the other rates that were $160 – $200 it was really a good deal. Coincidently, it was a stone's throw from where Graham lived! So it was the perfect place. We called David Oddie and said 'hey, we've got a studio now, I'm here, and we can do some vocals. Please send us the tapes'. So, kind of reluctantly I think, they agreed to send the tapes out to us. I booked the studio time and we started to work on the vocals there for the album and finish off what we had done on 'Liar' and we got that up to a point and mixed it there. Then there was the second single all ready to go. It gave us a little bit more time to go back and work on some more tunes."*

Two more songs came into the frame and were probably recorded at The Glade - 'Bad Days Are Gone', and 'Baby Don't Tell Me To Go', written by Bob Young and Micky Moody, with Dave Markee co-credited on the latter. These songs were never considered as album tracks as John Eden confirms: *"They were always set up as B-sides."* Both songs had a very live feel to them and seemed quite raw, alive and full of spirit. It was soon decided that 'Bad Days Are Gone' would be on the B-side of 'Liar'.

Not long after John had arrived back in the UK, Graham, his wife to be Jo, and his parents followed in early May to put any final touches needed to their wedding. The big day took place at Marylebone Register Office in London on May 13th. Jo's parents came all the way from Australia. David Oddie was best man, with Cozy Powell and Micky Moody also in attendance. The press were on hand too, and after the wedding reception, Graham and Jo went back to David Oddie's house and then flew home to Los Angeles.

'Liar' b/w 'Bad Days Are Gone' was released on May 29th in the UK, presented in a picture sleeve with a still clipped from the 'Night Games' video. The Russ Ballard penned A-side had been written as far back as June 1971 when he was still in Argent and the American band Three Dog Night had taken the song to No. 7 in the US Top 40 later that year. Graham was not too impressed: *"They just chose a single without really thinking about it, or asking me. I thought it was okay, but I think it was a last minute decision to put it out. Maybe that is why a video wasn't shot. It was totally the wrong choice. 'S.O.S.' should have been the follow up to 'Night Games'."* The problem was though that Phonogram only had three songs to choose from at this point. If they had been a little more patient and waited for 'S.O.S.' things might have worked out better, as these initial songs were album tracks and definitely not single material. They seemed to be hoping

The day after the wedding •
Graham, Jo with his parents, and brother Tony and his wife Gill.

A step up for groom

ROCK star Graham Bonnet took the appropriate step to keep in fashion yesterday.

His bride, 21-year-old model Jo Eime is the same height— 5ft 10 in—as he is. But if Lord Snowdon can cheat a little by picturing Prince Charles head and shoulders above Lady Diana, that's good enough for Graham, 33.

He stood on the steps of Marylebone Register office in London while Jo was happy to stand down on the pavement.

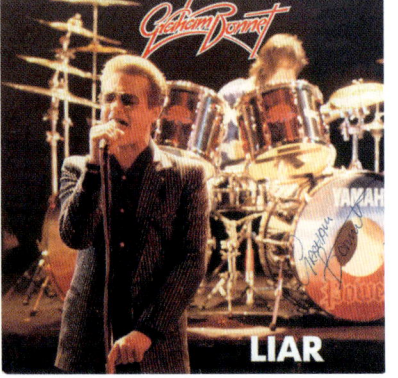

GRAHAM BONNET: Liar (Vertigo). Speak of the devil and . . . So here's the aforementioned Ballard R. providing a song for Graham Bonnet, who's been in the business long enough to know a winner when he hears it. Mind you, he heard this one a long time ago; in 1968, in fact, when Three Dog Night took it up the U.S. charts.

'Liar' would do quite well purely on the strength of its predecessor. But the NME was not impressed with the track and described 'Liar' as a *"messy old production of an old Argent song"*, saying that Graham "tries desperately hard to be clever and sees himself as a HM smoothie." Melody Maker were less harsh, suggesting that Graham had taken an unhurried casual approach to this version of the song, *"the voice is big and straining at the leash, but always held in check, and the same goes for his hooligans."*

Entering the charts at No. 65 on June 13th, 'Liar' rose to No. 51 the following week, which turned out to be its peak position. When the single was released in Japan, the songs were reversed, with 'Bad Days Are Gone' as the A-side. Masaya Uchimura explains: *"Culturally, the Japanese really love melodious songs in a minor key. Graham was marketed [here] as a pathos-laden pop singer, so the ballad-type track was pretty much in line with this image. The Japanese title for 'Bad Days Are Gone' was changed to 'Kodoku no Sakebi' which literally means 'solitary shout'!"* 'Liar' was later released in Holland and then France, where 'S.O.S.' was on the B-side.

Graham returned to England and John Eden booked RAK studios to work on three more songs, the newly penned 'S.O.S.' by Russ Ballard, the Phil Spector, Ellie Greenwich and Jeff Barry classic 'Be My Baby' and 'Don't Stand In The Open' by Bob Young and Micky Moody. John then booked time at Roundhouse studios where more vocals were recorded, and percussionist Martin Ditcham laid some parts down. Gary Twigg played bass on 'S.O.S.' and 'Be My Baby' and guitarist Kirby Gregory came on board to play alongside Micky Moody. Keyboard player John Cook was also drafted in for a day to play on 'S.O.S.' (having played on Cozy Powell's 'Tilt' album.)

John Eden adds: *"I remember working at the Roundhouse in Camden Town and being there in the room when we did 'Be My Baby'. I did some percussion in there on that and I think we actually did some vocals there."* For 'Don't Stand In The Open' Chrissie Stewart was on bass guitar duties and Adrian Lee from Toyah's band on keyboards, who also played on 'Be My Baby'.

On the day 'S.O.S.' was being recorded Russ Ballard decided to pay everyone a visit and ended up playing guitar on the track. Graham remembers the session also resulted in the recording of 'Be My Baby': *"It was one afternoon at Mickie Most's studio. We'd completed 'S.O.S.' and Russ came along to see how it was going. We were talking in the studio and he said something about the song 'Be My Baby' being the kind of thing that would suit my voice. So I told him that in one of my Skeggy bands we played a lot of Ronettes and Crystals songs. Then he started playing it on piano and John Eden said 'let's do that'. So Russ is playing piano and it was done in one afternoon!"*

Phonogram took a liking to Graham's version of 'S.O.S.' and talked about it being the next single, which might have got the project back on track as it had 'hit single' written all over it. The matrix numbers of Graham's singles started with VER 1 ('Night Games'), VER 2 ('Liar'), before jumping to VER 4 ('That's The Way That It Is'). Was VER 3 'S.O.S.' allocated but pulled at the last moment?

Even Cozy Powell commented about the decision to Kerrang: *"'S.O.S.' is great, but they didn't put it out as a single. They put out 'That's The Way That It Is' – that's a nice song but it's not a single. 'S.O.S.' was written as one. I often wonder who makes the decisions at record companies to put out singles. Maybe they ask the tea lady what she thinks."* Graham agrees saying: *"'S.O.S.' should have been the single chosen as it was new and fresh."*

By now David Oddie had decided on a title for the album, dropping the word 'Dangerous' and simply going with 'Line-Up', because there was so many different musicians featured on it. Not too long after the session at Roundhouse studios, David arranged for the team, which included Adrian Lee on keyboards, and Chrissie Stewart on bass, to continue recording at Rick Parfitt's RAMP studios. John Eden explains how the name was just an acronym: *"I was at the house with Rick when he came up with the name. Richard And Marietta Parfitt - simple! Rick loves to come up with silly stuff like that."* Three further songs were recorded – 'Dirty Hand', which was another from the pens of Bob Young and Micky Moody, a version of the little known Chuck Berry song 'Anthony Boy', and 'Set Me Free', written by Ray Davies, which The Kinks had taken into the UK Top 10 during May 1965.

Having suggested the last two Graham explained: *"They were old favourites from when I was playing in bands as a teenager in Skegness."* The version of Chuck Berry's 'Anthony Boy' was a good choice. It sounds punchy and the 3 mins

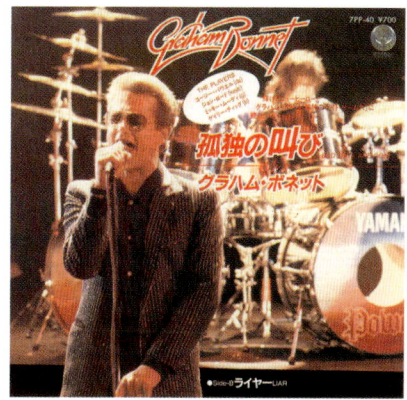

27 seconds or so really bounce along. You can hear Graham is really enjoying himself and so is everyone else. Mel Collins (who had played on Graham's unreleased album for DJM back in 1974) produced a tasty sax solo, followed by what Micky Moody excels at, a slide guitar break. The song became quite successful in Germany. There was actually talk about Graham going to Germany to perform 'Anthony Boy' on various TV stations, but it didn't happen.

John Eden says of RAMP: *"The thing about that was that I could spend a little bit more time there, because Rick [Parfitt] cut a reasonable deal. He wasn't in that commercial big studio league, because it was his home and a private studio. He and Marietta kindly agreed we could come and use it and the big bonus of course was having him play rhythm guitar on 'Anthony Boy', which we may not have got had we been working in London."*

Graham also recalls the session for 'Anthony Boy': *"It was originally in 6/8 time, similar to a fast waltz, but I changed it so it was in 4/4 time. So then it became more like a straight rock 'n' roll song and I love the words to it. Rick kept saying 'we're coming in at the wrong place' but I assured him that everyone wasn't and tried to explain it to him, but Rick was far from convinced. We all had a great time in Rick's studio, because everyone basically did everything there. It was like one big happy party."*

The final studio they used was Playground in London as John Eden remembers: *"That's where the mixing was done for a good section of the album. Of course this was after we'd done 'Night Games' and 'Liar', and I mixed those there. Graham also did vocals there at some point. He was around when I did some of the mixing and we worked together. I also did some saxophone parts there with Mel Collins on 'Be My Baby' as well. Everything finally got finished off there in that room."*

After Graham had completed his vocals and listened to a few mixes he returned to Los Angeles. The album was completed when keyboard player Adrian Lee was brought in and he laid down more synthesizer parts.

Looking back on why so many different keyboard players were used on the album, John Eden says: *"It wasn't me chopping and changing necessarily, it was down to availability of people. I'd loved it if Jon had continued on through the entire process just like Cozy had done."*

It is also interesting to hear John Eden's take on how Graham works in a studio environment, because Graham tends to sing songs slightly differently each take, which can be a producer's nightmare. Having worked with Graham from late 1973 at DJM, through his Ring O'Records and Mercury period, he says: *"I love working with Graham, always did. The main thing was in learning that you had to be very fast with Graham in terms of getting your sounds on him and getting the limiting and all the technical stuff done pretty fast, because it was very hard for him to hold back. Once he went in there he would be giving it his all and, being the mega-lungs that he is, the magic is generally in the first two or three takes. If you go beyond that point it can be a downward spiral. Especially around this period of time there was certainly some drinking that was going on in his life. One or two drinks would have a nice relaxing effect, enough to get him to feel comfortable, but if we didn't get the takes within that period and we started to go on more and Graham continued to drink, then quite often things would just go in a bad way and*

we wouldn't get anything at all that day. It didn't happen all the time, but there were occasions when that could have been an issue, maybe towards the later part of things."

Graham was providing a crate of Pils lager every day for everyone to enjoy and on occasions the bar was open as early as 10am! Micky Moody says: *"Because of his epilepsy, Graham had to take it easy on the booze. I think one-and-a-half bottles of Pils Lager was his limit, otherwise it affected him. I only remember one occasion in the studio when he had to call it a day. I also recall that he would smoke the odd Silk Cut cigarette and always pre-empted this by poking a few holes in it with his steel comb so he didn't inhale too much!"*

"Graham was always there for the basic tracking points" says John Eden. *"Graham has never been an artist that sits in the control room and listens and partakes in the entire process, whether it was with me as a producer, or Kaplan in the beginning as a producer or Pip in the middle period there, he's just never been that way. Of course, when we were in The Manor, and we were all there together in that old house, so he's around more. But he's never been, throughout all the period of time that I've known him, somebody who was around watching every note that was going down. His focus was always on his lead vocal and it was always in how he built the backing vocals up. He loves to do those backing vocals. He loves to multi-layer up. Those harmonies, when we start to stack up those voices, he has such an incredible blend with himself."*

Late 1980 had seen a new monthly pop magazine arrive on the scene titled 'Flexipop' and with every issue (as the name suggests) they gave away a free flexi-disc. The August issue featured a four-track flexi of Phonogram artists along with a special front cover featuring a photograph of Graham with Phil Lynott from Thin Lizzy and Tim Worman of rockabilly band The Polecats. Graham recalls the photo shoot: *"I remember Phil saying, 'you got dressed up for the occasion didn't you?' I was wearing just a white t-shirt, jeans and my leather jacket. It was a short session. The other guy didn't say much at all!"* Graham's 'Night Games' (new version) was the featured cut, with the magazine claiming (wrongly) the new version had actually been released in Japan. It was an exclusive alright, but not for long as it turned up as the opening song on 'Line-Up'.

As Graham was in the country, he was able to visit the second 'Monsters Of Rock' festival at Castle Donington, which AC/DC headlined. Phonogram had also organised the filming of three low budget videos for 'I'm A Lover', which included Graham playing his acoustic guitar, 'That's The Way That It Is' and 'Anthony Boy'. Graham and the band, which consisted of Jon Lord, Cozy Powell, Micky Moody and Chrissie Stewart deserved far better than this cheapskate approach, as Graham was quick to point out: *"They shot a bunch of videos in a cheap small studio when the money was running low!"*

With his album ready to face the world Graham was totally shocked when he heard the final mix for the first time. Gone was the hard edged sound that was in the can prior to him going home. He was unaware that synthesisers had been added to most of the songs, which had made the sound far thinner. *"It weakened the sound on the songs"* he says. *"It became a pop album, though it started off as very basic rock. Jon Lord was there, along with Cozy, Micky Moody, all rock*

and rollers. But John Eden got in the keyboard player from Toyah's band and made it flowery. He worked hard but I wasn't very impressed." Disillusioned, Graham returned home to Los Angeles.

In his defence, John Eden says: *"Graham never voiced this to me at the time. I didn't ever get any inkling whatsoever when the album was mixed and we did the playbacks that he was unhappy and that it had softened the sound of the songs. I don't think they have, they have their place and I think they work. I was trying to make, or I thought I was trying to make, an album that would be very commercially accessible to a wide range of fans and the public. For me, it wasn't meant to be a heavy rock album. It wasn't meant to be an Alcatrazz or a Rainbow album. That wasn't the idea behind it. So maybe my directive was completely wrong on that! I've read many, many comments from people who love this album. It's highly regarded now and it seems to have stood the test of time. Yes, there are a few bits here and there that show its age, but I still think it's a jolly good album. Adrian is a great player and a great arranger. He was in Toyah's band for a brief period, but did many other things including Mike and the Mechanics for many years. I don't think that the statement is justified. If I did, I would own up and say 'yes, you're absolutely right, it did soften', but I don't feel it did. I don't think the hard edge, what hard edge there is in those tracks, was lost in the mixes I did."*

'That's The Way That It Is' b/w 'Don't Tell Me To Go' limped out as the third single on October 2nd in the UK. The record had a very distinctive monochrome sleeve from his latest photo shoot and Phonogram did pay for the odd advert, but it didn't help much. The single didn't even chart and the low-budget video saw few airings. Graham says, *"I think they just chose a single without really thinking about it or, once again, without even asking me!"*

'Line-Up' was released towards the end of October in the UK and the album had a very striking sleeve showing five different photographs of Graham on the cover against a multicoloured rainbow background, with photographs of Micky Moody, Cozy Powell, Gary Twigg and Jon Lord on the back (plus the lyrics reproduced on the inner sleeve.)

With full page adverts in the press promoting the album (and single) Phonogram organised a tour - of radio stations. Graham visited London's Capital Radio, plus stations as far apart as Bristol and Scotland, ending up with an appearance on Radio 1's Roundtable: *"I did it with Donovan, Graham Stark and a few others. It was a strange day and evening. I was just back from Scotland where I'd done a radio tour and I was very hung over. I was literally taken from the airport to the studio not feeling very well at all!"*

All Graham's efforts didn't really help much. 'Line-Up' entered the UK charts at No. 69 on November 7th, climbed to No. 62 and then bombed down to No. 94 on November 21st.

Reviews in the music press weren't particularly enthusiastic either, with Carol Clark of Melody Maker suggesting *"this is an album of wandering moods"* and concluding *"as solo albums go, this one's fairly listenable, if inevitably lacking in direction or any attempt at originality."* Record Mirror's Robin Smith described it as *"another old boys outing for the likes of Moody, Lord and Powell on Uncle Graham's solo album. Granted, the man can produce immaculate singles, typified by 'Night Games', but an album is a different story. At best it's workmanlike. Bonnet makes a creditable job of the Ballard songs but the Phil Spector track 'Be My Baby' is painful candyfloss."* He formed the impression that Graham was at the crossroads and added *"as school reports used to say, he could do better."*

Back in his hometown of Skegness, Linda Blackburne of The Standard was far more upbeat: *"Apart from the dynamic hit single 'Night Games' there are a number of other songs, some old, some new, which are equally as powerful. It's difficult to choose a favourite track. 'S.O.S.' shows off Graham's distinctive vocals even more so than 'Night Games' and 'Don't Stand In The Open', both melodic and powerful, would make a good single."* She finished her review by adding: *"It's a very varied album with a song to suit all tastes but there's no doubt that the overall tone is heavy. I don't think any of*

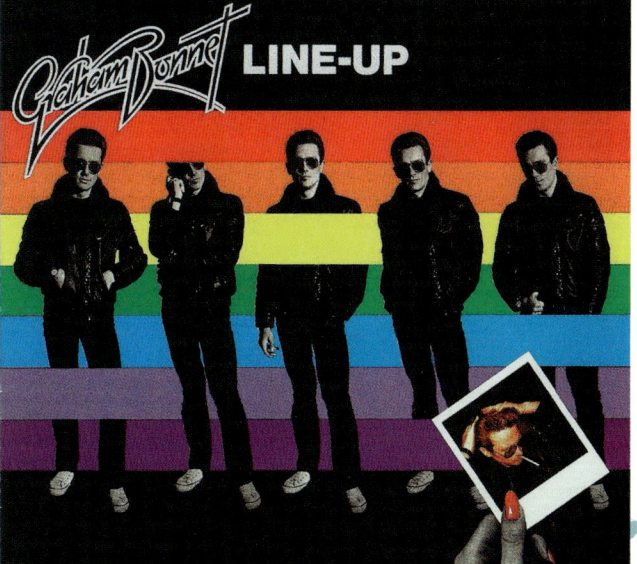

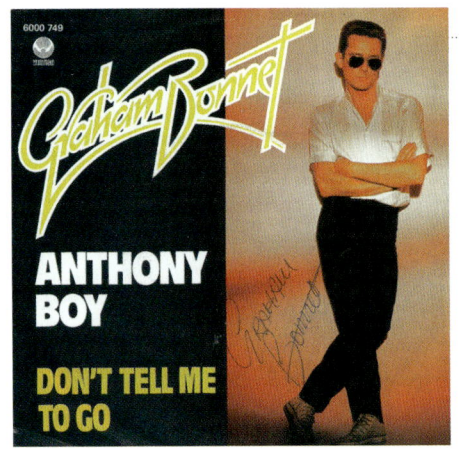  

the songs show off Graham's vocals to the full." For marketing reasons in Japan, the album title was changed to 'Kodoku no Night Games', although the sleeve still carried the title 'Line-Up' like everywhere else. The Japanese LP also had a gatefold lyric sheet issued with it.

Just prior to returning to Los Angeles, Graham found time to squeeze in an appearance on the manic UK Saturday morning TV show Tiswas, which was presented by Chris Tarrant and Sally James. In Tiswas tradition Graham was pulled up by his ears from underneath the desk for an interview and a competition to win the album and a promotional cap. They even aired two of the promo videos. Usually the guests jumped into a swamp, but Graham wasn't too keen on the idea while on air. But, as soon as the show had gone off the air, he dived headlong into it! Graham recalls: *"I travelled back on the train with drummer John Coghlan from Status Quo with my green slimed converse!"*

There was also a newly established Graham Bonnet Fan Club with Hazel McLean at the helm. An off-shoot of the Rainbow Fan Club, this venture only lasted around a year or so. 'I'm A Lover' b /w 'Don't Tell Me To Go' was released by Philips in Finland, and is possibly the rarest Graham Bonnet release from this period (shown on the top right) since less than 1,000 copies were pressed, Phonogram went with different A-sides around the world. Germany and Holland saw 'Anthony Boy', while Japan had something completely different, 'Set Me Free' b/w 'Be My Baby'. As always Graham was the last to find out: *"I didn't even know. I was in Los Angeles, and none of these things were told to me!"*

Obviously the real element missing from the promotional push were some live concerts, and on 'Line-Up' they clearly had the basis of a really powerful band. The press suggested that plans were afoot for Graham to tour Japan and possibly the UK in the New Year with Cozy Powell, Micky Moody and Jon Lord in his band but this never came to fruition. Graham had heard that Cozy, who had been with the Michael Schenker Group since August 1980, was going to leave very soon; as it turned out, he decided to stay. Apparently Cozy had been dithering about leaving and then staying for quite a while.

Back home in Los Angeles Graham was left thinking about the future of his solo career. He was considering making another solo album, then something happened to make him change his mind.

CHAPTER 6
Breaking The Heart Of The City (1982)

Featuring: MSG

FLASH, BANG, WALLOP!

On December 22nd 1980 Graham had been invited by Cozy Powell to see the Michael Schenker Group at the Country Club in Los Angeles.

The talk among Graham's friends at the time was all about whether he would be interested in replacing vocalist Gary Barden. Graham thought Gary (who'd been plucked from nowhere to front the ex-UFO guitarist's band) was doing a good job at the time and couldn't understand what all the fuss was about, and although he appreciated what was said he had just started to get his solo career going again having recorded 'Night Games' a few months earlier. And anyway, Gary stayed. Talking to Mick Wall in Metal Fury magazine about the situation, Graham commented: *"Somebody I was with said that he thought the band was about to split up because they were looking for a new singer and he also said that he thought they were going to offer the gig to me. Of course I thought, you know, no way!"*

In the event Gary stuck around for almost twelve more months. MSG had just had completed their UK tour promoting their successful second album 'MSG' when towards the end of 1981 a bombshell was dropped on Gary and keyboard player / guitarist Paul Raymond. Summoned to a meeting with manager Peter Mensch, Gary had a feeling for what was coming. The 'MSG' album had taken around seven months to complete with Ron Nevison at the helm, whereas their debut, 'The Michael Schenker Group', had only taken six weeks with producer Roger Glover. It is believed Michael and the band had been under tremendous pressure to complete their second offering for Chrysalis Records which, since the cost had already gone over the £250,000 mark, is hardly surprising. All this was taking its toll on the musicians and it was also suggested at the time that Gary was struggling to come to terms with his new found fame. Sure enough, Peter informed them both that their services were no longer required. The cost of keeping MSG together was running at a very high price, and in a bid to move further forward, this decision had been made jointly by the record company and the management (and also, presumably, the rest of the group) to replace Gary with a 'name singer'. Even Cozy Powell was pushing for this, as Michael told Steve Gett in the December 1982 Sounds' Guitar Heroes 'Schenker Schpecial': *"I had two conversations with Cozy Powell and he was one of them who actually brainwashed me as well. He said, 'Gary has got to go.'"* So the band was trimmed to a four-piece, provided they found a suitable vocalist, as with Michael now writing heavier and more powerful songs, using keyboards would only thin the sound out. Ironically Peter himself wasn't around much longer after dispensing with Gary and Paul, because Michael thought the time was right to split from the manager who had guided his career successfully since leaving UFO.

The remaining band members listened to many cassettes (700, according to a press release from Chrysalis Records!) in a bid to try to find a suitable vocalist. It wasn't just a case of finding someone to replace Gary Barden; it was also getting someone with a higher profile who could sing the new material that Michael was coming up with. Michael's heavier material had got the band thinking of vocalists like David Coverdale and Robert Plant, but it was Graham's impressive performance on 'Down To Earth' that the guitarist was attracted to. Since he was writing songs with a singer like Graham in mind, it only seemed natural to get him over to the UK and rehearse with him. This was left to Cozy Powell to arrange and, with the New Year barely underway, Graham received a phone call from Cozy in January asking him if he would be interested in joining MSG. Graham still wasn't 100% sure what to do at the time, but one more listen to his compromised solo album convinced him that being in a band again was the only sensible direction to take. He says: *"I was asked to see if I was interested, and that was it. They had been thinking of asking me, but took some time."* Having indicated that he would be up for joining, roughly one week later Graham received a cassette with three songs on it: *"The envelope was marked URGENT and basically all that was said was 'these are for you. Please listen and start thinking about melodies'."*

After listening to the songs and coming up with some melodies as requested, Graham agreed to travel over to rehearse with MSG during February. He had only met Michael Schenker once before, at the Donington Festival in 1980, and didn't know ex-Alex Harvey Band bassist Chris Glen either.

MSG used a rehearsal studio in London and Graham recalls their very first get together: *"The studio was somewhere in north London. There was a pub on the corner. Def Leppard rehearsed there too and Madness. We just played Rainbow stuff in the rehearsal to begin with. Then we started to make the new songs with me la-la-la-ing along."*

Commenting on Graham's audition to Steve Gett in Kerrang!, Cozy was quick to dismiss the suggestion that he had chosen the singer: *"Believe it or not it wasn't my idea. I didn't suggest Graham because I thought people would draw too many conclusions. We had a few singers on the shortlist before Graham was even discussed. In the end Michael said he was writing songs with someone like Graham in mind. So I said 'if you're writing with his voice in mind let's get him over. There's no harm in trying it'. I didn't know if he was going to carry on with his solo career or not, but he came over and is still working with us so hopefully it'll work out ok."* Since everything was going very well, Graham was offered the gig and temporarily moved in with the band, as he recalls: *"We all stayed in a house, which was rented, in London. Sometimes I would stay at Cozy's house though."* Graham was very pleased to be back in a band again, with 'rock 'n' rollers' as he put it.

The story was big news in the rock press, and naturally Kerrang! went after the sacked musicians to get their angle on the changes. Both were diplomatic. Gary Barden wasn't sure: *"Graham Bonnet is a very good singer. I personally don't think he fits, but then the proof is in the pudding"*. And Paul Raymond added: *"Graham's a great singer and it sounds very promising. But it's almost like starting at the beginning again."*

Graham's first outing with MSG came during March with a signing session at London's Virgin Megastore on Oxford Street to promote an album featuring his predecessor. 'One Night At Budokan' had sold very well as a Japanese import, so Chrysalis Records rush-released it in the UK that month. With Graham not being on the album it put him in a potentially awkward position but he was persuaded to go along to the store. All seemed to be going very well until one particular fan told Graham *"I don't think you'll be as good as Gary Barden."* Graham was under the impression it was because of the way he looked, but it really bothered him and he decided to leave the store and go to the local pub. Returning a while later much the worse for wear, Graham departed once again, this time for good. He told Metal Fury's Mick Wall: *"It really pissed me off at the time and I got totally drunk that day. Sometimes it does get to me. It shouldn't, but sometimes it does."*

Back in Los Angeles, Graham's wife, Jo, was pregnant and he flew back home to be with her when she gave birth to twins on March 22nd at Northridge hospital. Having not found out until quite late on that she was expecting twins, Jo gave birth to one boy and one girl, which they named Aaron and Keeley. Graham points out: *"We wanted our children to be American citizens."*

Graham then had to get back to the UK again. During rehearsals, Michael formed the impression that Graham wasn't comfortable improvising with the songs by adding some words and trying different melodies out. Since Michael wasn't writing lyrics at the time, he suggested that Graham should read some magazines for inspiration. Graham had never written full lyrics for a rock band before, so he drew from what he had learned during his time in Rainbow. However, reading the magazines triggered him off and there was no stopping him. The following few weeks saw him come up with several sets of lyrics and melodies to some of the backing tracks. One later became 'Desert Song', which was one of the first songs he wrote, and he claims it only took him around ten minutes. Others from this period were 'Samurai', 'Dancer', 'Rock You To The Ground', 'Broken Promises' and 'April Fool' (an early title for 'Girl From Uptown'). Some of the songs originally clocked in between ten and twenty minutes long and Graham was seriously wondering where the verses and choruses would fit. Eventually, as the songs were shortened,

things started to fall in to place, and he used a more husky and aggressive type of vocal which he felt suited the material. He says: *"It was my choice of melodies and the sound of the words. Michael's chord progressions were more in a dark mode. They were also very Germanic."* Graham generally only saw Michael at rehearsals, but he did hang out with Cozy and Chris.

Work progressed quickly and quite a few more songs were written as Cozy pointed out to Steve Gett in Kerrang! during the album sessions: *"We've written seventeen tracks for the new album of which we'll pick the best. Michael's obviously come up with the basic ideas and Chris and I have done our bit. I don't contribute much to the writing. I just add more to the arranging than the writing. But I've come up with a few bits and pieces here and there. Graham has now got to go and put his lyrics and melodies on. Then we'll get together in a week or ten days and get on with it."*

When asked whether they were getting a new keyboard player in the band, Cozy said: *"I don't think we need a keyboard player, we can get away with Michael and Chris using Moog pedals to give us all the colours we need. This band is a lot stronger and harder. Keyboards tend to knock the rough edges off and smooth it out. The material on the last MSG album was a lot better than people made out, but the production didn't bring out the best of the material. So the material on the new album will be a lot nastier. MSG go Motörhead or whatever!"*

Living in the rented house for quite a while, along with a couple of roadies, the musicians found that life was becoming a little stressful with everyone on top of each other. All of a sudden after less than a handful of rehearsals, if rumours are to be believed, Cozy suddenly decided to quit the band, claiming at the time that he had burnt himself out due to the pressure of work over the last eighteen months and needed to rest. He also said he wanted to concentrate on racing cars, but before you could blink he turned up playing on two tracks on Robert Plant's debut solo album 'Pictures At Eleven', released at the end of June. What no-one knew at the time was that Cozy and Michael had had a big argument during one of the rehearsals, which had apparently seen drumsticks flying. Graham remembers it well: *"I was there. It was a scene that left Michael in tears."*

Cozy's speedy replacement – if anyone can ever be said to replace Cozy – was Chris Glen's former Sensational Alex Harvey Band colleague Ted McKenna; apparently no-one else even auditioned. Ted had played with Rory Gallagher from 1976 to 1981 and since Graham knew Rory from his Quarry management days around that time, there was a little connection. Graham says: *"Chris got him in. He was the obvious candidate."* It was reported at the time that Michael had actually bumped in to Ted at the Funny Farm, a basement bar in West London and he persuaded him to come for a jam. And since that went very well, he asked Chris to persuade Ted to join. Although happy with Ted, Graham regretted the change: *"I missed my friend very much. He wasn't Cozy; no-one is."*

But Graham was now getting in to writing lyrics in a big way; it was as if the floodgates had been opened and Michael was very happy with what Graham was coming up with. Ted McKenna had settled in nicely too, and with the highly respected Martin Birch being brought in to produce the album everything was looking very positive. Martin, whose earlier production credits had included Fleetwood Mac and Deep Purple, as well as Whitesnake and Rainbow, had just finished working with Iron Maiden on the No. 1 album 'The Number Of The Beast'. Graham had never met Martin before but since they got on really well, he used to spend quite a bit of time at Martin's house listening to old MSG songs, which he knew he would have to sing live at some point in the future.

In May the band flew over to France to start recording at the Chateau d'Herouville, close to Paris. Many artists had recorded there over the years including Pink Floyd, David Bowie, Deep Purple, Stevie Wonder and Elton John who nicknamed it Honky Chateau, and even titled one of his albums after it. Never understanding why bands or artists should go to these types of places to record – miles away from civilization – Graham nicknamed it Chateau Horrible, with less than happy memories of his previous experience of recording in a castle with Rainbow still fresh in his memory. They were joined by ex-Gary Moore keyboard player Tommy Eyre, who was recruited for the sessions. In a bid to save time and money, and avoid the long delays which struck their previous album, Graham had already written most of all the lyrics and the melodies to the songs, which had now been whittled down from around seventeen to nine.

Recording started well, with everyone feeling relaxed. They were really enjoying working with Martin Birch, who Graham described as one of the band, claiming this is what it must have been like for The Beatles to work with George Martin. But they just had to give him a nickname, and called him 'The Ninja'. Graham says: *"Martin was into the martial arts and that was the reason. I remember his favourite track was 'Samurai' and I think it was me who gave him that nickname."*

Even though being in this out-of-the-way situation wasn't Graham's ideal choice of studio-venue, he did manage to complete most of the vocals there. And there was time for some fun and games, as Graham remembers well: *"Every session I would try to sing the song 'Misty' in French, before we would start the real singing. I used it as a kind of warm-up. And on one occasion, Martin and I were lying in the bushes, both of us drunk, because we couldn't quite make it to the house. When we left the studio, the air hit us and we both suddenly realised we were very drunk, and fell over, just yards away from the house. We started saying as we were lying there and looking up at the stars 'good 'ere, ain't it?' Eventually we staggered or crawled back to the main*

house to go to sleep..."

Graham spoke to Kerrang!'s Dante Bonutto about the how the recording was going, saying: *"So far so good. I'm enjoying it very much and getting on with the guys in the band rather than arguing. Well, not so much arguments, but in Rainbow we just didn't communicate. This group actually talks which is unusual and we all get on very well together."*

It is believed that the track 'Ulcer' was one of the last to be laid down during the sessions. Originally intended to be a song with lyrics, Graham wasn't sure what to do with it so he didn't write any and, with time running out, Michael changed the song around and turned it into an instrumental. During their time at the Chateau the record label also organised a photo session, with the band looking suitably mean and full of attitude. With the backing tracks now finished, along with most of the vocals, it was time to move on to Musicland studios in Munich, Germany to continue with the album. It was here that Graham completed his vocals and Martin finished all the necessary overdubs.

Chrysalis had been pushing hard for a single, and of the nine songs recorded the most commercial song the band had in the can was a song called 'Dancer'. The situation was identical to when Graham joined Rainbow; the management knew the band needed to have a big hit single which had so far totally eluded them. Only two previous singles had come close to being hits, 'Armed And Ready' and 'Cry Of The Nations', which reached No. 53 and No. 56 respectively in 1980. Graham agrees: *"They wanted a commercial hit, and that song was the obvious one."*

'Dancer', is actually about choreographer, singer, songwriter and actress Toni Basil (real name Antonia Christina Basilotta), known for the one-off worldwide hit 'Mickey', and someone Graham had met in America in 1974. As for the B-side, the band settled on 'Girl From Uptown', as Graham recalls: *"It was a bit of a throw or*

keep deal with that song. It didn't take up much of my time, word-wise or melody. It was very quickly put together, but a go or no-go track." As for who the 'Girl From Uptown' might be, Graham says: *"It can be anyone you like, or just about! It's a guy reaching for something he thinks he can never reach. The same thing Billy Joel wrote with 'Uptown Girl' later in 1983."* Martin Birch set about mixing the two songs, leaving the remaining seven until a later date, and the label was happy, setting a release date of August 27th for the single, and going to work on promoting it.

With everything looking so good, and the album largely finished, promoters were called in to prepare a world tour, starting off in Japan in October, followed by a British tour in November and December. Dates in America were also discussed. Prior to all this, since the band had been booked to headline the Reading Festival on Sunday August 29th, there was the simple matter of a 'secret' warm-up gig which for some reason was booked miles away at Sheffield Polytechnic's Phoenix Hall for Friday August 27th. The date tied in very well with the release of their new single, 'Dancer', which would hit the shops on the same day.

Live rehearsals had started roughly two months prior to these gigs. Graham basically only knew the songs he had written and recorded, so set about learning tracks from the previous albums. With his bad memory this was far easier said than done, even though he'd already heard quite a few at Martin Birch's house, and as time ticked by the pressure mounted as he tried in vain to remember all the lyrics. Anyone can read the lyrics off sheets of paper in the rehearsal room, but once on stage it is totally different. Unknown to his band members, Graham had been feeling the pressure on quite a few levels since he had joined, having to come up with all the lyrics and melodies, then having to put down his vocals and backing vocals, and now needing to learn a lot of old songs. Clearly this all comes with the job but nevertheless he began to get nervous. He had tried to talk to his band mates, but says they didn't seem to understand.

Graham opened up to Chris Watts of Kerrang! seven months later about his troubles: *"Since I joined the band there'd been so many pressures on me to learn 19 songs from the old set, not new ones, and I knew nothing of the old band. I was recording and writing lyrics for the new album as well as learning new tunes and I couldn't do it all at the same time.*

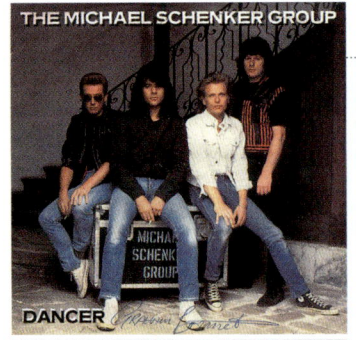
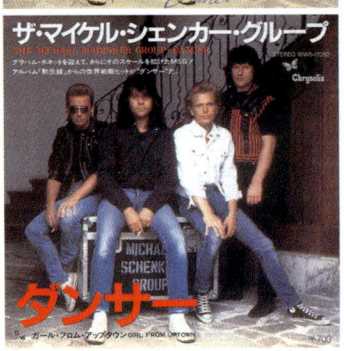

Sadly Bonutto wasn't the only journalist with reservations over the single and when 'Dancer' came under the spotlight in Kerrang! it couldn't have been given a worse review, courtesy of writer Peter Makowski's alter ego Toots Daley: *"And here we have it, at the fans' expense, the ultimate proof that the Kute Kraut and his James Dean clone sidekick may be immensely talented in their respective roles on guitar and vocals but totally incapable of writing songs. In fact, when it comes to melodies and lyrics, as with the subject matter of their co-writing partnership, these guys operate with two left feet."* He concluded: *"This is a total disaster and the final chapter on MSG as far as I am concerned."*

With friends like this, even with all the different vinyl pressings and a reasonable amount of publicity, 'Dancer' didn't do as well has everyone had hoped for. Whereas 'Since You Been Gone' had seen every DJ in the land playing it, 'Dancer' was hardly ever played on national daytime radio. The song did enter the UK charts on September 9th at No. 69 and climbed to No. 52 the following week, only to drop out of the charts a couple of weeks later. Even so it was still MSG's biggest selling single in the UK – albeit by just one place.

Over in Japan, Mercury Records saw the forthcoming MSG dates as an opportunity to capitalise on their Graham Bonnet back-catalogue, reissuing the 'Graham Bonnet' album and putting out 'No Bad Habits' for the first time there. They decided to add 'Bad Days Are Gone' from 1981 as the opening song on Side One, to lure in Graham's growing Japanese fan base who knew him only as a rock singer (it had been issued in Japan as a single). The album was not a big seller.

The band had decided to call their new album 'Assault Attack' and Graham remembers how the album came to be so named: *"Jack Magill, who was a roadie, was woken up one morning by Michael turning his amp up really loud while he was asleep in the rehearsal room. He jumped up and said, 'what's this, some kind of assault attack?' Michael chose the title from that incident."*

MSG arrived in Sheffield for their warm-up gig in the early afternoon and it wasn't too long before Graham had met up with some old friends for a drink. The afternoon saw them have a lot of fun, as well as a lot to drink, and the partying continued for a couple of hours. Getting back for the sound-check somewhat the worse for wear, Graham had managed to persuade one of the road crew to write out and then photocopy the songs, some fourteen in total, which he still wasn't too familiar with, as well as indicating the changes on separate pieces of paper, which were then taped onto the stage monitors, so he could glance down when he needed to.

Graham then tried to get Michael to come out of his dressing room for the sound-check, but he didn't want to know, and it was clear he had also been drinking heavily. An argument between them then broke out. Graham says: *"He had locked the dressing room and my jacket was in there. He wouldn't let me in to get it. He was drunk going by the sound of his voice. Then he passed out. I was also drunk and we had both taken Valium as well."*

Music journalist John Aizlewood attended the gig as a young punter. He recalls the events of the evening: *"It was part of a series of free gigs at Sheffield Polytechnic for the unemployed. I was at school, but me and my friends knew people with UB40 [unemployment benefit] cards (which you had to produce to get tickets), so we saw most of the gigs – The Fall, UK Subs and The Look are ones I remember. I had never owned a MSG album; we went along because it was there. Everyone knew they were going to be playing Reading and MSG playing the Poly (they were really a City Hall act) was a big thing in such a metal stronghold as Sheffield."*

Graham's parents had also been invited along but when the time came for the band to hit the stage, Graham was in a very bad way - in fact he was totally drunk.

I said to the band 'look, I have a really bad memory problem', which is dead true, 'and I can't remember all this'. Everybody laughed and thought I was joking, but it was the truth. I couldn't learn nineteen songs in two weeks. I had the same problem in Rainbow but I didn't have so many old songs to learn. We were rehearsing every day for about two months and I kept saying, 'look, I don't know the bloody songs to be comfortable in singing them, to be able to wander around the stage and to look as though I know what I'm doing.'

Part-way through rehearsals, around mid-August, Kerrang!'s Dante Bonutto was given a special early preview of 'Dancer' and 'Girl From Uptown' but wasn't won over: *"I can't say that I'm overly optimistic. My first and only impression was it lacked real character, though the B- side 'Girl From Uptown', not on the album, came across as a more consequential composition and Martin Birch, fresh from his triumph with Maiden, has certainly done his reputation another power of good, providing a rich, purposeful sound topped with a Bonnet voice showing subtle new dimensions in range and timbre."*

During the build up to the gig in Sheffield, Graham phoned his parents a few days before the gig, and explained he was really feeling under pressure in a huge way. Interestingly, three days prior to the debut, on August 24th, Graham spoke to Mick Wall of Metal Fury and explained that he was in the group for the long haul: *"I do see this thing with Michael as a long term project. At least, I hope so. I hope so very much because the band as it stands now is very, very good and I'm not saying that because I'm in it, when I saw the original band with Gary Barden I thought that they were really very good."*

Chrysalis certainly had faith in 'Dancer' and pulled out all the stops. As well as adverts in the press, the collectors were spoilt for choice. On the morning of MSG's warm-up gig in Sheffield you could buy the record in four different formats: normal black vinyl, a clear vinyl pressing (both in picture sleeves with the lyrics on the back), a picture disc edition and to complete the set a 12" version. As all sales counted towards chart placings, by getting these special versions into chart shops, if a fan would buy them all – and many did back then – it could help lift the single up the charts. 'Dancer' was also released in Japan but, for some reason, not throughout Europe.

John says: *"I was too young to grasp whether he was drunk or not. I did grasp instantly that something was odd about the whole set up, but people assume it's planned and a joke!"*

MSG opened up with 'Armed And Ready' but the carefully prepared lyric sheets began to come apart with Graham and the band walking over them without realising it, as well as the monitors getting moved because many people in the audience were right up at the front of the stage. The rock fans started to give Graham some abuse about his hair from the word go, and John remembers how the singer reacted: *"He started smirking, pulled out a comb and started preening himself in a manner unbecoming to a metal act! That was the sign that he and the fans weren't on the same side. From that moment it was war."*

Prior to the start of 'Cry For The Nations' Graham and Michael exchanged angry words with one another. Graham's answer was to introduce the song as a piece of shit, informing the audience that he had to sing it or he'd get fired. As soon as the number had finished Graham started to introduce the band but to stir things up, he also introduced the hidden keyboard player, Andy Nye, and Michael's guitar roadie, Steve Casey.

As 'Let Sleeping Dogs Lie' started, Graham was really beginning to lose it. He messed up the start of his vocals, and then began to panic over the lyrics even more. With the crowd swaying forward, and the monitors moving all over the place, he started to lose his nerve. Everything was building up to a crisis point; Graham was simply out of control and for some reason he now decided to get his penis out and begin shaking it about at the crowd, apparently showing the fans what he thought of them! John says: *"I always thought it was deliberate provocation to a hostile audience - and his band mates."* Worse was to come, as Graham then started swearing at the crowd. With loud boos from the audience echoing around Phoenix Hall, Graham couldn't get off stage fast enough though he needed help from the road-crew even to do this. The band carried on playing and did instrumental versions of the remaining songs and, to their credit, were even called back for a couple of encores.

On his way back to the dressing room, Graham hadn't a clue what was happening around him, let alone what he was doing. One of the crew met him and Graham tried to convince road manager Rob Cooksey that he was unable to carry on with the gig; Rob was not impressed and told him to get back out there, but it was no good. With the room spinning around him, Graham finally passed out. It was definitely the end of the gig as far as he was concerned: the rest of MSG saw it as the end of his job!

Eventually coming round, Graham was just about to leave in a taxi with one of the road crew and go back to the hotel, when he saw his Mum and Dad outside. Goodness knows what they thought of it all, though he was able to have a few words. Graham went back to sleep it all off and try to be ready to be picked up by the band as arranged the following morning to return to London in time for their Reading preparations.

With the gig and all the mayhem over, Rob Cooksey had other instructions and was quickly on the phone to ex-singer Gary Barden, arranging a meeting the following day. Being in a very desperate position, Rob offered Gary the Reading gig. They agreed a fee for this and also for two other bookings in Germany. The band fully expected Gary to say no, and had visions of having to pull out of the festival. Apparently, if Graham had done the Reading gig, it is thought that somebody from the road crew had already planned their revenge by throwing something which was 'not very nice' over him during the set!

When Graham woke up in his Sheffield hotel room the following morning, he came down to earth with a bang once he realised that the group had cleared off back to London and left him behind. After his behaviour the previous night, the band and management had clearly decided he was out, and had no intention of picking him up. Graham's own manager, David Oddie, had already been informed of what had taken place. Was there any sign of a rapprochement? During the morning, Michael Schenker's girlfriend phoned Graham a number of times, asking him if he still wanted to be in the band and do the Reading gig. Graham obviously told her yes, but according to him Michael himself never phoned. Michael later told Graham he did call at one point, but never got an answer.

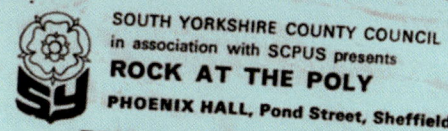

Checking out of the hotel with hardly any money in his pocket, Graham managed to get a ticket on his credit card and caught the next available train to London's St. Pancras, meeting David Oddie just down the road at King's Cross station. David had already spoken to the MSG camp and explained to Graham that the band had fired him. He didn't believe that and thought it more likely to be the management. Graham suggested that he could still do the Reading festival and even though David agreed, he told Graham that the band didn't think he could hack it. The following day Graham flew back to America: *"When I got back to Los Angeles, I had to think what to do next, as I realised I had screwed up big time."*

Despite the events both Graham and Michael have since put it behind them, with Michael commenting in Kerrang! in November 1982: *"I still have the greatest respect for Graham. Graham is one of the best singers in the world. It's a shame, mainly for what could have been something really special."*

With the album now at the mixing stage, the band hoped to persuade Chrysalis to wipe Graham's vocals and overdub Gary's, but there was no way they were going pay for this. They had already had their fingers burned when MSG's previous studio album had cost far more than expected. Having set an October release date months before, they were not prepared to have it drag on again into the New Year.

So in early September the band flew out to Munich to listen to Martin 'The Ninja' Birch putting the final touches to the mix. Instead of Graham's vocals powering out over the music, they had been buried. One has to assume somebody had asked Martin to turn it into more of a guitar album. It was a pity really, because this could have been an excellent 'group' album. Graham remembers the situation: *"They were so mad at me they almost got Gary to re-do the whole vocal tracks. So they took me down in the mix as punishment for my stupid behaviour."*

Two promotional videos had already been planned by the record company to support the release of 'Dancer' and for 'Desert Song' (which suggests they saw it as the next single) but not yet filmed. And while they would not fund new vocals on the album, they did want to have Gary redo the vocals on the videos while the band was in Munich to help promote the new album, which had now officially been given the title of 'Assault Attack'. With the songs not being in Gary's range he found them very hard to reproduce, and to save time Graham's backing vocals were left in place. No sooner had this been completed than the Japanese tour, which had been widely promoted was cancelled for reasons never fully explained.

Despite no longer being in the band, Graham was still a major part of the album and his name dominated the reviews. When 'Assault Attack' was released on October 15th, (with a limited edition picture disc also available), Michael told reporter Andy Secher: *"I believe that it's the strongest album this group's ever done."* But it met with mixed reviews, Dave Roberts of Sounds, for example, finding that it lacked something: *"Sure, 'Assault Attack' is a good LP, but considering that it contains one of the best guitarists and one of the best vocalists in rock music it's ultimately a bitter disappointment. The problem seems to be in the old chestnut of 'song writing'. There are certainly no bad songs on this album, but there aren't any classics either."* He also found time to comment on Graham's more aggressive vocal approach, compared to what he had done in the past with Rainbow, or on 'Line-Up', noting: *"Bonnet emerges with some credit, his voice attaining a new roughness, particularly noticeable on the bluesy 'Rock You To The Ground' which is snarled rather than sung. And Herr Schenker's contributions are as reliable as ever. Surprisingly, the songs that do stand out are the more commercial, lightweight numbers such as 'Dancer' and 'Broken Promises', both of which are not dissimilar to Rainbow's past chart successes."*

Melody Maker's Brian Harrigan also commented about how good Graham's voice was on the album: *"Gary Barden, as we all know, has replaced Bonnet as singer in the band and a good vocalist he is too, judging by his performance at Reading. But I'd reckon that this wouldn't be half the album it is without the strength and individual style of Bonnet's vocals. I'm not an enormous fan of Schenker and his type of guitar playing; I think he tends to be a little on the flashy and derivative side and rather short of originality. However, his deficiencies are compensated for by the earthy and daringly direct bass lines of Chris Glen and the impressively bicep-ridden drums of Ted McKenna. Add to that Bonnet's vocals and you have an album that is reasonably good - in fact better than it has much right to be. One of the major problems is that the songs simply aren't strong enough. 'Rock You To The Ground' is a good example of how the band should go. It's a great shame that Bonnet's gone from the band now, simply because I feel he could have helped to pull them out of the rut they've got into. I hate to say it but this is an album by a second division band."*

Steve Gett didn't seem to know what to make of the album when he reviewed it for Kerrang! As much as he admired Graham's amazing vocal range, he felt there was something missing in his delivery and he didn't think he sang from the heart: *"To be quite frank, I still can't work out whether I like it or not. There's plenty of bite and aggression in the music but it's the vocal work that leaves me mystified. Do I like the singing or not? I just can't tell. There are times when it seems to work and others when it becomes a shade aggravating. Bonnet has a tendency to shout rather than sing on certain tunes and this certainly puts a damper on affairs. And yet on cuts like 'Samurai' and 'Desert Song' one can't fault the man."*

The album was also released in Japan, America, Australasia, Europe, Scandinavia and Ireland during the same month. On October 23rd it entered the UK charts at No. 25, peaking at No.19 the following week before sliding back down to bow out on November 20th at No. 92. In Sweden it reached No. 24 and America No. 151. It might not have been as accomplished as the earlier MSG albums, but it did find support with some fans. In Japan the album reached No. 9, selling a respectable 44,000 copies. In Korea, 'Samurai' was not included as Government rules saw that references to Japanese culture were suppressed, an edict dating back to 1945 when Korea was released from 36 years of governmental rule by Japan.

Back in the UK, MSG went ahead with the tour as planned, starting at Bristol's Colston Hall on November 21st and concluding it appropriately enough with two nights in Sheffield at the City Hall on December 14th and 15th. It is a huge shame Graham missed this opportunity, and also that in later years Schenker and Bonnet couldn't get something together again. Australian music journalist, Ian McFarlane perhaps sums up the lost opportunity, writing in 2000 on the sleeve notes to a Schenker retrospective: *"'Assault Attack' can lay claim to being one of Schenker's best albums, an almost faultless synthesis of commercially viable melodies, scintillating guitar pyrotechnics and a palpable sense of drama, all backed by Martin Birch's dynamic production sheen. Bonnet's contribution to the project cannot be under-estimated, his vocals complimenting Schenker's playing with considerable dexterity. Almost every track is a winner, from the blistering title cut and the moody and magnificent 'Desert Song' to the lacerating 'Ulcer'. One can only speculate as to what else the Schenker/Bonnet song-writing partnership could have achieved."*

The album was re-mastered (but not remixed, which is a shame as many labels have provided fans with new mixes and original versions of the same album) by Chrysalis in 2009, and still stands up as being a strong, powerful, aggressive and very gritty rock classic. It has never sounded 'thin' like so many of the early Eighties' rock albums do now. The recording and production by Martin is first class.

Graham still remains proud of his work on the album, particularly as it was his first real go at writing a set of strong rock lyrics: *"All these songs are basically reporting on observations of things I have seen. Not your sex and drugs and rock and roll, but a different look as an insider and outsider. It's all in there, I did make up stories about mythical beings in some songs, but explained why they were there in the minds of believers."*

Once again, Graham found himself pondering about his future, as well as reflecting on recent events, which understandably were still preying on his mind. In an interview with journalist Chris Watts in Kerrang! in March 1983 he talked about his departure from MSG: *"I was very upset for a long time, I still have nightmares now about that bloody night! What went wrong? What did I say? I didn't think I was going to be sacked. I was mainly upset with the band because I thought they respected me as a musician,"* although he did concede that *"it was my fault."* Accepting that it was more of a management decision, he tried to sort out his relationship with Michael Schenker: *"I was hoping I could get in touch with Michael and speak to him myself and try to sort out what had gone on because I know I wasn't fired by the band at all. I was fired by the guy who was the manager, but who has himself since been fired,"* he told Laura Canyon, also in Kerrang!

With plenty of time to spend with his family, the cause of his sleepless nights soon became more as a result of attending to the needs of new-born twins than worrying about what had happened in Sheffield the previous August. If every cloud has a silver lining, this one helped to take his mind off his musical worries, if only for a short while. Changing nappies became a regular chore for him in the Bonnet household and, struggling to remember when he last had a decent night's sleep, Graham would try and catch up by catnapping during the day whenever possible, as well as taking up bike-riding as a form of exercise and relaxation to help him work out what to do next.

CHAPTER 7
Island In The Sun (1982 - 1984)

Featuring: The Royal Philharmonic Orchestra & Friends, and Alcatrazz

"This is kind of the 'thinking man's Heavy Metal'. It's got more melodies..."

Things were not all doom and gloom as Graham wondered what to do next. Offers still kept coming in and Graham turned down quite a few, including one to team up with Ted Nugent (a gig which eventually went to another Brit, Brian Howe.) One band who didn't get in touch was UFO, despite what was said at the time.

While this was all going on, one of Graham's old friends, Stuart Taylor, along with Tony Harding, had been working on an idea with the Royal Philharmonic Orchestra and various musicians to record a collection of cover versions of songs by The Police, who had become one of the biggest bands in the world. Don Airey was already involved, having called time on Rainbow after a gig in Honolulu, in early September 1981. The final straw came when after setting off on his nightly keyboard solo, the rest of the group left the stage – and kept on going, right back to the hotel! Don, who lived near to Stuart, was helping with the arrangements and conducting on the new album. With sessions getting under way in various studios around London, Stuart phoned Graham and asked him if he would like to sing on one of the tracks. It was a real lift to his spirits, because he knew he would be back amongst friends, in particular Don Airey, for the first time in quite a while. Stuart wanted Graham to cover 'Truth Hits Everybody'. Graham says: *"He chose that track for me. I didn't know the song. It was one of the lesser-known Police songs. I knew the hits, so to speak, and I didn't think it was much of a song - but I got paid!"*

During October 1982 Graham recorded the vocals in Los Angeles. The backing track featured a surprisingly stellar rock line-up with Gary Moore on guitar, Whitesnake bassist Neil Murray, Don Airey on synthesizer and Ian Paice on drums. Don remembers the session well: *"He recorded his vocal in Cherokee studios LA, which didn't take long. Chris Thompson was on first – then when it came to Graham's turn we couldn't find him, but located him by the snoring coming from under the mixer!"*

Having gone through a fairly lengthy period of soul-searching, wondering what to do next, and trying to decide if it was worth having another stab at a solo career, the New Year finally saw Graham decide the way forward was to get a proper band together. Graham had also parted with his long-standing manager David Oddie, so it was time to see if there was anyone else out there he could rub along with. A friend put him in touch with Andy Trueman, who was part of the De Novo Group. Andy himself was a Los Angeles-based Brit who had been in charge of tours by bands as varied as the Bay City Rollers to Jethro Tull. His instinct was that Graham should form a really impressive group and bring in as many names as he could.

Graham had also been introduced to Robin Le Mesurier during The Police covers sessions by Stuart and spent some time with the guitarist, who was currently working with Rod Stewart's band, at his house in Hollywood. Even though nothing really materialised from the meeting in terms of songs, it gave Graham an opportunity to start flexing his vocal muscles and getting used to working with someone musically again.

Around this time, Graham and his new manager saw an advert in a music magazine from a bass guitarist looking for work. The advertiser was ex-New England bassist Gary Shea who, after talking with Andy, was definitely interested. This sounded promising, and fitted in with the gameplan to get a band together that musically would fit into the Rainbow and MSG sort of mould, but if anything be even more tuneful and dynamic so people could identify it with Graham. Andy asked Gary if he happened to know a keyboard player, so he suggested his ex-New England colleague Jimmy Waldo. If New England didn't immediately strike chords, they were no slouches, having had a US Top 40 hit with 'Don't Ever Wanna Lose Ya' in 1979, followed by three albums between 1979 and 1981, and had toured with Kiss, AC/DC, Journey, Cheap Trick and Kansas over that time. After the band had run its course Gary and Jimmy, along with Hirsh Gardner, also from the band, decided to up sticks from Boston and move to Los Angeles where they teamed up with guitarist Vinnie Vincent. They formed a band called Warrior, but had hardly got started when Vinnie got a call from Kiss which he couldn't turn down. Meanwhile, Gary and Jimmy already knew Andy, having once nicked the prawns out of his cocktail backstage on a tour with New England! A meeting was soon scheduled and took place at 11am on Sunday March 13th at the Hyatt Hotel on Sunset Boulevard in West Hollywood, Los Angeles, with Graham, Andy, Gary and Jimmy in attendance to discuss the concept.

They agreed that the idea of putting together a hard-hitting rock band was a sound one, and Andy Trueman suggested that drummer Barry 'Barrimore' Barlow, who had played with Jethro Tull, and one-time Alex Harvey Band and Nazareth guitarist Zal Cleminson (who Andy thought would be up for it) should complete the line-up; Barry and Zal having played together in the short-lived Tandoori Cassette in 1980. The plan was that Graham, Jimmy and Zal would be the main songwriters and as far as everyone at the meeting was concerned it all looked very promising. The meeting over, everyone retired to the hotel bar to celebrate and got totally smashed.

Having recovered from their first band meeting (and lending their manager enough money to get his car out of the hotel car-park!) early rehearsals for the new band took place, with manager Andy Trueman overseeing affairs, as Gary remembers: *"The first rehearsal was in Graham's garage with just me, Jimmy and Andy."* Jimmy brought a song to the table he'd written which Graham liked straight away. The song later became 'Island In The Sun'. *"That song was a New England song that would have been on our fourth album,"* Gary says. *"The way Andy structured the song writing to Bonnet-Malmsteen-Waldo you get one impression Jimmy had little to do with it."* Talking about these early rehearsals to Sharon Liveton in Creem, Gary told her: *"It was like being back at school, except we're all 35 years old. The neighbours were calling up that we were making too much noise in the garage. One guy was freaking out. He kept asking if we had a permit."*

Another song that began life very early on was one that Graham had already written called 'General Hospital'. *"I did bits of some of the others, but that one was all mine."* Gary also remembers the song: *"The second song we worked on was Graham's, which he had music for and later lyrics. The working title was 'Plunk Plunk', the first two notes of the song!"*

The rock press were soon sniffing around trying to get the story, but Graham was playing it down to begin with: *"I've been in the studio recently with some friends, laying down some stuff in a rock 'n' roll context, but it's sort of here and there at the moment,"* he told Chris Watts in Kerrang! *"It's going to be good, I think. I don't know whether it's going to be called The Graham Bonnet Group yet, it's sort of 'well what shall we do?' you know."*

Managers are often less cautious and it wasn't too long before Andy Trueman was getting the three existing members of the new group some press coverage in Japan. Gary Shea recalls: *"We did press photos for Japan, just us three posing at my house in the Hollywood Hills next to my roommate's Harley Davidson."* They were still waiting for Barry and Zal to arrive from England but this didn't prevent Andy securing the new group a record deal with MCA subsidiary Rocshire Records, on the strength of a handshake and without a note being played.

Rocshire were based in Orange County and, although they had only been operating since 1982, had built up a busy roster of acts. The company was the creation of Clyde 'Rocky' Davis and his wife Shirley (hence Roc Shire). Ex-Rainbow keyboard player Tony Carey later signed to the label and recalled his first meeting with the people behind it all: *"They flew me over first class and picked me up in a stretch limo in Hollywood. But I lived in Hollywood in the Rainbow years and wasn't that impressed with it and I'm from California anyway. They took me to Anaheim where they had a million dollar state-of-the-art recording studio. All these artists were under contract there; including the singer from Tower of Power and Graham Bonnet. If you could sum up my opinion of Graham Bonnet in two words it would be 'Red Trousers' – I don't mean it meanly, it's all I remember!"* he told Fireworks' Rob McKenzie.

But it all went wrong when news broke that their prospective drummer and guitarist would not after all be making the trip over. Zal had decided to go on tour with Robert Palmer and Barry went off to work with Robert Plant. This knocked everyone back to square one and also threatened the band's future. Gary says: *"We got the record deal with no demo music on the strength of the line-up. It was then we learned Barry and Zal could not be part of it. We had to do some serious fast talking."* Gary, Jimmy and Andy started ringing round everyone they knew in a bid to find replacements quickly. They had no intention of crawling around all the clubs in Los Angeles checking out the local scene. Within a few days Andy had asked guitarist Laurence Juber to audition, but the feeling wasn't there for the others. The trio had been recording every rehearsal

and intended doing the same for the auditions, Gary remembers: *"We used Graham's song 'S.O.S.' to audition everyone. The Friday we auditioned Laurence Juber from Wings we also played with drummer Robert Williams from Capt. Beefheart. Laurence was not right; although Andy was quite keen to have Laurence join, as he could see that selling a band on the strength of Wings, Rainbow and New England connections would be great commercially."*

A stroke of luck came his way the following day when Andy happened to be chatting to a friend at a local vinyl store, Ozz Records, where he learned of an excellent young guitarist who was making a name for himself on the local club scene in a band called Steeler. That guitarist was nineteen-year-old Swede, Yngwie Malmsteen, who had been a fan of Graham's since the age of fourteen. Jimmy Waldo had seen Yngwie at the Roxy on Sunset Strip a little earlier and been impressed, and word was already spreading. Ronnie James Dio had been down to watch him on a few occasions, and so had Phil Mogg. Realising he needed to act fast, Andy phoned the guitarist straight away and invited him for an audition at Diamond Sound in Los Angeles. Robert Williams agreed to help them out so they could properly audition Yngwie. Gary says: *"We got Yngwie that weekend. I was really impressed with his burning enthusiasm, as well as his great playing. Andy vowed that he would go out and get the hottest guitarist in L.A., and have him here by the weekend, and he definitely delivered on that one. Those were the only guitarists we tried out."*

Graham came over for the auditions and sang some Rainbow material (which Yngwie knew) and solo songs, and must have been impressed at how things were shaping up already.

Gary explained that it was his New England connections which enabled the project to more forward so quickly. *"Some A&R friends of mine and Jimmy's at MCA who were big New England supporters wanted to see us put another band together. They were the ones who told us of Rocshire in the first place. Without that connection the whole thing would not have happened. Young Yngwie may not have heard of New England at the time, but we had already played every arena in North America two or three times and brought a lot of savvy and connections to the table, which we were able to use to promote the band. Andy knew of us beforehand when he was with ELO and daily pumped us for info and consultation. Graham stayed home and had little input on the day-to-day running of the group, but was the one who complained and whined the most!"*

Even though there was still no permanent drummer, the critical lead guitarist position was close to being settled, although Yngwie did agree to meet up with Phil Mogg and see what he had in mind. But at the end of the day he saw working with Graham, Gary and Jimmy as the perfect move forward for himself. He also had a batch of new songs he had written which he felt would work well for Graham. Once the deal was settled, Yngwie would also go over to Graham's house to write too. Graham described him as being *"just what we are looking for. A heavy sort of Ritchie Blackmore-type guitarist."*

Apart from the music, the musicians had been thinking about a name, but whatever anyone came up with it never seemed to stick. Gary says: *"Graham, Jimmy and I wanted a strong name like Tiger or Hunter, but Yngwie wanted dungeons and dragons and wanted our name to be Excalibur. One day we were sitting around I said that after New England always being in the 'N' section of the stores it would be cool to have a name that started off at the front with an A, somewhere between Abba and Aerosmith, something like (off the top of my head) Alcatraz. We could say 'no parole from rock and roll, disturbing the peace', etc. Trueman jumped up screaming what a genius I was. That was my fifteen seconds of brilliance."*

Alcatraz was now added to the list of band names as Graham recalls: *"Gary Shea came up with the name. We had a list of 'rock' names and that was one of them, along with animal names, etc."* Alcatraz was chosen but while Gary obviously had the San Francisco prison in mind when he thought of the name, not wanting to cause confusion, he added an extra 'z' to it. *"The name Alcatrazz sounds heavy metal, but we just wanted a tough sounding name,"* he told Mary Toledo in Faces magazine.

Rocshire had now been told about the line-up changes but still had enough faith in the project to keep it going, and allowed Alcatrazz to audition drummers at their own studio from now on. Over the following month quite a few put in an appearance, from local players to well known names. Reports were coming out of LA saying that Aynsley Dunbar, who had been with Jefferson Starship for four years, had got the position but that was only half true. In fact Aynsley had indicated that he would be happy to do the album, but did not want to join the band full-time. Bill Lordan, who had played with Robin Trower for many years, did audition but it didn't gell properly. They actually thought they had solved the problem when Clive Burr flew over from England. Clive had played on the first three Iron Maiden albums, and was apparently recommended by Cozy Powell. But, even though he lasted a week, in the end he too didn't fit, as Graham explained: *"Clive didn't seem to work well during rehearsals. I don't know if it was due to jet lag or what. He seemed very tired,"* he said to Hit Parader's Charley Crespo. One of the big problems with Clive turned out to be that he wasn't prepared to move out to LA on a reasonably permanent basis. Finding a suitable drummer was becoming a real issue, as Graham told Cozy Powell during a phone conversation. Cozy told him not to worry, and he would personally play on any recordings for an album if they couldn't find anyone, even though he had just joined Whitesnake.

Gary recalls the endless auditioning: *"Bill Lordan didn't want us to interfere with his going to an ashram in Israel. Ed Cassidy from Spirit was very cool but not right, and my good friend Jon Hyde, who went on to play in Detective, had a broken collarbone and fingers from a bicycle accident and he didn't play double bass*

drums, which we wanted."

However, just as they were starting to lose hope, someone heard a tape of Jannaro 'Jan' Uvena playing on Alice Cooper's 'Zipper Catches Sin' album from the year before. On the strength of this he was invited for an audition and, as it turned out, everyone was pleasantly surprised because he just clicked right into place, playing just the sort of loud, heavy drumming the band wanted to hear. Gary says: *"It took one month to find the right drummer. Eventually Jan came in and played brilliantly."*

Once again though, manager Andy stuck his oar in. He didn't think Alice Cooper (whose glory days, it seemed, were a thing of the past) was a big enough name, and wouldn't help his vision of a long list of groups he could reference in press releases. Rather than just come out and say so, he went round to everyone individually and said the others didn't like him. It was a while before the band realised what had been going on as Gary recalls: *"A few weeks later we talked among ourselves and found out we all liked him very much and that Andy had lied to all of us, a very big omen for the future of things."*

It had taken far longer than everyone had ever imagined it would to complete the line-up and for good or bad Andy Trueman now saw himself as the sixth member. Graham more or less had to go along with the situation. There was always an option for him to keep the musicians on a retainer but deep down he really didn't want that. Apart from it being very expensive, there was also a great deal of responsibility to take on board. In essence Graham just wanted to be in a band, not his band, but a band where everyone was equal, because he enjoyed being part of a team.

Meanwhile, The Police session Graham had done the previous October was released by RCA Records during April in the UK and Japan, appropriately titled 'Arrested: The Royal Philharmonic Orchestra & Friends Presents The Music of The Police'. It was an interesting take on their music, elevated by the use of an orchestra, and if you happened to be attending one of Ian Paice's drum clinics at that time you would have heard the album being played through the PA system before and afterwards.

Back in LA, Graham also took a job with locally-based hard rock band 3rd Stage Alert, who had contacted him to see if he would be interested in producing their demo tape. Quite why they approached Graham, who had no real production experience, isn't known!

At last though, the deal with Rocshire Records was finalised on May 13th and Alcatrazz immediately entered into an intense two-week rehearsal period for their planned album recording sessions. The producer was Dennis MacKay, who had previously worked with such artists as David Bowie, Judas Priest, Gary Moore, Jeff Beck and Tommy Bolin. Gary says now he can't really recall how Dennis got the job: *"I think he was doing work at Rocshire at the time. In hindsight Jimmy and I wish we had chosen Andy Johns instead. We felt he had a substance problem at the time, but he would have recorded it much better."*

At the beginning of June the band started recording in Rocshire's studios in Anaheim on the outskirts of Los Angeles. Graham had in his mind an album which might be seen as a progression or follow-up to Rainbow's 'Down To Earth'. Yngwie and Jimmy had come up with most of the music, although there were exceptions, with Yngwie only writing the bridge / break for 'Island In The Sun' according to Gary. Graham provided all the vocal melody lines and lyrics to the songs, and began with 'Hiroshima Mon Amour', where he drew inspiration from the film of the same name which he remembered seeing as a child: *"The words just came to me one afternoon"* he says. As for the lyrics for 'General Hospital', Graham dug into his past to recall his feelings when he was admitted to Whittington hospital in London in 1973 after one of his first epileptic seizures.

As was increasingly the case for bands at the time, firms soon came round to strike endorsement deals, a representative from Aria guitars even visiting them in the studio. A short while later, Graham, Gary and Jimmy were also endorsed by Randall Equipment. In the meantime, Andy had signed a separate deal for the band with Polydor Records in Japan, where Graham's past continued to reappear. This time it was Hideki Saijo releasing a speeded-up cover version of 'Night Games' in Japanese, which became a big hit. Naturally Phonogram there then re-released Graham's original version to try and cash in.

The new album sessions went very well and towards the end of July Alcatrazz had virtually finished recording their debut. Gary recalls: *"We wrote and rehearsed all the music within two months."* It was suggested at the time that Yngwie recorded all his solos in one take, and that the rhythm guitar parts were initially recorded through a Rockman amplifier then overdubbed with Marshalls, although in relation to the guitar solos Gary recalls: *"Yngwie's solos went quickly, but not necessarily all in one take."*

With the backing tracks and most of the vocals finished, the record company were eager to get the album completed, and Graham finished his parts off at Skyline studios in Topanga, including the final song: *"I had to make a song up in a hurry one afternoon as they wanted the album ready for pressing. So 'Big Foot' was a hurried song and it was all done in one day. Very quick for me, as my vocals take forever usually, because they are never good enough for me."*

The record was now ready for mixing while Alcatrazz did some publicity shoots, including one with photographer Diana Lyn at the prison itself in San Francisco bay where they posed in the very last remaining look-out tower standing (the others having collapsed through rust and old age.) It was a very windy day and that last tower was swaying horribly from left to right...

Money seemed no object for Rocshire Records. They had really gone to town promoting their artists and now they were talking about Alcatrazz being the next supergroup. While the label were deciding on a single, the band were trying to come up with a title for the album: one was simply 'Alcatrazz', but the excellent idea Gary Shea had come up with a few months earlier, 'No Parole From Rock 'N' Roll', was the obvious choice. Rocshire decided upon the commercial 'Island In The Sun' to lead the way, with the haunting and beautiful 'Hiroshima Mon Amour' as the B-side, and an October release.

Wanting to create a memorable promotional video, Michael Miner (who later went on to co-write the very successful film RoboCop in 1987), was asked to direct. Graham went over to Hawaii without the band, although accompanied by some attractive models, to film on the beach for a few days. *"The 'Island In The Sun' video was done with a severe hangover! I got to hang out with this millionaire's wife, who was the girl in the video. She took a bit of a fancy to me, which was quite surprising! But the whole thing was a lot of fun. The prison parts were shot on the Clint Eastwood Escape From Alcatraz set in Culver City."* In those days videos even used to have their own reviews and one writer enjoyed the offering: *"Good story and innovating special effects revolving around the group's name. One of the better heavy metal outings, helped by the group's catchy song."* A second, shorter video for the Japanese market, which just showed the band synching to the track, was also filmed, as were interviews with the members of the band about their careers and the group for promotional purposes.

As it would not be long before Alcatrazz would be performing to an audience, as they started rehearsing they knew they needed to extend their set as the ten songs from their album, even if they might all work live, wouldn't be enough. They quickly decided to cover two of Graham's Rainbow era hits, 'Since You Been Gone' and 'All Night Long', along with the album epic 'Lost In Hollywood'. MSG's 'Desert Song' was also included. Yngwie got to include his track 'Incubus' as a powerful set opener, and a new song he had come up with called 'Evil Eye' was added as a solo vehicle during the show.

It had been suggested that Alcatrazz would make their debut with some warm-up dates in the UK, then over to Japan in October, with Europe or America penciled in for November and December before a full-scale return to the UK in January. However, this schedule went out the window as the band's management favoured touring in America in a bid to try and promote the album there first.

A series of US dates were duly booked for the autumn but all the early gigs had to be cancelled, because Graham was showing signs of suffering from Bell's palsy (which can cause temporary paralysis of the facial muscles). While he took time off, promotion for the album started in earnest. One particular photo shoot, which became the front cover of the album, showed a slab of volcanic rock with a prisoner's arms (Jimmy Waldo's) reaching out from within the bars of the prison window, with the rock suspended in the air against the background of a burning sky. Rocshire came up with the line 'No Escape From Alcatrazz' for their adverts and Graham was suitably impressed by the work: *"They were promoting Alcatrazz like crazy, any way they could."*

The single and album were released on October 15th in America (and in Japan soon after, with a poster of pin-up boy Graham inside). 'No Parole From Rock 'N' Roll' crept into the US Billboard chart but struggled to just No. 128 and, after being in the charts for only seven weeks, it disappeared from view; a disappointing result given all the work. Graham described the music as *"the thinking man's heavy metal"* to Laura Canyon. *"It's got more melodies and I've got some good tunes together that help me, sort of, sing out more than I have done in previous years. Sort of operatic in a way – longer notes, proving what I can do, instead of just rasping rock 'n' roll licks. It's nice to sing out a bit and use your guts."*

If the album had a flaw it was in the production, which was workmanlike but lacked edge. Graham appreciated the problem, but argued that the album had been done in a hurry: *"We were looking for something individual, for an Alcatrazz sound but, since we'd been together for such a short time, there really wasn't such a sound. We went in and sort of copied other songs, in a way, and just did what we expected to do,"* he told BAM's KJ Doughton.

And for a debut on a limited budget it punched above its weight for some. One reviewer in America was more than happy: *"With nary a weak moment on the entire album, Bonnet has outdone himself as a lyricist, especially on the cruncher 'Hiroshima Mon Amour'."* As for the very catchy and commercial 'Island In The Sun', despite quite a lot of air play (and the video airing on MTV), it failed to break out and give them that important radio hit. Kerrang!'s Howard Johnson described 'Island In The Sun' as a *"tremendous hunk of US AOR power, bursting at its bubbling seams with power, precision and a positively irresistible melody. It's an undoubted rock gem that really aches and itches to be heard."* The enthusiasm ran out after that though, and he was far from impressed with the rest of the album: *"I don't think I can recall a time when I've been so disappointed with an album. Alcatrazz have as much idea of rock 'n' roll as Whitesnake do of a stable line-up, which is incredibly distressing when the potential should be there. Much of*

the material smacks of some pseudo-Japanese influence creeping in which is about as welcome as the Japs were at Pearl Harbour, but at least they were effective. 'Hiroshima Mon Amour', 'Kree Nakoorie', 'Big Foot'. Very good, but like, er … what's it all about? 'Too Young To Die, Too Drunk To Live' and 'Starcarr Lane' give a glimmer of hope," he suggested, but maybe he was missing the point as over in Japan the album took off, quickly selling 100,000 copies and going gold. This wasn't surprising as Graham was so popular there but it took this to wake his manager up to the possibilities, and Andy Trueman quickly started organising a Japanese tour. Masaya Uchimura recalls how much publicity the band were getting there: *"The record and tour was broadly promoted on major radio stations, by music magazines and by Udo, the top concert promoters in Japan. Masa Itoh, the editor of Burrn! magazine, also played Alcatrazz on his radio programme. He wrote the liner notes for the Japanese inlay and the notes for the tour programme. The record company set up a telephone service enabling fans to listen to three tracks down the phone. So, even before the record was released there was a huge Alcatrazz buzz in Japan. The 11,000 tickets for the shows were quickly sold out."*

In America, Rocshire's promotion department got Michael Miner back in for another promo video clip, this time for 'Hiroshima Mon Amour', the B-side of the single. Graham recalls the shoot: *"It was filmed in a big rehearsal room at SIR studios in Hollywood where we'd done the previous video. It is ideal for shooting videos. I rehearsed there with Rainbow. It was a long day of doing the same thing over and over. Nothing special, just lip-synching to the song and waving the flag at the end, which got a round of applause every time I did it. The camera guys thought it was a great shot for some reason!"*

Alcatrazz eventually kicked off their 'No Parole From Rock 'N' Roll' tour in Bakersfield towards the end of October. After a show in Fresno, the band played on home soil at the Country Club in Reseda on October 31st. Of those first shows, Gary says: *"We chose those because they are out in the desert, good-to-get-the-act-together kind of places."* The set for these early shows was 'Incubus', 'Too Young To Die, Too Drunk To Live', Starcarr Lane' (which was soon dropped), 'General Hospital', 'Kree Nakoorie', 'Island In The Sun', 'Evil Eye', 'Hiroshima Mon Amour', 'Big Foot', 'Yngwie Solo', 'Since You Been Gone', 'Suffer Me', 'Desert Song', 'Jet To Jet', plus a Rainbow double-header to close, 'All Night Long' and 'Lost In Hollywood'.

From here the schedule went to pieces a little though and during November both sold-out shows in San Francisco were cancelled because Graham was sick. Yngwie, though, flew to San Francisco and made an appearance with local band (and planned support act) Anvil Chorus after their set. Alcatrazz's planned return date at the County Club in Reseda on November 24th was also initially cancelled but rescheduled for December 8th (and is often wrongly cited as their live debut). Other shows in San Francisco, Fresno and Huntington Beach prior to Christmas and in Milwaukee on Boxing Day went ahead. The set remained basically the same, although some songs were juggled around or dropped in a bid to find out which worked the best for the live show.

Amazingly, given Graham's stint with Rainbow, the band still had not got a record deal in Europe. During December Andy Trueman opened negotiations to sign Alcatrazz to a major record label in the UK, Europe and Australasia, hoping to get one company to cover them all. It was well into the New Year when he eventually persuaded RCA Records to come on board, by which time any hope of a projected January 1st release had gone out the window.

On December 27th Alcatrazz teamed up on a triple bill with Saga and headliners Eddie Money for five shows in five days. Gary remembers the tour well: *"We did our first arena shows, Columbus Coliseum was December 27th, my birthday, and the New Year's Eve gig was in Cleveland, Ohio, at Richfield Coliseum, a gig New England had played five years before with Kiss. We had a killer show. The people are filing in and we have nine songs to play."* But things weren't going so well with Graham, as Gary recalls: *"At song eight Graham comes

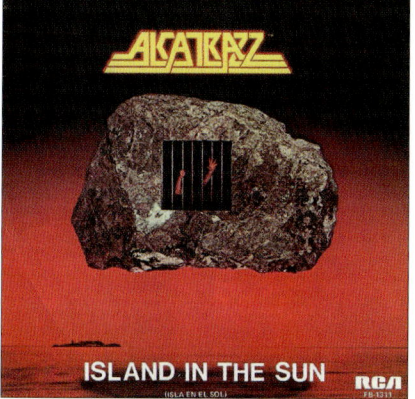

over to me and says 'I can't hear myself, I'm leaving'. He proceeds to walk off the stage in the dark. I look at Yngwie and yell 'solo'! We do the last two songs as instrumentals and the crowd is getting weird. We run down to the dressing room fuming mad and Yngwie clocks Graham right in the head full force. Jimmy is next in line but Andy blocks him. We take Graham back to his room and he throws the first of a series of epileptic fits, which Jimmy had prior experience of. We tie him to the bed while he is screaming out relatives' names in England. The next day Graham remembered nothing and besides a sore head we learned he cracked two ribs because he just walked off the back of the stage and dropped down fifteen feet onto road cases!"* Knowing of Graham's epileptic background, this was something the band took very seriously.

Through Michael Miner, Graham was approached around this time to be in a film called Another State Of Mind, playing two roles - a musician and, once again, James Dean. An Alcatrazz song was to be the theme tune and a host of top musicians were lined up for the soundtrack. Graham says: *"It never came to anything, but it was a great story. The idea was to have Alcatrazz music with a James Dean thing, including what would have happened had he lived. So it would have gone on to the guy being 40 or 50 years old. It was really a good idea to bring heavy rock music in to this kind of thing about poor James Dean."*

To keep momentum going for the LP, Rocshire Records came up with a limited 12" promotional EP at the beginning of the year featuring both tracks off the single on the A-side and the interviews the band had recorded a few months earlier on the reverse, and distributed it to a number of radio stations. Another stab at radio exposure came via one of the then popular live radio special albums. Alcatrazz played the Country

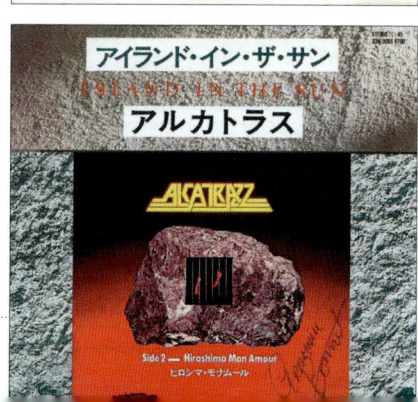

Club in Reseda on January 7th 1984 and their ten-song set was recorded by RKO radio in Los Angeles. RKO edited the set, added gaps for local DJs and commercials (or in this case cues added by DJ Jim Ladd for his Captured Live! show) and pressed it up to send to all the stations which syndicated the show on February 20th. Once aired, stations were supposed to return the album to RKO but inevitably copies went astray and fell into the hands of bootleggers who quickly pirated it. It was not released officially until 2010, and even then under the erroneous title of 'Live '83'. Later in January Alcatrazz appeared live on the American TV programme Rock Palace in Hollywood, performing three songs from their album: 'Too Young To Die, Too Drunk To Live', 'Hiroshima Mon Amour' and 'Island In The Sun'.

With the Japanese tour now booked, and sold out, Rocshire agreed to record one of the shows for an official live album (why they didn't simply use the RKO recording isn't clear). They also decided to have the show filmed as well.

Graham was really looking forward to returning to Japan where, back in 1980, with Rainbow he was very popular and won many fans over. As MSG's 1982 tour there fronted by Graham never happened, a lot of fans had been disappointed and were keen to see him live again. During rehearsals for the tour Graham's 'Night Games' was added to the set, along with the Eddie Cochran number 'Somethin' Else'. Graham says: *"It was my idea, just for the hell of it! Get a bit of Fifties' music in there. It was mainly for the Japanese fans' amusement."* It also enabled him to plug the Aria guitars the band had been supplied with: *"I did play it on stage in 'Somethin' Else'. That was the one made by Aria that looks like Chuck Berry's Gibson. I also used it sometimes when we played 'Jailhouse Rock'."* The latter was in fact only ever done during rehearsals for a

ALCATRAZZ IN JAPAN 1984

...esday, January 17th	Andy Trueman and Graham Bonnet depart for Tokyo
...aturday, January 21st	Remaining members of party depart for Tokyo
...onday, January 23rd	Rehearsal in Tokyo
...uesday, January 24th	OSAKA FESTIVAL HALL
...ednesday, January 25th	Travel to Nagoya
...hursday, January 26th	NAGOYA SHI KOKAIDO HALL
...riday, January 27th	Travel to Tokyo
...aturday, January 28th	TOKYO SUN PLAZA HALL
...unday, January 29th	TOKYO SUN PLAZA HALL
Monday, January 30th	Day off (Tokyo)
Tuesday, January 31st	Day off (Tokyo)
Wednesday, February 1st	Travel to Honolulu

ALCATRAZZ
FEBRUARY/MARCH DATES

DATE	CITY	VENUE
Fri. 24th February		
Sat. 25th February	HOLLYWOOD, CA	
Sun. 26th February	Travel to Tucson	The Palladium
Mon. 27th February	TUCSON, AZ	-
Tues. 28th February	PHOENIX AZ	Rockefellers
Wed. 29th February	Travel	-
Thurs. 1st March	ALBUQUERQUE, NM	Graham Central Station
Fri. 2nd March	DENVER, CO	-
Sat. 3rd March	Travel to Pu...	Graham Central S...
Sun. 4th March		
Mon. 5t...		

ALCATRAZZ
TOUR DATES — 5.10.1984

DATE	CITY	VENUE	CAP.	PROMO
Fri. May 18th	TULSA, OK	Brady Auditorium	2,771	Steve L (314) 56
Sat. May 19th	OMAHA, NEB	Music Hall	2,608	Steve I (314) 5
Sun. May 20th	JOPLIN, MO	Memorial Hall	3,000	Ted M (816) 3
Mon. May 21st	travel day			
Tue. M...	...OH	Sports Arena	5,000	Jules (216)
			9,000	Jules (216)

DE NOVO MUSIC GROUP INC. DE NOVO MUSIC GROUP INC. DE NOVO MUSIC GROUP INC. DE NOVO MUSIC GROUP INC. DE NOVO MUSIC GROUP INC. DE NOVO MUSIC GROUP INC. DE NOVO MUSIC GROUP INC. DE NOVO MUSIC
24514 CALVERT STREET   SUITE 210   WOODLAND HILLS, CA 91367   TEL. 818

ALCATRAZZ/U.S.A. 1983
BASIC PROMOTER INFORMATION

	CITY	VENUE	PROMOTER	BANDS
19th	SAN FRANSISCO	WOLFGANGS	QUEENIE TAYLOR (415) 441 4333	ALCATRAZZ ANVIL CHORUS
20th	FRESNO	WARNERS STAR THEATRE	ROCKIN CHAIR (JIM WORTHMAN) (209) 521 6310	GIRLSCHOOL ALCATRAZZ
21st	HUNTINGDON BEACH	GOLDEN BEAR	KEVIN KIRBY (714) 536 3192	ALCATRAZZ
26th	MILWAUKEE	SOUTH EXHIBIT HALL WEST ALICE	STARDATE RANDY McELRATH (414) 765 0133	ALCATRAZZ
27th	COLUMBUS	COLISEUM (VETS MEM)	JULES BELKIN (216) 464 5990	ALCATRAZZ SAGA EDDIE MONEY
28th	COLUMBUS	COLISEUM (VETS MEM)	JULES BELKIN (216) 464 5990	ALCATRAZZ SAGA EDDIE MONEY
29th	DETROIT	COBO HALL	JULES BELKIN	ALCATRAZZ SAGA EDDIE MONEY
30th	BATTLE CREEK	KELLOG ARENA	JULES BELKIN	ALCATRAZZ SAGA

MEMORANDUM

Wednesday, 25th April,

TO	: all ALCATRAZZ touring personnel
FROM	: JAKE DUNCAN
SUBJECT	: upcoming tour dates

Sat. 28th April	Pomona Valley Auditorium, Pomona, CA
Fri. 11th May	Radio City, Anaheim, CA
Sat. 12th May	Kabuki Theatre, San Francisco, CA
Sun 13th May	Sherwood Hall, Salinas, CA

bit of fun. The band also prepared for Japan with a couple of warm-up dates to see what the audience made of 'Somethin' Else' and Yngwie's new instrumental 'Coming Bach' which was added to the set.

Graham and Andy were the first to fly to Tokyo on January 17th, the rest of the band departing four days later. They were due to perform four shows in six days (unaware that they would also have to do a matinee in Tokyo on the final day), with a rehearsal in Tokyo on the 23rd and their first show in Osaka the following day. Alcatrazz then traveled to Nagoya for their second gig two days later, and then back to Tokyo for three shows in two days at the Nakano Sun Plaza Hall on January 28th and 29th. The Tokyo show on the 28th is the one they had decided to film and record, with the live album only for release in America and Japan and video for Japan only.

There was, however, one potential issue building up. Yngwie had started to develop his own fan following and seemed determined to build on this regardless of the band. In Japan he took his self-publicity a stage further and was constantly soloing over everything on stage, even standing in front of Graham while he was trying to sing. This didn't look good and it didn't sound good either, as Graham points out: *"Yngwie wanted to be a star, and wanted all eyes on him on stage."* The Japanese rock press duly featured him heavily, with interviews and the tab scores for the songs published. To give him his due he certainly had no issue reproducing the Alcatrazz and Rainbow material live, although his homage to Ritchie Blackmore in looks, guitars, and style did seem to be carried a little too far at times.

But the shows in Japan were a big success and proved to Graham that there was definitely a life after Rainbow. The set for the Japanese shows was 'Incubus', 'Too Young To Die, Too Drunk To Live', 'Hiroshima Mon Amour', 'Night Games', 'Big Foot', 'Island In The Sun', 'Kree Nakoorie', 'Yngwie Solo - Coming Bach', 'Since You Been Gone', 'Suffer Me', 'Desert Song', 'Jet To Jet', 'Evil Eye', 'Lost In Hollywood', 'All Night Long' and 'Somethin' Else', though again the songs were changed around at some shows. An impressive glossy LP sized tour programme was produced and Graham was interviewed on the famous TV show Best Hit USA, as well as doing numerous other interviews. Recalling the tour now, he says: *"We were huge with that first album. I didn't think Alcatrazz would get the same reaction as Rainbow, but it was a nice surprise. Even more adoration, I think, than the Rainbow days. We were followed everywhere by fans in taxis, etc… It was like The Beatles kind of following, really silly and quite unbelievable! All the guitar manufacturers were giving us freebees, and other companies gave us tape recorders, etc. We were young and the fans were just amazing and shaking with excitement when we spoke with them. It was a time that I won't forget."*

The shows over, and the live material in the can, the band had two days off to explore the city, flying back via Honolulu on February 1st for a show, a flight Gary sort of recalls: *"When we left Tokyo we had the whole downstairs first class lounge to ourselves, and drunk everything, and I mean everything, they had!"* The band played at the Honolulu Campus Centre Ballroom on February 3rd, before returning to Los Angeles the day after.

Once back in America, and with the band still on a high after all the Japanese excitement, Andy Trueman brought in Lester Claypool to mix the Tokyo show in Rocshire's studio. A few overdubs were necessary to correct mistakes but as Graham says: *"We did a few things, but not much."* With Andy and Lester producing the album, nine songs were chosen by the band and as far as the title was concerned, it was quickly christened 'Live Sentence'.

Meanwhile, Yngwie had always fancied learning to drive and had been practicing a little with his bandmates. Gary recalls: *"Jimmy was trying to teach Yngwie how to drive. After he almost drove us over a cliff we two former kamikaze cab drivers said enough is enough and took the wheel away, never again to try and*

teach him."

Back on the road, Alcatrazz continued to include 'Somethin' Else' in their encore, though not everyone was up for it. During a show at Graham Central Station on February 27th in Phoenix, things boiled over. *"Yngwie hated the fact that we elected to do 'Somethin' Else' for a third encore and Graham and Jimmy would also play guitars,"* recalls Gary. *"He even refused to have Graham's amp on his side of the stage! Graham sang the shit out of that song. It was so cool to hear him sing it and play the song. It all came to a head when we headlined in Phoenix and Rob Halford, who lives there, came to say hi to Graham. Yngwie refused to play the song and ran out the back door to the tour bus leaving the rest of us confused and angry."* This led to a huge row on the bus, with the driver joining in as Yngwie had scratched the bus furniture with a case and wouldn't apologise.

The band made a trip to Puerto Rico on March 2nd to support Canadian band Loverboy the following day at the Roberto Clemente Coliseum, a sporting and concert arena which seated 10,000. Alcatrazz took it to the crowd, so much so that the headliners were worried about having to go on after them. Gary remembers the show: *"It took them one-and-a-half hours to take the stage after we stirred up the crowd. The kids were lighting fireworks indoors while we played and it was a wild crowd. When Loverboy eventually came out – fourteen hit songs or not - the crowd was not the same!"* From there it was back to The States for six shows in Texas concluding at Nick's Uptown in Dallas on March 11th.

The group were then due a few days off but were offered a prestigious support slot in Seattle opening for Heart at extremely short notice. Gary recalls the event: *"We got a call on a Thursday afternoon at 5:00 pm wanting to know if we could do two shows with Heart at The Paramount Theater in Seattle on Friday and Saturday. It involved a marathon 24 hour overnight drive from LA to Seattle (just about the entire length of the west coast) to get there in time for a 5:00 pm sound-check. The shows went well, especially since we were in Heart's hometown. Mark Andes, Heart's bassist, and I were friends before he got the Heart gig and I got into Alcatrazz. New England had sold out The Paramount as a headliner during the summer of 1979, five years earlier."* The remainder of March saw Alcatrazz headlining more shows and gaining some valuable exposure.

The following month found them on the road with Night Ranger for half a dozen or so dates. The gigs went well, but when Alcatrazz played in Bakersfield they experienced the first onstage clash with Yngwie. Gary remembers the

incident clearly: *"Standing behind my bass rig are the bass player and the two guitarists from Night Ranger checking us out. A keyboard break is coming up for Jimmy. Yngwie comes dancing all the way across the stage from his side, behind Graham, past my front and proceeds to solo leaning against Jimmy's keys the whole time with a house spot operator following him against the cue of our light desk. Yngwie begins his retreat, unknown to Graham who is backing up and they collide. They both are going down to the floor, but are trying to keep their balance. The Night Ranger guys are howling behind me in laughter at amateur night!"* In the dressing room afterwards Gary remembers that all hell broke loose with the 'you're fucking fired' – 'no, I fucking quit' – 'fuck you' – 'no, fuck you!' routine. Gary feels their manager chose to take sides, at Alcatrazz's expense: *"In hindsight this is where Andy probably said 'fuck these guys, Yngwie. Graham is too hard to deal with. We'll get you your own band'. And they did."*

Despite this issue, April also saw Rocshire release the 'Live Sentence' album, which spent sixteen weeks on the US Billboard charts, peaking at No. 145. It was also released in Japan and again soon achieved gold status there, but was only available in Europe as an import. Kerrang! reviewed an import copy and came down hard on it, feeling it was perhaps a little early in their career for a live set, possibly missing the point that many bands were recording live albums for the Japanese market at that time: *"It might reap the odd yen in the Orient, Graham, but this is milking the Western public just a mite too much. There is very little difference between live and studio Alcatrazz."*

Towards the end of the month Alcatrazz headlined a series of shows mainly in the California area, but the clashes between the band and Yngwie, or more accurately, between Graham and Yngwie, continued. *"When we played live"*, Graham says, *"I'd be doing my verse and he's soloing over everything I'm singing. He had no stage presentation or anything. He would come in front of me and he is taller than me. He'd go and do his stuff while I'm singing. Then he'd knock the mic out of my hand. I mean, I gave this guy a job, he didn't hire me! He's treading on me and I got so angry."*

"It finally ended up with him trying to kill me one night," Graham told Chris Collingwood in Metal CD. *"I'd gone behind the speakers and accidentally tripped over a cable, so all his gear went off. He came running after me, grabbed hold of my neck, stuck his thumbs right where my tonsils were and told me he was going to kill me, or at least make it so I wouldn't ever be able to sing again."* Graham wasn't even sure what had stirred the guitarist up so much: *"It was an accident and I didn't even know I had done it."*

The Californian tour came to an end at Sherwood Hall in Salinas on May 13th and it was clear that Yngwie was now beginning to attract more publicity than the band and, even though he was enjoying it, it wasn't doing him any favours. The rest of the members pointed out to him that they wanted to go in a more 'radio friendly' direction. Not AOR or soft rock, but just enough so the radio stations would pick up on what they were doing. Experience was telling them this (it had after all worked well for Rainbow), but Yngwie wasn't happy with trying to curb his antics and wanted to carry on exactly as things were. The band wasn't having any of it. *"There's no room in rock 'n' roll for attitudes"* Gary told Sharon Liveton of Creem magazine. *"There's a fine line between having confidence in what you do and having an attitude."* Jimmy Waldo agreed: *"With Yngwie we had a Ritchie Blackmore clone thing going on. It just wasn't what we wanted – it was close when we started, and it could have progressed. It didn't progress."* By now 'Yngwie Is God' t-shirts were doing the rounds and something had to give. It was Yngwie who blinked, and told Jimmy that he wanted to leave the band to concentrate on his solo career, although he did opt to stick around for the band's up and coming tour with Ted Nugent. It would be wrong to just blame Yngwie though as occasionally Graham would get completely lost in some songs due to his alcohol intake, and simply didn't know what he was doing.

With all this going on, Andy Trueman took his opportunity to gain ownership of the copyright to all the band's songs, though quite how he managed this isn't known. If that wasn't enough he then told the band he was totally against the idea of holding auditions for replacements for Yngwie prior to the tour with Ted Nugent. The band ignored this of course, but replacing Yngwie wasn't as easy as they thought, as Gary explained to KJ Doughton in BAM: *"I was on the phone for months talking to different guitarists, but they all had the same thing in mind. They were all out to play just like Van Halen, or just like this or just like that. I kept asking who they listened to, or who they wrote like, and they kept referring to the same influences. They were all too influenced by*

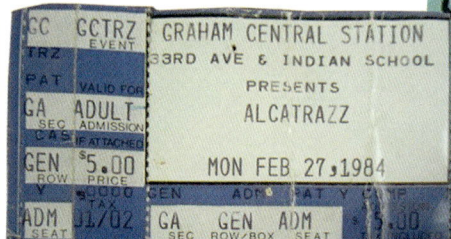

Previous page • L-r: Yngwie Malmsteen, Jimmy Waldo, Jan Uvena, Gary Shea and Graham. Next page; Graham and Yngwie live, June 8 1984, Jackson, New Jersey.

other people. All of us in Alcatrazz like all kinds of bands and musicians, but none of us are hung up on anybody. We just do what we do, whatever feels good."

Jimmy Waldo was a good friend of David Rosenthal, Rainbow's keyboard player at the time and who suggested Steve Vai as a replacement. Steve had just left Frank Zappa's band after being with them for five years and was currently working in a trio. Steve recalled the approach in Kerrang!: *"I heard that Alcatrazz were looking for a guitarist and I knew of Graham just by reputation, Yngwie was still in the band at the time but they had decided to replace him and Jimmy gave me a call. I don't think that the fact that I'd been with Zappa helped a lot and it had crossed my mind that it might obstruct me getting involved in a rock band again. In fact I had submitted tapes to Ozzy and Kiss but I never got calls and heard later that the Zappa background had put them off."*

In fact the Zappa stint was something Alcatrazz were more than happy with, as Jimmy Waldo adds: *"We needed a real musician. Of course we wanted flash, someone who could play his ass off, but we also wanted a musician who understood all about writing and arranging. Someone who just didn't think about guitar, but about music and vocals too – about the whole band. With a background in Zappa's outfit we knew he'd be a great musician."*

With a few days off before they opened for Ted Nugent at the Brady Auditorium in Tulsa, Oklahoma on May 18th, they decided to audition not just Steve Vai but another young guitarist who people were talking about called Chris Impellitteri. Gary and Jimmy thought they would have a little fun with Chris first and called a number he gave out for guitar tuition, as Gary recalls: *"Jimmy put on his heavy southern drawl and asked him if he was any good. And could he play like that Wing Wang guy from Sweden?"* Waiting until Chris ran out of patience they finally confessed who they were and asked him to come down the next day with Steve.

In preparation for the auditions, the full Alcatrazz stage rig was set up at Burbank studios, but the result was something of a dead heat. Gary says: *"Jimmy, Jan and I thought Chris, although a very personable guy, was too similar to Malmsteen in style and we wanted something new. We thought Steve's unique style and energy was refreshing and would take the band in a new direction, but Graham felt he was totally wrong for the band and was impressed with Chris. A heated discussion ensued between Jimmy and Graham, with Jimmy insisting on Steve and Graham pushing Chris. After 'two hours and ten beers' at the Holiday Inn bar in Burbank, Jimmy won the argument and Steve was in the band."*

Steve had actually done his homework and been to seen the band play live and, despite his first solo album having been issued, he seemed up for the gig.

With a suitable replacement now found, the band with Yngwie could look forward to the tour with Ted Nugent, which had now grown to over thirty dates including two shows in Ontario, Canada. The size of the venues ranged from 1,600 at the Club Casino in Hampton Beach, New Hampshire to 16,939 at the Poplar Creek amphitheatre. Yngwie's time in Alcatrazz might be coming

to an end, but it was still no surprise when the band received great reviews for their shows due to the energy they were putting into them, along with the quality of their musicianship. Graham remembers the band being very tight on stage during the tour: *"One day we would be playing in a big arena and next a small hall to about 100 people! It was a very good time. We were all on top form, singing and playing, because we played every day and every place across America. So everyone was well rehearsed and warmed up. Ted liked our band. It was a lot of fun with him and we were grateful for the exposure."*

Alcatrazz needed to trim their set but as is sometimes the case this just gave it more impact. They settled on 'Too Young To Die, Too Drunk To Live', 'Island In The Sun', 'Hiroshima Mon Amour', 'Night Games', 'Kree Nakoorie', Yngwie Solo' and 'Since You Been Gone'. To help break the routine sometimes 'Jet To Jet' would be dropped in instead.

Back in Los Angeles, Steve Vai had been left a batch of songs to learn so when Alcatrazz had completed the tour they could start rehearsing with him immediately and piece everything together quite easily. Meanwhile the band's Japanese tour video was being launched in Tokyo, titled 'Metallic Live', on VHS and Laser Disc. For some reason it retailed at an incredible 13,800 Japanese yen ($172.00). Few fans had that kind of spare cash around.

Yngwie's final show with the band took place at the first ever summer festival in Milwaukee, Wisconsin, on July 7th. He left on good terms with the band as far as he was concerned, but hadn't made many friends, and certainly not with Graham. Having worked with the real thing, he was quick to point up Yngwie's strange crusade, talking to Mick Wall in Kerrang!: *"It wasn't really anything to do with musical differences. He's a little sod, a starstruck little arsehole who started believing everything that the press had to say about him almost before the press had even learned to spell his name. It's just that he thought he was the son of Blackmore or something equally ridiculous!"* But Graham realised, as did the others, that Andy Trueman, who had now been personally managing Yngwie for a few months, saw a much bigger potential paycheck with the Boy Wonder: *"He seemed more bothered about him than us,"* he told Andy Secher in Hit Parader. *"It got to the point if anyone called him concerning us, he'd actually say 'forget about Alcatrazz, let's talk about my other band'."*

CHAPTER 8
God Blessed Video (1984 - 1987)

Featuring: Alcatrazz

ALCATRAZZ ARE BREAKING OUT!

Only six days after Yngwie's departure, the new line-up had the first of a couple of local shows booked, at the De Anza Theater in Riverside on July 13th followed by Perkins Palace in Pasadena two days later. Designed to give Steve Vai the opportunity to get settled in, the band's set was pieced together over three days of rehearsals and as before included songs from 'No Parole From Rock 'N' Roll' and Graham's back catalogue with 'Night Games', which hadn't been played for a while, coming back into the show. Steve was also given a solo slot in the set to show everyone what a talented guitarist he was and, deep down, Graham knew that he was the right choice for Alcatrazz. From the very start of Steve's first show, Graham and the band were in blistering form as they powered through 'Too Young To Die, Too Drunk To Live' and 'Jet To Jet' with absolute perfection. Steve might have been nervous beforehand but was certainly enjoying himself, and Graham was on top form vocally. The recent Ted Nugent tour had certainly kept everyone on their toes and really tightened the band up; plus, Steve was playing Yngwie's parts very well indeed. Inevitably throughout the show the band was met with cries of 'where's Yngwie?' and 'we want Yngwie' but they took it in their stride and Steve certainly made the crowd stand up and take notice. By the end of the gig the audience knew they had seen a great show and one hell of a guitar player. The set for this first show was: 'Too Young To Die, Too Drunk To Live', 'Jet To Jet', 'Night Games', 'Island In The Sun', 'Kree Nakoorie', 'Steve Solo', 'Desert Song', 'Hiroshima Mon Amour' and 'Suffer Me'.

After their great reception in Japan there were plans for Alcatrazz to return to play the Summer Rock Festival, but since Yngwie was no longer in the band, the show was cancelled. Instead the promoters opted for a tour in October, by which time the new line-up would be better known. Masaya Uchimura says: *"Yngwie's departure came as a huge shock to the Japanese fans. The tickets for this tour didn't sell out as quickly as the previous tour, but they were still very hard to get hold of."*

With Steve's feet now firmly under the table, it was clear they would need to cut a new studio album soon, and Steve started writing some songs, leaving room for lyrics to be added by Graham. The singer had now really warmed to Steve, because his song-writing and playing was completely different to Yngwie's. Steve seemed far more in tune with what the band wanted, while his inventiveness and a very different way of working with chords certainly impressed Graham: *"Because of his time working with Frank Zappa he came up with a lot of unexpected things, what you wouldn't call the normal things. He certainly brought the best out of me and I think me out of him. The band had our own individual style and we moved away from that Rainbow Mk 2 thing with Steve. The songs we did were more crafted and thought out because of his ability. It was certainly my favourite time in the band, without doubt."*

On the record front, RCA Records finally began pushing the first album in Europe and Australasia with 'Island In The Sun' as a single, though most fans had probably already bought the album on import anyway. In the UK they brought copies of the album over from Germany rather than press locally. No sooner was the studio album out than 'Live Sentence' was available as an import in the UK, Europe and Australasia.

Across the pond rehearsals were going well with new songs being knocked in to shape. All the band members were contributing and everyone felt optimistic. On the business side, however, and unbeknown to the band, things were in a complete mess, and it was only later that they discovered what was going on, as Gary points out: *"Andy Trueman had stolen tens of thousands of dollars from the band. He was making secret side deals, and was a heavy substance user. Important record sales, merchandise sales and concert gross information were totally unknown by the band, and the band's bank accounts were in complete disarray."* But then, if things weren't bad enough, Rocshire Records was suddenly closed down by the US Federal Marshalls. Incredibly, it was alleged that the record company had been financed by money which had been embezzled from the Hughes Aircraft Company where Shirley Davis had worked. As a result all the label's assets including master tapes were confiscated. It was reported on August 11th that Rocshire Records had been placed in court receivership pending an FBI investigation into charges by the Hughes Aircraft Company that label founder Rocky Davis and his wife Shirley had diverted more than $3 million from the Hughes accounts to finance the label. As Alcatrazz had built up a good reputation and a decent following over the past twelve months or so, luckily they secured a release from their contract with Rocshire just a few days before the scandal broke, and avoided being left in contractual limbo. It wasn't too long before they had several labels chasing them down. They had spoken to Capitol Records before anyone else, and as they seemed really keen on the band, Alactrazz decided to sign a worldwide deal with them.

When the talk got round to who should produce their new album, legendary South African Edwin H. (Eddie) Kramer's name cropped up, a man whose credits included Led Zeppelin, Jimi Hendrix, Kiss and John Mayall. On being approached he had just finished producing Fastway and Triumph and was keen to give it a go. Prior to going in to the studio, it was arranged for Eddie to go to Japan with the band in October and get a feel for the music. Yet again there was also talk in the press about Alcatrazz playing in the UK, but other territories had prior claim, as Graham told Sounds' Sylvie Simmons: *"Before the end of the year there's Japan, Australia and the States to fit in first."*

Pre-production work for the band's second studio offering took place at Pacific Sound in Chatsworth. *"The songs that we're writing,"* Graham told KJ Doughton in BAM, *"to me have the same kind of feel that The Beatles had –*

Alcatrazz Mk 2 • *L-r Steve Vai, Jan Uvena, Jimmy Waldo, Graham and Gary Shea.*

'something different' that incorporates heavy guitar playing with other kinds of music which is basically what The Beatles did. They covered all the bases and reached every kind of audience."

With the second Japanese tour looming, the band took a break from studio work for a few rehearsals and even a warm-up gig at their regular venue, the Country Club in Reseda, on September 29th. No fewer than eight new songs were included in the set, alongside five from 'No Parole From Rock 'N' Roll', plus the two Bonnet-era Rainbow classics and Graham's UK solo hit 'Night Games'. For a bit of fun at rehearsals the band did another cover, as Gary recalls: *"We did do a pretty good version of Rare Earth's 'Get Ready' with Steve in the band but, again, only at practice."* The new set list, debuted at the Country Club, was 'Breaking The Heart Of The City', 'Jet To Jet', 'Skyfire', 'Sons And Lovers', 'Hiroshima Mon Amour', 'God Blessed Video', 'Will You Be Home Tonight', 'Kree Nakoorie', 'Steve Solo' (including 'Lighter Shade Of Green'), 'Since You Been Gone', 'Painted Lover', 'Suffer Me', 'Stripper', 'Too Young To Die, Too Drunk To Live', 'Night Games' and 'All Night Long'.

On October 1st, the band flew out to Japan and the following afternoon rehearsed for three hours at Leo Music's B Studio in the Tokyo suburb of Shibuya-ku. The Japanese fans got a very big surprise, because none of them had any idea that the band's set list would include any new songs. And they got an even bigger surprise when Alcatrazz included 'Kojo no Tsuki' ("The Moon Over The Lake'), a Japanese folk song which the Scorpions had also pulled out of the bag when they played in Tokyo in 1978.

All shows began (as is traditional in Japan) at 6:30 pm and the opening night of the tour saw Alcatrazz play the Kinrou Kaikan in Nagoya on October 3rd. The following evening the band were in Osaka at the Amagasaki Archaic Hall, then they travelled to Tokyo the next day for a weekend off prior to three shows across four days beginning at the Shibuya Kokaido on October 8th. With another day off it was time to prepare for the filming of the concert at the Kosei Nenkin Hall the next day, the real reason Eddie Kramer had been flown out. A sound-check took place at 1:00 pm and this was followed two hours later by a rehearsal for the cameras at 3:00 pm. With Eddie at the controls, the show went very well with everyone on top form. The video was released by Shochiku in Japan on VHS, titled 'Power Live'. Because Alcatrazz hadn't recorded their new album at the time of the show 'Stripper' was titled 'Jack The Ripper', which was actually the working title for the song, while Graham sang a slightly different lyric in 'Skyfire'.

Masaya Uchimura attended the final show in Tokyo, at the Sun Plaza Hall: *"At the time of this tour nobody knew about the new material for the second album. Accordingly, everybody in the audience was very curious to see what kind of guy this Steve Vai was, and what kind of new music they would play. Most people seemed to be expecting to see and hear a similar musical direction. When the show started*

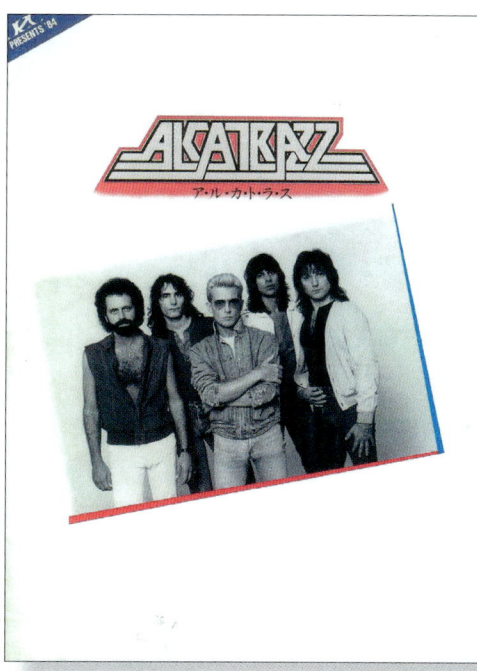

and Steve Vai appeared on stage, everybody's jaw dropped. He had dreadlock hair like a reggae musician. He was completely different from Yngwie, that's for sure! As for the new material, my impression was that the new songs were in major keys and very different. [People] seemed to like the new material, but were confused. With respect to Graham, he was perfect; powerful yet precise."

The set for Japan was as the warm-up, with 'Kojo no Tsuki' dropped in before 'Night Games' and 'All Night Long'. Despite the line-up change the tour was another huge success and once again a large glossy tour programme was produced. The band returned to Los Angeles on October 12th. *"It was a better return to Japan than expected,"* Graham said about the visit. *"There were even more fans and the venues were excellent. We did great and we were all very happy on that tour."*

Back in America, Jimmy Waldo, Gary Shea and Steve Vai started to put plans in place for a full re-organisation of the band's management, because they wanted their finances straightened out. They also wanted to give manager Andy Trueman a standard manager commission but he wasn't having any of it. Meanwhile in October, in Los Angeles, Shirley and her husband Clyde Davis pleaded guilty to charges arising from the embezzlement scheme. Later, a federal judge sentenced them to ten years in prison for embezzling more than $12 million from a Hughes Aircraft Company employee medical benefit plan.

The band now concentrated on recording, mostly at Cherokee studios in Hollywood, with some additional work at Skyline studios in Topanga, then back to Cherokee for the mixing. Steve Vai had arranged all the songs and even contributed some backing vocals, as did Jimmy Waldo and Jan Uvena. Graham says: *"The recording was uneventful really. It took a long time as we wanted this to be the best album, because the songs to me were much better."* When the recordings were sent to Sterling Sound in New York City to be mastered by George Marino there was talk of calling the album 'From The Inside'.

Graham spoke to journalists prior to the album being released. *"The melody lines are a little more interesting, I think,"* he told Faces' Shelley Harris. *"This time we went for something more 'commercial' on a couple of songs, but the real out and out heavy stuff, whatever you want to call it, that's still there. What we wanted to do was reach a wider audience."* To Sharon Liveten of Close-Up, he said: *"Once you label a band heavy metal, you might as well be calling it limited. We have lots of different kinds of influences and musical tastes and it all sorted of melted together. If we want to kick out all the stops and be a heavy metal band we can. But if we want to be a sweet band we can do that also."*

Chatting to Paul Suter in Kerrang! about the new album, Graham admitted the band had hurried their debut: *"It was a rush to find a guitar player. After the first album we realised that there had to be some sort of improvement and we took much more time to work out the songs this time. I think the album is 100% better than the first because of all the preparation which went into it and we have managed to steer away from that heavy metal tag to [reach] a wider audience."* Jimmy Waldo wasn't too keen on the 'heavy metal tag' either, as he told Paul: *"Even with the first record I couldn't see us as a metal band. Heavy metal is like Walt Disney caricatures, like Mötley Crüe and so on – it's a role I don't want to play."*

But if the new album was shaping up, things were stressed on the managerial front. *"The band met and all agreed it was time to set things straight",* Gary says. They confronted Andy Trueman at a rehearsal to try and find a way forward but he just walked out. Jimmy Waldo followed him to the car park and asked him straight how much it would cost the band to get rid of him. He said $20,000. The band's attorney Ken Krauss was immediately contacted, along with the head of Capitol Records, and within three days Andy Trueman had been paid off, returning everything to the band. This left Jimmy Waldo fully in charge and, along with Gary Shea, he started to organise tours, although that turned out to be easier said than done.

The departure of Andy Trueman inevitably had repercussions on the album release, promotion and just about everything else imaginable. Now finally titled 'Disturbing The Peace', which Gary Shea had thought up, Capitol Records released the album on March 22nd 1985 in America. Musically, 'Disturbing The Peace' certainly raised the bar. Capitol planned to release 'God Blessed Video' as the first single and promotional copies of the album all carried a sticker mentioning this. The song was supported by a promotional video, which once again Michael Miner was to direct.

However the release elsewhere was delayed, so Howard Johnson had to rely on an import copy again for his review in Kerrang!. Having rubbished their debut one wonders why he bothered, but to say the band had won him over with the follow up was an understatement: *"Alcatrazz are at last in the big league. Here the band wave noo (Kerrang! had their own way with words.) colours and come up with one red hot noo album. 'Disturbing The Peace' is a real giant among minnows. It's accessible, it's complex, it's musical, it's heavy as hell, it's all things to all men … it's a BLOODY GREAT ALBUM!"* In particular he described 'God Blessed Video' as a *"stunning opener"* and *"the cream on the cake"*; 'Mercy' as an *"all-time epic"*, 'Desert Diamond' as having *"vocal gymnastics"* and 'Skyfire' possessing *"thoughtful lyrical fare"*. He concluded by saying: *"There are really no low points, especially with Vai pasting the opposition with his incisive play."*

In America the album also found support albeit in the more niche music magazines. Rock Scene reviewer, Maxx Havick, said of the album's opener 'God Blessed Video': *"Solid riffing, and Mr. Bonnet's vocals show signs of good things to come."* He talked of 'Mercy' as *"head bopping with its infectious rhythm,"* and rated 'Painted Lover', reckoning it *"is arguably the best song on the album."* It wasn't all smooth sailing however, and he felt that 'Will You Be Home Tonight' and 'Wire And Wood' were both *"tedious keyboard numbers."* KJ Doughton in BAM called it *"one of the year's most solidly satisfying rock collections"*; Andy Secher of Hit Parader said: *"Such cuts as 'God Blessed Video', 'Painted Lover' and 'Mercy' show Bonnet, Vai, keyboardist Jimmy Waldo, bassist Gary Shea and drummer Jan Uvena ready to join the top ranks of metal mavens"* and Sharon Liveten of Close-Up said: *"The disc has a bunch of headbangers. The best of those is 'Wire And Wood'. Vai soars through the entire song."*

The album deserved far better than seven short weeks on the US Billboard chart, where its highest position was No. 133, below even their studio debut. Talking to Andy Secher of Hit Parader, Graham put much of the blame on a lack of live shows at the time: *"If we had gotten the proper managerial support that album would have been much more successful than it was. Instead of going on tour and supporting it we were spending most of our time in court getting out of our deal with [Andy]."* Very happy with the reaction to the album, Graham told Sharon Liveten of Creem magazine: *"We got the best reviews we ever had, but we were firing a manager just exactly at the same time as we were planning to go out on tour*

and, suddenly, we had no-one fighting for us at the agency."

For the 'God Blessed Video' video, Michael Miner had developed a detailed storyline, something more and more promo videos were now leaning toward. The video has a one and a half minute introduction with an angel talking to the devil on the phone, before the song even starts (and they keep cropping up throughout). The video lasts over five minutes and is very well produced. The band was filmed at SIR studios as before and they all put in great performances. It is interesting to note that the album instrumental 'Lighter Shade Of Green' was planned as the introduction to 'God Blessed Video' but then separated off. However, all of a sudden Capitol Records began to have second thoughts about releasing the single and put it on hold. It seems that some of the more conservative radio stations wouldn't play the song because they were put off by a title which mentioned 'God'. Instead they waited to see what the reaction was to the video on MTV and elsewhere. Sadly, it didn't get high rotation, and the label shelved the single.

'Disturbing The Peace' was released in Japan during April but it didn't do as well as expected there either. Maybe more fans there had been followers of Yngwie than the rest of the band realised, as his first solo album was a huge hit there.

The Japanese were also wary of issuing a single, but towards the end of spring 'Sons And Lovers' b/w 'God Blessed Video' was pressed up as a promotional only 7". It got little airplay beyond the heavy metal discos that existed in Tokyo at the time.

Meanwhile Graham found the problem with Bell's palsy affecting him more and became very conscious of it. A form of facial paralysis, it affects one side of the face and makes it virtually impossible to control the muscles as Graham recalls: *"It was the right side of my face that lost muscle tone and movement. It really annoyed me. I am so vain, we all are. It has made one side of my face very wrinkly and people say nasty things about how old I look sometimes, which hurts, but it was a medical condition, that slowly made me look older than I am as years pass. I have sort of recovered from it, but now I am older the muscles it paralyzed are more evident and has caused me to look older in the face as the skin droops. It has put years on my face."*

The band should have gone out on tour in America during January but because of the managerial problems, it didn't happen. Nor did a talked-about fifty-date tour starting in June as the middle act between headliners Uli Jon Roth & Electric Sun and Los Angeles band Odin. Instead a one-off gig took place at the Roberto Clemente Coliseum in San Juan, Puerto Rico on May 31st supporting ex-Kansas guitarist / keyboard player, Kerry Levgren. Kerry had just moved into playing Christian rock as Gary remembers: *"He was forced by the angry promoter to learn some Kansas songs before he got there. We smoked them!"*

The album track 'Will You Be Home Tonight' found unexpected exposure through a campaign group called Mothers Against Drunk Driving, so much so that Capitol pressed a special 12" promotional single in June. The A-side featured an edit from the LP, while the B-side had a 30 second introduction to the song about a kid going out and his mother asking *"will you be home tonight?"* Then, when the car sets off, a voice says *"have a beer."* Graham then appears: *"This is Graham Bonnet of Alcatrazz: before you drink and drive, ask yourself, will you be home tonight?"* A real curio, indeed.

Finally, 'Disturbing The Peace' was released in Europe on July 15th by Capitol, with the UK pressing sporting a unique inner sleeve (America got a lyric / photo sheet). A single 'God Blessed Video' b/w 'Wire And Wood' also came out, but neither had any chart success, despite a great review in Kerrang! courtesy of Mark Putterford: *"I've never been a Graham Bonnet fan – all mouth and sunglasses – but I must admit to being totally bowled over by his band's new album 'Disturbing The Peace'. New guitarist Steve Vai throws in a breathtaking performance that puts Malmsteen right into perspective, and the whole package is set up by the suitably-storming single 'God Blessed Video'. As a satirical dig at Duran 'Nice Video, Shame About The Song' Duran, 'GBV' is hard, harsh 'n' heavy, yet cool, classy and commercial, with Vai flitting all over the frets and Bonnet busting his lungs in familiar fashion. Brilliant! Break into the new shit-hot Alcatrazz immediately."*

Others were picking up on Vai, who was now offered the role of Jack Butler, the devil's guitarist, in the Columbia film Crossroads, released in March 1986.

Alcatrazz finally began to shape up for a headlining tour, which began at The Golden Bear in Huntington Beach on August 6th (after a warm-up gig at the Country Club on July 29th). The same day though, as Steve Vai was on his way to The Golden Bear, he received a phone call from singer Dave Lee Roth, wanting to know if he would be interested in a job. Despite his current commitments, Steve accepted: *"I wanted to develop it into something a little more interesting than commercial music … but everybody was afraid – [so I] had no second thoughts when the call came from Dave Lee Roth. Ted Templeman heard a tape of mine and sent it on to Dave. When Dave finally called I was on my way out of the door to an Alcatrazz concert,"* he said in an interview in Kerrang! He

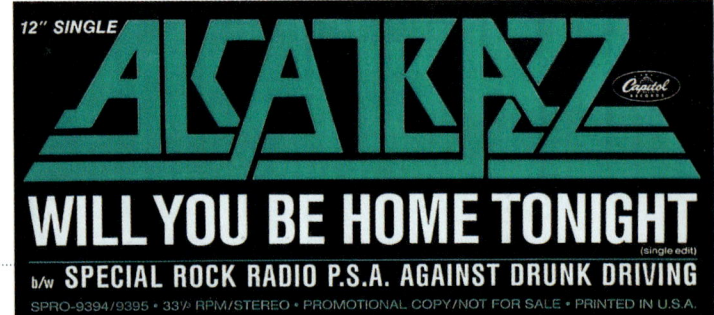

informed his fellow musicians after the gig and they were devastated, but it was decided not to say anything to Graham until after the tour had been completed. Alcatrazz did five more headlining shows, the final one at Cardi's, in Houston, Texas, on August 15th. Gary Shea recalls: *"The opening act, Odin, came along from LA with us after I talked them into providing a tractor trailer truck for both bands. We were both driving motor homes. They hired two of their friends to drive for them. We drove ourselves. All our crew got to ride on the bus. They loved me!"* The set-list on the headlining tour was 'God Blessed Video', 'Island In The Sun', 'Painted Lover', 'Lighter Shade Of Green', 'Sons And Lovers', 'Skyfire', 'Will You Be Home Tonight', 'Wire And Wood', 'Steve Solo', 'Since You Been Gone', 'Suffer Me', 'Stripper', 'Attitude Song' (from Steve's solo album) and 'All Night Long'.

The following day, Alcatrazz joined up with Helix in McAllen, Texas for three consecutive support gigs, again with Odin opening. The short tour concluded at Opry House in Austin. It had been an incredible ten long months since Alcatrazz had undertaken their last tour, and that was in Japan. It had been even longer on home soil.

With Steve's mind made up, it was down to the band to inform Graham. He had really grown to like Steve and knew he was a big part of the way the group had progressed. *"The other guys told me, much later on, as Steve was a bit nervous on how I would take it. He had a good offer from David Lee Roth so we couldn't compete with that. It was shattering, to be honest, as I thought this was the best line-up of the band. I always liked Steve more than the other guy because he was very original and that's what we needed."*

Steve would explain things from his own point of view a little later, saying in Guitar Magazine in March 1986: *"We went out on a scorching two-week tour. There was no money to survive on the road and because we weren't out sooner, which I blame on the management, it became time for the band to start working on another record. We [had only] played three gigs before they asked us to make another record. I didn't feel comfortable with that. When you sit around for a year you get stagnant. I had to play live. On top of that Capitol wanted me to start work on my solo album, which would have meant I had to stay in the studio for another six months! That was one reason I left the group."* The band had actually done around a handful of basic instrumental demos for a second offering, and one song was completed with vocals titled 'Emotion'.

Alcatrazz were now back to square one, and it was left to Jimmy Waldo to talk to potential replacements. Some were very interested, but something always seemed to get in the way. Gary recalls: *"We did audition Robert Sarzo, Rudy's brother, but he wasn't right."* They turned their attention next to ex-Derringer and Rod Stewart guitarist Danny Johnson. Gary and Jimmy were very much in favour of him joining the band, although Graham wasn't. Looking back on the situation Gary recalls: *"In hindsight, Graham was correct about Danny, whom Jimmy and I spearheaded, not being right for us but we were running out of time."*

So during November the band eventually decided on Louisiana-born Danny Johnson, who was interviewed about joining: *"They're all good musicians and good people and we hit it off. I wanted to get a solo band together with a good singer,"* he told Mary Toledo in Faces magazine. *"I even got a singer to share the duties, but then he flaked out so I didn't look anymore. Then I heard about Alcatrazz. I thought it would be a good opportunity. In Alcatrazz, there's room for everybody to write and experiment. The band is hard to write for but I was excited because it's not just one person who participates, it's everybody. It's a mixture of the Louisiana overtones of my heritage, Graham's artsy vocals and Jimmy's classical roots. Alcatrazz has the potential to be a really good group, because they have the guts to say they want to try this as opposed to sticking to one sound."*

Coinciding with the arrival of Danny, Alcatrazz signed a management deal with Wendy Dio at Niji Productions. Wendy was married to former Rainbow singer Ronnie James Dio, who Graham had replaced almost seven years before, and had set up her own management company initially to look after Ronnie's career. There were immediate hopes that this would find Alcatrazz supporting Dio in the UK and even though it was mentioned in the press during February 1986 as a possibility for May, the slot went instead to Keel, the band formed by Ron Keel who, as Steeler's frontman, used to share a stage and dressing room with Yngwie Malmsteen. It was perhaps the best chance for Alcatrazz to make their UK live debut, but it was destined not to be.

Instead February saw the band enter the American Recording studios in Woodland Hills, California, to begin working on their third studio album with producer Ritchie Polodor, who Danny Johnson already knew. With just a handful of songs written, Alcatrazz knew it was make or break time and so did Capitol Records. Graham told Creem Metal's Sharon Liveten: *"This one has got to make it. It has to do really well. 'Cause I don't know what's going to happen to the band if this album doesn't make it. We made a good album last time and nobody got to hear it. The radio thought we were a heavy metal band."*

Capitol also tried to persuade the band to use some outside song-writers in a bid to secure a hit single. Graham was against the idea of using outside material, and based on the songs he had listened to he still felt the band could do the writing themselves, and told Capitol so. They replied by more or less saying, 'it's your funeral!'

Alcatrazz knew they had to go in a more commercial direction than before and started throwing ideas around in the studio. Richie Polodor had previously worked with the Grateful Dead, Three Dog Night and Steppenwolf, and he had his own ideas of how things should be done in a recording studio and how he should record the band. He thought it was important for them to be able to see and hear Graham even if he was in a different room.

With the sessions progressing, Gary took a short break to be his wife as she gave birth to their first child, after which he was back in the studio to finish a track: *"My daughter Tyler was born in the morning. Later that day I went out to the studio to put a bass track on the song 'No Imagination' as our A&R guy, Ray Tusken from Capitol, was coming out later that evening to hear our progress. I laid the bass on, Ray was happy, and when we came back to review it a month later there was nothing to fix up. I'm very proud of that track!"*

This time, the songs weren't based as much around the guitar during the song-writing process, and Graham realised having a star guitarist had perhaps detracted from the band: *"Most of our audiences were just guitar players,"* he noted to Faces' Mary Toledo. *"They just wanted to see what the new guitar player was like. Half of the audience were kids grabbing at this guy's feet, whoever it may be at the*

time. This version of Alcatrazz is more song-based. The songs are not played around a guitar like the last two bands have been. It's still us. It still has, if there is one, an Alcatrazz stamp. This time it's more straight down the line rock 'n' roll. It's heavy rock 'n' roll. It's not heavy, heavy metal. I think it's a little more commercial than the stuff we've done before. We've tried to be commercial, but it's unpretentious."

Capitol Records might not have been able to persuade the band to use outside songwriters, but they did have a think about doing a cover version or two. One of them which Graham came up with was 'It's My Life' by The Animals, which Bruce Springsteen had played live during his 'Born To Run' tour at the end of 1975. Graham spoke to Andy Secher in Hit Parader about the song: *"It's a great tune that has a lot of character and has a very commercial feel to it. That's something that the record company was very interested in. They were the ones who recommended we find an old tune we'd feel comfortable with covering. But we like it. Our label, Capitol, had a great deal of success with Heart last year by having them record a lot of other people's work, so they thought it might work for us as well."*

Another contender was Graham's old Marbles hit 'Only One Woman'. Graham was arranging a vocal in the studio, and started strumming the chords to his old hit on his guitar and singing along. The rest of the band wanted to know what it was and, when he told them, they all insisted that they did it. Even producer Richie Polodor agreed it had to go on the album, although Graham wasn't keen.

As it was the new album was taking far longer to record than planned, because of the way Richie Polodor worked, and Alactrazz ended up being in the studio for around three and a half months. The album had originally been scheduled for release during early summer but that date had now passed, as Danny Johnson explained to Sharon Liveten in Rock It: *"We concentrated on keeping the feel, and that's what took such a long time. To me, the feel is always more important than the technical aspect."*

The album was actually recorded in a more piecemeal fashion than had been the case before, something Gary mentioned in the same feature. *"Usually we do the bass and drums first and the guitars and vocals get done last. This time we've been doing a bit of everything."* Graham was also finding it hard to keep up, as he elaborated: *"I can hardly remember which songs I've sung. We've been doing a little bit here and a little bit there - a guitar here and a keyboard there and a vocal down there and a harmony over there."*

The album had been given the title of 'Dangerous Games', a song Danny had brought to the table and the band had been keen to record. During the sessions there were a couple more cover versions and new songs laid down which still haven't been released. The covers were played by The Graham Bonnet Set back in the mid-Sixties. Graham says: *"We did the Percy Sledge song 'When A Man Loves A Woman' twelve keys up from Percy's version. When we started to record it I remember Richie Polodor, the producer saying, 'that's too easy for you to sing.' But I said 'it's still high.' He said, 'it's still too easy, take it up.' We did another one, which was an old Ike & Tina Turner tune called 'A Love Like Yours'. We thought it could have been a single."* Another song they recorded was 'Lonely Rider', an original.

Out of the blue, the BBC in the UK contacted Graham to see if they could travel over to America to interview him and also film him singing with Alactrazz for their music programme Rockschool, designed to help children keen on becoming a rock musician. Programme producer Chris Lent flew out to California and talked to Graham about various vocal techniques and how he approaches his singing. Some of this also ended up in a tie-in book for the series. Graham explained about his vocals on 'Dangerous Games': *"On the album, we went out of our way to feature the lead vocals and to bring in harmonies – sometimes with the other guys in the band and sometimes me overdubbing myself. So we're still a heavy rock band but also vocal, which most bands aren't."* As regards to how he tackled live gigs, Graham told Chris: *"It's really hard to keep in tune with guitarists nowadays, because they're bending strings and one thing and another. So what I usually do with Jimmy is, I have him really loud through my monitors, like you wouldn't believe. I have him as loud as myself, because the keyboards are pretty constant pitch-wise. So that's how I tune. But there have been nights when I can't hear anything and I've had to pitch to the bass drum!"*

As is often the case with the BBC they filmed hours of material and showed only a few minutes when the show went out in October 1987 on BBC 2, but it did have Graham singing in a number of styles to show what could be done in a rock band.

'Dangerous Games' was eventually released in early September in America (with a limited edition picture disc also available.) The album is lighter and far more mainstream than their earlier albums. In Kerrang! Maura Sutton described it as being a *"highly polished FM radio production; an entertaining if not particularly outstanding release."* Commenting about Danny's playing she said: *"Sensibly enough, Johnson has not tried to emulate the incomparable Vai. There's nary a trace of flamboyant soloing within these grooves. Call me perverse if you like, but it's Johnson's rhythm work that pleases me most on this platter. Album opener 'It's My Life' boasts a deliciously infectious riff whilst 'That Ain't Easy' features equally fine rhythm, venturing into Billy Squier/Big Beat territory. 'No Imagination' is yet more of the same. And when Johnson does solo he's short, sharp and deadly."* As for Graham's vocals, Maura was upbeat: *"His voice is certainly as strong as ever; check out the remake of 'Only One Woman' for evidence. Even better, listen to the menacing tones of 'Double Man' – Bonnet at his soaraway best. Lush vocal harmonies abound on 'Undercover' and 'Dangerous Games', conjuring up fond memories of the last Toto opus. In fact it is Bonnet's peculiar sense of humour that rescues the album from being dismissed as just another slick AOR release. Here is a man with tongue wedged so firmly in cheek it's a damn miracle he manages to sing at all. Who else would write a song about the Blue Boar service station?!"*

Others, however, were less complimentary: *"The title is already synonymous with what they are doing"* said Reinhard Harms in Metal Hammer. *"Graham Bonnet's band delivers a poor, not very inspired, work. The new axeman, Danny Johnson, doesn't even come close to what Steve Vai achieved when he was in the same position. The songs have no power and they don't sound like 1986 hard rock. The only attraction is still Graham Bonnet's voice."*

September also saw Capitol release the album in Japan. The UK had to put up with import copies again but it was issued in France (and possibly other European countries.) The label were still in a cautious

Alcatrazz • *Live at The Ritz, New York, Dec 1986.*

mood when it came to singles, but felt 'It's My Life' would be worth a try. To test the waters they pressed up a batch of promotional 12" copies up (with the same song on each side) but there was very little reaction, positive or otherwise, so the single was not issued commercially.

The band went out on the road as support to Starship doing seven shows in eleven days to help promote the American release. It had been over a year since Alcatrazz had played live; their first show was at the U.T. Pavilion in Martin, Tennessee on October 16th and the run ended at the Ollign Coliseum in Wichita Falls, Texas on October 26th. They travelled back to Los Angeles the next day, but had only a week's break before opening up for San Diego band Rough Cutt on a two-month tour. Alcatrazz were still getting column inches in the press and had a following, but airplay, which was critical to building their sales, was a completely different matter. Capitol tried a second promotional 12" single, 'Undercover' (with the same song on both sides), in October, but once more to little effect.

The tour with Rough Cutt ran through most of November and December. Alcatrazz might have been the support band for most of the tour but they did headline the last four shows. It was certainly the longest tour the band had ever undertaken, ending in Riverside on December 21st at the De Anza Theater. The set list as support was: 'Island In The Sun', 'It's My Life', 'Undercover', 'God Blessed Video', 'Double Man', 'Wire And Wood', 'Danny Solo', 'Since You Been Gone' and 'All Night Long'. It was a very long, hard slog for the band, and as far as Graham was concerned it couldn't have finished soon enough. *"It was a very cold winter and a horrible experience playing with Rough Cutt and being the opening band. It was a lousy tour,"* he says.

Incredibly, December saw Capitol Records issue a third promotional 12", 'Dangerous Games' b/w 'Double Man', but it was a last throw of the dice. Alcatrazz did a few one-nighters over the Christmas period, including one on Boxing Day at The Omni in Oakland. A short tour with Stryper fell through, but Alcatrazz eventually teamed up with them on New Year's Eve for a show at the Civic Auditorium in San José, though working with Christian rockers wasn't quite the harmonious experience you might imagine. Graham remembers it well: *"We were booed off and had pennies thrown at us, because we were not that well known I guess. It was horrible and what an awful crowd. That's the believers in mystical beings for you!"*

Gary too recalls the show: *"That was the worst gig ever. Never in any band I ever played in were we booed. They wanted Graham to sing different lyrics to 'All Night Long', a very, very dirty song! They were funded by a Christian mega church and had a tour bus and fancy roadcases of gear just like us, except we earned ours the hard way in the real world. When we got on stage the idiots in the audience started yelling that we were the Devil and began booing and hissing. They actually started throwing coins at us; I got hit a couple of times by quarters and it hurt. I made an extra 10 dollars that night though!"*

Irrespective of this, Alactrazz supported Stryper the following day. A journalist from Metal Hammer was at this New Year's Day show at the Santa Monica Civic: *"After their last album, that was unanimously agreed as being one of the weakest ever, the band seem to be getting their act together on this tour and are hitting their critics where it hurts. Many had written Alcatrazz off but now they seem to be a force to be reckoned with. What is obvious though is that their strength lies in their live appearances."*

These duff support slots were the final nail in the coffin as far as the band were concerned though. Since mid-October the band had played over forty shows and it had taken its toll on everyone, as Graham says: *"We were touring, but we weren't making any money and it just became very depressing and awful. It just came to a natural death, because things weren't going very well for us."*

On January 6th Gary and Jimmy parted company with the band, although it wasn't announced officially until March. Graham says: *"Danny Johnson said to me 'let's fire a couple of the guys out of the band'. So we fired Jimmy Waldo and Gary Shea. Jay Davis, Danny Johnson and I got together with Jan Uvena on drums."* Jay Davis, had actually been around for a short spell during the sessions for 'Dangerous Games', along with another bassist Jimmy Heslip. Jimmy Waldo wasn't replaced at all because the band wanted to go in a heavier direction. This all meant that Graham and Jan were now the only original members.

Despite this attempt to streamline the operation, time was running out. There was talk of the new line-up going to Japan to do some shows, and pre-production rehearsals got under way for a possible new album (three songs being 'The Dancer', 'Tonite I Fly' and 'Reel To Real') but the hammer blow came when Capitol Records didn't renew their contract. Although the band did manage to limp on for a little while longer, the new line-up started to fall apart quite quickly, and Graham points out why: *"Eddie Van Halen called up Danny and Jay and said 'how about Danny's girlfriend and you two guys doing an album?' So they disappeared to Eddie's house and Jan and I were left looking at each other. Drummer and singer: it doesn't really go very far does it? It's Don and Phil! It was a bit of a shock actually. I found out from somebody else that this was going to happen and I called up the guys and said 'are you gonna leave the band?' And they said, 'how do you know that's going to happen?' 'Well, I've heard.' I replied. And they said 'Graham, what can I say? I've got to go.' So they went. So that was the end of that."* A call to Wendy Dio elicited the response that they couldn't do anything to help either, so that really was it.

Alcatrazz arguably tried to ride the crest – or undercurrent – of a huge metal wave in America, when dozens of bands attempted to slog it out on lengthy American tours and out-pose each other in the magazines which served the market. They had never really fitted into that scene (or wanted to be part of it) but nevertheless got lumped in with it. And you have to feel that without a solid European presence Alcatrazz were always going to struggle.

Never entirely happy with the band's final offering, Graham told Alex Solca in Italy's Heavy Metal magazine: *"To be honest, 'Dangerous Games' is an album more for the record company than for myself. I'm not completely happy with this disc, because there are songs on there like 'It's My Life' which I thought were never worth the effort wasted on it. But the record company was of a different opinion. Our record company was putting on pressure until we made a commercial disc, but, can you tell me, what in reality is a commercial disc? When I write a song I don't think in the least of the etiquette; it's only music. Another classical 'stroke of luck' was the decision of the record company; they wanted us to change dramatically, because the previous discs hadn't sold well. And that was another error. When the band formed we were heavy metal, but the radio didn't have the least interest in this type of music. Then when Steve joined the group we became more experimental and less heavy, but the radio still had no interest in us because the name Alcatrazz was always synonymous with heavy metal. In the end we made a commercial disc just when the radio started to accept heavy metal. So this time we were not heavy enough. I really think in the music business, you have to be in the right place at the right time, otherwise you've had it."*

CHAPTER 9
Undercover (1987 - 1989)

Featuring: Impellitteri, The Party Boys and Graham's solo career

Disenchanted Bonnet starts again

Having fronted Alcatrazz for for over three years to little international success, Graham now wanted to go in a different direction vocally and musically, telling Alex Solca of Italy's Heavy Metal magazine: *"I think I must make some kind of change to my music to attract more fans."* He and Jan Uvena had now gone their separate ways, so Graham started to write some new songs with a view to negotiating another record deal, whilst discounting unfounded rumours that he might be forming a new group which included Cozy Powell and ex-Thin Lizzy and Whitesnake guitarist, John Sykes.

During the spring Graham was asked to do backing vocals on a couple of songs for Danish heavy metal band Pretty Maids who were recording their second album 'Future World' in New York with 'Disturbing The Peace' producer Eddie Kramer. Graham featured on the tracks 'We Came To Rock' and 'Loud 'N' Proud'.

Meanwhile Chris Impellitteri, who had unsuccessfully auditioned for Alcatrazz at the same time as Steve Vai, was starting to make waves via his self-titled four-track EP released in January 1987. On the back of it Relativity Records offered Chris a one-off album deal, but allocated a budget of around $4,000 to make it. Chris knew if he wanted to do it properly he had to surround himself with quality musicians, so he financed much of it himself. He also realised he needed a name singer of a certain calibre and soon focussed his attention on Graham, having heard that Alcatrazz had broken up. *"He called me up one day and said, 'hello Graham, it's me.' And I said, 'hello Chris, it's me too!' The money was right and it was a session."* Chris was pleased: *"I've always loved Graham's voice. It gives me chills. When you hear it, you know right away it's his. His range is incredible. As I was composing, I would think of his voice,"* he told Laurel Fishman in Rip. Graham was equally impressed, telling Paul Suter in Creem: *"It was great to get back to my roots and when Chris played his stuff to me that was what I wanted to do."*

"There were a lot of people out there who really weren't seasoned," said Chris in the same article. *"They had all the right elements but hadn't learned how to put them together, so I had to find players who were musically mature. Graham's influences are great for my stuff, they complemented my own. I'm into stuff like Al DiMeola, Allan Holdsworth and classical music, whilst Graham's into the Beatles, the Beach Boys and stuff like that."* In Kerrang!, he elaborated: *"We get along very well, we're both tough and demanding musicians – but I think we respect each other enough to know when not to take matters to extremes. I know Graham's had a tough time with guitar players, most of that has been down to personality and ego clashes, but at least in this band we've both agreed that I'm going to play my guitar as fast as possible and he's going to sing as hard as it takes to impress."*

Next to join the project was ex-M.A.R.S keyboard player Phil Wolfe ('ex-' because Rudy Sarzo and Tommy Aldridge – the 'A' and 'S' in the acronymic name alongside – had just left to join Whitesnake). Former Ted Nugent drummer Pat Torpey soon came on board and finally, to complete the line-up, ex-Quiet Riot, Giuffria and Ted Nugent bassist Chuck Wright signed up: *"I had just left Quiet Riot and got a call from Chris. I had never met him before. He said he heard I was a good bassist and asked if I'd be interested in coming over to jam with him at his apartment. Things went great and I agreed to work with him."*

Chris began to put songs down on his portastudio for Graham to listen to. From there Graham started writing lyrics as he wandered round his house. When he felt he had something to share he travelled over to Thousand Oaks where Chris lived (and indeed Graham had too for a while) in southern Ventura County. For a bit of fun prior to getting down to some serious rehearsing, Chris suggested 'Since You Been Gone', which he had actually been playing since he first heard it in 1979. *"Ritchie Blackmore's been a big influence. I'll be the first to admit that I got a lot of my stuff from him,"* he admitted to Paul Suter in Creem. The song then became a regular warm-up piece for the band, while Graham recalls them doing 'All Night Long' as well. Chuck Wright also recalls the rehearsals: *"I remember them being VERY loud and very tedious. Chris is a real perfectionist. I have a clear memory of Graham sitting on the couch in front of us at Mates Studio just staring off into space, just a blank look. This was a common occurrence back then. I'm not sure what was going on with him, perhaps he was working on melodies or words in his head. He did come up with some very intriguing lyrics."*

Perhaps also Graham was mulling over the idea he and his wife had discussed of leaving America and moving somewhere else. While the Impellitteri work progressed, Graham teamed up with a Japanese guitarist called Kuni, with a view to putting a new line-up of Alcatrazz together and doing a one-off festival in Tokyo in early October. No sooner had this been agreed than Graham had to pull out as the Bonnet family finally decided during April to up sticks and move to Adelaide in Australia. Graham had spent seven years in the Los Angeles area and it was time for a change, but he remained committed to the Impellitteri project, and flew back after they'd settled in to finish some more material. It wasn't too long before pre-production rehearsals began. The album was recorded mainly in Los Angeles, where they moved between Record Plant, Cherokee and Sound City studios, and everything went without a hitch according to Chuck Wright. *"Graham was always pleasant to work with. The thing about Graham that always stays with me is his intensity when he sings. I mean his head looks like it's going to explode!"*

Chris Impellitteri sat in the production chair, with Cliff Cultreri overseeing things as executive producer. Nine songs were recorded in total, including two instrumentals. Talking in America's Rock Scene magazine about the writing Chris explained: *"I usually come in with a bar and Graham will end up writing the melody and the words. Or sometimes it can be vice versa."*

They had originally planned more songs but some weren't finished vocally, as Chris explained to Fred Verhoeven in Powerline: *"Because of some problems with Graham, a few tunes didn't make the album because the vocal lines weren't done."* 'Over The Rainbow' didn't have a particularly good introduction and 'Secret Lover' didn't have a great ending so Chris decided to edit the two together; as the latter finishes, Chris brought 'Over The Rainbow' virtually straight in. He also added the bell at the beginning of 'Stand In Line'. *"It took four hours but it turned out very good and boosted the excitement. It makes you think, 'what's gonna happen next?' and that's the purpose,"* he told Koh Sakai in Burrn!

The band had completed the album, but the label thought otherwise. *"The record company asked us to record one more number,"* Chris said in an interview with Derek Oliver for Kerrang! *"We had some material left over but nothing as powerful or as obvious as 'Since You Been Gone'. So, with that in mind, we decided to record it but in the manner it should have been done by Rainbow. Our version is much heavier, more intense and I think my solo is a little more apt – it's extremely classical in structure."* Graham wasn't too keen on the idea of recording the old hit again saying: *"I didn't want to do it. Chris had to heavy up 'Since You Been Gone' to make it a bit more evil. He was probably right in a way to do it like that."*

The inclusion of the Rainbow track certainly cheered up the record company. As for including 'Over The Rainbow' Chris told Derek Oliver: *"I always found [Ritchie's] version of this tune very enchanting and I wanted to do it. My rendering is a lot faster and heavier – I really went all-out to make it as riffed-up as I could."*

Without a work permit, Graham needed to return to Adelaide, although group and individual photos for the album sleeve with Glen La Ferman were shot before he left. Graham dug out the blue suit from his Alcatrazz days, one of a few he had accumulated over the years: *"I had the suits made because on outdoor shows a coloured suit shows up great in daylight, or night gigs. I have a silk light pink suit, a light green one and a black saffron one - the more colourful the better!"*

Impellitteri Mk 1 • *L-r Pat Torpey, Phil Wolfe, Chris Impellitteri, Graham and Chuck Wright.*

Unsurprisingly, given the potential Chris was now beginning to think along the lines of having a permanent band, rather than hiring musicians. Session drummer Pat Torpey moved on to another project and Chris immediately started looking for a replacement. Having seen Stet Howland bashing away on the New York club circuit with Run 21, he put the idea to him. Stet didn't need asking twice, and was also able to contribute backing vocals. Speaking to Laurel Fishman in Rip, he said: *"It's hard not to drown Graham in compliments. Now Graham's voice is better than ever. People are dying to see him perform again."*

Graham was already anticipating a follow up: *"The band name Impellitteri may be changed for the next album"*, he told Burrn!'s Kaz Hirose. *"When we recorded the album, we got together for a session, so it was Chris Impellitteri's album. The record company wanted me and Chris to be the main guys. So it may be Bonnet Impellitteri."* However it was apparent to him that Stet and Chuck weren't seeing eye to eye on things, so Chuck Wright departed (for Giuffria again, the band Kiss's Gene Simmons later dubbed House Of Lords) and Chris started thinking of bass players to contact. Dave Spitz's name came to mind, because he had met him at the NAMM show. *"Dave had been in Black Sabbath and recorded two albums with them, but decided to quit the band in 1987 and was still keeping his options open,"* he told Burrn! *"He played a bit in my living room, and was really great."* Graham was also a fan: *"It was very good. I wanted to sing to his bass and certainly wanted to work with him. Other bass players don't play chords, but he does,"* he pointed out to the magazine. *"It was unbelievable. I thought the songs recorded for the album were revitalised. I personally thought they were better than the ones on the album."* Dave Spitz was also fired up while talking to Burrn!: *"Graham and Chris have been together for a while, but the other members have not. We are finally doing it as a unit. Everybody is saying that they want to record the album with the current members."*

Flitting between continents, in early autumn Graham returned to Los Angeles to film a promotional video for 'Stand In Line', now the title track for the album. A large stage set was used with lots of props as Graham remembers: *"It was filmed in Los Angeles on top of an old department store from the 1930s or so. It was completely empty. We were there for many hours on the set, until the sun came up next day. Lots of climbing gear was used to get us up to the roof, mountain climbing gear, as it was a very small thin old ladder that was inside the tower of the building, and this was the safest way to be hoisted up."* It is interesting to see Chris doing a Ritchie Blackmore impersonation at the end of his guitar solo when he turns and points to the drummer!

Bill Freesh, who was one of two engineers used on 'Stand In Line', had now finished mixing it while Graham, who was over 8,000 miles away on the other side of the world, had been struggling to occupy himself: *"I was hanging around doing nothing!"* No sooner had 1988 started though than he received a call from ex-Status Quo bassist Alan Lancaster. He'd heard Graham was in Adelaide, and since John 'Swanee' Swan had suddenly left his band, The Party Boys, he needed a replacement very quickly. John was already a successful singer in Australia and amongst the first recordings he did with The Party Boys was a cover of the John Kongos hit 'He's Gonna Step On You Again', which reached No. 1 on the Australian charts. Graham found himself involved in rehearsals during the first week of January for a Party Boys show at Kitchener Park in Northern Sydney on January 8th. As well as learning a batch of cover songs Graham introduced 'Only One Woman', his own version of Bob Dylan's 'It's All Over Now Baby Blue' and 'All Night Long'. The band did try out his hit 'Warm Ride', but it was one step too far, as Graham says: *"They couldn't manage that. It was too difficult! We had two drummers so can you imagine what that was like?"*

The Australian press soon got hold of the story about Graham joining The Party Boys. He told Paul Suter in Creem: *"I had to learn so many songs in one week. Alan, who is an old friend, wanted me to do it. He said 'you get money every night.' I thought 'oh, that's good. A wage packet!' That's what happens out there. You get it straight in your hand. It's amazing. Two thousand in cash in your hand at the end of every night. Nobody has management there, no agencies, and no commissions to pay because the bands manage and book themselves."* Not bad money for a covers' band, but, at most, Graham only did about three gigs with The Party Boys. His second was at Selinas in Sydney and Juke magazine was there to review it: *"Considering Bonnet has only done one other performance with the band, it was the band itself that was sloppier than I'd expected. Fair enough on the unfamiliar songs from Bonnet's store, the massive 'Only One Woman' from his time with the Marbles, and a woeful execution (literally) of his Rainbow hit 'All Night Long', but you'd expect mistakes from Bonnet, not the band on 'Hold Your Head Up' and 'He's Gonna Step On You Again'. Best of all, we got the chance to see one of rock's finest ever voices in action again, after too long. The Party Boys, you couldn't have hoped for a better choice than the remarkable Graham Bonnet. The enormous strength and range of his vocals should have made him a greater force than he has ultimately been, but in an all-too-chequered career, Graham Bonnet has delivered some real gems, and he delivered them with a vengeance tonight. From the moment he came on to an unfortunately under-par version (from the band) of his biggest hit 'It's All Over Now Baby Blue' you were aware of his awesome strength and professionalism. In fact it was the two Englishmen in the band that shone through the whole performance."*

Yet after just two weeks Graham was told Swanee was re-joining. *"I was fired because they got John Swan back. One morning Alan said to me 'I don't know what's going on, but they want to get John Swan in again.' So I said, 'why, what have I done?' Alan said, 'it's nothing to do with you.' They all phoned me up that night and said 'we're really sorry about this, but it's just one of those things.'"*

Still at least The Party Boys had got him back gigging and whetted his appetite. Meanwhile, after sitting on the album for ages, Relativity Records eventually released 'Stand In Line' on April 29th in all formats – vinyl (with an embossed cover), cassette and CD. The album peaked at No. 91 on the US Billboard charts, spending a total of eighteen weeks there, while the video for 'Stand In Line' had some airplay on MTV, serving as a good introduction to the band and their album. Chris had wanted to do some gigs and, with Graham being very popular in Japan and the line-up which had recorded the video all available, they were booked to appear at the Tokyo Dome in July with Billy Joel headlining.

The album came out on Music For Nations in the UK and Europe in June with full page adverts in the press, and in Japan via CBS / Sony on the Relativity Combat label, and met with mixed reviews. Hit Parader in America were very complimentary: *"The group contains several big-name performers who give the band a multi-dimensioned sound that is both heavy and appealing."* Kerrang!'s Jon Hotten was far from impressed though, describing the album as: *"All flash and no feel and boring because these people, for all their technical perfection, can't play with any heartfelt passion."* Dave Ling of Metal Hammer commented: *"'Stand In Line' is a guitar player's album desperately in search of material to make it world class. The closest we come to a genuine tune is the souped-up cover of 'Since You've Been Gone' [sloppily rendered as 'Since You've Been Gone' on the cover]. If Impellitteri is seriously searching for mass acceptance then next time he'll have to spend more time concentrating on his songwriting. It's good to see Bonnet back in the saddle, but this sure ain't the project that will bring him back into the spotlight."* Blast magazine was more upbeat: *"Impellitteri is now a collection of firepower musicians. 'Stand In Line' boasts songs with big hooks, memorable melodies and excellent back-up from his band. Listen and believe."*

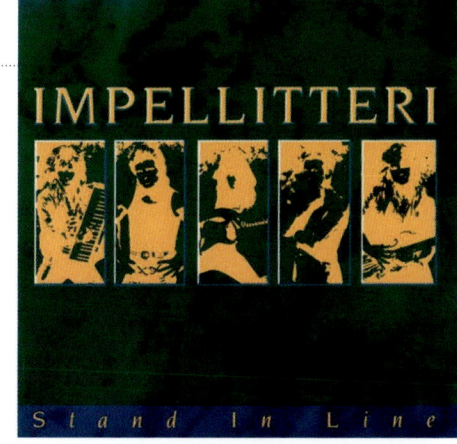

In June Graham returned to Los Angeles as the band re-grouped for rehearsals for around a month before they flew to Japan for two shows. Impellitteri appeared at the Nissin Power Station in Tokyo on July 17th, a warm-up gig, which also served as a showcase for the media, invitees and a limited number of fans who had won a ticket via a radio phone-in. The band performed nine songs in total; seven from the album, 'All Night Long', plus a slow blues improvisation, in the following order: 'Stand In Line', 'Tonight I Fly', 'Leviathan', 'All Night Long', 'Secret Lover', 'Somewhere Over The Rainbow', 'Goodnight And Goodbye', 'Since You Been Gone' and 'Blues Song'. Once he saw what was happening, Graham improvised a set of lyrics about Tokyo with a chorus around 'goodnight Tokyo'. The show was broadcast on Kanagawa TV (minus the blues ad-lib), and quickly bootlegged. Rarely seen Japan-only promotional videos for 'Stand In Line' and 'Since You Been Gone' were recorded on the stage of this club before the audience arrived, and mixed with live footage. The bootlegs show that Graham's performance at this gig was superb, one of the best live performances of his entire career. It won the praises of many in the Japanese media at the time.

The band were in Japan for several days, allowing them plenty of time to undertake promotional work across a number of TV stations. The gig at the Tokyo Dome, a huge baseball stadium that holds more than 50,000 people, on July 24th was a big event for all concerned. Impellitteri had the difficult task of opening with various CBS/Sony artists following before the headliner, and their set was the same as before (minus the blues ad-lib encore). At the end of Billy Joel's set all the vocalists from the other bands got on stage to perform a Beatles song. Recalling the event, Graham says: *"It was amazing. Billy Joel, Art Garfunkel, Boz Scaggs, The Hooters and ourselves. You couldn't believe the noise from the audience. Such a strange sound, it was like a jet plane landing. And when we played 'Since You Been Gone' they loved it. Then we all got on stage at the end and did 'I Saw Her Standing There'. Billy Joel was playing piano and he said to me 'what key do you think?' And I said 'I don't know, what do you do it in?' He replied 'D' so I said 'fair enough.' Boz Scaggs did a verse and Billy did a verse. Art Garfunkel*

went home, it wasn't really his thing! We did the whole thing twice through. I remember when we all went back to America, Billy Joel's guy came up to me and said 'Billy would like to say he thinks you're amazing'." It was one of the biggest crowds Graham has sung in front of, second only to the Monsters Of Rock festival.

Masaya Uchimura also recalls the show: "*The festival was called 'Kirin Dry Gigs 88'. It was CBS/Sony's 20th anniversary music festival sponsored by Kirin Beer. All the artists did a press conference before the gig. Billy Joel was in the centre of the desk, obviously, and the Impellitteri members sat on the right hand side. Impellitteri's performance was again excellent, just like in the previous 'secret gig'. I went to the show alone and I still remember that people around me were talking about Graham, saying 'who's that cool guy with a GREAT singing voice?'*"

Two days later Chris performed a guitar seminar then the band returned home. Graham had a couple of months off in Adelaide before he returned to Los Angeles so the band could rehearse a set for their American live debut, which was at the Civic Auditorium in San José on September 24th. The blues ad-lib was now part of their set and once again Graham made up some lyrics.

Long time Graham Bonnet fan, Rick Oswald recalls the occasion: "*It was part of a weekend-long event called the 'KOME Rock Expo'. Every couple of hours a band would play across the courtyard in the Auditorium, which had a capacity of 3,100. There were probably only a few hundred people in the audience for each act including Impellitteri's show, which was included in the admission price.*" Impellitteri played a new song called 'Here Comes The Night'. Graham says: "*I wrote it while I had depression in my rented apartment alone. The song was a reflection on my thoughts at the time and I remember my tears falling on the paper as I made up the words very quickly, but very much in the way I felt in that instant. It wrote itself, nothing too poetic about it, just raw sadness.*" The full set was 'Stand In Line', 'Tonight I Fly', 'Leviathan', 'All Night Long', 'Blues Song', 'Here Comes The Night', 'Secret Lover' (with a keyboard solo prior), 'Chris Solo' (including 'Somewhere Over The Rainbow'), 'Goodnight And Goodbye', (including drum solo) and 'Since You Been Gone'.

October saw Relativity Combat release 'Since You've Been Gone' b/w 'Stand In Line' in the short-lived 3" CD single format in Japan, in a 'make your own sleeve' pack! The cover featured a photograph of the latest line-up of the band. Back home in Adelaide though, all the flying Graham had done over the last twelve months was beginning to take its toll. It wasn't just a case of being on the shortlist for the 'Commuter Of The Year' award; Graham was having big problems in his personal life. "*I'd had enough after those gigs. I wasn't in the best of shape. My marriage was suffering and I was going through a bad time. It was because I was away so long. It was a depressing time if I'm honest.*" 'Stand In Line', which had only been available on import in Australia, was now issued there by CBS in October. Reviews were mostly very complimentary, the Daily Sun commenting: "*Impellitteri is a superstar metal act.*

The group displays boundless talent and will go a long way in the metal field on the strength of this debut." However this release would mark the end of Graham's stint with the band.

Australia is rightly seen as the original home of the tribute band, largely a way of giving music fans access to music they would rarely get to hear otherwise. Graham now found himself involved in this phenomenon. Guitarist Rob Pippan had been gigging around Australia with a band he co-founded in 1987, The Zep Boys (no prizes as to what material they were covering), playing large venues. Rob was also involved with the Australian Formula One Grand Prix set-up. The F1 day included a rock concert featuring some of Australia's biggest artists and Rob was in charge of sorting out the backing band. Initially he didn't even believe Graham was living in Australia but once he was convinced he began to make plans: "*Towards the end of 1988 I was told that Graham Bonnet was living in Adelaide. I was contracted to do a big concert in Adelaide for the Grand Prix, the Rock Of Ages concert. The promoters put together several big Australian artists on the bill and I had to form a backing band for it. I met Graham on a social level through some friends. We had a chat, and Graham ended up being included on the bill for this event.*"

Graham went to see The Zep Boys at the Tivoli in Adelaide and he told Patrick McDonald of Entertainment magazine: "*I was really surprised because the bands I'd seen before around this town I wasn't very impressed with at all. I met them backstage and we got on very well.*" The Zep Boys' drummer John Zak remembers meeting Graham after the gig: "*It was quite a surprise after the show; our friend John Pemberton said 'Guys, meet Graham!' It's actually him! We talked for about 45 minutes.*" Rob was more nervous: "*He was one of my biggest idols of all time! I was one of the only people I knew who had everything he had ever done*

Impellitteri • *with new members Stet Howland (top left) and Dave (The Beast) Spitz far right.*

with Alcatrazz, MSG, Rainbow, all the solo stuff, all his Seventies' solo stuff too, which a lot of people didn't really get."

A meeting was set up to discuss what songs to play and where to rehearse for the Rock Of Ages concert. Graham began to dig into his back catalogue for songs which were big hits in Australia. Rob says: *"We had some rehearsals with Graham and a band I'd put together with members from The Zep Boys, plus extra girl singers, keyboard players and a horn section etc."* Rehearsals took place at Artec studios and the main keyboard player, Sean Timms says: *"They had a great space and we could leave our gear set up there. My first impressions were that Graham was very highly strung but had an enormous voice."* John recalls the rehearsals: *"Graham's voice was unbelievable every rehearsal, despite a nagging throat infection. I would ask him hundreds of questions about his career. Graham opened up his crusty little phone book while we were driving one day. As I glanced over at him flicking through the pages I remember thinking that it looked like someone had created a fake phone book with the name of every famous rock star on Earth. But it was real!"*

The Rock Of Ages concert took place on November 13th in Adelaide, and Rob recalls Graham's slot: *"We did 'Warm Ride', 'It's All Over Now Baby Blue' and the Marbles big hit 'Only One Woman'. Graham also did 'River Deep Mountain High' as a duet with The Party Boys vocalist John Swan. When Graham came on stage he wiped the floor with everybody who had been on before him. His performance was on such a higher level than the Australian singers who were quite big at the time; it was almost embarrassing for them. When Graham walked on stage with about 4,500 people in front of him, the first thing he said was 'G'day motherfuckers'. This was a family type show. It certainly got everything off to a rousing beginning! Graham used to say he just took the performance as if he was doing another show in LA or Europe. He just went for it. I think the Australian audience were a little bit shocked, but he performed brilliantly."*

John also recalls the occasion: *"We mentioned to Graham that swearing was not allowed and to keep talking to a minimum, because of the tight schedule. Graham marched out, called the crowd motherfuckers about ten times then blasted out three songs leaving most of the audience stunned with mouths agape! In a very quiet voice he asked me after the show, 'was that ok?'"*

Rob asked Graham if he had any plans for the future. He hadn't, apart from wanting to record some new songs and look for a deal. Rob says: *"Around the beginning of 1989, I had a bit of spare time between The Zep Boys' commitments. So I thought to myself, I'd love to do some shows with Graham. I wonder if he's got a band or anything. He hadn't. So I suggested we do something. We decided to get a line-up together and do some shows."* Rob brought in John Zak and bassist, Warwick Cheatle from The Zep Boys, and keyboard player, Sean Timms. Graham also made an appearance with the re-formed Master Apprentices, who were a big Australian band during the late Sixties and early Seventies. Joining them during their encore at the Colonnades Tavern in Port Noarluga, Graham performed 'River Deep, Mountain High' and 'All Night Long'.

With the end of the year approaching, Graham decided to officially call time on Impellitteri: *"I came back to Australia and, to be honest, I was a bit fed up of travelling backwards and forwards. I thought about it for a very long time. I called their management in New York and said 'I'm sorry, I just don't think I can do this anymore. I'm missing out on being with my family. My kids are growing up now and I want to be around them a bit more than I have been the last couple of years. I didn't really wanna leave the band as such, but it was just one of those things that I think had to come around eventually. For a long time it just seemed like a lot of rehearsals and no playing and I thought it was about time for me to change my musical direction a little bit and do something for myself, instead of being another hired hand, promoting another guitar player,"* he told Byron Smith in Juke.

Looking back, Chris recalled to Fireworks' Rob McKenzie: *"I got to spend a lot of time with Graham. Graham is one of the nicest, considerate human beings I have met. He is extremely compassionate and easy to befriend. As a performer, Graham seemed to have fun. I recall he did not take himself too seriously and even enjoyed joking around while on stage. Of course he was a true professional and when it came time to deliver he gave it everything he had and delivered musically."*

During January 1989 Rob Pippan started organising a series of rehearsals and took on managerial duties for Graham, as well as the role of band leader. He says: *"I organised sessions, rehearsals and gigs, touring schedules and road crew."* He certainly gave it everything, right down to the photo shoots (by Sue Hedley) for the band. Around this time Graham also made a one-off appearance at Cartoons in Adelaide as part of a vocal-only evening.

In a bid to get create some interest for the upcoming shows Graham did quite a few interviews. *"I basically still wanna have that kind of hard rock edge, but I don't want it to be over-the-top,"* he told Byron Smith. *"I mean, the Impellitteri album just about takes the top of your head off. It's balls-to-the-wall right from the word go and I don't particularly want to do that. I want some more colour to play with. That music is just so heavy and fast that it gets a bit ridiculous and tiring to listen to, let alone go out and perform. Chris Impellitteri is one of those guitar players who thinks that the faster he plays, the better, which I don't always agree with. It's very clever, but so what? It's like singing high all the time or something. You've gotta sing in mid-range as well as high-range, otherwise it becomes monotonous."*

Graham was under the impression he was still remembered in Australia for how he was in the late Seventies. *"I've expanded my vocal range and I think my vocal has become more powerful. I wanna make a change, but don't want to get completely away from the heavy rock thing, which people in America think is all I do now. I can do other things and I think it is time to give it a try, to be my own person and to do my own music again. One time I was younger and I could afford to live by the seat of my pants, but now is the time to be more secure and make money as well as play the music I like. All the other things in the past have been non-starters. All I was doing was paying hotel bills and tour bus bills and management and agents, etc. I was coming out of tours with nothing for myself, but plenty for my manager."*

To earn a little income Graham also did a couple of TV adverts for a paint company and for Mount Thebarton Ice Arena, which had a purposely written rock jingle. Even his wife Jo was getting in on the act as a bourbon promotions girl.

Rehearsals for the tour were going really well as John recalls: *"Every rehearsal was an experience. Graham's voice was always incredible and he would just quietly thank everyone very politely after every song and we never saw him lose his temper or get annoyed for any reason. It was quite unsettling as we knew who he had worked with in the past. After a while we just realised that he really was just an easy-going guy and we relaxed. Until he blasted some vocals out the next time that is!"*

When it came to choosing what songs to play the set list basically picked itself, although the band did rehearse some songs which weren't performed. Obviously Graham had to include the massive hits he'd had in Australia in the late Seventies, as well as 'Only One Woman', plus a selection of songs from Rainbow, his 1981 solo spell, MSG and Alcatrazz. Rob says: *"We did learn 'Night Games', but we never got it sounding right. So we didn't do that live in the end, I think the band didn't really cut it. I really like 'Night Games' but we weren't good enough!"*

Prior to a warm-up gig, Graham spoke to Phil Thornton of NewScene, an Adelaide newspaper: *"The rehearsals are going fine and a definite sound is emerging. The band sounds really hot. We have our heart in rock 'n' roll but it won't be just another heavy metal band with long hair and guitars."* The band hit the road on February 16th with a warm-up at The Westlands Hotel in Whyalla, before the Night Of The Shooting Star tour officially kicked off the following evening in the ballroom at The Old Lion Hotel in Adelaide, followed by three more gigs back to back in the city. After a three-day break, the band moved over to Melbourne playing at Chasers on February 23rd, then The Palace and Richmond Social Club. Rob says: "The attendances were great. We had a lot of hard-core Bonnet fans turn up with all their albums to get signed. The live show we did was basically a Graham Bonnet's greatest hits package. We did songs from all his albums, but all of his really well-known songs. We did 'God Blessed Video' from Alcatrazz, which was our opener. That always got the crowd revved up. Also, 'Will You Be Home Tonight', which I believe was the song they used in America for a 'don't drink and drive' campaign and 'Island In The Sun' from their first album. We did some Schenker stuff too, 'Dancer' and 'Desert Song', we had that pretty well down." 'S.O.S.', was also included in the set, plus 'River Deep Mountain High' by Ike & Tina Turner and the Lovin' Spoonful's 'Summer In The City'.

Sean says: "During one of the Adelaide gigs a guy at the front was headbanging so much he cracked his head open. There was blood everywhere! He didn't seem to notice and just kept on going until someone led him away for treatment."

"I booked us a tour of Melbourne", says Rob, "We had a big production, big lights, the whole thing. We wanted to make sure that Graham was seen in the international light that he deserved to be. We didn't want him to look like he'd come down ten steps. We had to make sure this was going to be on the money. We played a 1,800 seater gig called The Palace." The Richmond Social Club date was reviewed for a Melbourne newspaper by C. A. Barnes: "The man took to the stage with as little a fanfare as I have ever seen. Nonetheless, Bonnet displayed a stage presence and voice that left no doubt in my mind that he has definitely earned his reputation as an international performer."

One particular song that was going down with the audience better and better every night was the old Marbles hit, as Graham remembers: "'Only One Woman' was probably the show stopper. I don't think we included any originals at that stage. We wanted to keep it purely greatest hits. The shows were fun. There was a party every night... My drinking days!"

John also recalls his time on the road: "We had to travel vast distances in Australia to get to shows. The travelling did seem to wear Graham a little, but I never heard him complain. I do recall the looks of absolute awe from fans at gigs everywhere as Graham belted out those vocals." The core of the tour set was 'God Blessed Video', 'Island In The Sun', 'S.O.S.', 'Will You Be Home Tonight', 'It's All Over Now Baby Blue', 'Only One Woman', 'Desert Song', 'River Deep Mountain High', 'Summer In The City', 'Since You Been Gone', 'Lost In Hollywood', 'Dancer' [Melbourne shows only], 'All Night Long' and 'Warm Ride'.

Rob was actually offered more shows: "We had offers from promoters who were friends of mine around Australia to do gigs in different cities," he says, "but Graham didn't really want to do it. He felt he wanted to have some sort of product out, or at least a good fee, which was fair enough. We had offers from Perth, Sydney and a return offer from Melbourne."

They returned to play The Bridgeway Hotel on March 26th, The Old Lion on March 31st and The Tivoli on April 15th, all in Adelaide. The problem with this was it was easy to spoil the magic by returning to the same venue too soon. Graham now started to focus his attention on recording a batch of songs – some were recent, others from a couple of years back. Rob says: "Graham asked us to do some demos with him on some songs he'd written, because he wanted to get another record deal. We were basically the Graham Bonnet Band for a while here in Australia."

The band entered Bartels Street studios in Adelaide, owned by Tony Elliott. They quickly rehearsed around a dozen songs and laid them down, as John remembers: "We got a lot done. And on a shoestring budget, Tony gave us a great deal and we went way overtime as we were all excited about working with Graham. It was a totally new and incredible experience for us. We couldn't help but feel a little pressure considering who Graham had worked with in the past. We must have told Tony a hundred stories about Graham's voice before we got to the studio, so seeing him experience it up close for the first time was very funny indeed! It was also quite an experience sifting through Graham's vocal takes as every one sounded perfect. He would regularly nail most parts first or second take. Graham also had trouble figuring out why we collapsed with laughter in the control room after the first of his vocal takes. He didn't know how impressed we were and thought something was wrong. It took a bit of explaining..."

"The first time we heard him sing in the studio the voice came out," remembers Rob. "We just realised at that point there was never any studio trickery. That was Graham. He can out-sing anybody I've ever heard. He's louder and the volume is amazing in his voice. He had an unbelievable ability to harmonise in the studio and double-track himself immediately.

"We recorded about ten to twelve songs altogether and probably did three or four sessions in the end. The titles included 'Rider', about American bikers, 'Midnight Crossing', which was very Michael Schenker-ish, and 'Reel To Real', which I think came out of jam Graham had had in Los Angeles with Danny Johnson and the bass player Jay Davis. He wanted to take the song further. We did a cover of an old song

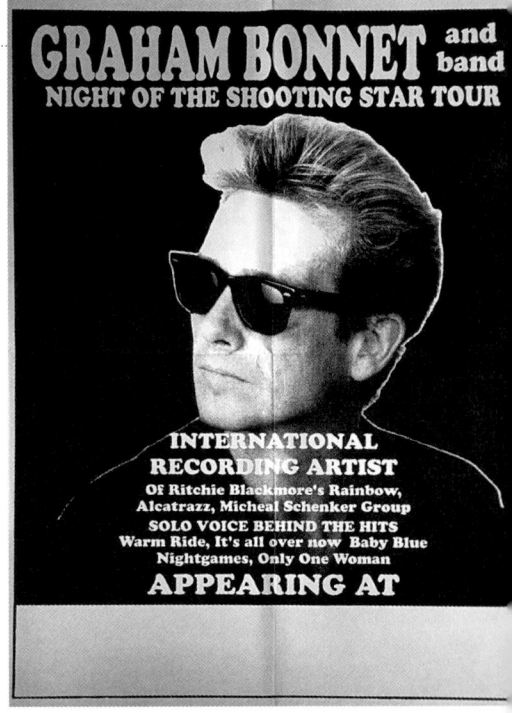

called 'Summer In The City', the old Lovin' Spoonful hit. Graham wanted to do a cover as he thought record companies might like it as summertime was coming in Australia! 'Long Time Gone', which he later recorded with Ray Fenwick, and 'Whiplash', was a damn good song which Graham had from LA when he'd finished with Impellitteri. We did a version of that and it was fabulous. Another one was 'Look Don't Touch', which we really didn't get a proper vocal on. It was just a rough vocal but Graham was sick that day, so he didn't want to take it any further. We'd got another track which was just done instrumentally. We just didn't do a vocal on it. He didn't want to come down to the studio that day for whatever reason. The fact that we were doing demos with him was just mind-blowing. For me personally, as a guitar player, I had to somehow measure up with all the greats he'd played with. Also our first efforts from a band point of view weren't up to Graham's probable normal standard, but we gave it our best shot and he seemed pretty keen to allow us the space to develop. We quickly grew and developed as a band from working with Graham, and some of our later demos I think were really strong." 'River Deep Mountain High' was also recorded during the sessions.

The band also had their input into the songs as Rob explains: *"We helped out with the arrangements. Graham brought his acoustic guitar in to the studio. Graham always called it his 'ca-hoostic guitar'! What he'd do was sit down at the table and strum these chords, and sing the song to us and say 'that's the song, let's make it into something.' He had a structure pretty well set for how it would go for verse, chorus, melodies, etc. What we did was start arranging it for guitar, bass, drums and keyboards. So we kept the arrangements pretty faithful to what he'd suggested and we just put our own bits in. He said to us, 'do what you think will fit', and every now and then he'd say 'Cozy would do something like this, John', or 'Michael or Ritchie would have done this on guitar, Rob, what do you think?' He'd*

Graham on the Australia tour • *February 1989.*

sort of guide the way to how he'd like to hear the song done."

John adds: *"Melodies and basic chord structures were Graham's. We collaborated on the instrumental parts and arrangements. Graham gave us a lot of freedom and genuinely considered every suggestion."*

There were plans for a single and album, provided a deal could be sorted out, but it didn't happen. The idea of a live album exclusively for the Japanese market was also mooted as Rob says: *"This was right at the height of when we were gigging and doing demos. Basically Graham and Jo were waiting to hear of a further commitment from Japan. Graham rekindled an old friendship in Australia with Barry and Maurice Gibb and he gave them stuff that we'd recorded together. There were a few conversations between Graham and Barry about the possibility of another solo deal in America."*

There was also talk of a supergroup being formed in Britain with Graham as the singer, as Rob recalls: *"It was going to be a super-session. Bob Daisley was going to be the bass player, Simon Phillips was going to play drums, Graham was doing the singing and there was a young guitar player. I think Relativity Records in America were involved. Graham was sent all these songs and he spent weeks working on lyrics and melodies. There were to be five singles coming from the album."* It all fizzled out, but The Zep Boys now went back on the road without Graham, although they did team up with him for a twenty-minute set, as well as performing a set themselves at the Bridgeway Hotel in Adelaide on May 6th which, as it was an evening featuring Adelaide's top groups, also saw Graham do a rock 'n' roll medley with all the singers from the other bands.

"We tried to help Graham achieve the next step," is how Rob sums up his time with Graham. *"Australia was fairly isolated, but he kept scouting around looking for other options. I could hardly blame him. After working with the world's greatest musicians it's pretty hard to come to a country like Australia and expect things to happen. It's pretty quiet down here."*

Graham Bonnet • *with his band in Australia 1989. L - r Warwick Cheatle, John Zak, Graham, Rob Pippan and Sean Timms.*

CHAPTER 10
Dangerous Games (1989 - 1994)

Featuring: Forcefield, Graham's solo career, Wind In The Willows and Blackthorne

A Monster Yet to be Heard

Graham seemed to have settled down well in Australia and his musical endeavours there had been well received, although they had not made much of an impact elsewhere. Throughout June 1989 he even did a few Q&A evenings with various DJs in Adelaide, mainly at Lennies Tavern and the Marion Hotel. Graham would chat about his career and answer any questions put to him. He had also become good friends with someone who had gone to the same school as his wife: *"Rocky and his family became my best friends. We would always hang out together. He came to gigs and was just a great friend. So too was his Dad, Tony and he was very close to me also. I would spend many nights on the back porch eating peppers and cheese and drinking homemade grappa with them. Their family have been my closest friends for years. Prior to Rocky getting married, he and his brother used to come and visit me and my family in America."*

Graham's next musical project came once again as the result of a phone call out of the blue towards the end of the Australian winter. Ex-Spencer Davis Group, Fancy and Ian Gillan Band guitarist Ray Fenwick contacted him about recording the vocals for a new album he was producing for his Forcefield project. As his old friend Cozy Powell was involved, Graham was happy to do it and Ray sent him the demos of the songs.

The Forcefield name dated back to 1986 when Ray had the idea to record a cover of the Deep Purple song 'Smoke On The Water' for President Records, which lead to an album the following year. Ray: *"It was just after Far Corporation did 'Stairway To Heaven'. I took the track to David Kassner. The next thing I knew he'd got the Japanese interested. That was Polydor who had heard it and really liked it."* They asked for an album of mostly covers, and it sold well enough to suggest a follow-up. The idea was to have a different rock singer on each album, hence the call to Graham.

During 1989 Ray, Cozy Powell, Jan Akkerman, Chris Cozens (keyboards), Mo Foster (bass guitar), Terry Pack (bass guitar) and Johnny Mars (harmonica) set about recording ten backing tracks for the third Forcefield album at Redwood studios in Camden Town, London. Polydor in Japan had suggested Graham to David Kassner probably because he was still very popular there and David managed to track him down in Paradise, a suburb of Adelaide. There was a rumour at the time that this was to have been a Graham Bonnet solo album, but that was never the case; it was always planned as a Forcefield release.

Graham went through the tapes: *"They were complete demos or just album tracks I covered. I changed them a little, not too much. They were very straightforward songs really and they didn't need much messing with."* Ray then flew to Australia with the master tapes so Graham could record his vocals at Soundtrack studios in Adelaide. Graham says: *"I'd never met Ray before and he stayed at a hotel. I was just working every day. It wasn't really my thing. I just treated it like a session."*

Back in London, Ray returned to Redwood studios to mix the results, and the album was given the appropriate title 'To Oz And Back'. Ray was very happy with how the album came out, especially the song 'Who'll Be The Next In Line': *"I think that's great. A very unusual version. I think it sums up Graham's energy. It's a real energy track."*

President Records released 'To Oz And Back' in the UK on October 30th on LP, cassette and CD, with Jan Akkerman, Cozy Powell, Ray Fenwick and Graham all featured on the front cover. It was released later in Germany and then, on November 25th, in Japan by Polydor.

The press release made much of the star musicians in a hyperbole ridden offering: *"After a perfect Rainbow, 'the eyes of the world' see the car with its Bonnet open and there's a Cozy sound of the engine roaring – and sometimes purring – keeping pace with Ian Gillan's one-time band member, a Ray of light named Fenwick, plus in and out of Focus, Mr. Jan Akkerman. 'Forcefield III' is a powerful machine and President hopes you'll want to do more than test drive!"*

The acid test was the reviews, and mostly it was well received. Ray appreciated that not everyone got the Forcefield concept: *"Some people hate what we do. I think the reviews have been about half and half. There have been some fabulous reviews. 'Hit And Run' would have made a good choice for a single. Alan Freeman played it a couple of times on the radio."*

"We've had a couple of serious offers to go to Japan, but we could never get it together because Cozy couldn't get the time off from Black Sabbath. They were put off and put off and in the end, the people just went cold because every time a date was set we had to change it. It's not Cozy's fault. It's just that his commitments to Black Sabbath were his number one project."

Back in Australia, the Forcefield LP aside, Graham was struggling to get anything together. He tried to form a band playing chart material, but found it hard to cope: *"I had a vocal problem, which was all in my head. I couldn't sing. My voice kept failing me as I was going through a bad time. I got vocal tension during rehearsals every time, because I was unsure of the way my life was going. It's amazing what self-doubt can do to you physically. I would start croaking away for no reason. I had my throat checked but there was nothing. It took me a while to regain my confidence, but it eventually was something I had to do in my own head."*

While dance music started to elbow out almost everything else back in Britain, Ray, Cozy and Graham (who had flown to the UK for a couple of months) were keen to buck the trend and set about putting together a fourth Forcefield album during the summer. The concept of a having a different singer on every album was out the window, because everybody wanted Graham to remain part of Forcefield, as Ray recalls: *"Graham has a great knowledge of music, which I am impressed with. He was brought up right from The Beatles era. The other*

Australia • *Graham in the Soundtrack studio, 1989.*

two singers - with the greatest respect to them - were younger than Graham and they didn't know that whole era. So they didn't have the background. There is a little musical barrier sometimes, but with Graham he has a wide variety of styles."

Another mixture of covers and originals was chosen (though Graham had no input into the final selection), including Bad Company, Jimi Hendrix, Don Henley and The Temptations, with two by Denny Laine again. The originals included a song by Ray co-written with Chris Cozens, and two written by Ray, Cozy and Graham, 'Women On Wings' and 'Living By Numbers'. Russ Ballard wrote 'Let The Wild Run Free' specially for the project and it became the title track. Talking to Rob McKenzie of Fireworks, Russ says: *"I think they made a good job of an average song."* Graham agrees: *"I didn't think it was the best from Russ."*

With Ray in the producer's chair again, Cozy recorded all his drum parts at Impact studios in London in between gigs. Graham did his lead and backing vocals at Watershed studios, also in London: *"I wrote the songs there. It was a terrible time too. Ray was driving me nuts. Nothing I did was good enough. Don Airey liked 'Women On Wings'. He came down to record on that day. It was just hard work trying to sing things the way Ray wanted them."* Graham's parents did get to come by and see what went on in a studio, and someone brought in a Sooty puppet (which even gets a credit on the sleeve!) for a laugh to relieve the tension. Part of the problem was that there was no band as such, and the album was being done at the behest of a Japanese label and designed to turn them in a profit.

Overdubs were done at Chapel studios in London and Graham also remembers going to The Manor studios in Oxfordshire. An impressive list of guest musicians helped out; Bernie Marsden (guitar), Tim Hinkley (organ and keyboards), Micky Moody (slide guitar), Terry Pack (bass guitar), Mario Parga (guitar), Don Airey (keyboards) and Chris Cozens (keyboards) with Barry St. John adding additional backing vocals.

Born in Lytham, Lancashire, guitarist Mario Parga had got to know Graham earlier in the year: *"I was mostly a guitar instrumentalist at that time. I played many sessions on the London circuit, recording guitars for several acts that were not necessarily in the hard rock or metal genre. I'd been offered a major solo recording contract back in 1990, and the record company wanted to base a band around me. My first choice of vocalist was Graham, so my then manager tracked him down to Australia and that's how we got in touch. The record company pulled out of the deal the day before I was scheduled to sign the contract [but] Graham and I kept in* touch, and later that year he called me and mentioned the Forcefield project." Mario played on four songs and this was actually the very first time they had met: *"It was as if we'd known each other for ages. We got on very well and have remained good friends ever since."*

'Let The Wild Run Free : Forcefield IV' was mixed at Farmyard studios in the Cotswolds by Andrew Scarth and Ray Fenwick, and President were amazed to be able to take a photo of all three of the main musicians together in the same place for the first time.

The session over, Graham returned to Australia to find things were very quiet, with just a few radio and TV commercials to help pay the rent. Vertigo in Australia issued a Graham Bonnet career-crossing compilation covering 1968 to 1981 titled 'The Rock Singer's Anthology', promoted via TV adverts, but while he was flattered by the idea it wasn't going to pay the rent (it was later released in Germany and Japan.)

The new Forcefiled album was released by President on November 30th in the UK, then in Germany and Japan on December 15th by Polydor Records. Metal Hammer's Tom Oakes quite liked the album: "Slightly soft, considering the power that is available, the unit does deliver some great songs, aided and abetted by Don Airey. Sadly, much of this album sounds like what it is: a group of great session players laying down some old standards and new material, but the whole gets dragged from total boredom by spirited performances from Bonnet (who hasn't lost any edge to the old vox). High points include 'Money Talks' and 'Living By Numbers'. Low points are a ludicrous cover of 'The Wind Cries Mary' and a fairly lifeless title track."

Kerrang! hated it: "'Let The Wild Run Free' amounts to little more than a week out with The Lads. A slack, sterile exercise in an ungraceful search for Eternal Youth."

Polydor in Japan however were very pleased with the end result, which fitted their target market ideally, and now approached President for a solo album from Graham. Having not enjoyed the Forcefield session, he nevertheless agreed. It was, as he put it, a question of *"money and desperation."*

So, early spring 1991 saw Graham travel to England to start recording, with Ray as producer. Graham hadn't really thought about what songs to record but Ray had some in mind. *"We chose them together and decided on them in England,"* Graham recalls. It was a mixture of old songs that Graham liked from his younger days, along with two of his own compositions, 'Long Time Gone' and 'Look Don't Touch', which he had recorded with the Zep Boys a couple of years earlier. He also co-wrote a couple with Ray, 'Please Call Me' and 'What She Says, You Hear It Means'. *"I added the melody and the words to those songs,"* Graham points out. Another from the pen of Denny Laine, 'Eyes Of A Child' completed the twelve-song track list.

Ray also suggested Graham should tackle 'Only One Woman' again reluctantly Graham agreed: *"I didn't want to do it again! Alcatrazz did it on the last album and that is my favourite version, because we played it live every night. The original is the best though, because it was new and exciting for me."*

Graham recorded across three different studios; The Watershed, Farmyard and Joe's Garage. *"Ray was okay in the studio, but it was a mis-match really,"* recalls Graham. With Ray on guitar and additional keyboards, Don Airey joined the

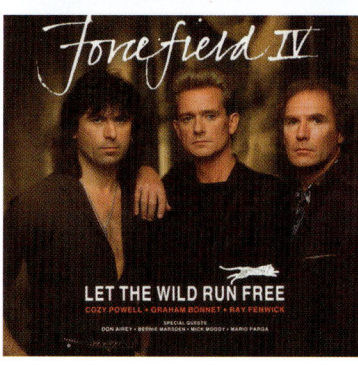

Forcefield • *Graham with Cozy Powell (left) and Ray Fenwick.*

troupe contributing keyboards to seven songs. Terry Pack was on bass guitar, Frank Mead alto sax and Dave Storey added some drum overdubs. Tony Rivers, Anthony Thompson Rivers, Michael Clarke and Barry St. John sang backing vocals. Dave Storey recalls his part: *"I was drummer for the American blues artist Johnny Mars. With me in Johnny's band were bassist Terry Pack, who I had previously played with in The Enid, and Ray Fenwick. Ray asked me if I would do some session work. I was there for two days and did the 'live' drumming on three or four tracks. Ray did all the programming. I didn't meet anybody else and I have never met Graham! I did get a copy of the finished album and I really liked it."*

Graham though was far from happy with the finished result. Once he had completed his vocals, he couldn't return to Australia fast enough. Ray, on the other hand, seemed more than happy with how things were progressing and after getting everything as complete as possible, flew out to Australia. Ray wanted a modern sound for the album and opted for drum machines which, although they certainly sounded modern, were definitely not the sound to have behind Graham's vocals. Back in the UK, Ray did the final mix at Rockford studios, with help from Paul Cobbald and Sean Lynch (who had earlier worked as the engineer on some of the backing tracks and vocals.) Graham was dismissive of the end result: *"I hated the album. It's awful. I didn't have much interest in it at all. It was a bit of a throwaway. Ray did the drum bits at my house on the keyboard in Australia. This album was crap to me and always will be."*

It all seemed even more insignificant when Graham heard that his mother had died. This came as a massive shock to him. *"It changed my whole perspective of the world."* He returned to Skegness for the funeral and stayed as long as he could with his Dad *"until my money ran out and I had to book a flight home."*

Mario Parga proved a good friend at this difficult time: *"I travelled up to Skegness and stayed at Lou's house for several days during this period. I remember going shopping with Lou. He was always very proud of Graham and he introduced me to just about everyone he knew, bless him. One day Lou decided that his house needed cleaning, no doubt to take his mind off the loss of his wife. I vacuumed, Graham dusted and Lou tidied the kitchen. I imagine we looked pretty comical!"*

In May, back in Adelaide once more, Graham was approached to record a live album and to write the score to a biker film with Bob Daisley and Lee Kerslake from Uriah Heep involved but the project never got off the ground.

Graham's session solo album 'Here Comes The Night' came out at the end of May and irrespective of Graham's feelings about it, he still felt strongly enough to dedicate it to his Mum, Irene Bonnett.

It came out in Germany and in Japan on July 25th, where it received a lot of press. Ray Fenwick had his own idea why Graham's career was stalling, and said at the time: *"It is 1991. You see the thing that has always happened with Graham - he has never been able to make a career in Australia because he would go to the radio stations with his albums, Alcatrazz, Impellitteri and they would say 'great Graham, but how are we going to play this on day-time radio?' You can't."*

Elsewhere it took the press months to pick up on the album and reviews were few and far between, but many seemed to like it. Tim Harrison of The Gazette in London said about the title track: *"Insistent and relentless, it slows the original tempo down to a powerful grind and is one of the finest cover versions of any Sixties song to emerge in the last decade."*

Dave Thompson commented in Seattle's City Heat magazine: *"Twenty-five years since his first hit and he's still kicking them out and 'Here Comes The Night' – which may or may not be an album of nearly all Sixties covers, all the songs I recognised were – is as worthy a smasheroo as anything else he's done. Worth more than a simple listen, I think."*

"If you are into soulful bluesy sounds then this set of crossover songs might just be of interest," said Brian Glossman of Cab News Trader magazine (President's press office was really working overtime!). *"There is one track which is a real peach of a song, 'Look Don't Touch', a mellow haunting song with a melody to cherish. It is an album which delivers more than you might have hoped for and one which I have played more than I thought I would."*

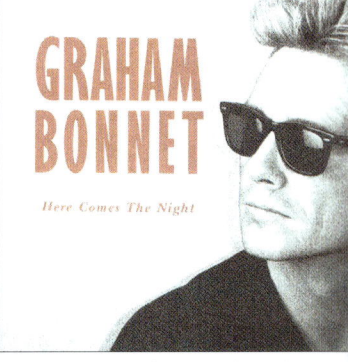

Needless to say Polydor were keen to keep the twin strands of the Forcefield and Bonnet projects going, as they were clearly lucrative. Graham was keen to try some original material but faced an uphill struggle convincing them as Ray recalls: *"The Japanese would like us to do other people's material. We have always fought against it. We'd rather write the whole album ourselves, but are being forced into it. It's never been by choice, believe me. It's always been the Japanese wanting that kind of thing. Having said that, I think a lot of the songs we've picked out are good ones"* In the end the series was not continued.

Of more interest from Graham's side was a plan to relaunch Alcatrazz on the back of a reissue of their second studio album on vinyl in America. Graham said: *"Jimmy Waldo and Gary Shea have been in touch with my wife and it looks like we could probably put the band back together again. But would it work again? I don't know."* This rhetorical question was answered fairly quickly and the idea was kicked into touch.

One project that did get off the ground though was the Kenneth Gordon-inspired 'Wind In The Willows' rock show, which ex-Spencer Davis keyboard player Eddie Hardin had put together. Graham says: *"Eddie got in touch with me while I was in Adelaide, he was a fan as was Zak Starkey."*

Eddie gathered together an impressive cast. Along with Graham, the other vocalists were Joe Fagin, Val McKenna, Donovan and Maggie Bell. Ray Fenwick (guitar), Tony Ashton (piano and vocals), Steve Richardson (bass guitar), Jon Lord and Don Airey (keyboards), Pete York and Zak Starkey (drums) and Raff Ravenscroft (tenor saxophone) also took part. During the first week of June rehearsals took place in Sunningdale (where Eddie lived) at a sports complex just behind the Red Lion pub where Graham was staying, for two shows at the Zeltfestival in Freiburg, Germany on June 14th and 15th.

The project was inspired by a 1974 album 'The Butterfly Ball' put together by Roger Glover, which Eddie had contributed to. Such rock adaptations of children's books were not an easy sell, but there was a crossover market for them. Eddie had enjoyed huge success in Germany in the early Seventies with his duo Hardin & York, and both players had a lot of clout in a country where promoters were more open to such esoteric ideas. Graham had a big part in the new show: *"I'm The Badger. I'm doing four songs myself, two with Maggie Bell and another with Joe Fagin and Maggie from 'The Butterfly Ball'. We'll probably end up doing harmonies as well. The music is so good, very varied, it's great."* Graham's songs were 'The Badger', 'Piper At The Gates Of Dawn' 'Life's A Dream' and 'Why Can't We Go Home'. He also featured in 'Good Morning To You', 'I'm Looking Forward To Tomorrow' and 'Wayfarers All'.

The 'Wind In The Willows' shows took place in a circus tent and went down so well that each night resulted in four encores, with 'Love Is All' from 'The Butterfly Ball', which Graham performed with other singers, and the Spencer Davis hit 'Gimme Some Lovin' with Graham on backing vocals. Both shows were filmed, and the plan was to record an album.

Graham flew back to England and visited his Dad in Skegness, full of enthusiasm about the gigs: *"'The Wind In The Willows' shows did go great, after all the teething troubles were ironed out. It was good fun and everyone was very pleased with the outcome. The show was in a huge circus tent with about 4,000 capacity*

Graham • with his father Lou, April 1993.

and all the best moments from the two nights were edited together; it's already been shown on German TV. I had some very complimentary remarks from Pete York and Eddie Hardin about my performance in the show. It's very nice when you get rewarding remarks from other respected musicians. It's supposed to be performed in Japan in September. There is talk of doing it in Disneyland in Europe next year." Sadly neither got to go ahead. Nor did an idea to tour it in Europe the following year. Inak Records later released an edited fourteen-cut CD titled 'Wind In The Willows - A Rock Concert'. Graham says: *"Some of the other singers in England had to re-do their vocals, but they couldn't re-do mine as I was an expensive plane ticket!"* In fact Graham sings very well on his songs; he wasn't given compliments at the time for nothing.

After spending time in Skegness, Graham arrived back in Adelaide in time to guest on the panel for the Miss Metal Angel competition at The Cathouse in the Tivoli Hotel on June 29th. But after the buzz of the solo album and the Eddie Hardin project, Graham's career looked moribund for the rest of the year. There is no doubt that had he been able to move back to Britain, many more options would have been open to him, but in Australia even if people did want to use him, few knew how to get hold of him. *"I'm playing the nerve-wracking waiting game right now, which seems an all too common experience that I'm getting tired of. This seems to be the way things go with me. People get excited about doing some kind of project and then nothing happens,"* Graham ruefully commented at the time.

Apart from going to see a rare appreareance by Ian Gillan in Adelaide on his March 1992 Toolbox tour (while Ian was on an enforced sabbatical from Deep Purple) and meeting him afterwards, it was another proposal to re-unite a new line-up of Alcatrazz which got Graham's career moving again. After chatting on the phone, Jimmy Waldo sent Graham a cassette of songs he had written with guitarist Bob Kulick as a precursor to a possible reunion. It was Graham who instigated the idea as Jimmy Waldo told Player magazine in Japan: *"He said to me that he wanted to start a band again in the States, so I sent him three demo tracks. He liked them very much so we asked him to join the band."* Graham added the lyrics and melodies to the songs, which later became 'Cradle To The Grave', 'Sex Crime' and 'Love From The Ashes'.

There was no Gary Shea or Jan Uvena and Graham understood that the project would have a new name: *"It won't be called Alcatrazz, because Jimmy Waldo doesn't want to have the old drummer and wants to start a new thing. The reason I am going along with this is because he has organised the whole thing, getting the ball rolling, talking to management and getting me an apartment! Jimmy has been working with another guitar player named Bob Kulick, who worked with Meat Loaf and others, and they have written songs together. So I'm kind of joining a new band. We have to do the ever popular demos and shop for a new deal, which will be helped by our old record producer, Eddie Kramer. He's offered to take our tapes to all the major labels, so we don't have to knock down doors ourselves. It'll be a great help because he knows everyone in the recording industry - and he's a fan, which helps too!"*

On May 7th Graham left for Los Angeles for a two-month stay but couldn't really afford the trip until one of his friends came to the rescue. He says: *"They had no money to bring me over. So I borrowed $3,000 from my friend Bob Tarca and I still haven't paid him back yet!"* There was no album deal yet but ideas for songs and an album were bounced around. Rehearsals started around two weeks after Graham arrived in the States.

Jimmy Waldo knew Bob Kulick through playing on the guitarist's Skull album 'No Bones About It' in 1991. Things looked promising, and Bob had turned down a permanent position in W.A.S.P. because he wanted to get this project off the ground. The rhythm section was comprised of two ex-White Lions, bassist James LoMenzo and drummer Greg D'Angelo. After a few rehearsals, the question of a name started to crop up in conversation. With Hellbent already on the shortlist, Graham says: *"The band was having a beer in a bar in Los Angeles and we were trying to think of band names. Greg saw an advert on the wall for Blackthorn cider and said, 'what do you think of Blackthorn for a name?' And we said, well, why not? We added an 'e' on the end and Blackthorne is a hard sounding*

Graham • at the Wind In The Willows rehearsal and concert, 1991.

Auditioning for Lord Of The Rings • Graham, Ian Gillan and fans, Adelaide, March 1992.

name. It's hard finding a name for a band that doesn't sound Spinal Tap!"

Blackthorne busied themselves putting together a set so they could go out and do a few shows in California to tighten the band and get them working together. They also recorded a demo tape of a few songs in a bid to tour Japan. The set was built around some songs Bob and Jimmy already had; 'Wild Inside' (written by Bob, Steve Plunkett and Donnie Nossov), 'We Won't Be Forgotten', 'Hard Feelings' and 'Baby You're The Blood'. Others picked themselves; 'Breaking The Chains' from Bob's ex-band Skull, 'Will You Be Home Tonight' by Alcatrazz, and the Golden Earring classic 'Radar Love' which White Lion had covered on their 1989 US Top 20 album 'Big Game'. The set wouldn't be complete without some Rainbow songs so the two hits were included. Graham says: *"Of course Bob knew we had to do those songs."* 'All Night Long', was sung with a more gravely and aggressive approach (looking back today Graham says: *"We took it into a higher key. It was horrible!"*). Another cover was 'Wishing Well' by Free and Graham liked doing this, a slightly slower version, which saw him change the melody in places. The band used to encore with a song that Jeff Beck covered in 1972 on his 'Jeff Beck Group' album, called 'Going Down'. Don Nix wrote the song and it was originally recorded by blues/rock musician Freddie King. Deep Purple had done this as an encore on their 1974 tour, after Blackmore picked up on Beck's version, so Blackthorne were in good company.

They lined up a few shows in Los Angeles and San Francisco during July but bassist James LoMenzo suddenly quit and joined Zakk Wylde, to be followed by Greg D'Angelo. Bob told Chris Collingwood of Metal CD: *"We played the tiniest, most awful places to begin with, just to see if we could make it work, whether we could pass the 'all for one and one for all' test."*

The departees were quickly replaced with ex-Pat Benatar and Lita Ford bassist Donnie Nossov, and drummer Kevin Valentine (who was actually still a member of Cinderella and had previously played with Kiss on 'Revenge'). Kevin says about joining: *"That was through Eric Singer who knew Bob Kulick. In Cinderella there was plenty of spare time - months waiting for Tom Keifer's voice to get to a point where he could sing!"* Graham had also known Kevin Valentine for a while.

On August 22nd the new line-up made their debut at The Marquee in Anaheim, California and the band's shows were very well received. Their set was 'Wild Inside', 'Since You Been Gone', 'Hard Feelings', 'Wishing Well', 'Baby You're The Blood', 'Will You Be Home Tonight', 'Breaking The Chains', 'We Won't Be Forgotten' and 'All Night Long'. Graham said at the time: *"We'll be ready to face the tough LA audience. Not that we've ever been slammed by our audiences, but we just want things to go smoothly. A large number of the people that are out and watching bands are 'other' band members. And they are sometimes out to pull their peers apart!"* In all with the two different line-ups they did about ten gigs around LA and San Francisco. *"All of which were our own gigs, not supporting, but they were only at small clubs as we had this new-named band. They were all very different, some good crowds along the way and some a little iffy."* The band felt it went okay, but as Bob said: *"No one was impressed enough to make a difference."* Kevin adds: *"It was a very short tour without any really good or bad things - just a well done club tour."*

As soon as the second batch of live shows had come to an end the rhythm section changed yet again. Kevin Valentine moved on and Donnie Nossov was sacked. Graham recalls: *"Kevin had other work and Bob fired Donnie for some reason. Then he hired Chuck Wright."* Talking to Michael Van de Moosdijk of Metal Hammer, Bob commented: *"After our first gig Chuck Wright told me that he thought we were a good band but the rhythm section was all wrong. He suggested that he should do it instead."* Graham of course knew Chuck from the recording of 'Stand In Line' with Impellitteri. Kevin was replaced with another ex-member of Quiet Riot, Frankie Banali, and Blackthorne quickly signed a one-off deal with Music For Nations in the UK (who helped fund an album), and Polydor in Japan.

In Los Angeles more rehearsals were arranged so the new members of Blackthorne could cut their teeth, and sort out song arrangements. As mentioned, some of the new songs had been contributed by outside writers, including Steven Rosen, whose credits are longer than your arm, and Steve Plunkett, once a member of the band Autograph. There had been talk about issuing a live debut album as they had been recording all their shows, but once Music For Nations had confirmed everything they wanted a studio album.

Graham was becoming a bit disillusioned with all the changes: *"Steve Plunkett had had success in writing silly heavy metal tunes for movies and for other bands, plus Bob Kulick didn't get my words, and since I knew Steve Rosen we thought we would make up the words and melodies together to get the song-writing done as quickly as possible. Neither of us were Bob fans and I think he knew I wanted out of there as fast as possible!"*

The nucleus of Blackthorne, Bob Kulick, Jimmy Waldo and Graham, whittled down the songs to ten for the album. Five were from their live set, including 'All Night Long', plus five new ones, with Graham contributing to four of them: 'Cradle To The Grave', 'Afterlife' (born from the keyboard of Jimmy Waldo), 'Sex Crime' and 'Love From The Ashes'; the final new song was 'Over And Over'.

By the time the new line-up entered Soundchamber studios, North Hollywood, on October 25th, with Bob Kulick handling the production, they had formed their own company, Blackthorne Music, for publishing purposes. Bob explained to Riff Raff magazine: *"Even though my name is down as producer I never acted as dictator. I was the logical choice, having the biggest mouth and having co-written most of the songs."*

Graham started recording but was getting homesick: *"I hope to have my parts finished by the end of November. It seems a long slog. It's very lonely for me, as usual, without my wife and the kids but hopefully this 'long sentence' will get us all back to Los Angeles again in the New Year. I got really sick during the whole thing and had an epileptic seizure during a vocal. I had to stop. I didn't like the songs and Bob Kulick wanted me to sing like the guy from AC/DC. So it was all a bit stupid - and insulting really."* There was only one track left over from the album sessions, 'Wild Inside'.

On one occasion while Bob was out of the studio Graham got together with the engineer and recorded a vocal track for a song in a more regular Bonnet style. The engineer was surprised and very impressed with Graham's efforts. Bob wasn't though, so that was the end of that.

Chuck also recalls the problem: *"My issue with the Blackthorne sessions was with Bob Kulick. I love Bob and we're good friends, but during those sessions he insisted I copy all his guitar riffs, which is not how I play bass. I always create my own parts to work with the vocal, the drums and the vocal melody. It was very frustrating. However, it was cool playing with Frankie Banali again. Graham was his usual self,*

Blackthorne • *San Diego, June 30th 1992.*

calm and vocally intense."

Still, it wasn't all hard work, and the band ordered from the local pizza place so often during the sessions that they even mentioned them on the album! Having originally planned to stay a couple of months, Graham ended up being in LA over seven months in total, returning to Adelaide on December 1st.

Blackthorne's album was finished at the end of January 1993, mixed at A Talon Recording studio. The album was given the title 'Afterlife' and the band now signed to Stagefright Management, with Neil Levine becoming Blackthorne's personal manager. The band now began to look at shows and promotion. During early February Graham flew back to Los Angeles before he, Bob Kulick and Jimmy Waldo set out on a ten-date Japanese promotional tour on February 27th, with the album due for release there in March. This involved a lot of TV interviews, and even a short acoustic gig in front of around 500 people. The trio did Sony Music TV, playing 'Afterlife' and 'We Won't Be Forgotten', and repeated the songs on other shows. They also appeared on Waratte Iitomo! which is one of the most popular variety shows in Japan, but is the last place you'd expect Graham and other rockers to turn up. Masaya Uchimura caught their performance: *"On the show the three played humorous games with Japanese pop stars and comedians. Bob carried an electric guitar with him and Graham sang the chorus part of 'We Won't Be Forgotten'".*

Bob recalls Graham making a rather expensive phone call: *"He spent all his Japanese money on one phone call direct from the hotel when we were there!"* Graham says: *"We played a few songs at small rock clubs acoustically and did pretty well. It is strange doing hard rock songs acoustically, but it was appreciated."*

Polydor Records issued 'Afterlife' on March 25th in Japan. The market there is generally receptive to well-played rock music and this album was just that, and sold very well. Bob was in two minds about what they had achieved: *"I thought a few songs met expectations, otherwise not so much."*

In Los Angeles, Graham and Bob were ready for taking in a European promotional trip in early April, but ended up in England having been thrown off the plane to Germany after complaining about their seats! Nevertheless they managed to speak to lots of magazines from their London hotel room, incluging Kerrang! who made it quite plain that they wouldn't publish the interview unless the album sold more than 15,000 copies. Talk about Catch 22…

Still, they managed to perform an acoustic version of 'We Won't Be Forgotten' for TV show Raw Power at the Gibson Guitar Centre in London on April 15th, after which Graham returned to Skegness to see his Dad. Word soon got around though that he was in town and it wasn't long before he was interviewed for the Skegness Standard. Metal CD magazine included 'Afterlife' as an exclusive track on their May covermount and Blackthorne's album was scheduled for May 31st across Europe. It seemed to miss the mark as far as most reviewers were concerned, many wondering why Graham had ditched his normal rock vocal style. Liz Coldwell of Metal CD said: *"Five men better known for the people they've played with than anything they've achieved on their own. Their sound is beefy, yet commercial. The weak link is, surprisingly, Bonnet's voice. He sounds here as though he's gargled with a cheese grater before entering the studio. Blackthorne are at their best on the more restrained 'Baby You're The Blood', where the keyboards are allowed to emerge from the mix and Bonnet lays off the vocal histrionics."* Kerrang! reckoned it boasted *"some great moments"* but felt Graham needed better material.

The album went down far better in Germany, with an excited Blasius Wiesbaur of Metal Hammer saying: *"This album is so good I am continually listening to it in my boss's office. No wonder with these musicians because they are all experienced. Older musicians can still show the young musicians how to play hard rock. The music sounds good without being dated. The songwriting, arrangements and production all come together. The individual musicianship is excellent."*

"This is a long term venture," Bob told Steve Beebee of Rough Diamond, and Graham added: *"He's just the kind of guitarist this type of band needs; someone who can write songs with a sting in the tail."*

Back in Los Angeles, while Blackthorne set about preparing to tour drummer Frankie Banali got married in May, with Graham in one of his famous suits performing 'Going Down' at the reception. Graham felt he needed to be back in America for his career to progress, and in June his family arrived from Adelaide.

At the beginning of August Blackthorne were due to sign to CMC International. *"At the last moment they said they didn't have enough time to help the band,"* Graham recalls. *"They had offered us tour support and a video to coincide with the release date."*

Blackthorne as a band seemed to suffer unduly from cancelled tours; South America, Japan in September and a UK tour supporting Black Sabbath all fell through. *"The band is playing the waiting game,"* Graham said, *"and*

Blackthorne • L-r Jimmy Waldo, Graham, Bob Kulick and Chuck Wright.

it's a real drag!" The band's management were really struggling to get anything moving, so Blackthorne started to look elsewhere for representation.

A US release for the album continued to elude them, despite a great review in US magazine Metal Edge; *"Blistering. Ten tracks range from the fast and furious 'Breaking The Chains' and the raw and ballsy title track to the heavy but melodic 'Baby You're The Blood' and 'We Won't Be Forgotten'. There's also a cool cover of Rainbow's 'All Night Long'."*

The year had seen the band continue to record demos and on into into the first few months of 1994, resulting in eight songs ('Paralyzed', 'Insanity', 'Man In The Black Hat', 'Judgement Day', 'Sanctuary', 'Save Me', 'Twist The Blade' and 'Dreaming In The Hideaway') for a possible second album, with a far darker sound.

With CMC having recently signed Yngwie Malmsteen, they invited Graham and Bob Kulick to an Yngwie gig in Los Angeles in early spring which prompted one magazine to invent an 'Alcatrazz to reform' scoop, though there was nothing in it. Finally, CMC got around to releasing 'Afterlife' in early June via a one-off deal, long after any die-hard fan would have bought an import.

The band had by now got a new manager, Todd Singerman, who was also looking after Motorhead. To help promote the US release Graham, Bob and Jimmy did interviews but CMC refused to fund any tour support so the band were left kicking their heels. Rather than sit about, they decided to work on new material, rehearse it and try it out in a studio to see if they could get some interest from Japan, a country now seen as a lifeline for many rock bands who were struggling back home. Blackthorne entered the studio in early June with drummer Jay Schellen helping them to record two songs, 'Skeletons In The Closet' and 'Don't Kill The Thrill'. It was basically a do-or-die situation, as Graham said at the time: *"We are finishing up new demos. Then maybe get a real deal here or in Japan. But we really don't know what the reaction to the new songs will be."*

Blackthorne got on the bill of the annual showcase for heavy rock at the Burbank Hilton Hotel in Los Angeles, the Foundations Forum, on September 9th. This was a last throw of the dice for the band and their first gig in over two years. Amongst seminars and trade stands, the Foundations Forum featured some thirty live performances from Dream Theater, Biohazard, Paradise Lost, Bruce Dickinson, Machine Head and Yngwie Malmsteen (who by a twist of fate appeared on the main stage immediately before his old singer's new band topped the side stage).

Music author John Tucker, who is a fan of Graham's, was on holiday in the area and decided to take in the event, even at the best part of $300 for a ticket: *"Taking part in a hotel the size of a town in Devon, the Foundations Forum was THE place to be seen at the time, a place where deals were done and the futures of bands and labels alike secured or lost. Nine bands played each night; as late additions to the bill, Blackthorne neither figured in the event brochure nor the original running order. Bonnet, Kulick, Waldo, the ever-reliable Wright and drummer for the evening, Jay Schellen, took their places on the smaller side stage and launched straight into 'Afterlife', followed by 'We Won't Be Forgotten' and 'Hard Feelings.'"*

However, Malmsteen's unscheduled pyrotechnics, setting fire to his guitar at the end of his set, had alerted the local fire department who arrived and insisted that the hall be cleared to check out the alarm. As a result Blackthorne had to restart their set well after midnight where they had left off. *"Very few people came back in to see them. Which is a great shame, because the band kicked back into 'Cradle To The Grave' and dispatched another three songs with an aggression and energy that had been lacking in the evening's previous performances. Those that did watch Blackthorne witnessed a furious assault by a band keyed up to the max and ready to explode. A handful of songs off. 'Afterlife' were accompanied by 'Breaking The Chains' from Bob Kulick's 1991 Skull album 'No Bones About It' and the ever-faithful 'All Night Long'. It's hard to see how a band that played so well under such conditions could fold so quickly."* But, as John himself admitted, grunge was riding high, nu-metal was on the horizon (Korn was the major showcase of the event) and it was difficult for traditional hard rock bands of any calibre to get a look in.

Chuck Wright also recalls the show: *"Malmsteen was on before us. He had set his guitar on fire during his last song. When he ended we started, but there was a delayed fire alarm response to his stage smoke and they cleared the room. When we started back up most everyone was gone!"* The band's full set on the night was 'Afterlife', 'We Won't Be Forgotten', 'Hard Feelings', 'Cradle To The Grave', 'Desert Song', 'Breaking The Chains' and 'All Night Long'.

Blackthorne • *at their hotel, September 1994.*

Neither their appearance at such a prestigious event nor their demos sparked any interest. With literally nothing happening Graham decided to knock it all on the head. He had been hiding his feelings about things for far too long and wanted no more involvement. *"It was a time I wanted to be out of,"* he recalls. *"It was one of the worst times of my life!"* The rest of the band members tried to talk Graham out of leaving, but he told them he wanted to be with his family.

Chuck Wright adds: *"There was no reason at that time to rehearse. We had no shows and everyone went their own way,"* which included him and all the other musicians starting up a new band, Murderer's Row. Their first album was in effect the second Blackthorne album, but with all trace of Graham's writing contributions removed.

Before the year was out 'Afterlife' was re-released by D Rock Records in America, even though the original CMC version was only six months old and the band wasn't even together anymore. Hit Parader in America picked up on the reissue and was quite complimentary: *"Unfortunately, their combined efforts on their self-titled debut album fail to match the stellar heights one might expect. This is a very good album, filled with stirring guitar solos and gut-wrenching vocals, but occasionally it seems to be case of 'hard rock by the numbers' and in the Nineties that won't cut it."*

Off-stage • *Stourbridge, November 2001.*

CHAPTER 11
It's My Life (1995 - 2005)

Featuring: Graham's solo career, Anthem, Impellitteri, Graham Bonnet & Don Airey Band, Moonstone Project, Elektric Zoo, Iain Ashley Hersey and MSG

GRAHAM BONNET
+ SUPPORTS

Graham's time in Blackthorne had really ground him down, more than many people realised at the time. Throughout 1995 and well into the following year, Graham wrote nothing at all and instead concentrated on his home life, spending time with his family and leaving his guitar to gather dust. This period of musical inactivity changed around July 1996 when he received a phone call from his old Alcatrazz guitarist Danny Johnson. Graham was led to understand that Danny had got himself a recording deal with Samsung Music in Korea and was looking to form a band. Kevin Valentine from Blackthorne was already on board and Danny wanted Graham to be the lead vocalist and write some tunes with him.

Graham decided it was time to pick up the threads again and having agreed to be part of the project the trio met up and, as Graham says: *"We spent a few weeks making up tunes together."* The first songs they worked on were 'Cajun Pink' and 'Model Inc' which ended up on the back-burner later.

Although he hadn't written anything for the best part of two years, Graham did have some material in his songbank. One of these was 'Whiplash', written just after his days with Impellitteri, which he thought would fit the emerging project. It had been recorded during his time in Australia in 1989, but never released, and now he and Danny worked on it together.

With writing sessions mainly taking place at each others' houses, keyboard player Pat Regan became involved in proceedings. A friend of Danny's, he had previously worked with Billy Thorpe, Quiet Riot and Lion. He had also worked as a producer with Doro Pesch, Kiss, Deep Purple and many others.

When Kevin Valentine was told that Graham was on board he instantly wanted to go in a completely different direction to anything he had done before: *"I thought about recording a blues record with Graham. I don't recall now why I wanted to do that. Maybe I had a connection with a blues label. Looking back, I think Graham would have sung the death out of it, but not sure if his fans would have liked it! It did turn into a typical Graham record because of the studio owner Pat Regan. He had a connection with Samsung Records, who wanted a new recording from Graham. We did the record and Samsung really didn't do much with it. They were VERY hard to deal with."*

All four members now started to bring ideas to the table and a couple of songs came to fruition in the shape of 'The Strange' and 'Underground'. Graham had also been working on two more which he titled 'Movin' On' and 'Breakaway'. Danny came up with 'Sail On' while off-and-on he and Graham were working on 'Winter Skin' together. 'The Wind Cries Mary' by Jimi Hendrix was a song Graham had always liked ever since he had first heard it back in 1967, and it was he who suggested that they cover it: *"The Hendrix song was just something of his I had liked for a long time. I was never a big fan even though he was obviously very talented."* The others came back with the idea of re-working 'Lost In Hollywood' which, after some thought, Graham eventually agreed to. They now entered Pat Regan's New Century Media studios in Los Angeles. Graham says: *"We wrote most of the songs first and made up a few along the way, but we had most of the album."*

With Pat in the control room, twelve basic tracks were put down. 'Model Inc' and another song, 'Killer' were put to one side leaving the rest to be worked on for the album. Apart from Pat, who added keyboards to a couple of songs, Jamie Carter, Tony Franklyn and Todd Jenson completed the bass guitar parts and Eric Gorfain added violin on a couple of tracks.

Everyone was very happy with the backing tracks, so it was now time for Graham to record his vocals and once again he found himself alone within the four walls of a recording studio. He recalls: *"It was just straight ahead boring days of singing alone when everyone else had done their parts!"*

Pat had to look after something else during this part of the recording, so with Kevin and Danny having been helping him behind the desk he left Kevin to continue recording Graham's vocals. When Pat returned he wasn't too pleased with the results and decided to start again. As Graham usually nails it very early on, he was very fed-up: *"I had recorded stuff in an orthodox manner with Kevin while Pat was away, not using headphones and recording in the control room so it felt more real. When Pat returned he decided this was technically wrong and made me re-record everything. So my best performances were lost as far as I was concerned."* With the sessions over, Kevin was presented with a song from guitarist, John Thomas. Realising its potential, he added his drums. The song would later become 'Spiked!'.

The album was mixed by Pat then mastered by Brad Vance at Quadim. Potential titles for the album had been talked about and one that always seemed very popular was 'Underground' which Danny had suggested. The album was now finished, with Graham still under the impression it was a band offering. All of a sudden this changed and it became a Graham Bonnet solo album. To this day Graham doesn't quite know how it came about, but he does have his suspicions.

A photo shoot for the album took place in Hollywood, with one shot of him looking naked wrapped around a large pot! *"It was a small studio and hot outside, that's why the shirt came off toward the end of the session. It looked as though I was naked, so we used that."*

Samsung released 'Underground' in Korea on February 29th 1997, on their popular Orange label, but it wasn't issued anywhere else at the time. Nor did Samsung bother to promote the album at all. There had been talk of a few shows in Korea, as Kevin recalls: *"It never materialised. Samsung is a strange company.*

They might make great washers and dryers but to deal with them in the music field - very strange!"

While left pondering the whole experience, Graham suddenly found himself in the middle of a Beatles event. Ex-City Boy and Steelhouse Lane guitarist Mike Slamer was putting together a seminar for Sir George Martin in Los Angeles and told Graham he was trying to get various musicians and singers involved to recreate The Beatles sound as it was in the Sixties, performing around half-a-dozen songs. Agreeing that this was something that he would like to do, Graham explained the set-up: *"I got a phone call from Mike, as he had worked with Danny Johnson. The show was done at the Palace Theater next to the Capitol Records building. Mike's wife Susan was the organiser. She had something to do with the George Martin people. I chose to sing 'Oh Darling'. Mike was the band's musical director, making sure the guitar chords were played in the same positions as done by The Beatles and the harmonies were the same with no added thirds or whatever. George talked about how he made The Beatles recordings and all that. Then we all did about seven Beatles songs after his seminar. It involved Steven Bishop, Andrew Gold, Brad Delp and David Sikes from Boston, along with two other guys plus two girl singers. The music was played exactly as The Beatles did it, same key, and everything else. I did harmonies with the others when I wasn't doing 'Oh Darling'. It was a great night. Quincy Jones was there, Tom Petty, Jeff Lynne and all local news stations. It was two days of rehearsals then the show. I will never forget it. On the last night before he went back to England, George Martin ran across the room as he was leaving and kissed my hand with a huge smile on his face. What a thing to remember. Amazing!"*

Six months after 'Underground' came out in Korea, Victor issued it in Japan on August 21st but again there was virtually no publicity apart from a phone interview for Burrn! magazine. Graham and Danny talked about the album and also a couple of other songs, 'Rider', which Graham had actually recorded in Australia in 1989, and a (still unreleased) love song from 1985, 'Set Me Free'.

Despite feeling very let down over the album, Graham did pick up his pen and paper again and start writing a few songs. He was fairly convinced that no-one would be interested in what he had to offer, but wanted to keep the momentum going. Before long Kevin Valentine was in touch again and liked what he heard, so much so that he took it on himself to try and get Graham a deal in Japan, with Victor agreeing to fund it. Graham: *"It seemed like I was done with, but I was wrong."*

Although it was far from brilliant financially, at least this time it was a Graham Bonnet album from the word go. Kevin offered to produce it and Graham was happy to let him get on with it. They still had the three tracks left undeveloped from the last project, then met up to talk about various new songs Graham had written and also listened to some demos from guitarist/keyboard player John Thomas. Graham had got to know John and bassist Tim Luce when Kevin brought them along to a party Graham had hosted during the summer.

The first song Graham played him was called 'The Day I Went Mad'. He had come up with the title inspired by the WC Fields quote 'the day I drank a glass of water', as he too was an alcoholic and Graham had begun to acknowledge his own issues in this area.

More ideas from Graham quickly became 'This Day' and 'Flying Not Falling', while 'Killer' and 'Model Inc', which had been on the back-burner from the 'Underground' sessions was dusted off. Kevin presented the John Thomas song, which became 'Spiked!', and he also suggested recording a cover of the Mick Ronson song 'Don't Look Down', and Graham decided he wanted to include a version of The Beatles' 'Oh Darling', since he had enjoyed singing it so much at the seminar. 'Greenwich Meantime' and 'Hey That's Me' soon followed, along with 'Lolita Crush'. They now had eleven songs and the album was sounding good. As Graham says: *"We always made them up before recording in a studio. Time was money!"*

Victor suggested Graham should go for an all-star line-up and it was agreed that they would try and involve an array of players, then they could market the album to a wider audience. John Thomas was the first to come on board. Kevin then phoned ex-Guns N' Roses axeman Slash, as well as Vivian Campbell, while Graham contacted Bruce Kulick, formally of Kiss, and Mario Parga, who he was still in touch with: *"Mario was an obvious choice. Kevin got in touch with Slash as he knew he was a fan. Plus Viv, as Kevin knew he would like to contribute, and I knew Bruce through his brother."* Kevin adds: *"We wanted to play with these people, but also needed name appeal for the Japanese market."*

In February 1998, Tone King studios on West Sunset Boulevard, Hollywood was chosen to record the backing tracks. John Thomas was involved in a big way. He played rhythm guitar on eight songs, and laid down three guitar solos. Interestingly, what became 'Spiked!' doesn't feature an actual bass player. Kevin explains: *"It was cut after all the others at a temporary studio Pat Regan had set up; it was the first time I recorded without analogue tape. John Thomas had written the song so I played to his guitar tracks and synth bass he had recorded at his studio. We liked the bass track so we kept it."* Danny Johnson plays the guitar solo on 'Killer' and rhythm guitar on 'Model Inc'. Bassist Tony Franklyn features on 'Killer' and Jamie Carter, who played bass on half of 'Underground', features on 'Model Inc'.

As well as putting his guitar down on four songs, Mario Parga also recorded a solo on each of them as well. *"Graham and I had always kept in touch, and we were chatting on the phone when he mentioned the album. He was living in Los Angeles at the time, and by coincidence I was going to be in LA in February of '98. We recorded my guitars at Kiss's studio in Hollywood. I think the entire album was recorded there. I was visiting Graham during the 'El Nino' storms. I remember us sat in his living room watching the storm on TV; houses were literally sliding down the Malibu hills. Then, all of a sudden, the same weather hit us. The rain was so torrential that water started to seep through the patio doors and we all had to grab towels, buckets and pans to prevent a flood!"*

"Another great moment," Mario adds, *"was when Graham visited me in Las Vegas a few years ago. I drove him out to see the Valley of Fire, which is a beautiful and sacred valley once inhabited by Moapa Indians in Nevada. The echo there against the rocks is amazing, and when we were stood in the most acoustic area, Graham sang 'Day-O' at the top of his voice! Anyone who knows Graham knows that he sings LOUD … I'm sure on that day he woke several ancient spirits!"*

Back in the studio, with Kevin playing drums on all the songs, Mark Eric came in to add a third guitar part to those Mario and John had already put down on 'Greenwich Meantime'. Ex-Kiss guitarist Bruce Kulick joined Graham and Kevin in the studio over a couple of days. Bruce knew they wanted him to be playing bass rather than guitar and ended up recording his bass lines for 'The Day I Went Mad', 'Don't Look Down', 'Oh Darling' and 'Hey That's Me'. Graham says: *"He was a great bass player and we needed some tracks re-done."* Tony Franklyn played bass on 'This Day' and 'Lolita Crush' and ex-Vanilla Fudge bassist Tim Bogert played on 'Greenwich Meantime', as did Matt Boyd, as Kevin recalls: *"I felt the song did not have enough drive, so I brought my friend Matt in to pump it up!"* Matt also played on 'Flying Not Falling'.

Slash laid a guitar part down on 'Oh Darling' as well as a solo for it, and Teddy Andreas also played keyboards on the song. Vivian Campbell did guitar on 'Don't Look Down', and Michael Alemania played keyboards on 'The Day I Went Mad', 'This Day', 'Flying Not Falling' and 'Lolita Crush'. The credit list Victor were looking for was certainly growing!

It was during the writing of some of the lyrics that Graham received the very sad news that his good friend Cozy Powell had been killed in a car crash on April 5th. He had apparently been driving his Saab 9000 at just over 100mph in bad weather on the M4 motorway near Bristol. He hadn't been wearing a seatbelt, was over the legal drinking limit and was also talking to his girlfriend on his mobile phone when it happened. He might have got away with all this, but one of his rear tyres had a slow puncture and blew out. Graham reflected on the news and penned 'Flying Not Falling' about his friend.

Cozy's death not only shocked Graham, but the rock music world in general, because he was such a likable person and a great rock drummer. Graham recalls the moment: *"Don Airey phoned me and I couldn't believe it. I started crying. I lived on the hillside and when I looked out the next day I saw two rainbows. I thought that was unusual, but one of them was touching the hill. I asked my wife to get the video camera and I filmed it. I said 'Is that you Cozy saying goodbye to me?'"*

Graham was quickly back to work and the next stop was his own home studio to record all the vocals, though he did cause a scare one day: *"I passed out from loss of lung power on one song and fell over. Kevin was calling to me over the headphones asking where I had gone. He thought I had walked off from the mic. It's happened a few times in my career when I have been in the studio, you know, like when you blow out too much air you get dizzy. I wanted to make something worthwhile and I concentrated all the time."*

"He was more comfortable there," recalls Kevin, *"making the recording process smoother, plus he didn't have to leave his home! Graham is a sweetheart, one of the best singers I've had the opportunity to work with, and the LOUDEST singer ever! He can hurt you if you're standing next to him when he belts it out. Unfortunately for me, he is also a pain in the ass in the studio! He has such a powerhouse, killer voice, but is somewhat insecure. We all are at times, but he is more so. So it just means it takes a little longer to lay it down, but when he does … look out!"*

Come the start of 1999 the album was given the title 'The Day I Went Mad' after Graham's song, and shipped over to Victor Entertainment in Japan. They didn't think it was heavy enough but were still happy to go ahead with its release. Graham says: *"I knew it wasn't what they were expecting, but I wanted to do something a little different."*

Kevin had the idea of filming many of the recording sessions, with thoughts of a video release, but it was never finished which is a shame as it would have been a unique insight into Graham's studio technique. Kevin remembers working on it: *"I got Slash's permission and we sat down and talked for an hour or so and videotaped it. The following day I was very excited in checking out the footage. Booted up the camera, put in the tape, fairly good video... NO AUDIO!"*

Graham also had to invent a name for his home studio to use on the credits and came up with Black Dog, after his newly acquired Newfoundland called Cooper. The artwork for the album cover was left in the hands of Mario Parga, who as well as being an excellent guitarist was also a very accomplished artist. He'd just about finished the detailed oil painting when his dog knocked it over, leaving it covered in dog hairs! He had to redo it very quickly overnight as Victor were screaming for the sleeve.

'The Day I Went Mad' was released on June 23rd but, yet again, Victor seemed to think it would sell without proper promotion. With nobody to hassle

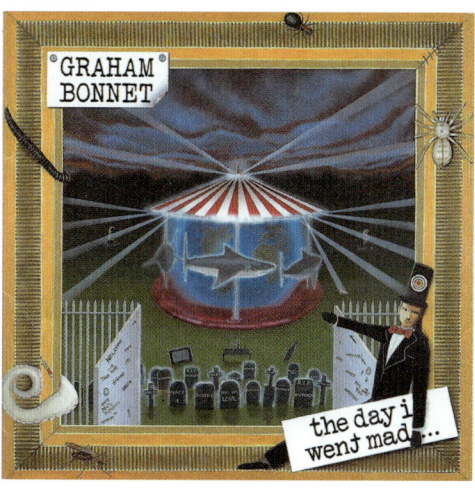

on his behalf, Graham expected the label to get behind it. Kevin Valentine points out: *"Graham needed a manager but was burned badly in the past so was reluctant in doing so."* Kevin though had also been thinking about setting up an official website for Graham and in July Bonnet Rocks went live.

Without a deal anywhere else, Graham and Kevin decided to release the album themselves in America. It was a real DIY job, and because they had only been given a small advance Graham even ended up folding the booklets himself to go in the cases: *"We thought we would make more money by selling the album ourselves for some reason, although I don't remember why I came to that decision!"* With no way to properly promote it, their plan ran out of steam. *"We put it out but it was a dismal failure!"*

It's really hard to know why one of the independent labels didn't jump in and offer to take the work on, but Graham had little time to ponder what might have been. His wife Jo was pregnant and on August 11th gave birth to a baby girl whom they named Tayla. Graham recalls: *"Jo and I thought of the name, after the singer Taylor Dayne. I wasn't a fan, but liked her name and we thought it would be cool to spell it with 'la' at the end instead of the usual 'or'."* The arrival of baby Tayla put and end to Graham's musical activities for a few months as he pitched in to help look after her.

He had though been busy adding English vocals to a homegrown Japanese rock album. Anthem, who had originally formed in 1981 and issued quite a few albums before calling it a day in 1992, had reformed to re-record a collection of their songs for the Victor label. This time they wanted the songs to be sung in English. Their second singer Yukio Morikawa had actually been quite similar in style, vocal range and ability to Graham, and the current line-up of Naoto Shibata on bass guitar, Takamasa 'Mad' Ohuchi on drums and Akio Shimizu on guitar contacted Kevin and asked if Graham would be prepared to sing on their new album.

After agreeing, the band sent Graham a cassette of eleven songs which they wanted to record, and the translated lyrics: *"They sent me a tape down the octave. The bass player did it for me and said to add my own inflections and ad-libs, etc. So I sang it up the octave from the demo. The songs also had English lyrics, but we had to change some of them as some sentences were backwards, so some of the words were made up!"*

Graham recorded his vocals at Black Dog studios with Kevin engineering, but along the way Tim Luce stepped in: *"Kevin had a good paying gig happen and Tim took over!"* Naoto Shibata travelled to Los Angeles to see it kick off: *"Naoto came with one of the other guys just to see the beginning of the recording, but they only came for two days. I was drunk on the day we started, so very bad vocals. I embarrassed myself!"* Eventually, Graham completed all the vocals to the backing tracks and sent them back, this time via the internet.

Naoto produced the ten track album and backing tracks at Mit, Taihei and Prime-Mix studios in Japan. There was also an EP was issued on March 23rd

2000 with 'Gypsy Ways (Win, Lose Or Draw)', 'The Show Must Go On' from the forthcoming album and 'Love In Vain', a non-album cut. The album titled 'Heavy Metal Anthem' was released on April 21st. Plans were quickly put into place for three shows in Japan, one in Osaka and two in Tokyo, with Graham fronting the band in July.

It never rains but it pours, and Chris Impellitteri suddenly got in touch with Graham and asked him if he would be interested in recording another Impellitteri album as Victor Entertainment had put forward his name. Graham agreed to this. On top of everything else, Graham and Kevin also started to talk about putting a band together to do some shows in California with bassist Tim Luce (who had worked with members of Quiet Riot, Kiss, Mötley Crüe and Scorpions), plus John Thomas on guitar and keyboards. Graham hadn't sung live for three years and knew he needed to warm up, so with the shows coming up with Anthem in Japan, a local gig would serve a double purpose.

Rehearsals took place in the Van Nuys area, with the band looking at a cluster of songs from Graham's back catalogue from the Marbles up to 'The Day I Went Mad'. As Graham says: *"It was a bit of everyone suggesting something. We all had our favourites!"*

Their debut took place at Joxer Daley's Irish Pub in Culver City on May 12th. The eleven-song set included three songs from 'The Day That I Went Mad' (although two of them were covers), plus songs from the Marbles, Rainbow, MSG, and Alcatrazz, as well as the highly underrated 'S.O.S.' from Graham's 1981 solo album. The set was: 'Spiked!', 'Don't Look Down', 'Island In The Sun', 'S.O.S.', 'Only One Woman', 'God Blessed Video', 'Will You Be Home Tonight', 'All Night Long', 'Dancer', 'Since You Been Gone' and 'Oh Darling'. Reacquainted with the stage, Graham flew out to Japan for a couple of rehearsals prior to the first of the three shows in four days with Anthem. The opening night was at Heat Beat in Osaka on July 11th then two at On Air East in Tokyo on July 13th and 14th. All the tracks on the album except one featured in the set list, together with the non-album cut 'Love In Vain'. They shook things up by including songs from Graham's Rainbow days giving the shows the following set: 'Gypsy Ways (Win, Lose Or Draw)', 'Evil Touch', 'Midnight Sun', 'Love In Vain', 'Yoshitaka Mikuni Keyboard Solo', 'Blinded Pain', 'Lost In Hollywood', 'Akio Shimizu Guitar Solo and Takamasa 'Mad' Ohuchi Drum Solo', 'Hungry Soul', 'Cryin' Heart', 'The Juggler', ['Shout It Out', 'Wild Anthem' sung by Yukio Morikawa on the last night], 'Hunting Time', 'All Night Long', 'The Show Must Go On', 'Will You Love Me Tomorrow?' and 'Since You Been Gone' [last night only]. Graham doesn't remember the first show too well: *"I fell off the stage on the first night as I was drunk. That's all I remember. The other two shows were good though."*

Back home, during September a couple of rehearsals took place for a second Graham Bonnet show in California, this time in Hollywood at the Coconut Teaser on September 23rd. The band introduced three 'new' songs, 'Lost In Hollywood' and 'Love's No Friend', along with 'Killer' from Graham's solo album. The line-up was the same as for the show in May, although the set's running order was changed around to accommodate the new songs and they started with the old Alcatrazz biggie 'God Blessed Video', while 'Killer' replaced the Beatles cover of 'Oh Darling'. 'Only One Woman' was dropped in favour of 'Love's No Friend', and interestingly the band closed the show with 'Lost In Hollywood'. The full set was 'God Blessed Video', 'Island In The Sun', 'Don't Look Down', 'S.O.S.', 'Spiked!', 'Will You Be Home Tonight', 'Love's No Friend', 'Killer', 'All Night Long', 'Dancer', 'Since You Been Gone' and 'Lost In Hollywood'.

Despite all this, Graham still had time to work on the melodies and lyrics for the new Impellitteri album when he had a few free days, and come November he had completed seven songs. The talk was that the album was to contain around twelve songs and all boded well for the New Year.

The new millennium celebrations brought a pause to the Impellitteri album project, but what was confirmed a little later when Graham was staying at Don Airey's house in April was Graham's inclusion at the Great Gransden Blues & Soul Festival in England on July 14th. Don was organising the event and wanted Graham to headline with him. They hadn't seen each other for ten years but while Graham was staying at Don's, the two of them decided it would be fun to go out and do some shows performing a set of Rainbow songs. They knew they needed to put a band together which would do the idea justice and after a few phone calls drummer Gary 'Harry' James and bassist Chris Childs from Thunder and Italian guitarist Dairo Mollo agreed to come on board. Four shows were booked to follow

after the festival and make Graham's UK visit worthwhile. These gigs would also serve to test the water for further excursions.

April 2001 also saw Masaya Uchimura take over the running of the official Graham Bonnet website. *"Kevin set up the original website. I met him for the first time in LA after Graham did a warm-up gig. We met for the second time at the Coconut Teaszer club in Hollywood in September, again after Graham did the show there. Kevin asked me what I did. When I replied, 'I am working for a Japanese software company' he then said 'would you like to run the official site for Graham? I am a musician and I am not a website specialist'. I instantly said, 'yes!'"*

Not long after, Escape Music in the UK released 'The Day I Went Mad' on June 27th, and this time it started picking up a few reviews too. Record Collector said: *"'This Day' is a sweet ballad, the pace quickens with 'Flying Not Falling' and the other tunes are likable melodic rockers, particularly the intricately-syncopated 'Lolita Crush' and 'Spiked!'. With a rather diverse selection on offer, it'll take more than one play to absorb this, but perseverance should repay."* Drew Orbison of The Groove Machine also liked it: *"There is nothing here that matches Rainbow or Alcatrazz - but this is not by any means a bad album, in fact it's pretty good. Graham's voice in particular is superb - as good as I've ever heard him sing in fact. The man has also put together an excellent band that helps add a cool groove element throughout."*

Back in Los Angeles, Graham was busy learning a batch of soul songs for the UK festival, along with some by The Beatles. As well as this he was reacquainting himself with some Rainbow oldies, plus a few other songs from his back catalogue and some standards for the subsequent tour of England. Don Airey, meanwhile, had put together an excellent band in England for the festival at Great Gransden, which alongside Gary James and Chris Childs now also featured the likes of Rob Harris from Jamiroqui on guitar and former Whitesnake bassist Neil Murray. Graham flew over in early July and stayed with Don for rehearsals for both the festival and the short tour to follow.

It's unlikely that the picturesque village of Great Gransden, eleven miles west of Cambridge, had ever seen anything like it, as several hundred rock and pop fans descended on the village. With Graham headlining, also featured was ex-Scorpions guitarist Uli Jon Roth, and they chatted about Graham joining him for another festival later in Wales, although this didn't materialise. Graham hit the stage at 11:00 pm. The set was very different to what fans would have been used to, and the soul covers and Beatles songs brought a very welcome change. The set was medley: 'Sweet Soul Music' - 'Soul Man' - 'Midnight Hour', 'My Girl', medley: 'Hold On, I'm Comin' - 'Knock On Wood', 'When A Man Loves A Woman', 'Since You Been Gone', 'All Night Long', 'Beatles medley' and 'Twist And Shout'. These were songs Graham had grown up with and to him it was bread and butter stuff. He says: *"It was so nice to play something different. I cut my teeth on this kind of music."* Don also enjoyed the festival saying: *"Graham could sing the phone book and make it sound great!"*

Five days later Graham was on the road with Don and the boys. Everyone concerned was expecting the shows to be billed as the 'Graham Bonnet & Don Airey Band', but the promoter had other ideas and slapped 'Graham Bonnet's Rainbow' on most of the flyers. They kicked off in County Durham at Easington Colliery on July 19th and ended at the Rock Café 2000 in Stourbridge on July 26th (a final show in Portsmouth was cancelled). On the strength of it a longer tour for November was booked.

Rainbow biographer Roy Davies was at the show in Stourbridge: *"In stifling heat the band kicked off with 'Eyes …' very much the Eighties' version. First surprise of the night was B-side 'Bad Girl' arranged as the studio version but far heavier. By contrast, a sparse version of 'Only One Woman' was very impressive vocally, though in comparison the acoustic Beatles cover was a mite disposable. The crowd almost exploded with 'All Night Long' which included a typical sing-along-Graham spot. Bonnet sang unaccompanied through the first verse of 'Since …' before counting the band (and the crowd) in. Graham seemed genuinely affected by the warmth of the vociferous crowd and it certainly seemed to spur the band (particularly Bonnet) on. Graham was in great shape and sounded better than I recalled; much richer and a touch lower in register, and if anything more scary than ever!"*

The set was 'Eyes Of The World', 'Love's No Friend', 'Bad Girl', 'Don Airey Solo - Maybe Next Time', 'Night Games', 'Stargazer', 'Don Airey Solo - Difficult To Cure', 'Only One Woman', 'Eight Days A Week', 'All Night Long', 'Lost In Hollywood, 'Since You Been Gone' and medley: 'I'm Down' – 'Lucille'.

It must have been good to get back out there, and as soon as Graham got back home to Los Angeles he completed all the lyrics to the remainder of the songs for Chris Impellitteri. He started recording his vocals over the finished backing tracks at Track Recording studios in Hollywood and at Impellitteri Studios. Chris had put together a rhythm section of bassist James Pulli and drummer Glen Sobel, along with Ed Roth on keyboards. By the end of August Graham had recorded six songs and completed all his vocals by mid-October. As soon as this was sorted he was back on a plane for England so the Bonnet / Airey band could get a couple of rehearsals done prior to the busy seventeen-date UK tour, with one extra date tagged on at the end in Spain. The band line-up was the same, as was most of the set although they decided to drop the cover of 'Eight Days A Week'.

This time the posters and publicity correctly announced The Graham Bonnet & Don Airey Band, with 'Rainbow Revisited' tagged on just in case anyone didn't know. The opening two shows in Stourbridge were sold out but four of the gigs (including London) had to be pulled when Graham caught a chest infection. That aside he was quite pleased: *"The shows were all pretty good except for the first, which was really fucked up, but most of them went very well. People were glad to see Don and me together."* The band finished off the UK tour at Chinnery's in Southend. The next morning they flew to Spain to play at The Bikini Club in Barcelona, where Girlschool were the support. The size of the crowd even surprised the band, as Don recalls: *"They had to open up the other half of the club during the show as there were so many people coming through the door!"* This set included a tribute to George Harrison who had passed away two days earlier, a version of 'Something' from 'Abbey Road'. The full tour set was: 'Eyes Of The World', 'Love's No Friend', 'Bad Girl', 'Don Airey Solo – 'Maybe Next Time', 'Night Games', 'Makin' Love' [not at all gigs], 'Dario Mollo Solo', 'Stargazer', 'Don Airey Solo – 'Difficult To Cure', 'Only One Woman' [early gigs only], 'Night Of The Shooting Star' [later gigs only],

'Something' [Barcelona only, dedicated to George Harrison], 'All Night Long', 'Lost In Hollywood', 'Since You Been Gone', Instrumental medley: 'Spotlight Kid - 'Light In The Black' - 'Kill The King' and medley: 'I'm Down' - 'Lucille'.

With the tour finishing that night, Graham flew straight back to Los Angeles. There had been some serious discussions about recording a live album with a studio album as part of a deal but Graham wasn't happy with the idea. The band were offered plenty more shows too but these were declined for the time being. Negotiations were also in place for an Alcatrazz reunion with Yngwie but disagreements over the fee put paid to this; allegedly he wanted 50% of any income, leaving the remaining four members to split the other 50% between themselves. Obviously Yngwie had learned more than just his guitar licks and moves from the Man In Black!

Christmas came and went and on March 21st 2002 Impellitteri's new album 'System X' was released in Japan by Victor. Of the ten tracks on the album, six were co-written by Graham. The album still stands up very well today. Talking to Rob McKenzie of Fireworks, Chris said: *"Graham's vocals on the two Impellitteri albums are different due to the musical direction of each record. On 'System X' Graham showcased his vocal talent really well. His power, range and vocal tone is amazing. A few of the songs that really stand out vocally are 'Rock & Roll Heroes', 'She's A Nighttime Lover', and 'End Of The World'. Moreover, these songs demonstrate Graham's ability to roar like a lion, yet have an amazing sense of melody and emotion. His range is also incredible on this record. I also love the fact that Graham's writing style and vocal tone complemented my guitar playing really well. It is definitely a very cool record that fits somewhere in between heavy metal and hard rock."*

"On the 'Stand In Line' record, the musical direction was really (more of) an attempt to be an extension of bands like Rainbow. In fact, I did not want to call the band Impellitteri at that point since my first record was pure heavy metal in the direction of Iron Maiden, Judas Priest, mixed with shredding guitar solos. Whereas 'Stand in Line' was more of an album that paid homage to bands like Rainbow that I grew up listening to. Nonetheless, 'Stand in Line' has amazing vocal performances all over the record thanks to Graham Bonnet."

As what Graham was like to work with on the two albums, Chris recalls: *"Graham Bonnet is one of the greatest vocalists I have had the pleasure of working with; and that is saying a lot as I have worked with some legendary singers! Graham's tone, power, and vocal range is incredible. Interestingly, he actually uses his real voice (not falsetto) when he hits the extreme high notes. In addition, his unique vocal style makes him one of the most identifiable singers in rock music. His lyrics are also captivating and always have an interesting story or plot, unlike so many lyricists that have traditionally written about the same old sex, drugs, and rock and roll clichés."* And as regards Graham's contribution to the world of music, Chris added: *"Graham is a legend. I easily classify Graham as a vocalist that belongs with people like Ronnie Dio, Rob Halford, Bruce Dickinson, and even Pavarotti. Graham has also created a style that is his own. He does not mimic other vocalists and that makes him unique, original, and exciting. I think Graham still has a lot to deliver to the music community. I always will have fond memories of the two Graham Bonnet eras of Impellitteri."*

There was one unissued track from the album sessions, 'Anti Social Disease', which Victor saved up for their 'The Very Best Of Impellitteri – Faster Than The Speed Of Light', released on September 21st. In Japan this album and 'System X' received quite a bit of promotion and publicity but no live shows were forthcoming and with nothing happening on that front, the month saw Graham take a trip to England where he stayed again with Don Airey for a while.

Back in LA bassist Tim Luce had introduced guitarist Howie Simon, then working with singer Jeff Scott Soto, to Graham. They got on well and when Graham and Tim decided to put a live show together for early 2003, Graham's first since December 2001, they offered Howie the position of guitarist. Having worked with Glen Sobel on Impellitteri's 'System X' album, Graham suggested they offer him the drum stool. There was talk of keyboard player Ed Roth who had also played on the album joining but, since he couldn't make it, John Thomas came back in on guitar and keyboards.

February 21st saw Graham take to the stage at Paladinos in Tarzana, in the San Fernando valley. The gig went very well and the set was far longer than Graham's previous two shows in 2000. The band were quickly re-booked for another show towards the end of July. The set was 'God Blessed Video', 'Stand In Line', 'Don't Look Down', 'S.O.S.', 'Love's No Friend', 'Island In The Sun', 'Spiked!', 'Glen Sobel Drum Solo', 'Dancer', 'Will You Be Home Tonight', 'Night Of The Shooting Star', 'Desert Song', 'All Night Long', 'Since You Been Gone' and 'Lost In Hollywood'.

Other possible projects came and went, including a rock opera called 'Rasputin' and talk of Impellitteri playing at a festival in

Graham • *Pennington's, Bradford, November 2001.*

England during June, but a repeat of the Gransden festival did go ahead on July 12th. The set was virtually the same as two years earlier: medley: 'Sweet Soul Music' – 'Soul Man' – 'Midnight Hour', 'Day Tripper', 'Try A Little Tenderness', medley: 'Hold On, I'm Comin'' – 'Knock On Wood', 'When A Man Loves A Woman', 'Since You Been Gone', 'All Night Long', 'Land Of A Thousand Dances' and 'Will You Love Me Tomorrow?'.

More rehearsals then took place for a second show at Paladinos on July 26th. It had been decided that the set needed shaking up, so consequently 'Night Of The Shooting Star' was dropped and very interestingly replaced with a medley of 'Only One Woman' - 'The Walls Fell Down' - 'I'm A Lover'. The set was 'Too Young To Die, Too Drunk To Live', 'God Blessed Video', 'Stand In Line', 'Love's No Friend', 'Samurai', 'Island In The Sun', 'Spiked!', 'Will You Be Home Tonight', medley: 'Only One Woman' - 'The Walls Fell Down' - 'I'm A Lover', 'Night Games', 'Desert Song', 'All Night Long', 'Since You Been Gone' and 'Lost In Hollywood', and both the show itself and the new songs

Say cheese • *Photographed for Powerplay Magazine 2002.*

included in it were very well received.

The success of this was knocked though by the news that Graham's Dad Lou, who had been suffering from Alzheimer's disease for quite a while, passed away on October 27th. His funeral took place on November 6th and he was buried next to his wife Rene in Winthorpe church graveyard.

There had been talk of Graham and Don doing a 'Rainbow Revival' gig in Lochgelly, Fife, Scotland on December 6th and adverts had even hit the UK press but, due to Don's touring schedule with Deep Purple, the gig never took place.

Towards the end of the year Graham addressed his own problems and gave up drinking. It had been a major part of his life for the last three decades. After falling over and landing in the mud at the back of his house one day, and having to be dragged out of it and helped back inside by his son, Graham eventually realised he had a problem. His wife Jo discussed it with him and it made him realise what he had put his family and his friends through over the years. It was a big decision to quit and he found it hard at times, especially in a business where it is almost part of the life, but he started attending Alcoholics Anonymous meetings and to this day has stayed on the wagon.

A third show at Paladinos was due to take place in January 2004 but a sinus infection put Graham out of action and the gig was cancelled at very short notice, although the rest of the band played a short set to assuage fans. Once he was well, a gig was booked at the Club Vodka in Hollywood on March 11th. The band's line-up was exactly the same as before with the exception of Steffan Svensson, who replaced Glen Sobel on drums. The set was more or less the same as the last gig: 'Too Young To Die, Too Drunk To Live', 'God Blessed Video', 'Stand In Line', 'Love's No Friend', 'Samurai', 'Island In The Sun', 'Will You Be Home Tonight', 'Night Games', 'Night Of The Shooting Star', 'Desert Song', 'All Night Long', 'Since You Been Gone' and 'Lost In Hollywood'.

It was to Italy that Graham owed his next projects. Long a country which admired Seventies' rock, many of the new generation of players there were keen to work with older, well-regarded musicians. It was now announced that Graham would be joining guitarist Dario Mollo's new project, Elektric Zoo, for gigs in

Graham • *Bradford Rio club, May 2004.*

Spain, Austria, Belgium, Italy and the UK from mid-April to mid-May (with a possible extended UK twenty-five-date tour in October and an album, neither of which happened). As well as this, Graham agreed to guest on 'Moonstone Project', brainchild of Italian guitarist Matteo Filippini. He cut the vocals for a track called 'Not Dead Yet' at Tim Luce's house during mid-March.

Going into April, he focused his attention on learning new songs for his tour with Elektric Zoo. The Alcatrazz song, 'Mercy', had never been played live before so that was an interesting choice. Two songs by The Cage ('Life, Love & Everything' and 'Poison Roses') which Dario had recorded with ex-Black Sabbath singer Tony Martin in 2002 were also in the set. Graham flew to Italy for the ten-date tour (gigs in Belgium had been dropped) with Elektric Zoo which kicked off at the Vox Pub in Milan on April 17th. He and Dario already knew a lot of the material, having played most of the Rainbow songs on their 2001 tours, so it was just a question of Dario's fellow Italians, bassist Guido Block, keyboard player Maurizio Belluzzo and drummer Roberto Gualdi, getting up to speed during the handful of rehearsals. Dario had also decided to include 'Race With The Devil On A Spanish Highway' by Al Dimeola and 'Make Believe' from the second Voodoo Hill album he had recorded with Glenn Hughes; Guido Block took the lead vocals on this one.

By the time Elektric Zoo hit the UK, 'Makin' Love' by Rainbow and 'Night Games' had been dropped to shorten the set, as was a proposed acoustic sequence from Graham. The UK set was therefore: 'Eyes Of The World', 'God Blessed Video', 'Love's No Friend', 'Life, Love, Everything', 'Bad Girl', 'Mercy', 'Guido Block Bass Solo', 'Desert Song', 'Stargazer', 'Race With The Devil On A Spanish Highway', 'Roberto Gualdi Drum Solo', 'Poison Roses', 'Maurizio Belluzzo Keyboard Solo', 'Make Believe' [sung by Guido Block], 'Lazy' [instrumental], 'All Night Long', 'Since You Been Gone' and 'Lost In Hollywood'.

The band were driven from their show at Bradford Rio's to London for a gig the following evening at the West One Four. Record Collector reviewed it: *"The great man hit the stage at 10:30 and kicked off with Rainbow's 'Eyes Of The World'. Some excellent keyboard work and Graham's strong vocals made it a fine start. Tracks from Alcatrazz, Rainbow and some solo work followed, including 'All Night Long'. Also welcome was a superb 'Stargazer'. It was soon apparent that Graham wasn't in the best of health. Despite the criminal omission of 'Night Games' (when he hits the right note he can blow anyone off stage – the voice of rock) with Don Airey in the audience and guesting for 'Since You Been Gone' it was truly a memorable experience."* The tour concluded at Café Drummonds in Aberdeen, Scotland, on May 10th. After the tour Graham returned to Los Angeles. Looking back on it, he says: *"It all went very well. The live shows were maybe better than I have done in a long time."*

Graham spent a couple of months taking it easy before returning to the UK for his third appearance at the Great Gransden Blues and Soul Festival on July 16th with another ex-Rainbow singer Doogie White also on the bill.

Before Graham's next US gig at Paladinos on September 24th, he was again able to relax and spend time with his family before getting back to rehearsals. Glen Sobel was back on drums and the band began working up a set. Graham had always known that 'Eyes Of The World' was a great opening song right back from his Rainbow days and, having just experienced it once again on the Elektric Zoo tour, it was in his mind so the band set about learning it. MSG's 'Assault Attack' was brought in to replace 'Samurai', but as a lead into it Graham sang the first verse of the Alcatrazz song 'Suffer Me'. 'Oh Darling' was also drafted back into the set for the first time since May 2000 as part of the encore. Graham was in mighty fine form and the new running order worked very well. 'Night Of The Shooting Star' would also have been included, had Graham not forgotten to take his guitar! The full set was: 'Eyes Of The World', 'Too Young To Die, Too Drunk To Live', 'Love's No Friend', 'God Blessed Video', 'Bad Girl', 'Suffer Me' [intro only], 'Assault Attack', 'Will You Be Home Tonight', 'Island In The Sun', 'Desert Song', 'Stand In Line', 'Glen Sobel Drum Solo', 'Lost In Hollywood', 'Oh Darling', and Medley: 'All Night Long' - 'Since You Been Gone'.

In the build-up for the show, American guitarist Iain Ashley Hersey contacted Graham to see if he was interested in singing on the remaining three songs on his planned second album. Graham agreed, as Iain recalls: *"Most of the CD was done. If I'd had the opportunity of running into him earlier, I would have had Graham do the whole thing. I have always been into Graham's voice. The power, range, control, as well as having that edge! Also, serendipity, to get to run into him and ask him."*

Iain wanted to include 'Going Down', and since Graham had already sung it live with Blackthorne, that worked out very well. The other two songs were originals titled 'The Holy Grail' and 'Walking The Talk'. He took the backing tracks up to Graham's house himself (after the courier had screwed up delivery the first time around!). Iain had written all the lyrics and melodies, but encouraged Graham to put his own spin on them and even gave him a co-writers' credit on the two original songs. *"I presented him with just the musical tracks as a blank canvas, which is what I like to do with all vocalists that I work with. I presented him with a guide track with me singing an octave lower, as I never would have been able to sing in Graham's range. He changed some lyrics and lines so they would work better from a vocalist's perspective and he obviously put his own style or twist on the melodies."* Graham worked on the tracks in his studio with Tim Luce, tackling 'Going Down' first.

Meanwhile, in Finland, and the start of the New Year guitarist Asko 'Daffy' Terävä and his friends were putting a new band together. Daffy, who had previously played with Michael Monroe and was still heavily involved with Finnish band Yö, was a huge fan of Graham's: *"There was me, guitarist Lamppari Lamminsivu and drummer Lacu celebrating the New Year. We'd all played in Michael Monroe's band at the same time during 1999-2000 and we were talking about putting a band together. First we thought about an artist who we could do a tribute to. That's when we started talking about Graham Bonnet. I believe it was me who started that because 'Down To Earth', 'Assault Attack' and 'Disturbing The Peace' are in my all-time top ten favourite albums. Then we had a problem, who could sing these songs? We couldn't think of anyone from Finland!"*

There was only one thing left to do and that was to contact the man him himself, which Daffy did on January 2nd. He couldn't believe his luck when Graham got back to him virtually straight away saying he would really like to go ahead with his idea. *"Graham gave us his phone number in his first email,"* recalls Daffy, who's first ever rock album was 'Down To Earth' which he bought in 1980.

It was going to be a very busy year. January saw Graham complete the songs for Iain Ashley Hersey, 'Walking The Talk' and 'The Holy Grail'. Iain was more than happy with the results: *"After Graham did his tracks, Bobby Kimball of Toto was willing to do a guest track. I'm sure he would have been into doing 'Going Down', as he has been doing that song for years, but Graham had done such a killer job on it I did not want to replace it."*

Graham was also contacted by Michael Schenker to be part of the MSG show at the NAMM 'Night Of Guitar' concert at The Vault 350 in Long Beach in January, singing 'Assault Attack' with the band. However, come the day of the show he became ill and couldn't make it.

He had also been asked to play three shows in Russia and Lithuania which was quite exciting as he had never been there before. The backing outfit for these was the Green Town Band, a pretty competent covers outfit featuring Stanislav Michailov (guitar), Vadim Vintsentin (bass guitar), Igor Turkin (keyboards), Alexey Saveliev (drums) and vocalist Andrey Charmov. Ten of the songs were actually in the set that Graham had done at Paladinos the previous September, but one surprise was the inclusion of 'Hold On' from Graham's time with Forcefield, which had never been played live before. In mid-February Graham travelled by himself to Moscow, where he was met at the airport and unbelievably taken straight to a rehearsal. He recalls: *"The band was waiting for me that afternoon. You can imagine how awful I was at that rehearsal. Jet lagged and spaced out!"*

The short tour began on February 22nd at the B2 Club in Moscow (where the fans turned out in force, some passing Graham photographs to sign during the gig, which he did!), followed by another show at the City Park in Kaliningrad, and the final concert in Lithuania on February 27th at the Forum Palace Galaxy in Vilnius. Graham says: *"Once the jet lag had gone the shows went very well and we played large venues. The band was very good and there was a great response from the Russian audiences."* The set was 'Eyes Of The World', 'God Blessed Video', 'Love's No Friend', 'Bad Girl', 'Hold On', 'Assault Attack', 'Stargazer', 'Maybe Next Time', 'All Night Long', 'Since You Been Gone', 'Will You Be Home Tonight', 'Oh Darling' and 'Lost In Hollywood'. Green Town Band were their own opening act, doing a short set of rock covers by Whitesnake, Deep Purple, Uriah Heep and Kiss with their own singer, who later joined Graham and the band on stage for the encore, 'Lost In Hollywood'.

Graham's next venture was as a special guest at another Paladinos show, fronting Iain Ashley Hersey's album pre-launch on March 26th, with everyone who had appeared on the album plus Jerry Beller. Iain and his band had two rehearsals without Graham, one on the eve of the gig: *"I had to keep suggesting to Graham that we do one of the Rainbow tracks from 'Down to Earth'. At the eleventh hour Graham said 'let's do 'Love's No Friend'', a tune I've always loved. So everyone in the band, including myself, is scrambling to learn it the night before the gig! Regardless, at the end of the day, it came out well. We started the show and Graham showed up just in time for his part."*

Although Graham had missed the MSG gig, their planned 25th anniversary album titled 'Tales Of Rock 'N' Roll' was now well under way. Graham had been a little nervous about working with Michael again but contributed the melody and lyrics to a song that Michael had given him: *"I wrote a song called 'Tales Of Rock 'N' Roll', but he changed the name to 'Rock 'N' Roll' so I wouldn't look like the star on the album because I had the lead song!"* Graham recorded his vocals in what now was the Bonnet Rocks studio with Tim Luce. Michael and Graham began to chat a lot on the phone.

Over in Finland, Daffy had been working extremely hard piecing together a five-date tour for May which also included Sweden and Estonia. Daffy says: *"I booked the gigs and made the contracts myself. I took care of radio promotion, newspapers, fan clubs, merchandise, posters, hotels, flight tickets, boat tickets, transportation, PA, crew and tour managing etc. I took the financial risk."*

Daffy put a very experienced band together consisting of himself and Mika 'Lamppari' Lamminsivu on guitar, Jay Lewis on bass, Pate Flintstone on keyboards and Lacu Lahtinen behind the drum kit. They quickly nailed the songs and the set soon came together as Daffy points out: *"Graham asked me which songs are popular in Finland. I suggested some and we made the list together on the phone. I don't think Graham was too keen on singing 'Stargazer' or 'Assault Attack', but we played them!"*

Graham arrived in Finland on May 3rd, three days before the opening show at Tullikamarin Pakkahuone in Tampere. Daffy remembers: *"We did two rehearsals with Graham and several before he arrived. He didn't sing anything seriously at the rehearsals. In fact, he didn't want a microphone. Graham was doing impressions of old British sitcoms and he sung some lines with Monty Python type funny voices! The first time we heard him singing at full power was at the first gig at the old customs house in our hometown Tampere. There were about 500 people, and I remember getting goose pimples when he started singing 'Eyes Of The World'."*

The tour wasn't without its ups and downs, including Graham sending his luggage – and passport – ahead, thus causing anxious moments at the Estonian boarder. Graham recalls: *"I left my passport in my suitcase. I'd never heard of Estonia! Nobody informed me I should have had my passport with me!"* Graham thought it was a town in Finland. That aside, however, Daffy says: *"People were very thrilled everywhere. All the gigs went well. It was the first time I'd seen middle aged men crying during the set. They were so happy to hear those songs."*

Graham returned to Los Angeles on May 11th and was contacted about teaming up with his former MSG colleagues from 1982, bassist Chris Glen and drummer Ted McKenna. This was to form a Michael Schenker type band (but with another guitarist, obviously) for some shows in the UK. It got no further than the drawing board. But as that idea folded, another resurfaced, albeit a year later than planned, as work eventually began during the summer recording vocals for the Elektric Zoo album in Graham's own studio. He was also in demand back in Britain too, and a ten-date tour started in Nuneaton, at the Queens Hall, on October 21st. The format was similar to before, with a greatest hits set, and gigs were mainly in the Midlands or the South, apart from one in Scunthorpe and the final gig in Newcastle on November 1st. Midlands-based band Rock$tar were backing Graham. They had been spotted by promoter Mark Wheatley who had been bringing Graham over to these shores since 2001.

Rock$tar certainly had their work cut out. The band was made up of Tony Nicholl (lead vocals), Dave Rothan (guitar and backing vocals), Darren Yates (guitar & backing vocals), Mark Baker (bass guitar) and Simon Mac (drums & backing vocals). Tony recalls: *"We knew we had a great band, but this was the ultimate compliment for us. We were originally asked to be the support act, but the question was then asked whether we would do both the support and the headline show as backing to Graham. How could we turn it down? We covered everything including Impellitteri, MSG, Rainbow and Alcatrazz songs. Then we set about recreating the whole vibe, adjusting our guitar sounds, etc and creating vocal harmonies."* All being fans of Rainbow made their job even more enjoyable and, as for Tony, he was always impressed with Graham's vocal capabilities: *"We had three months of some of the hardest work I have been involved with to reach the standard that we would be happy with, let alone Graham. We were going to give him a backing band to remember."*

Graham arrived in the UK just a few days before the tour was due to start. Not being the biggest fan of rehearsals, Graham only did a couple with the band. There was one slight complication, though. Rock$tar featured two guitarists but no keyboards. To get round this they recorded midi files with keyboards and some backing vocals. Tony says: *"It was kind of strange, because of the big keyboards that featured in Graham's back catalogue. It took absolutely hours of programming. Obviously, we hoped the audience would forgive us as they could see the size of the problems we had come up against trying to reproduce the show!"* The set was quite long, but they cut it down from the two-hour original to take some of the pressure off as they progressed. As in 2001, Graham included 'Lucille' / 'I'm Down' during the show at the Queens Hall in Nuneaton. 'Only One Woman' was also played acoustically at some early shows, but soon dropped. The set-list was 'Eyes Of The World', 'God Blessed Video', 'Love's No Friend', 'Stand In Line', 'Bad Girl', 'Desert Song', 'Dancer', 'Night Games', 'Stargazer', 'All Night Long', 'Since You Been Gone' and 'Lost In Hollywood'.

Tours like this were a good way for Graham to earn a living. There was a ready audience for this material, overheads could be kept down and the promoter took most of the risks. After returning to Los Angeles, the remainder of the year panned out nicely. Graham continued to work on Dario Mollo's Elektric Zoo tracks, and during November, Lion Music released Iain Ashley Hersey's album 'The Holy Grail'.

CHAPTER 12
Will You Be Home Tonight (2006 - 2008)

Featuring: Taz Taylor Band, Moonstone Project, Elektric Zoo, MSG, Graham's solo career, Alcatrazz featuring Graham Bonnet, Tomorrow's Outlook, J21 and Lyraka

GRAHAM BONNET
SUPPORT BY PLANET OF WOMEN

The next two years found Graham busier than he had been in a long time, as he balanced interesting projects and sessions with the need to earn a living. His next significant collaboration was with another strong guitarist, albeit one who didn't carry with him some of the attitudes which seem to go with the territory. In 2006 British guitarist Neil 'Taz' Taylor decided to approach Graham to see if he was interested in working with him on his next album. Taz originally hailed from Walsall in the West Midlands but had decided to seek warmer climes: *"I had played in a band or two in my late teens and early twenties, but had more or less withdrawn from the scene when the Nirvana thing hit. I fell in love with San Diego on my first visit. After coming back a handful of times, I moved over in January '97. I had just a backpack, a guitar and $2,000."*

Knuckling down, Taz issued an instrumental debut album 'Caffeine Racer' on his own label in 2004, then put his own band together with a view to doing some shows. *"I was very much into doing my own thing, just working on my craft, as they say, in solitude. I put the Taz Taylor Band together so we could go out and play the material live."*

That band came together both through word of mouth and internet hook-ups, and crystalised around bassist Dirk Krause, Bob Miller on keyboards and Taz, plus drummer Calvin Lakin who didn't last the course. Taz also began to want to explore new directions as Dirk remembers, *"He started presenting ideas in a verse/chorus/bridge format. We had already gigged an instrumental called 'Enchanted Voyage', which turned into 'Haunted'. I also remember jamming around during rehearsals with what would later become the title track, 'Welcome To America'."* They needed a singer, so Taz and Dirk got together and bounced a few names around, as Dirk explains: *"We were hanging at my house discussing our favourite singers and who would be the proper 'voice' – Graham was definitely near the top of that list due to his Rainbow and MSG connections, but we didn't know what he was up to. We believed he lived somewhere near Los Angeles so, if he was available, why not give it a shot?"*

Taz went for it: *"I had a short list of vocalists in mind whose style I liked. I emailed three guys, and Graham responded immediately with his phone number. We spoke for about 45 minutes that first time. I sent him a track the next day in the mail and he was instantly into it. That track became 'Haunted'."*

Dirk was really surprised Graham had responded. *"I was absolutely floored. He said the conversation went smoothly and they hit it off from the start. There was never a formal agreement to join the band; Graham was willing to get involved for a straight fee."*

There had been talk of the album being half-instrumental, half-vocal, but with Graham on board the band decided to go for it. Even though they were still without a drummer, Taz set about writing a batch of material. Dirk recalls: *"Taz wrote at home, recording his guitar ideas to programmed drum patterns, then adding bass and keyboards. He would simply hand us the demo and we would work on the songs individually. When it came to do the formal recordings each one of us played our parts separately to the original drum patterns – the final drum parts were added afterwards."*

As soon as a few ideas had been recorded they were sent to Graham as Pro Tools files over the net so he could then set about writing lyrics and recording his vocals in his own studio, with Tim Luce as his vocal engineer. *"All of the tracks were completely written and recorded prior to Graham hearing them,"* Taz says. *"As far as vocals, however, they were a blank canvas. Graham came up with all the lyrics and vocal melodies. I think he did an amazing job. He was obviously very much into the project. He told me one time that he found it very easy to come up with his parts to my songs. I replied that it was because I learned to play guitar whilst listening to records he sang on!"*

The band used Blitz studios in San Diego to record. Dirk says: *"Richard Livoni owns Blitz studio and he volunteered to add the drum tracks since we were still having difficulty finding a permanent drummer."* Richard also acted as engineer and producer. Inspiration for the lyrics came from all over as Dirk recalls: *"One of the bigger music news stories of the moment was the impending Phil Spector murder trial, which Graham captured in the song 'Wall Of Sound'."*

'Goodbye Mr. C' coupled 'Goodbye To Romance' with 'Mr. Crowley', both songs from Ozzy Osbourne's 'Blizzard Of Ozz'. *"'Goodbye Mr. C' had always gone over well as part of our instrumental set,"* says Dirk. *"So, I recommended that we include it on the album – Graham did a fantastic job but when he sent us his vocals he had completely overlooked the 'Crowley' bridge! So we made him go back and sing some more, although we never asked him to sing it live – we always played it as an instrumental medley."*

"I was truly impressed with both the speed and quality of his work," Dirk continues, *"learning that many of the lyrics had come from ideas he had written down previously, but which fitted the songs now. He has a unique spin on words and can be quite personal too – I think his humour shows through in his writing and fits the band well."* Incredibly Dirk didn't even get to meet Graham until the photo shoot for the record at Vazquez Rocks State Park near his home.

Graham finished recording eight songs around mid-April, and completed by two instrumentals 'Welcome To America' was snapped up by Escape Music in the UK on the strength of hearing just a couple of songs.

If Graham had impressed the group with his commitment, they only discovered later that he had been struggling with a divorce at the same time, his long-time marriage to Jo having come to an end. Once the vocals were complete, Graham let Taz and his colleagues get on with it, and returned his attentions to Elektric Zoo. Only having recorded one song so far, the band was looking to tour extensively once the album was complete. A set of shows in Finland for Graham had been booked

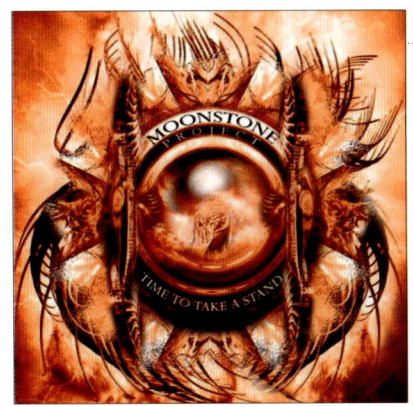

in for August.

In the UK, Majestic Rock Records released the Moonstone Project album 'Time To Take A Stand' on May 8th with Graham singing 'Not Dead Yet'. On the same day the worldwide release of the MSG album 'Tales Of Rock 'N' Roll – Twenty-Five Years Celebration' took place, issued by Armageddon Music in Germany, which featured Graham singing 'Rock 'N' Roll' (also included on a three-track EP).

Graham's foresight on concentrating on confirmed projects and sessions proved to be very sensible. The music business was in a period of real change, with big mergers between the major labels, and smaller ones going to the wall. The days of big advances and huge sales were still there for the very top bands but elsewhere everyone was beginning to cut back or hedge their bets. Talk of Graham fronting the Taz Taylor Band supporting MSG, and even of him joining Michael for a tour (as well as doing some solo acoustic shows) all came to nothing. He did play a one-off covering a couple of Rainbow tracks at the UCLA Ralph Freud Theater in Los Angeles on May 26th for Uli Jon Roth though, singing 'Love's No Friend' and 'Lost In Hollywood' and backed by Uli's band.

Graham also made a fourth appearance at the UK Blues & Soul Festival on July 1st at the request of Don Airey. Doogie White was on the bill for a second time and could not resist helping Graham out on backing vocals. The two former Rainbow singers had never met before the festival as Doogie points out: *"He was rather cool and friendly, just as I hoped he would be. I would watch him singing 'When A Man Loves A Woman' and thought his head would explode at the key change! But he just threw his head back and opened his mouth wider and roared it out."*

Doogie had come up against similar issues in Rainbow himself. *"I can still hear the band laughing as I spluttered though 'All Night Long'. Trying to come close to the sound that Graham produces, for me, is impossible. He has such range and power, and at times I expected to explode trying to give authenticity to the songs he sang!"*

In the meantime Cleopatra Records in America issued 'The Greatest '80s Metal Moments Of All Time' in July. This featured Blackthorne's version of 'All Night Long', which interestingly included guitarist, George Lynch. The performance was credited to Graham Bonnet (Rainbow) with George Lynch (Dokken / Lynch Mob). Bob Kulick sums it up by saying: *"Because it was no longer Blackthorne."*

With Graham now back in Los Angeles, he started to prepare for his second tour of Finland which he was looking forward to. The band line-up was exactly the same as in 2005. Daffy: *"We did two weeks of Wednesday to Saturday. Graham doesn't like to do more than four gigs in a row. We did seven club-sized (200-700 seater) shows and one outdoor festival."* The tour began on August 9th at the Foxia in Oula and concluded ten days later on August 19th at the House Of Rock in Kouvola, the set being: 'Eyes Of The World', 'God Blessed Video', 'Love's No Friend', 'Bad Girl', 'Into The Arena', 'Night Games', 'Assault Attack', 'Stargazer' - 'Catch The Rainbow', 'Weiss Heim', 'Desert Song', 'Too Young To Die, Too Drunk To Live', 'Since You Been Gone', 'All Night Long' and 'Lost In Hollywood'.

On August 26th, Escape released 'Welcome To America' which Graham described at the time as *"much poppier and a little different from the heavy music I've been known for."* Reviews were excellent. The Heavy Metal Addiction website said: *"Anytime an album featuring Graham Bonnet is released, I have to buy it. An album laden with melodic hooks and superb guitar. One of the best albums of the year. The songs are well written, full of melody. Nothing overdone, nothing too excessive.*

The band provides excellent music while Bonnet provides great vocals that singers half his age cannot master. This album will easily be in my Top 10 of 2006." Scott Jeslis of Metal Express Radio website commented: *"Bonnet fans will be thrilled to hear that Graham sounds better then ever on this release. The whole album has that sort of 'Bonnet-era MSG feel', à la 'Assault Attack' without the 'Schenker-esque' guitar, not that Taz Taylor is a slouch; he's just an ever so slightly different type of player."* *"I think it is a superb album"*, commented Buz Gaden in Fireworks magazine, *"which brings out the best of everybody involved. For fans of Alcatrazz, or Bonnet's tenures in MSG or Rainbow, you'll probably love this. Highly recommended."*

As ever, Graham was still interested in developing a band of his own again, and had been considering resurrecting the name Alcatrazz instead of going out under his own name. Before he could do so, his former 'bandmates' quickly blocked the idea by registering the name. In the end it was agreed that if he did tour with a new line-up, he would have to call the band 'Alcatrazz featuring Graham Bonnet'.

In the meantime he had by now written the melodies and lyrics for six Elektric Zoo songs, although his vocals still needed to be laid down on five of them. *"The songs are in a much heavier vein and contain progressive elements,"* he commented. Recording of his vocals eventually got underway again, with four tracks cut by the end of October, followed by Graham's live debut with the Taz Taylor Band (with their new drummer Val Trainor) at the Brick By Brick in San Diego on November 3rd, preceded by rehearsals in Los Angeles, as Dirk recalls: *"Several of the songs were still being arranged. We moved Graham's vocals around to fit the tracks – Graham would show up at rehearsals with his original lyrics all written down on paper, but he hadn't listened to the final mixes yet. The name of one song was changed and verses completely deleted, so he was a bit surprised (and lost) at times! Those rehearsals were also the first time for us to learn the old Rainbow tunes – the set would continue to evolve over the next year, but it was definitely a fun time. We rehearsed (and stayed) in Los Angeles to make things easier for Graham. I drove him down to San Diego the day of the gig, because Graham does not have a driver's license. That show was literally the third time we had played together and Graham did a great job joking with the audience about it being a rehearsal (for him), while still having to read words from a music stand. 'If you know these songs then you are a better man than me,' he said, 'and I wrote the fucking things!'"*

The gig saw the band play quite a few instrumentals which broke up the flow, and in hindsight it would have worked better if they had played an instrumental set first and then had Graham come out to sing for the remainder of the show. The set list was 'Lightning Strikes', 'Fighters Fist', 'Happy Hour', 'Pot Of Gold', 'Parisienne Walkways', 'Wall Of Sound', 'Haunted', 'Right Back Where I Started', 'Chilling Times', 'Radio Luxembourg', 'Silent Fall', 'The Reprise', 'Goodbye Mr. C', 'Caffeine Racer', 'Will You Love Me Tomorrow', 'All Night Long', 'Since You Been Gone', 'George's Song' and 'Welcome To America'. The concert was filmed and recorded, and some fans even flew all the way over from Japan to be there. Taz also recalls the band's debut gig: *"We were a little worried at first because Graham did not really participate much in the rehearsal and did not appear to know the songs too well and the show was the next evening. But we soon found out that is just the way he is, he does not like to rehearse. He always gives the impression of being unprepared but, come show time, he comes out all guns blazing and gives 100%".*

Uncertain about how committed Graham actually felt about things, the Taz Taylor Band actually had another singer in for a while, but Graham explained that he was happy to tour once everything was together. You can understand Taz's situation, with Graham still keeping himself very busy with other work.

Graham spent January 2007 cutting more vocals for the Elektric Zoo album, and re-recording others. Their plan was to have at least eight tracks for the album and now had songs called 'Dead Man Walking', 'Colder Than Cool' 'Feeding The Beast' (an 11 minute epic), 'You Are Your Money' (also called 'You Are Your Wallet'), 'The Mirror Lies', and 'Motorbike', which saw Graham use the lyrics from the 1986 unreleased Alcatrazz song, 'Rider'. There was three other backing tracks recorded, but Graham never got around to adding his vocals. Interestingly, the band also recorded three Rainbow songs in-between gigs on their 2004 European tour. These were 'Eyes Of The World' and 'All Night Long', which includes some additional crowd noise at the beginning and end to give them a live feel. A backing track for 'Since You Been Gone' was also laid down, but Graham never put a vocal on it. It isn't clear why these recordings took place or what they were for and Graham can't remember anything about them.

It was then announced in February that Alcatrazz featuring Graham Bonnet would be touring Japan during May and June, with yet another ex-Rainbow singer, Joe Lynn Turner, on the bill. Alongside this a lengthy UK visit for the Taz Taylor Band was put together, much to everyone's delight. *"Mark Wheatley had put a UK tour together for Graham using a UK covers band,"* says Taz, *"and because of the success of 'Welcome To America' he felt that a tour featuring Graham performing with us was a more legitimate way to do another UK tour."* This news spurred the band into learning more Rainbow songs, along with some of Graham's back catalogue, knowing that those would be fan favourites in England.

Graham played another one-nighter, this time in The Netherlands on March 23rd as a guest at the Classics In Rock show in Rotterdam. This franchise basically did what it said on the tin, bringing name players together to interest rock fans across Europe. The show featured Chris Thompson, Jon Anderson, John Waite and Glenn Hughes as well as Dutch singers and musicians less well-known outside their home country. Graham sang three songs, 'God Blessed Video', 'Since You Been Gone' and 'All Night Long' with a backing band led by Spike Edney on keyboards, and which included bassist Neil Murray.

Back in Los Angeles Graham concentrated his thoughts on the trip to Japan with his new version of Alcatrazz towards the end of May. There were four shows planned, starting at O-East in Tokyo on May 30th and finishing at the Zepp Sapporo in Sapporo on June 4th, but since Howie Simon, Tim Luce and Glen Sobel hadn't played together since September 2004 rehearsals and a set needed to be sorted out. A warm-up date for the tour was also booked at Paladinos in Tarzana for May 25th.

With Joe Lynn Turner (backed by a Japanese band) on the bill the tour was advertised more like a boxing match as 'Alcatrazz featuring Graham Bonnet vs Joe

Graham with the Taz Taylor Band • *2006 and on-stage at the Brick By Brick Club, 2006.*

Lynn Turner with Akira Kajiyama'. The shows were a huge success though and very enjoyable with every venue sold out and at least a thousand fans in attendance at each one, some apparently reduced to tears (of pleasure) when they finally heard Graham singing their favourite songs after 23 years! The set was 'Eyes Of The World', 'Too Young To Die, Too Drunk To Live', 'God Blessed Video', 'Night Games', 'Big Foot', 'Jet To Jet', 'Kree Nakoorie', 'Hiroshima Mon Amour', 'Will You Be Home Tonight', 'Island In The Sun', 'Desert Song', 'All Night Long', 'Since You Be Gone' and 'Lost In Hollywood'.

The two singers were then signed up for a tour of Finland in August, while Graham was also booked to sing a pair of his hits ('It's All Over Now Baby Blue' and 'Warm Ride') in Australia on the seven-date Countdown Spectacular 2 Tour from mid-August to early September.

But for now, back on home soil, he swapped hats and turned his attention to the Taz Taylor Band tour. Dirk says: *"Graham seemed genuinely pleased about staying active and involved with the project. He would thank us often for everything we did and was looking forward to the tour. I think part of it was also because of the 'happy distraction' it created, a healthy diversion from the other issues in his personal life."* Around mid-May, Graham was hit with the very sad news that his good friend from Skegness, Kenny Bray, had passed away.

Graham and the Taz Taylor Band arrived in Stourbridge prior to the tour, staying at The Talbot Hotel. It soon became apparent that the equipment the band were supposed to use for the tour, supplied by the main support band Planet Of Women, simply wasn't good enough, as Dirk points out: *"We ended up driving to Birmingham to rent our own gear for the tour."* The hired van was also too small: *"I remember going to a hardware store looking for spanners so that we could remove the rear seats in order to load our gear. I spent several hours in the rain trying to loosen the rusty bolts from that old van. We left two seats at the first venue and [the promoter] had to go back at the end of the tour to retrieve them!"* Ah, the glamour of life on the road! *"Apart from a few shows, I would say the gigs were fairly well attended,"* says Dirk. *"Performances were steady and Graham was in decent voice most nights. The opening band Planet Of Women were going to sing back-up for Graham on some of the songs, but that was quickly snuffed out. We were not intending it to be a cabaret show!"*

At Riffs in Blackpool the stage at one end of the room wasn't big enough to swing a cat and it was on the same level as the floor. The following evening saw the band in Sheffield at The Boardwalk. This was a great venue and the stage was a good size, which enabled the band members to have space and move around freely. Sheffield had recently been subject to terrible flooding, due to the torrential rain the UK had been experiencing, and Graham made a point of mentioning it and that he hoped everyone would soon get things back to normal. This, of course, was the first time Graham had played in the city since 'that' night with MSG back in August 1982.

The Royal Standard in London saw Graham and Taz doing a meet-and-greet after coming off stage at the merchandise stall, as well as signing autographs and posing for photographs. This became an ongoing event throughout the tour, as did trying to make sure Graham had all his medication, as Dirk remembers: *"Graham had been sober prior to becoming involved in our project but was still reliant on a few meds – I'm not fully aware of all the differences in European healthcare but we spent a lot of time in search of doctors. One day, we had to wait around while a motorcycle courier delivered his prescription from another town. So much energy (and frustration) went into this quest throughout the tour that it became a running joke and the old Golden Earring song was affectionately transformed into 'Xanax Love'!"*

The final gig was in Nottingham at Junction 7 on July 14th. The gig went well even though it was a small venue. *"I don't think anyone could fault Graham for needing lyric sheets to help him remember the 'Welcome To America' songs,"* Dirk says. *"But I think the audience was a bit surprised to see him reading the words to some of the older material like 'Stargazer' or 'Desert Song'. It turned problematic when the lyric sheets would get damaged or mixed up on stage. We had to re-write those things a few times throughout the tour!"* The set itself was mainly 'Eyes Of The World', 'Love's No Friend', 'Fighters Fist', 'Welcome To America', 'Desert Song', 'George's Song', 'Parisienne Walkways', 'Suffer Me', 'Stargazer', 'Happy Hour', 'Pot Of Gold', 'Caffeine Racer', 'Night Games', 'Will You Love Me Tomorrow', 'Radio Luxembourg', 'All Night Long', 'Since You Been Gone' and 'Lost In Hollywood'. Occasionally though certain songs were dropped or replaced by others.

Three weeks later, Graham was flying out to Helsinki for four shows in four days, sharing the bill with Joe Lynn Turner. The band line-up was virtually the same as on the two previous tours, except Pate Kivinen replaced Pate Flintstone on keyboards and two backing singers had come on board. (The same band backed both singers, so they certainly had their work cut out!) The first show was at Klubi in Tampere on August 8th and the short tour concluded in Imatra at the Rock To The River Festival. The set for the four dates was 'Eyes Of The World', 'God Blessed Video', 'Love's No Friend', 'Stargazer', 'Makin' Love', 'Desert Song', 'All Night Long', 'Since You Been Gone' and 'Lost In Hollywood', with Graham and Joe sharing the encore 'Long Live Rock 'n' Roll'.

Graham with the band • *Stourbridge on the 2007 UK tour. Opposite: Sheffield Boardwalk.*

Graham with the Taz Taylor Band • *Sheffield Boardwalk, June 2007.*

Graham Bonnet • The Royal Standard, Walthamstow, June 2007.

The 2007 U.K. tour set-list and flyer.

just a European tour through April instead.

But the final night of the year saw Graham's Alcatrazz play at The Avalon in Santa Clara as support to Y&T. *"It was great,"* recalls Graham. *"We won the night, even though we opened up for them. The next day we saw a lot of their fans in the street and they were overwhelmingly nice with their comments. I was not sick, which makes a change. The bronchitis had been a problem these last four years. It just cripples me, along with my asthma."*

Four days into 2008 and Graham was back with the Taz Taylor Band for a gig at the Knitting Factory in Hollywood. Due to the bad weather on the day of the gig it wasn't very well attended, as Dirk points out: *"A torrential downpour and very few people in attendance, because of the weather. In the end it felt more like a bona-fide rehearsal than a gig! I remember Graham showing up much later in the day, but he was in good voice and good mood."*

Two weeks later Graham was back on stage, but this time with his version of Alcatrazz again. The band only did a short, condensed set at Loffler's in Anaheim on January 18th but the reaction was excellent, fans saying it was the best they had seen Graham perform for many years.

Another quick session took place for Norwegian band Tomorrow's Outlook for a Lizzy Borden tribute album covering 'Red Rum'. The band had contacted Graham towards the end of the previous year to see if he would be interested in recording the vocals, and he went for it. The recording took place in February, but support for the project folded and the album remains unissued.

His next 'odd job' was for Spanish guitarist J21 who asked Graham about singing on a couple of songs for his debut solo album. Agreeing to go ahead with this, Graham was sent the song 'The Edge Of Now' in February and he recorded it the following month. Having been a big fan of Graham's from a very early age, J21 says: *"I recorded the vocals on those demos myself and I am probably the worst singer in the world, so I had a hard time sending him those rough recordings! Graham helped me a lot - he changed the melodies, added background vocals and improved them in every way."*

The same month also saw Graham start focusing his attention back on the European tour with the Taz Taylor Band, due to start in early April with twelve dates, mostly in Germany. Sadly, keyboard player Bob Miller couldn't do the tour due to ill health so Los Angeles session player Eric Ragno was brought in. The tour opened at the Gladhaus in Cottbus, Germany on April 4th. With Dirk having family in Germany everything really fell in to place for him: *"I was thrilled to be playing in Germany as it gave me a chance to visit my relatives – let me tell you that being able to have a proper meal, getting a good night's sleep and doing some much needed laundry is the key to any tour!"*

Graham still needed his medication on the tour as Dirk adds: *"As in the UK, a good deal of time was spent driving around and making sure Graham had all of his medications – in Berlin, I was chosen to be the designated 'translator' and took him around to the various hospitals; what an adventure speaking broken German with the Turkish taxi drivers!"*

The more the tour progressed the more bassist Martin Motnik from support

Less than one week later Graham was back on a plane heading for the Countdown Spectacular 2 Tour in Australia, which started on August 18th at the Entertainment Centre in Newcastle. Graham wasn't in the best of shape for the shows: *"I had bronchitis before I left and it got worse while I was there. They begged me to do it on the phone and I told them I wasn't well."* The show was a massive production and featured a dozen musicians and backing singers in the house band, and what was effectively an old-style package tour, hung on the famous Aussie TV pop show Countdown. The tour came to an end in Perth at the Burswood Dome on September 5th. 'It's All Over Now Baby Blue' was later issued on a live compilation by Liberation Music in November.

Giles Lavery was at the show at the Acer Arena in Sydney on August 24th: *"Not many artists would get me to go along to see an evening of acts I was for the most part pretty oblivious to, but Graham Bonnet IS one such performer. I was excited to see the man in person, regardless of how small his role was to be in this production. His set on previous dates included both 'Warm Ride' and 'It's All Over Now Baby Blue', but due to so called 'time issues' it had now been reduced to just '... Baby Blue'. One thing that was apparent right from the moment Graham opened his mouth is that he had not lost one bit of the vocal power he is known for. In fact, compared to the other acts which obviously casually cruised through their numbers, Graham's performance took many unawares. I recall looking around at a few bewildered faces, obviously expecting some smooth pop rendition of a hit they recalled from days gone by. Not so, Graham launched into the song with a huge intensity. He seemed to be enjoying himself and the performance of the track was well received."*

Recalling the tour, Graham says: *"I was told by the show's director to change the keys of the songs, because they sounded so strained so I eventually did. My voice though was really bad. I was coughing violently every day. I shouldn't have been walking around being so sick, let alone singing. I wasn't in great shape at all. The money was okay, but I thought I needed sick pay too!"*

Graham now had time to rest his voice, wrap up work on a couple of side projects and turn his mind to material for his new version of Alcatrazz, as the band would be supporting Y&T on New Year's Eve, followed by another a Taz Taylor Band gig in January. Prior to that though he also had a one-off gig in Argentina, at the Niceto Club in Buenos Aires, on December 5th, along with the usual round of TV spots. Towards the end of the month it was reported that Graham would be touring the UK and Europe with the Taz Taylor Band the following March. Venues in the UK were even advertising dates, but this soon changed and it became

Graham Bonnet and Joe Lynn Turner • *August 2007 Finland.*

band The Roxx felt at ease chatting to Graham. *"I enjoyed talking to him and listening to his stories a lot. It was like being a part of rock 'n' roll history,"* he says. *"Being on the road with someone who has influenced my musical upbringing and who has been touring with so many musicians that have been instrumental to my playing made me very proud. But also on a very personal level I did enjoy our conversations a lot. Graham is a very deep and sensitive person with a big heart and an incredible talent."* The set for the tour was: 'Eyes Of The World', 'Love's No Friend', 'Fighter's Fist', 'Radio Luxemburg', 'Pot Of Gold', 'Chilling Times', 'Blackmore's Blues', 'Stargazer', 'Desert Song', 'Happy Hour', 'Wall Of Sound', 'Doctor Doctor' [instrumental], 'Goodbye Mr. C', 'Caffeine Racer', 'Night Games', 'All Night Long', 'Since You Been Gone', 'Welcome To America' and 'Lost In Hollywood'. Sandwiched in-between two German gigs in Bruschal and Rosenheim the band had a day off. It was on this day, April 14th, that Graham became a Granddad for the first time when his daughter, Keeley, gave birth to a baby boy who was named Asher.

Given how well it all went musically with the Taz Taylor Band a second album with Graham wouldn't have been surprising, but that wasn't to be. The tight finances of the tour were causing issues, with the band often only on a percentage of the ticket sales. Dirk says: *"During the European tour I remember Graham sitting on the bus and jotting down song ideas for a new Alcatrazz album. Because of that I don't think there were ever any discussions about doing another album with us and it was splintering apart quickly. The whole vibe of the band had already started to change during the UK tour in 2007. I don't think the monetary terms of the European tour were clearly understood by everyone involved and, because most of the money was contingent on 'door-deals', Graham ended up spending more on his hotels, food and phone calls than he took from the shows, and things started to get a bit contentious. The last night of the tour, Taz and Val approached me to ask if I would be willing to give Graham and Eric my share of the monies to help make up some of the difference. So I did. I boarded the plane home with virtually nothing left to show for the work or investment I had made – just the smile on my face!"*

The tour thus marked the end of Graham's involvement with the Taz Taylor Band but it wasn't long before he was back out on the road, heading for Helsinki in Finland during early June for a seven-date tour with Joe Lynn Turner, using the same band and backing singers. They kicked off at Teatria in Oulu on June 4th and Daffy says it was the best tour they did, the highlight being playing in front of 7,000 people at the Sauna open-air festival with many people saying they outshone headliners Whitesnake.

Back in Los Angeles, Graham recorded the vocals for a second J21 song, 'The Truth Behind The Veil' in June, and the album 'Yellow Mind : Blue Mind' was issued as a download on iTunes by Voiceprint in the UK in August. It was issued on CD during September 2009.

Then towards the end of the month, Graham began to prepare for his trip to Russia, having sorted out a couple of shows. Not having been there since February 2005, he was certainly looking forward to it. He played the BikeFest-2008 in Maloyaroslavec on June 28th and the following day at the Club Grafit in Moscow.

Back in California the session requests kept coming, and Graham had adapted to this new strand of his career well. This kept the wolf from the door, helped support his own projects and meant his name was still out there; and besides, it was flattering that a new generation of rock musicians held him in enough regard to want him involved in their projects. He was in good company, with Joe Lynn Turner and Glenn Hughes to name but two treading a similar path (with Glenn very open about how this type of work was funding his solo albums). Guitarist Andy DiGelsomina and his girlfriend Jasmine Lyraka now contacted Graham about an ambitious 3D computer-animated movie project which they had been developing. Andy says: *"Jasmine started brainstorming on the concept for 'Lyraka' in the spring of 2006. Her concepts regarding an empress of mermaids and fantasy realm fell right in with my Ritchie Blackmore and Richard Wagner obsessions! We contacted Graham first on July 8th 2008 through Rockville. Graham was interested from the beginning. We sent him extremely rough home demos, but they weren't enough for him to really gel with things. So then we put 'Beyond the Palace' and 'Coronation' into production for him. 'Lyraka' is actually Jasmine's movie screenplay. I just set it to music and lyrics."*

Although the project was announced publicly in November 2008 they sent Graham his agreed fee in September. *"He wanted to get paid up front!"* quips Andy. In November he sent Graham 'Beyond The Palace', the first of four quality backing tracks, and over the next three months Graham worked on the song with Tim Luce. It was finished by the following February and sent back with Andy then sending Graham the next song, 'Coronation', to work on.

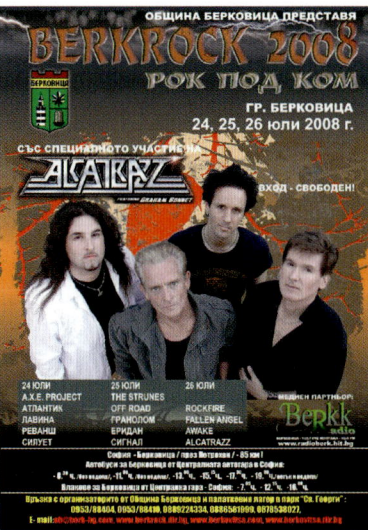

On the live front, Graham was trying to push forward his new version of Alactrazz, who headlined the BerkRock Festival 2008 in Berkovista on July 26th. With a couple of rehearsals under their belt, Bulgaria became the eighth different country Graham had played in over the last four months. He realised it was difficult to maintain consistency: *"It's been hard getting started, because of everybody's other commitments. I think it will be great when we can just concentrate on the band and put out some new stuff. I think we have something a bit different this time around. We need to be new sounding. Bring the band into this century, but with elements of the original sound of Alcatrazz in the mix with new stuff."* It was not long before they started to record some backing tracks, with an eye to getting an album together as soon as possible.

Meanwhile Bulgaria went crazy for the group: *"We were The Beatles for the day! They don't get much out there and it was in the middle of nowhere. A three-hour drive down a very pot-holed narrow road,"* says Graham. *"It was like a trip back 300 years with goat carts and all. But we had a great night."*

Top : Graham with the Taz Taylor Band, and support band The Roxx, Germany 2008; Graham and Martin Motnik on the tour bus 2008. Below : Graham / Turner Band, Finland, 2008.

CHAPTER 13
Jet To Jet (2008 - 2012)

Featuring: Pushking, Mario Parga, Alcatrazz featuring Graham Bonnet, Lyraka, Graham's solo career, Natasha Lea Jones, Tomorrow's Outlook, Sunset, GBS and Osmo's Cosmos

Ozzy a Potkan presents
GRAHAM BONNET & ALCATRAZZ

Having been approached earlier in 2008 by Russian band Pushking to record a couple of songs, 'God Made Us Free' and 'Kukarracha', Graham finished them in his studio during mid-September, with Tim Luce at the controls as always. Largely unknown outside their own country, Pushking had been around for a long time and were putting together a celebratory album, reworking their older material and featuring a selection of guest appearances by world famous musicians. The final version of 'Kukarracha' actually features a host of different singers: Joe Lynn Turner, Eric Martin, Glenn Hughes and Paul Stanley, so Graham was in good company.

He was now looking forward to appearing at the NAMM show in Anaheim on January 17th 2009 with guitarist Mario Parga. They had a five-song set, which included one instrumental, already worked out, but Graham wasn't in the best of health due to a lingering cough and cold. Looking to arrive the day before so they could run through the songs, Mario and his family set off early in the morning from their home in Las Vegas with a truck full of equipment. They picked up Graham in north Los Angeles en route (he travels quite light these days, only needing a suitcase and his acoustic guitar). Mario remembers that leg of the journey: *"My wife Shawna and daughter Skye were also in the car, and Skye at the time was one year old. She was sat in the back in her car seat and 'Uncle Graham' (my nickname for Graham) was next to her. We got stuck in a traffic jam from Hell due to road works that lasted for five hours, and Skye had a screaming tantrum session that lasted for almost as long! We tried everything we could to calm the baby, and Graham even sang to her; she went quiet for thirty seconds then resumed the screaming!"*

A rehearsal followed in Mario's hotel room with Tim Luce on bass and Eric Rango on keyboards. Graham soon went off on a tangent when he burst into versions of Elvis's 'Viva Las Vegas' and Buddy Holly's 'It's So Easy', showing everyone the chords along the way. The gig itself took place inside a noisy Fishman Acoustic Amplification trade booth (drummer Kevin Valentine was to have completed the line-up but his drums wouldn't fit on the stage!) and even when they began their now four-song set (the instrumental being dropped) at 2pm, the racket continued. Nevertheless, the band opened up with 'It's All Over Now Baby Blue' with Graham playing acoustic guitar. This was followed by 'Desert Song' and 'Will You Be Home Tonight' and they wrapped up with a version of 'Love's No Friend'. A lot of people turned out to watch the performance and the band themselves seemed happy with how things had gone. As ex-Black Sabbath vocalist Tony Martin had moved on from Mario's band Savage Paradise, Mario talked Graham into becoming their new lead singer - if the project ever resurfaces!

With two 'Alcatrazz Featuring Graham Bonnet' shows on the East Coast coming up at the end of February, a couple of rehearsals took place for the traditional warm-up show at Paladinos on February 13th. These gigs were the first shows the band had played since July last year, and they performed to modest audiences, first at The Haunt in Yonkers, New York on February 27th and the following evening at Jaxx in Springfield, Virginia. The band continued to occupy his thoughts over the year and Graham got in touch with Russ Ballard via journalist Rob McKenzie of Fireworks who had recently interviewed Russ. Rob explains: *"We discussed the 'Line-Up' album. I mentioned that Graham had said to me he loved 'Hold Your Head Up' and wondered if Russ could write a contemporary song in a similar vein for Alcatrazz. A few phone calls later and Russ and Graham were back in touch, and Russ wrote the song 'My Kingdom Come'."*

Graham discussed his idea with Russ half-a-dozen times on the phone and when he received the song it was an eleven-minute epic. Graham wanted something meandering and contemporary, and he certainly got it as the track wanders in and out in a progressive vein with a great hook in the chorus, which is what you expect from Russ Ballard.

There was another chance to go and see his friend Mario Parga, and they worked on a couple of songs including 'Desert Rose'. Once back home, Graham also finished track two for Lyraka, who promptly sent him 'Palace Guard' to get stuck into.

Towards the end of June, Graham set off to Brazil, another country he had not visited before, for three shows in just over a week, and he managed to take in a couple of rehearsals prior to the first show at the SESC in Santos on July 2nd. With a week to kill before the next show, Graham was able for once to take in some of the sights before he and the Paulo Zinner Rockestra headlined the Araraquara Rock Festival on Friday July 10th.

The free five-day indoor festival began on July 8th, but took off on the third day when ten bands appeared with Graham headlining. The following day he also played at the interestingly named Blackmore Rock Bar in Sao Paulo. *"It went very well,"* he recalls. *"Lots of trips by road, but I had a great time. The band wasn't too bad, they did a good job. I of course was sick from the plane, but got antibiotics and got my voice back…"*

Graham was interviewed on Brazilian TV and played an acoustic 'Night Of The Shooting Star' and a short version of 'Love's No Friend' with the band's guitarist and drummer as accompaniment. They also performed 'Since You Been Gone', but it was cut.

Towards the end of August Graham repeated his tour of Finland, albeit just for four shows in four days, and with the band featuring a new bassist and keyboard player, Klaus Wirzenius and Jani Kemppinen. They opened at Osmo's Cosmos Bar in Imatra on August 26th, with the final show taking place in Kouvola at the House Of Rock on August 29th. Graham had to rely on the band having rehearsed as he was late getting into the country so only had time for a few run-throughs.

Over the last year or so Graham's new version of Alcatrazz had been persevering with writing in their spare time and had worked up several songs. Glen Sobel had been offered a job with Alice Cooper, and was replaced in early September by Dave Dzialak, who had previously played in the Jeff Scott Soto Band. With two shows coming up in Mexico, the band rehearsed to get Dave up to scratch. Their first show took place in Monterrey at the Arena Santa Lucia on September 12th, with the following day's concert being in Mexico City at the Salon Vive Cuervo, with Testament headlining. Graham says: *"We had a great time except for the terrible sound on stage and losing it all sometimes. It was fun apart from that."*

Graham's back-catalogue continued to reappear as record labels increasingly began to trawl their archives to keep a diminishing industry going. There was a Rainbow 'Anthology 1975 – 1984' with Graham's era represented by four studio tracks and 'Will You Love Me Tomorrow' from the Donington Monsters Of Rock show (the TV version of this performance would follow in an overblown box set in 2015) and a 'deluxe edition' of 'Down To Earth' with an early version of Love's No Friend' ('Ain't A Lot Of Love In The Heart Of Me') and 'No Time To Lose' ('Spark Don't Mean A Fire') with different lyrics sung by Graham. EMI who now owned Chrysalis Records remastered Michael Schenker's albums including 'Assault Attack' (and included the B-side 'Girl From Uptown'). Voiceprint tackled some of his solo offerings but in a slapdash fashion. On 'No Bad Habits' they managed to miss off his biggest hit 'Warm Ride' by using a Dutch tape to master from, and only included a skimpy four-page booklet of dubious merit. Considering it was the album's first time ever on CD the label did a terrible job. It was issued properly in Japan later in the year by Air Mail Recordings with two extra B-sides, who also released 'Graham Bonnet'. Voiceprint tackled the same LP but forgot to list the bonus track, 'Heroes On My Picture Wall'. Over in Australia a triple DVD celebrating their music show Nightmoves included a rare promotional video for 'Danny' from 1977, as well as an interview with Graham on the banks of the Yarra River in Melbourne.

November also saw the start of the fourth and final track from Andy DiGelsomina for his Lyraka project. Graham had finished 'Palace Guard' in September and 'Errandia' was the last (he finished it in April 2010). It wasn't easy to get a vision of what was in effect a concept album but Graham did his best as Andy says: *"We had melodies, lyrics and guide vocals for Graham and then Graham added his own unique style to the interpretation. He also helped with the backing vocals."*

Graham was then able to look forward to touring with his version of Alcatrazz in Europe for six shows, beginning at Kult 8034 in Germering, Germany on November 25th then Essen Zeche Carl, before travelling to The Rock Temple in Kerkrade, Holland on November 27th. With four days off, the next stint began on December 2nd at the Orpheum in Graz, Austria followed by Szene in Vienna, and the tour came to an end in Prague on December 4th with a show at Exit Chmelnice. The set list was 'Eyes Of The World', 'Too Young To Die, Too Drunk To Live', 'God Blessed Video', 'Night Games', 'Howie Solo', 'Big Foot', 'Jet To Jet', 'Kree Nakoorie', 'Hiroshima Mon Amour', 'Will You Be Home Tonight', 'Desert Song' [inc drum solo], 'Island In The Sun', 'All Night Long', 'Since You Been Gone' and 'Lost In Hollywood'. Graham's recollection of the tour amounts to: *"The gigs went well. You know, gig, hotel, gig! But the shows were well received."*

2010 saw a big slew of Alcatrazz back-issues. Cleopatra Records in America released 'Live '83', though it's actually from the band's performance at the Country Club in Reseda, California, on January 7th 1984, broadcast by RKO. In Japan the two heavily bootlegged 1984 concerts from the band's appearances in Tokyo were officially released on DVD, and in May Columbia Music Entertainment issued the audio from the two concerts. You would think some label manager might have wanted to sign the current band up for an album on the back of what was in effect free publicity but not so.

Instead, with the band inactive on the live front for over five months, drummer Dave Dzialak also decided to move on. His replacement was Jeff Bowders, who had previously played with Paul Gilbert. There was a tour of Russia on the cards for the end of May, so a few rehearsals took place to bed Jeff in followed by the customary warm-up show at Paladinos on May 22nd.

The band arrived in Russia just prior to the opening show at the Jaggar Club in St. Petersburg on May 27th. The following night saw them play in Moscow, with another show three days later in UFA City. The short tour concluded at the News Pub in Volgograd City on June 3rd.

Graham wasn't very happy with some of his performances: *"Great audiences, but these were terrible gigs for me. I was told how bad I was on one of the shows. I lost my sound on stage, the ear monitors. I could not hear the band or myself so my voice was all over the place. I didn't know, but I should have just taken them out. So I would like to forget some of those shows, but the others were okay. I'm too honest about my performances, always putting myself down. But when the band complains then I know something is wrong!"*

They tried unsuccessfully to get on the Sweden Rock Festival in Solvesborg again – the sixth time the band had approached them. They also tried to get on the bill of the prestigious Download festival in England, but received the same cold shoulder. There was however a short three-date tour of Japan in September, featuring Graham, Joe Lynn Turner and Doogie White, billed as 'The Voices Of Rainbow'. Doogie White recalls the concept: *"The Japanese came up with the idea. In certain territories the Rainbow name still sells tickets and there is a market for people who want to hear these classic songs sung by the guys who originally sang them."*

Graham's version of Alcatrazz became his backing band for the four-day visit. The opening show was at Big Cat in Osaka on September 27th. Two days later they played in Nagoya, at Bottom Line, and the following evening they finished off at the Shibuya C.C. Lemon Hall in Tokyo.

Doogie says: *"For the fans, Graham is an enigma. He is rarely seen in public and tends to stay in the hotel. So it adds to the mystique. We all joined up [for the encore] and did a couple of songs together and paid tribute to Ronnie James Dio, the very best of us, who had died earlier that year."*

"I called Graham a bastard one night," Doogie continues. *"He was bemused and asked why. I mentioned that Yngwie made me sing 'Hiroshima Mon Amour' every night at the end of a two-hour set! But I have always enjoyed Graham's company*

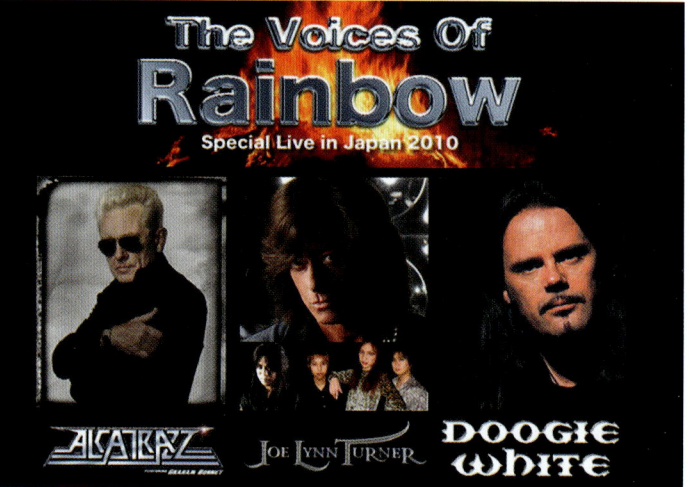

and singing. He still looks and sounds the same as he did when I heard him in '79. Bizarrely, I picked out his ties for the Japanese shows. What a weird thing to be asked to do!"

The set list was 'Assault Attack', 'Too Young To Die, Too Drunk To Live', 'Since You Been Gone', 'God Blessed Video', 'Love's No Friend', 'Kree Nakoorie' / 'Hiroshima Mon Amour', 'Will You Be Home Tonight', 'Skyfire', 'Suffer Me', 'Bad Girl', 'Jet To Jet', 'Lost In Hollywood', 'All Night Long' and 'Long Live Rock 'n' Roll'. The final two songs were encores which featured Joe and Doogie. Graham and the others agreed to donate a portion of the tour's finance's to Ronnie's 'Stand Up And Shout Memorial Cancer Fund'.

When Graham returned home he got worse and bronchitis was diagnosed. The year had seen Graham's divorce from Jo come through but they both had a bit of good news on October 10th when their daughter Keeley gave birth to a second baby boy who was named Shiloh.

The Lyraka album, titled 'Lyraka Vol. 1', was finally released on November 2nd. The reviews were very favourable indeed, with writer Martin Popoff describing Graham as *"a god amongst mortals."* Flushed with success Andy and Jasmine quickly approached Graham again to sign him up for the next volume.

Meanwhile Tomorrow's Outlook had been steadily recording tracks for their debut album on a song by song basis since 2007. Sometime in late November their manager, Trond Nicolaisen, sent Graham the very last song for their album as a backing track with a few ideas about how the melody should go, and Graham came up with a set of lyrics. Trond says: *"This time I only sent a sketch with some midi melodies. I came up with a lyrical idea myself, but Graham is responsible for all the words."*

Graham still wasn't well but battled on and Trond was over the moon with the results: *"The man was not properly healed from bronchitis at the time of the session, but even with a sore throat he did a killer job. I love his singing style so much and I'm probably very influenced by how he arranges vocal melodies. The stuff he did with Alcatrazz, for instance, is awesome. Graham has only recorded two songs with us so far, but we have already been talking about doing some more collaboration with him in the future."*

The album was titled '34613' and with the artwork virtually complete and just a little mixing required, they began to consider approaching record labels. It didn't appear until May 2012 in Australia, and was issued by Battlegod Productions but it did include the cover of the Lizzy Borden track Graham had recorded for them, 'Red Rum'. Mark Ashby of Uber Rock said: *"The unmistakeable vocal of Graham Bonnet takes over what is otherwise a fairly ordinary sub-power metal mid-pacer and lifts it into the stratosphere with an immense performance."*

Another session Graham took in was for Italian rock band, Sunset. They had originally contacted him in early September 2010 and sent him the song, 'Lunghezza d'onda' (translated means to be on the same wavelength) one month later. Lead singer Simon Locatelli says: *"Since hearing Rainbow's 'Down To Earth', Graham has been one of my favorite singers of all time. My good friend Robert Gualdi who was the drummer in Elektric Zoo told me about the experience he had touring with Graham and Dario Mollo in 2004. He said he loved Graham and that he appreciated the great feeling they had together. From that moment I knew I had to do something with him. When the occasion arrived for Sunset to record their first record 'Viaggio Libero' we decided to take the risk and sing in Italian instead of English and also include some guests. Graham Bonnet was the name I suggested, and after Jennifer Batten he was gladly chosen by everybody to be the second international artist to be part of our new release. When I spoke to Graham I explained what I had in mind and he accepted with enthusiasm, saying that the only problem he had was that he couldn't speak Italian very well! Don't worry I told him, your parts will be in English. When Graham sent the song back via Tim Luce on December 17th, he said he'd added a 'little surprise'. When I listened to it I was totally shocked …Graham was singing in Italian in time with me on 'sei sulla mia lunghezza d'onda'! It was the best gift I could receive."* 'Viaggio Libero' was later released by Rawlines on February 20th 2012.

Graham's next project was a one-off live show with Argentinean guitarist Walter Giardino, one of South America's most renowned guitarists and leader of the hugely popular Argentinean hard rock band Rata Blanca. Rudy Sarzo, who Walter knew, came on board so he decided to call the band GBS (Giardino/Bonnet/Sarzo). There was a hiccup when Sarzo had to pull out but they managed to recruit Greg Smith (ex-Alice Cooper, Ritchie Blackmore's Rainbow, Blue Oyster Cult, to name but a few) in his place, with the bonus that they could still use the name GBS!

On December 12th Graham flew to Buenos Aires, and rehearsals began the following day. Ainhoa Prieto, who had helped get the project together, says: *"The band only rehearsed for three days so it was a lot of work. Greg was a huge help working out the harmonies and it was a very tight band. They also had Rata Blanca's drummer, Fernando Scarcella, and their keyboard player Danilo Moschen."*

There was lots of interest locally and plenty of promotion, while prior to the show Graham and Walter had worked out a set list that included a lot of Graham's back catalogue as well as two songs from Walter's solo albums, which needed translating. Also included was the Jimi Hendrix version of 'Red House' which Greg Smith was to cover. An interesting choice was 'Danger Zone' by Rainbow, which hasn't had much of an outing since 1979.

"I actually translated the lyrics", says Ainhoa about the two songs by Walter. *"On the actual night they only performed one, 'Heroe de la Eternidad' ('Hero Of Eternity')."* Graham recalls receiving the songs: *"The words were sent to me by Ainhoa and she sang the melody, with the Spanish track in the background."*

GBS performed their one and only show at Teatro Flores in Buenos Aires on December 18th. On the night there were only around 400 tickets sold due to the short notice and proximity to Christmas. It seems a lot of work for one gig but everyone had a great time, which was the main thing. Graham was very pleased with how everything went: *"Greg Smith was a great asset to the show. The audience in Buenos Aires were amazing, just as I expected they joined in everything. All those Spanish smiles lit up the room for us. It's so incredible to play for the South America audience. They are very emotional, all have a passion for music, and they are always so welcoming to whoever is playing there."*

Back home, 2011 started with Graham's Alcatrazz putting in a couple of rehearsals for a show at Ventura Theater on January 20th while over in Europe Pushking's album 'The World As We Love It' was released on January 28th by Ear Music, and via deals in America, Japan and other countries. Graham certainly made his presence known on 'God Made Us Free', as well as contributing to 'Kukarracha'.

There was also a re-vamp of Graham's official website Bonnet Rocks, as Mandy Wheatcroft and Ainhoa Preito took it over. Masaya Uchimura had looked after the site for virtually ten years and put his heart into it, but thought it was time to hand it on to someone else. Mandy says: *"Graham asked me to help him in applying for gigs as I knew several promoters, and then we talked about what direction he should be going in with the music, etc. At that time he was about to do the GBS gig, so I was emailing Ainhoa a lot and we just got on so well. So I said to Graham that I would like to ask Ainhoa to work with me and set up the new website."*

On March 31st Graham's Alcatrazz were part of the Scrap Metal line-up at the Wolf Den in the Mohegan Sun Casino, Uncasville, Connecticut (an event co-founded by Gunnar Nelson). During the spring Graham wrote a song about Rory Gallagher, as a personal tribute to him, called 'No One Ever Sang For Rory'. Graham and Rory's paths had crossed in the Sixties and the Seventies. But cutting a new Alcatrazz album was no nearer completion and none of the band's new tracks had even made it into their live set.

They played again at the 4th & B in San Diego on June 11th with Mike

Vanderhule of Y&T as the band's 'guest drummer' for the show. Doing their usual set, Graham still used ear monitors and says: *"I got croaky towards the end and lost my in ear monitor sound and couldn't hear the band or me. So it wasn't real great as I couldn't hear what I was singing! It got raspy and the drummer got lost in one song. The other guys were lip-syncing me the words, so I could tell where we were. I just don't know why the sound got so messed up, but it ripped out my throat towards the end. Then it came back a bit, but it went well apart from those two bad things happening."*

Graham had been holding on to a Natasha Lea Jones song 'Come To Call' since the previous June, and now completed his vocals on it. The story behind the track was quite touching. Previously half of the duo Pooka, Natasha was getting ideas together for her second solo album and one was doing a duet with Graham: *"I saw him sing when I was nine years old at the Donington festival when Rainbow performed. When Graham came on stage it was just before dusk and his mic did not work for the first song. My brother and I were flabbergasted that we could still hear his voice! I do love Dio, but for me Graham became the soul of Rainbow."*

Natasha had written a few songs with Graham in mind and, after receiving them, the one which he was really impressed with was 'Come To Call'. *"Many of my friends have commented on Graham's vocals on 'Come To Call' and say they think his voice is even better now than ever, that there is a maturity in the sound."* It was finally mastered in early 2013. *"It was quite daunting mixing Graham's vocals in with mine, because he really does give the mic some shaking."* Natasha's album 'Soar' was released on her own Dantalian label on September 19th 2013.

Alcatrazz featuring Graham Bonnet were soon off on their travels again, but this time they hadn't very far to go; the House of Blues in West Hollywood, Los Angeles on July 2nd, supporting Hurricane. This was their fourth gig in just over five months. As before the band had a rehearsal a few days earlier, which Graham remembers: *"We had to do an acoustic rehearsal as the drummer, Mike Vanderhule, didn't fly in until the day of the gig! It's all a bit worrying not having proper loud rehearsals. I don't like having to sing softly for rehearsals as it doesn't strengthen my voice enough."*

Behind the scenes, the second Lyraka album, titled 'Lyraka Vol. 2', was starting to take shape, and Andy was overjoyed to have the singer on board once more: *"Graham Bonnet is one of the only 'old school metal' vocalists that has all the unique tone and power that he had early in his career. Because Graham's work has been a huge inspiration to me, he is the main vocalist in Lyraka, with most songs being written for him."* As to exactly what Graham would be doing on the album, Andy was relaxed: *"We are giving Graham all the time he needs, no rushing. There is no real time limit for him or the other singers. Jasmine and I rushed the first album - and then it ended up taking two years to make it anyway! Graham's got the duet with Veronica Freeman and a trio with Mark Boals and Liz Vandall, none of whom have appeared on record with him before. Tracks like 'Volcano' are too intricate to be finished in a few months. When I gave Graham the backing track for 'Volcano' I told him that there was absolutely no rush. It's a duet I wrote for Graham and Veronica."*

Graham also got a little media exposure, appearing on That Metal Show, hosted by Eddie Trunk, in July. Then, with Andy DeGelsomina on the Kenny Pick radio show Turn Up The Night the following month where they discussed the second Lyraka album, now being laid down at West Street Digital, in Fairfield, Vermont.

The following day, August 24th, producer John Eden contacted Graham after hearing a song by Karla Davis, who he has produced and worked with since March 2010. Karla was recording her second album at John's studio and the song 'Unbroken' really jumped out at him. He thought it would be perfect for Graham and suggested that they record it as a duet. Graham found himself travelling to Hendersonville, Tennessee, on January 7th to cut this but the recording didn't work out: *"The track that I did they aren't going to use. I wasn't on top form and to me the voices didn't really match."*

Graham had also been planning a trip to England, and his two-week visit took in trips to see his brother and his family in Skegness, as well as a few business meetings, one of which was to discuss the possibility of touring the UK in 2012 performing a set of Rainbow songs once again.

During late September, Graham's version of Alcatrazz drafted in ex-Nelson and Vinnie Vincent's Invasion drummer Bobby Rock for a short four-date European tour. Graham thought it would be a good idea to flex his vocal cords at home since he hadn't sung for quite a while. *"I just overdid it, so it's me getting more antibiotics and anti-inflammatory drugs to use in case I get the cords inflamed again. It's too long to go without singing and, of course, like any other muscles you don't use for a while they will suffer."*

Their first gig was on November 28th, at the Hard Rock Heroes Festival at the Spodek in Katowice, Poland, which Whitesnake were headlining. Recalling the gig, Graham says: *"Apart from the snow and freezing temperatures, it went very well. We wiped the floor with Whitesnake. The voice was fine. I didn't use in-ears. It was the worst thing I ever did for many years. All the distortion and not hearing everything properly. The doctor told me that was what was destroying my voice – over-compensating by singing louder. After Whitesnake had finished playing, Howie went out with their bass player and he was very complimentary about our show!"*

The following day saw the band begin a series of headlining gigs, starting off at the Golum Club, in Zlin, Czech Republic, on November 29th. After shows at the 7er Club in Mannheim, Germany on December 1st and at the Rock Temple, Kerkrade in The Netherlands two days later, Graham and the boys returned home on December 4th.

Japanese fan Junko Ogawara had never seen Graham sing live before, even when he had been in her native country, and due to an illness she'd had for fifteen years, it was very difficult to travel. She says: *"When Alcatrazz announced their European tour I really wanted to go, because I'd never seen one of Graham's gigs before. I was going to go to the gig in Italy, but it got cancelled. I decided to go to the gig in the Czech Republic because it was the nearest, and I really wanted to meet Graham and tell him that his music and singing always gave me encouragement and support. The club they played in was very small. I sat at a table near the front of the stage. It took me nineteen hours to get there from Japan and Zlin was a five-hour bus journey from Prague. Their performance was great and I enjoyed their gig very much!"* That's dedication. The set list was 'Assault Attack', 'Too Young To Die, Too Drunk To Live', 'God Blessed Video', 'Howie Solo', 'Big Foot' / 'Jet To Jet', 'Kree Nakoorie' / 'Hiroshima Mon Amour', 'Will You Be Home Tonight', 'Desert Song', 'All Night Long', 'Since You Been Gone' and 'Lost In Hollywood'.

Before the year was out Graham and Howie performed a set of acoustic songs at the United Rockers 4U American Red Cross Benefit Concert for Disaster Relief, as well as being part of a full-on jam later in the evening at the Hard Rock Café in Hollywood, on December 15th.

On the live scene Graham's Alcatrazz were struggling to draw a crowd on some occasions and, on February 10th 2012, they played at the Marquee 15 club in Corona, California to an audience of around fifty people. *"The place was still being built,"* recalls Graham, *"and is not really well known but we were told that some bands have packed the place out. We were also told one band who played there had three people turn up! So we made sure we got paid before we went on!"*

One week later Graham flew back out to Russia for a show in Moscow at the Music Town club, an indoor festival on February 22nd, which featured an array of singers backed by a house band. Graham performed five songs: *"It was a bit like a jam session really, just five songs, the usual 'All Night Long', 'Since You Been Gone', 'Lost In Hollywood', 'Long Live Rock 'n' Roll' and 'Oh Darlin''. It was a long way to go for just four days though. I paid for it with jetlag and a cold!"*

There was another repeat of the Finland scenario, with a mini-tour beginning in Tampere on March 14th at Klubi and concluding in Imatra at the Osmo's

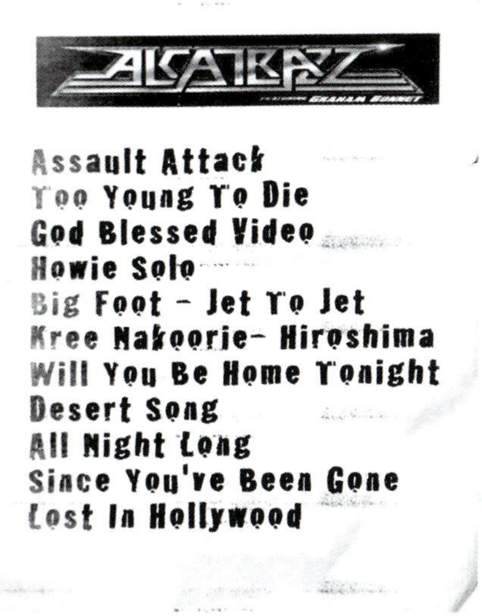

Assault Attack
Too Young To Die
God Blessed Video
Howie Solo
Big Foot – Jet To Jet
Kree Nakoorie – Hiroshima
Will You Be Home Tonight
Desert Song
All Night Long
Since You've Been Gone
Lost In Hollywood

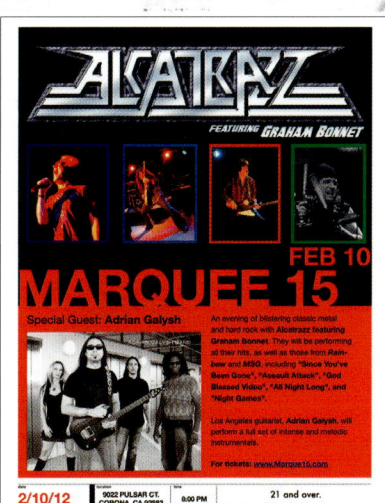

Above : Graham with Japanese fan Junko Ogawara; Set list Zlin, Czech Republic, 2011: flyer Marquee 15, California. Left : on stage, San Diego, June 2011.

Cosmos Bar with Graham returning home to Los Angeles the day after on March 18th. He was starting to feel the effects of all the touring, especially without the little luxuries and support some of the bigger names get on the road. *"I, of course, was jetlagged to death when we played. We had just one short rehearsal the day before the first gig. I need more time to get my energy back. The shows went well, even though I was not happy with my tiredness, although no-one complained. The crowds were great and there were lots of signing sessions and photos, etc. It is so hard getting out of bed one hour before a gig, and then going and shouting my head off and jumping around and doing the thing I do. I wish I didn't have to travel so damn far to do these gigs though. It doesn't always make for a good performance from me as I'm always afraid of letting them down by being so tired. People want to see that you still do the same work you did years ago. Singing is something that needs rest and proper warm-ups. The more gigs you do the more you are keeping the instrument in use and you know when to lay back and when to really go for it. It's that kind of thing you forget to do sometimes and the energy is lost before you get to the end. It is the same with drummers. If they are tired they drag and then come back to life in the middle of a show. That is what I'm like."*

While in Finland and playing at Osmo's Cosmos Bar in Imatra, Graham was approached about another duet, this one on a song called 'Seven Years' by Jaska Miikki, the singer of the band named after the bar, Osmo's Cosmos. He cut it quickly back at home, but only sings the second verse of the song. It appears on 'Show', which AXR Music later released in May 2012.

Realising that getting any label support to enable his Alcatrazz to get into a studio would be almost impossible, Graham had been thinking about recording another solo album. It had been around thirteen years since his last offering, and he thought the Russ Ballard song 'My Kingdom Come' would be better off on his album than as an Alcatrazz song. He also wondered about getting his childhood hero on board for a duet. *"I would love to do a track with Helen Shapiro,"* he said at the time. *"I've always wanted to sing with her. She was my hero! Her voice influenced my style when I was a kid, but it would be great to do something with her. A duet with her would make my life's dream perfect. I know she's into jazz and R & B stuff now, Amy Whitehouse was going for that sound, but never quite did it. Helen was the original and a much greater singer."* Sadly, despite his enthusiasm, Helen declined his offer; one childhood dream wrecked! He also expressed a big interest in working with ex-Michael Jackson guitarist Jennifer Batten, and wanted Michael Schenker to feature on a track.

One more proposed UK tour for Graham's Alcatrazz fell through as the financing of small tours is a real problem for bands and promoters, since it is so easy to end up out-of-pocket. But the band were approached to play the more established 2013 Monsters Of Rock Cruise in The Bahamas in March. The Russians were soon back in touch as well, though a show in Sergiev Posad, Russia, at the Dubrava Hall on June 30th, turned out to be a bit of a self-aggrandising project for the local town governor, playing bass in his own band, The Michael Men Band, backing Graham primarily on a batch of 'Down to Earth' songs. The set was 'Eyes Of The World', 'Over The Rainbow', 'Since You Been Gone', 'Love's No Friend', 'All Night Long', 'Desert Song', 'Dmitry Kuznetcov Keyboard Solo', 'Lost In Hollywood' and 'Long Live Rock 'n' Roll'.

The Scrap Metal event came round again and Alcatrazz featuring Graham Bonnet appeared on November 17th: *"I sang 'Since You Been Gone', 'All Night Long', 'Island In The Sun' and a Ricky Nelson song called 'Hello Mary Lou', which was way too low for me so I sang it an octave up. Gunnar Nelson – Ricky's lad – said we should have done it higher, but it worked out okay. His Dad was obviously someone I admired as a teen and sang his songs. It's a funny world; there I am standing on stage with his twin boys!"*

Out of the blue on December 2nd

Graham in Finland • 2012.

Graham was hit with news that his long-time friend from The Missing Links, The Blueset, The Bluesect and The Bluesecte, Roger Sleath, had passed away suddenly in his hometown of Guisborough, England.

Another Russian promoter now signed Graham up for a makeshift band called Rockstar, along with singer Chas West (ex-Bonham and Foreigner). The band comprised of guitarist Keri Kelli (ex-Alice Cooper), bassist Phil Soussan (ex-Ozzy Osbourne, Dio), drummer Chad Stewart (ex- L.A. Guns) and keyboard player Scott Warren (ex-Dio and Heaven & Hell). The shows carried the billing 'Rockstar is the world's most powerful super project, Worldstars in Moscow!' It was clearly a bit of a one-off money-spinner but even with two individual sets to be worked out for Graham and Chas, everyone managed to make the rehearsal in Los Angeles. Except Graham! *"We left early Sunday morning on December 16th,"* says Graham, *"but I had an epileptic seizure on the plane on the way out. Most of my time there was spent in the hotel having a drip in my arm and all that kind of stuff."*

Two short sets at various private parties reinforced the vanity nature of the set-up. *"The audience were very young well-to-do Russians, very weird,"* recalls Graham. *"We were all confused about us appearing in front of these people when they didn't know who the hell we were!"*

The final, public, show was another matter and took place at the Music Town Rock Club on December 20th. Graham said: *"Under the circumstances, amazingly, the shows were great as far as energy and fun was concerned. The band was great. They are all seasoned players and knew how to avoid a train wreck if someone missed a cue! We did two separate sets and then we all sang a couple of things together at the end. The usual kind of thing, 'Paranoid', 'Smoke On The Water' and 'Highway To Hell', where I just joined in the chorus. When I got home I was sick from the travelling and still suffering with bronchitis. Living The Dream, eh?"* he queries.

Having celebrated his 65th birthday there was the not-so-simple matter of a gig with his Alcatrazz at Studio Seven in Seattle on December 28th: *"The guys rehearsed without me and I just hoped I'd have the energy to sing. I felt terrible. I'd been to get some things for my stomach and some vitamins to go with the antibiotics I got from the doctor. I'd also been feeling dizzy and weak and coughing a lot because of the bronchitis, which is hard to fight."* The show went far better than anyone could have wished for but, it was followed by some very sad news.

Graham in Finland • *2012.*

Graham in Finland • *2012.*

CHAPTER 14
Wire And Wood (2013 - 2016)

Featuring: Alcatrazz featuring Graham Bonnet, Graham's solo career, Don Airey, The Doors Tribute, Stardust Reverie, Bonnet, Graham Bonnet Band, Rough Rockers, Wishing Well, Elektric Zoo and The Michael Schenker Fest

Night Game
(2 quad in, v-2c-4lead,4out)

The New Year had hardly got under way when Graham was told his cousin, Trevor Gordon, who he had played with in The Graham Bonnet Set and the Marbles, had been found dead in his house in London on January 9th. Graham was devastated.

The first two months of the 2013 were very quiet, but before long confirmation came through of three further shows in Japan for Graham's version of Alcatrazz as part of 'The Voices Of Rainbow' with Joe Lynn Turner and Doogie White again.

"We rehearsed on the Friday before we left. No new songs as such, but we added 'Dancer' and 'Assault Attack' from my MSG days to the set list, along with 'Only One Woman'. The only thing about Japan was the likelihood of getting sick again and bronchitis. I have to be real careful."

They started out at the Nakano Sun Plaza in Tokyo on March 12th, followed by the Bottom Line in Nagoya, and a final show at the Club Quatro in Osaka on March 14th. Graham says: *"It went well. We won them over again and we got the usual shower of gifts. They were very attentive when I sang 'Only One Woman' for Trev. They were moved with respectable applause, which was very nice; you know, without yelling; a quieter type of applause."* From Japan the band flew straight to Florida for the 'Monsters Of Rock Cruise', which departed from Ft. Lauderdale on March 16th. These rock cruises have gained quite a following in recent years, with some very big names taking part. The promoters theme each cruise and book appropriate bands, and word has gone around that they are very different from the old style cruise entertainments! The ships have multiple stages, proper rigs, and everything runs like clockwork. Although not cheap, fans do get to see a number of bands as well as signings, question-and-answer sessions and other special events. It certainly beats standing in the rain outside a hall for an autograph! Graham and the band had an excellent time and admit it was much more professional than they had expected: *"The cruise was amazing. The fans and other band members were ultra-kind with their praise. It was really good as we were warmed up from the Japanese shows. Lita Ford watched us at the side of stage from the beginning to the end. Other bands also came to watch us and were very complimentary. Our drummer Bobby played for Lita on the boat and now has a few gigs with her. Nelson were also on the cruise and they sang 'Since You Been Gone' with us. I signed lots of albums… And had some naughty nights!"*

Graham was next offered another package vocalist tour as one of the 'Legends - Voices Of Rock' with Bobby Kimball, Bill Champlin and Steve Augeri, because Jimi Jameson had pulled out. By sheer coincidence the backing band for the tour, Alien, had had a No.1 hit single in their native country Sweden with a cover of 'Only One Woman' back in 1988.

Hitting Slovakia, Austria and Spain, Graham was offered an immediate rebooking after covering 'All Night Long', Since You Been Gone', 'Only One Woman' and 'Lost In Hollywood'."

While this was all going on people were working to bring Graham over for a nine-date tour of England and Wales during August backed by Rainbow tribute band Catch The Rainbow. The first date had been pencilled in for August 16th at The Patriot in Crumlin, Wales, with Camden Underworld on August 20th being the standout venue. It was mainly a pub tour and all the shows were on consecutive nights. Even though the tour wasn't properly finalised, the dates still appeared in the press during early June, although soon afterwards they were all cancelled. The idea went on the back-burner for now.

Graham's next live appearance was something slightly different as he was a guest for mainly all-girl band Hardly Dangerous at the Whiskey A-Go-Go in West Hollywood on June 25th. He shared the vocals with Tomi Rae Brown on 'Oh Darlin'' and the Badfinger song 'No Matter What'. Graham also got to share the stage with bass player Beth-Ami Heavenstone who he had contacted in late 2012 about the possibility of forming a trio with another guitarist. *"I want to get away from this heavy rock label I have been stuck with and do some new things, along with a new band that doesn't have any drums. This will be a three-piece, two acoustics and an acoustic bass guitar. We'll do some covers though and our favourite tunes, alongside some acoustic versions of a couple of my rock songs,"* he said at the time. The event would also have lasting repercussions for Graham on a personal level too.

A couple of days later Graham flew to the UK to appear again at Don Airey's Blues & Soul Festival in Great Gransden on June 29th. It had been seven years since he'd last done the show and while here he nipped into a local recording studio with Don to record vocals on a track titled 'Mini Suite' for Don's upcoming solo album. The song was a tribute to Gary Moore, who had cut his part at Don's house not long before he died ('Keyed Up' was later released by the Mascot Label Group on February 25th 2014).

Firefest • Nottingham, 2013.

covered 'The Soft Parade'; 'Light My Fire – A Classic Rock Salute To The Doors' was released by Purple Pyramid Records on June 24th 2014. Graham also laid down a vocal for the European-based project Stardust Reverie on a song called 'Conqueror Of Both' and this appeared on 'Ancient Rites Of The Moon' issued by Foque / Avispa on April 8th 2014. Next up was the vocals for Canadian-based guitarist and songwriter Patgirl's song 'Enjoy The Show' in Mario Paga's studio but Patgirl later decided not to use Graham's recording. He was also approached to do another track for the second Tomorrow's Outlook album, titled 'Through Shuttered Eyes', but having been sent a demo of the song in mid-August he turned it down, feeling it wasn't right.

On August 29th Graham's Alcatrazz left for San Paulo in Brazil for a rescheduled gig on September 1st. But it was a bittersweet trip, as Graham had made his mind up to knock the band on the head after nearly seven years struggling to get the project fully off the ground. *"After I quit the guys sent me links to great reviews. Howie said 'the reviews were the best we'd ever had'. I will still do my guest heavy rock things but I am ready to sing again with my real voice. I am really looking forward to doing all the new stuff. The limitations of heavy rock are very evident - all a bit 1980s, big hair and spandex!"* The final set for Alcatrazz featuring Graham Bonnet was 'Assault Attack', 'Too Young To Die, Too Drunk To Live', 'God Blessed Video', 'Love's No Friend', 'Stand In Line', 'Howie Solo', 'Big Foot' / 'Jet To Jet', 'Skyfire', 'Kree Nakoorie' / 'Hiroshima Mon Amour', 'Will You Be Home Tonight', 'Desert Song' [inc drum solo], 'Night Games', 'All Night Long', 'Dancer' and 'Since You Been Gone'.

Graham was soon back on a plane to Sweden to rejoin the 'Legends – Voices Of Rock' tour for a month beginning in Lycksele on October 18th: *"I was doing 'Love's No Friend' instead of 'Only One Woman' then and the Alcatrazz song 'God Blessed Video' had been added. This is as well as Rainbow's 'Lost In Hollywood' and the two hits."*

The 25-date tour took in just about every big town and city in Sweden, punctuated with one break to headline Firefest at the Rock City in Nottingham on October 20th after Joe Lynn Turner had pulled out. Graham opened with 'All Night Long', followed by MSG's 'Desert Song' and 'Lost In Hollywood'. He finished his short but dynamic set with 'Love's No Friend'. Graham loved every minute of it, as he recalls: *"The venue was packed and everyone certainly enjoyed themselves. It was a pity the Swedish venues weren't the same. They were theatres where everyone was sat down, which makes it difficult for the fans to get into!"* The numbers weren't good either. The tour was due to finish in Bollnäs on November 17th but only ran until November 2nd. After a show at the Hotel Tanumstrand in Grebbestad the musicians were told the rest of the dates were being pulled due to lack of sales. With some unplanned free time Graham and Beth-Ami met up in London and visited family and friends in both the UK and France, and also used the time to look at some new material and discuss covering a couple of Beatles songs.

Before the year was through Graham parted

Back home and after a couple of rehearsals with Beth-Ami, Graham could see a lot of potential so during mid-August he met up with Mario Parga, who loved the idea, and the two jammed on various ideas and then started to rehearse more frequently at Beth-Ami Heavenstone's place. Graham explained about the emerging project: *"I really want to do something different. I have played so many different kinds of music growing up and been in different bands so why ignore the roots of all the learning I got from those early years? It's all music just in a different order of notes and feel."* When it came to choosing a name, Graham said: *"We are using our last names, Bonnet, Parga & Heavenstone. There were too many bands with similar names to what we came up with so last names will do!"*

At the beginning of July it was confirmed that Graham would be headlining the Hard Rock Hell Festival the following year in North Wales. Around the same time as this announcement, Mandy Wheatcroft became Graham's manager, and the first thing she did was resurrect the tour with the Rainbow tribute band Catch The Rainbow.

A few more sessions popped up during the summer, including a Doors tribute album which multi-instrumentalist Billy Sherwood was putting together. Graham

company with his manager, Mandy Wheatcroft. Back in the States Graham, Beth-Ami and Maio were confident enough to have some promo photos taken but recording didn't go so well. They tried again in December but it wasn't gelling. Beth-Ami said of the trip: *"My parts felt very staccato when I was playing them and Graham also felt disenchanted with his playing, but Mario assured us that it would sound great after it was mixed."* A possible management deal was in place but with a showcase at NAMM in Anaheim in January 2014 coming up, Mario pulled out. Beth-Ami suggested Brazilian guitarist Conrado Pesinato from her band Hardly Dangerous and he was more than happy to oblige, but when they got to the venue they all decided it was way too noisy for their music, so they spent their time networking instead.

With offers bubbling in Graham, Beth-Ami and Conrado began working on recording some acoustic songs: *"I moved all my pro tools equipment to Beth-Ami's, because Conrado lives out that way. So it was best for everyone."*

His *"rock thing"* now kicked back in, the long-awaited UK tour with Birmingham-based Catch The Rainbow. It does seem a strange thing at first, an original member playing with a tribute band, but the concept seems to be growing. The band's drummer Bob Richards is a big fan of Bonnet-era Rainbow: *"I formed Catch The Rainbow in 2010. I wanted to base it on the 'Down To Earth' tour as that was my first introduction to Rainbow."* Apart from Bob, the band consists of Ian Richardson (guitar), Neil Taylor (keyboards) and Pete Knight (bass guitar). Their singer, Persian Risk's Carl Sentence, also fronts Don Airey's band, when Don isn't busy with another group he's involved with! Bob recalls: *"I knew Graham had worked with different bands in the past. A local promoter called Ray Williams had originally contacted Graham and put us in touch. Later Dave Clough from EMA contacted Graham and myself and the tour was born."*

The band had been quite nervous about playing with Graham but he soon put them at ease. There was only one planned rehearsal, as Bob points out: *"We knew our songs and I guessed that Graham knew them as well. We had an afternoon at Madhouse rehearsal rooms in Birmingham. We ran through several songs. The first we did was 'Love's No Friend' and Graham nailed it! It was a surreal moment for me as you can imagine. We decided to play 'Bad Girl' and 'Makin' Love' as these were not really played at all by Rainbow on the road, but are good songs and I thought the audience would like to hear them."*

Beth-Ami travelled over with Graham and prior to the tour starting the pair visited his family in Skegness and stayed at the North Shore Hotel where Graham had worked as a teenager back in 1963. On their return train journey to Birmingham they found themselves completely alone in their carriage on the leg to Boston in Lincolnshire. So what did they do? They got their guitars out and had a jam!

The tour itself kicked off at Fibbers in York on March 16th, nearly 35 years since Rainbow had released 'Down To Earth'. More shows were added and they ended up playing nine in nine days, although some of the venues were changed. The show at The Garage in London – where Graham got a great reaction from a virtually sell-out crowd – was attended by two ex-Graham Bonnet Set members, drummer Steve Hardy and keyboard player Bob Turner. This was the first time Graham, Steve and Bob had all been together since 1968.

It was a good decision to headline the HRH AOR 2 Festival in Pwllheli, North Wales, too, as Graham again put on one hell of a show and got a tremendous reception from a sold-out crowd, with over 2,000 people in attendance. Throughout the tour, and taking pride of place on stage, was Bob's drum kit: *"I've had Cozy Powell's kit since June 2000. It was for sale in a drum shop. It is the one from the Whitesnake 'Slide It In' tour from 1984. I saw Cozy playing it in Cardiff and I never in a million years thought I would actually own it."* The set for the Catch the Rainbow shows was 'Eyes Of The World', 'Love's No Friend', 'Since You Been Gone', 'Bad Girl', 'Makin' Love', 'Neil Taylor Keyboard Solo', 'Kill The King' [instrumental], 'Bob Richards Drum Solo', 'Stargazer', 'Catch The Rainbow', 'All Night Long', 'Lost In Hollywood' and 'Long Live Rock 'n' Roll'. 'Stargazer' wasn't performed on early shows and occasionally a couple of the songs were juggled around.

Away from the rock scene, Graham's acoustic trio had decided to call themselves simply Bonnet and made their debut performance at Beth-Ami's son's school's music night on May 2nd. The idea of performing without a drummer had now gone out of the window, and Anthony 'Tiny' Biuso was brought in. Their short set was 'Here There And Everywhere', as well as 'Eight Days A Week' by The Beatles, 'No Matter What' by Badfinger and 'Since You Been Gone'. *"Graham had a rough night,"* says Beth-Ami, *"and I predicted it which is why I wanted this to be our first gig, to get that out of the way. I wish I could help him but he has to go through what he has to."*

Bonnet set about trying to get their sound down again: *"More recording was done during late June and early July at Studio Boudoir, the room that used to be my bedroom!"* says Beth-Ami. *"Graham's voice was so loud. He was literally rocking the house."*

In and amongst work for Bonnet, Graham recorded the vocals for a track called 'Imagining Confusions' by Jesus Arjona, who is based in Spain. He had actually contacted Graham quite a while earlier. Graham says: *"The song was way low for me but I did the best I could. The vocal is not that inspired. In fact, I think it may be the most average vocal I have done!"* Conrado Pesinato was now Graham's vocal engineer and the song features on the second Stardust Reverie project, 'Proclamation Of Shadows', which Kuiama Records issued on November 15th 2015.

On July 8th Graham and Beth-Ami set off to Stuttgart in Germany as three days later he was appearing at the Bang Your Head Festival at Messegelände in Balingen, Axel Rudi Pell's 25th anniversary show. A self-confessed fan of Ritchie Blackmore and, also like Yngwie Malmsteen, a guitarist

Graham and Beth-Ami • *London, 2014 with Bob Turner and Steve Hardy from The Graham Bonnet Set.*

who started out in a band called Steeler, Axel had invited a host of singers and musicians to appear alongside him. Backed by Axel's band, Graham only sang one song by himself, 'Since You Been Gone', but covered 'Long Live Rock 'n' Roll' with Doogie White and was part of the final encore, 'Smoke On The Water'. The whole show was later released on both CD and DVD under the title 'Magic Moments' by SPV on April 28th 2015.

Almost one month later, on Monday August 4th, Graham headed for Gothenburg in Sweden for three shows in Scandinavia. Guitarist Sayit Dolen had pieced a band together to back Graham and, with just enough time to take in a couple of rehearsals, the first show took place at Stopp Pressen in Oslo, Norway on August 7th and the following evening saw them appear at Restauarang, Vasterhus, Gothenburg, Sweden. This was a very intimate gig with VIP tickets, which included a buffet and a glass of wine or a beer, costing 495 SEK. It also included an opportunity to meet Graham before and after the show enabling you to get his autograph and have a photograph taken with him. He performed a selection of his hits for one hour. The final show on August 9th saw Graham as part of Bonna Rock (Anthems of Rock) with Bobby Kimball and Nik Kershaw at an outdoor event in Kopparberg, Sweden, despite undergoing some emergency dental treatment for problems which he'd been suffering with for a while.

Mid-August saw Graham working on Bonnet songs with keyboards added by Eric Rango. Drum auditions too were held along the way for the up-coming gig at the Whiskey A-Go-Go in West Hollywood. Graham says: *"We decided on Ronnie Ciago. He was recommended by Beth-Ami's friend who went to the Julliard Music Academy in New York with Ronnie. Our first rehearsal with him and the whole band was on September 1st and went very well."* By now the band was more electric than acoustic with only Graham playing acoustic guitar on a few of songs.

Most of September was taken up with rehearsing at Amp Rehearsal studios for their gig, part of the Sunset Strip Music Festival on September 20th. This was the band's 'official' live debut and included Eric Rango on keyboards. Bonnet played for around 30 minutes and Beth-Ami says: *"I had a great time. The stage sound at the Whisky notoriously sucks so I think that was what was tripping Graham up. We got great feedback from the crowd and I think despite a snafu or two, the show went well."* Two brand new songs, 'I Thought They'd Always Be There', which is a tribute to The Beatles and the Sixties and 'The Mirror Lies', a much rockier song were included with some Rainbow songs. Graham used the lyrics for 'The Mirror Lies' from the Elektric Zoo song since it had been decided along the way that their planned album was going no further. He says about the song: *"This is about being over-confident and about the way you appear and your vanity."*

This high contrasted with the low of more bad news, as on September 30th Graham's brother Tony passed away after suffering from Alzheimers for a while. Although it was not unexpected, and Graham had been over to visit him a few times while he was ill, it was still a huge personal blow.

During mid-October Graham teamed up with Jørn Lande and Doogie White, who had replaced Joe Lynn Turner for two gigs in Norway. Graham arrived in Oslo on October 15th, and the first show took place inside a mountain at a rock club called Stormbringer in Gjovik on October 18th. The following day saw Graham appear at a blues festival in a sports hall in Fauske. He says of the trip: *"It was a very stressful time for me as I was thinking about Tony quite often. I did my usual jetlagged performances."*

Bonnet now parted company with Ronnie Ciago. *"Ronnie just wasn't the right guy,"* says Graham. *"He was good but too light on some songs."* This left Bonnet in a bit of predicament, with a European tour only a matter of three weeks away. Local drum teacher Justin Lack joined and numerous rehearsal sessions took place. He says: *"I've known Con for over two years. We played in a band together and became fast friends. He has been telling Graham about me for a while. At my audition we played 'All Night Long' and 'Love's No Friend' and they were happy."* Graham said: *"Justin has really studied hard to be ready so quickly."* They left for Spain on November 11th for a gig at the Bikini Club in Barcelona two days later. Two more Spanish shows took in Madrid and Bilbao over the next two days and the band had decided against using a live keyboard player on the tour. Graham says: *"The keyboards have been recorded by Eric Rango and backing vocals too, which Beth-Ami and I did. The fans were ecstatic and everything went very well indeed. We won a lot of people over to the new songs."* The set included 'The Witchwood'. Alcatrazz had never been performed it live, so better late than never!

The band stayed in Barcelona for just over a week with four days rehearsing at Motor Music Records before travelling to The Netherlands for a show at The Patronaat in Haarlem on November 28th. They added another Rainbow song to the set, 'Bad Girl'. On the spur of the moment 'Johnny B. Goode' was also performed. From there the band flew to London for a short five-date UK tour. Bonnet performed the same songs, although they were juggled around at times. For the London show Doogie White joined them on stage for 'Since You Been Gone'. The set list was 'All Night Long', 'Love's No Friend', 'Makin' Love', 'Bad Girl', 'I Thought They'd Always Be There', 'Eight Days A Week', 'The Witchwood', 'The Mirror Lies', 'Seven Deadly Sins' [instrumental including guitar and drum solos], 'Since You Been Gone', 'Night Games', and 'Lost In Hollywood'. As Graham had been getting to know Dragonsclaw vocalist Giles Lavery, he was asked to tag along for the UK dates. One thing led to another and Giles took over their management. An official band website had also started up, but soon disappeared, but come the summer of 2015 a new one graced the internet. Graham decided to take advantage of the web and make some of his archives available as downloads. His unreleased album from 1974 was one of the first, and titled 'Private I – The Archive Vol. One' it also included the tracks from the film soundtrack 'Three For All'.

Returning home the name Bonnet was top of their debriefing list. They immediately changed it to the Graham Bonnet Band. In January 2015 the newly-named band parted company with drummer Justin Lack. They still continued to record, however, and Graham decided to resurrect 'My Kingdom Come', with ex-Fates Warning and Warlord drummer, Mark Zonder on hand to help out. The keyboards were supplied by ex-Alice Cooper and Dream Theater member, Derek Sherenian. Graham says: *"I have a great history with Russ Ballard, having recorded several of his songs for bands and projects I have been involved in over the years."*

For a change of scenery Graham appeared at a jam night at Lucky Strike on

Beth-Ami and Graham • *Glasgow, December 2014.*

Hollywood Boulevard on March 11th even though he was suffering again from bronchitis. He says: *"I had to do it as I had let Chuck Wright down the first time he asked me. I just did the one song, 'All Night Long' and stayed half an hour and then went home. It's fun for everyone to mingle though!"*

It was back to more recording and around early spring the band tackled 'The Mirror Lies'. Even though they had now decided on drummer Chase Manhattan after numerous auditions, it was left to Mark Zonder to do the recording and Eric Rango to supply the keyboard parts. Both new recordings were mixed and mastered by Alessandro Del Vecchio.

During late March and into early April, Graham turned his attention to recording the vocals for 'Unleash The Beast' for the Swedish rock band, Rough Rockers. Bassist, Peter Ljungberg says: *"I wrote the song (music and lyrics) and guitarist; Magnus Hällström helped me to develop it. I sent Graham a demo with my singing on it. He followed it to a big extent, but developed some parts to fit his voice and his way of singing."* The song is featured on their third (self-financed) EP, 'A Safe Pair Of Hands' and was released on December 11th.

Graham flew to Prague on May 4th and two days later he began a seven-date tour of the Czech Republic, Russia and the Ukraine as part of the 'Living Legends Of Rock' tour. Opening up at the Velka Synagoga in Pilsen in the Czech Republic, the middle five shows were all in Russia, with the final one talking place at the October Palace in Kiev, Ukraine on May 24th. On the days off prior to each gig a rehearsal with the local Philharmonic orchestra took place. Also on the tour were John Lawton and Dan McCafferty.

It was manager Giles Lavery's job to look after Graham, and his experiences on this tour give a real insight into the problems such a job can entail, especially touring in Eastern Europe: *"The lead up to these dates was filled with communication issues and a lot of email back and forth between the promoter (a Ukraine woman who seemed to have a monopoly on the classic rock live market in her territory). The proposed dates were cancelled at least twice before May 2015 became the agreed timeframe. The fee came at the last minute so it was uncertain if it would even get off the ground. Flights and ground transportation were booked as we went along. It seemed that promoter was having to borrow money along the way and pay for things piecemeal - she sold off the shows to other promoters in local areas but seemed to wield her power behind the scenes. Our tour managers were nice enough but were terribly inept young people, one had never been on a plane before, let alone tour managed. The promoter was paying these kids on promises to hang out with 'rock stars' and taking advantage - something that made Graham very angry as he isn't one who likes to see people exploited. Per-deims were frequently short or begrudgingly given and the contracted '4 star minimum' hotels were switched with much lower standard accommodation - resulting in loud arguments in the parking lots of several hotels until we got the correct agreed upon lodging sorted out. The shows themselves were well attended mostly - with enthusiastic fans happy to see the three singers. Myself, Graham and John provided backing vocals for Dan McCafferty and a good time in general made up for the many short comings on the organizational front. Graham, at about the halfway point, needed a refill of some prescription medication, which ended in a fruitless search across some very run down hospitals that looked like a scene out of a Hammer horror film. Finally, after being told that the only way to get this medication would be to fly back to Los Angeles and get it there, we realised just how remote things were. It wasn't until one of the local promoters told us he 'knew a guy' who could obtain the meds that we solved that problem. All this of course was nothing compared to what awaited us in the Ukraine. After a very long day's travel we finally arrived at passport control in the Kiev airport - everyone was able to be sent through apart from me, as the documentation I was provided with by the visa agent was not appropriate. So off I was taken - and this turned into a 20 hour ordeal that had soldiers with guns pointed guarding me for the whole night and relieving me of my passport, though strangely not my iPhone. Finally, at around lunch time the next day the promoter's son had arrived with promise of my release. The singers had stated that without my release there would be no show. This had angered the promoter, who had called upon some heavyweight muscle to ensure that the singers did not go anywhere but the gig - and if they did not perform then they would be held until the lost revenue was repaid in cash. So I told Graham to 'do the show as there is no point getting in further strife just to make a point'."* Back at the airport the authorities told Giles he would have to leave and not come back. *"Graham was very worried. I advised him to get out, however, he stayed and performed (as did everyone) and thankfully they were all allowed to leave. I only relaxed when I knew he was at the airport ready to board for LA."* The set list (just for the record!) was 'All Night Long', 'Since You Been Gone', 'The Witchwood', 'Love's No Friend' and 'Makin' Love'.

June saw the Graham Bonnet Band on more familiar ground, travelling to Japan as 'special guests' on Michael Schenker's Temple Of Rock Spirit Of A Mission tour. With five shows in six days, the opening night was in Osaka at the Zepp Namba on June 14th and coincided with the release of 'My Kingdom Come' and 'The Mirror Lies' as internet downloads. The Diamond Hall in Nagoya came the day after, and the short tour closed in Tokyo at the Nakano Sun Plaza with three shows on June 17th, 18th, and 19th. The set list was 'All Night Long', 'Love's No Friend', 'God Blessed Video', 'Makin' Love', 'Since You Been Gone', 'Suffer Me', 'The Mirror Lies' 'Night Games' and 'Lost In Hollywood'. Graham also joined Michael on stage each night and performed 'Assault Attack' and 'Desert Song'. This made it the first time the pair had performed any songs from their 1982 MSG album together. Graham says: *"We know that this record holds a very special place for many fans, especially in Japan. So this made the debut shows there of the new band even more special."* They returned to Los Angeles on June 22nd. One month later as a good-will gesture to the fans the band released a 6-track EP from the tour called 'Escape From Alcatrazz - Live In Japan' as a free download on the internet.

Cleopatra Records in America chose this moment to release Rainbow's 1979 show from Denver on their Purple Pyramid label. It was issued as a double LP in a holographic gatefold sleeve, pressed in red, green or blue vinyl, and limited to 1000 copies per colour. They simply titled their offering 'Denver 1979 Down To Earth Tour'. Later, on August 21st, they released the same show but as part of a 3 CD box set, which also included 'Long Island 1979' and 'Chicago 1979'. In the UK, Hear No Evil Records, through Cherry Red, set about plans to release a large selection of Graham's back catalogue and these began to see the light of day from October 2015 on a fairly regular basis and were set to continue into 2017. Included amongst them was Graham's 1974 unissued album, 'Back Row In The Stalls'. All the releases include extra tracks, some of which are unreleased or have never appeared on CD before. A CD / DVD career retrospective is also planned.

More excitingly for him and his group, the summer saw the Graham Bonnet Band agree a deal with Frontiers Records for a new album and also a bonus disc of re-recorded past hits, well known songs and personally chosen tracks like 'Here Comes The Night', which Graham had only ever performed live once back with Impellitteri at the Civic Auditorium in San Jose in September 1988. Work began in July on recording these new cover versions first with Conrado Pesinato handling the production. As for the new material, once again Graham opted to use the lyrics from past Elektric Zoo songs, 'Dead Man Walking', and 'Motorbike' (a song from Graham's 1989 Australian sessions originally called 'Rider') where he just retained the verses.

On July 22nd the band returned to Lucky Strike in Hollywood for the jam night where they performed 'Lost In Hollywood' and 'All Night Long'. It was a good warm up on local soil as three days later they then headlined The Cruefest at the Whiskey A Go Go. The event was in aid of pediatric cancer research and the set was the same as in Japan, minus 'Suffer Me'.

Graham was soon on his travels again and was joined by his partner Beth-Ami. He teamed up with Michael Schenker's Temple Of Rock in Seebronn, Rottenburg, near Stuttgart, Germany for the Rock Of Ages 10th anniversary 3-day event on

Japan, June 2015 • Graham and Michael Schenker, Graham Bonnet Band, Graham and Doogie White.

August 1st. As in Japan, he sung 'Assault Attack' and 'Desert Song'. Graham and Beth-Ami took in various sightseeing trips in Germany and stopped off in New York for about a week before heading back to Los Angeles.

On their return the band continued to record but, come early September they parted company with drummer Chase Manhattan. He was replaced with Mark Zonder and it wasn't too long before he started laying down his drum parts for the cover songs in his own studio. He says: *"I am fortunate to have a 900 sq ft studio in my house with tracking room and control room."* As for being in the band, he adds: *"The one thing that really struck me while working with Graham on new material is actually how musically gifted he really is. We all know about his days with Rainbow, MSG etc … as a singer with that powerful voice, but to sit down with an acoustic guitar in his hands and watch him come up with ideas and melodies is simply amazing. He's one of those guys that have nothing but great melodies and harmonies coming flying out of him. It is a true pleasure and honour to play with him and the band."* For a breather from recording, Graham appeared at Count's Vamp'd in Las Vegas on November 12th as a special guest with the band Sin City Sinners.

As soon as Graham returned to Los Angeles he re-recorded his vocals for a song by Finnish rock band Wishing Well titled 'Hippie Heart Gypsy Soul' with Conrado Pesinato at the controls. The song appears on their album, 'Chasing Rainbows', released on February 5th 2016 by the Finnish label Inverse Records. The song was also released as an internet download as Wishing Well featuring Graham Bonnet. Guitarist, Anssi Korkiakoski says: *"I first heard Graham's unique voice in 1981 when I heard both 'Down To Earth' and 'Line Up'. I do regard 'Assault Attack', which is also a band favourite, to be Graham's greatest achievement."* As for 'Hippie Heart Gypsy Soul', he points out: *"I came up with the song in early April and wrote the lyrics in a couple of weeks, which is an exceptionally short time for me. 'Desert Song' was a key influence for it."*

Wishing Well had originally planned for Graham to sing three songs (the other two being 'Sands Of Time' and 'Fire In My Soul') and to record them in Finland but, after realising the costs involved decided against that. Graham says: *"The guys got in touch last summer and after I heard the song I was immediately ready to give it a go. It's a catchy tune and perfect for my range."*

As 2016 began, the Graham Bonnet Band took a break from recording to work out and rehearse a set for their appearance at Malone's in Santa Ana, California

on January 22nd as part of the NAMM event. Conrado says: *"It was a lot of fun. Unfortunately we didn't have a sound-check, but all things considered it went really well. It was the first time we'd played live with Mark and he killed it! It is a pleasure to be on stage with these 3 great musicians."* The excellent Russ Ballard song 'S.O.S.' had now been added to the set, which was 'Eyes Of The World' 'All Night Long', 'S.O.S.', 'God Blessed Video', 'Will You Be Home Tonight', 'Night Games', 'Suffer Me', 'Dancer', 'Love's No Friend', 'Desert Song', 'The Mirror Lies', The Witchwood', 'Island In The Sun', 'Since You Been Gone', 'Assault Attack', and 'Lost In Hollywood'. The band had planned to include 'Only One Woman' and 'Stand In Line', but these were dropped at the last minute.

Before the month was through there was some renewed interest in the previously recorded Elektric Zoo songs (including the Rainbow covers) for an album, and Dario started to remix them, adding some more guitar and giving the songs a makeover.

The Graham Bonnet Band now set off to the U.K. on January 24th for a 17 date tour which with a slot at the Giants Of Rock weekend at Butlins in Minehead on January 29th and ran through most of February. The tour included a special hometown show at The Suncastle in Skegness on February 3rd. Remarkably this was the first time Graham had played on home turf since June 1967 with the Graham Bonnet Set. What was even more noteworthy was that it was almost 49 years to the day since the band had performed at the venue itself on February 16th 1967. Prior to leaving Los Angeles, he said: *"It's important for me to play in my hometown this year because Skeggy means more to me now than ever. My dear brother Tony passed away a little over a year ago and it made me realise that you can take the boy out of Skeggy but you can never take Skegness out of the boy. It all started here and I want to pay tribute to my friends and family. This is where I first discovered my love of music and more importantly, that I had a talent for singing, playing and writing music. My last show in Skegness was as a young man at the old Festival Pavilion with The Graham Bonnet Set. We were a group of fresh faced lads with a burning desire to rule the world and it was one of the best times of my life."*

Many of Graham's friends, relatives and ex-band members turned up at the Suncastle, some of whom he hadn't seen for several decades. Ex-Graham Bonnet Set drummer, Steve Hardy was there and said: *"It was a very nostalgic evening for everyone, especially Graham with it being nearly 49 years to the day since The Graham Bonnet Set last played there with The Peter Tomlinson Band. Two other ex-members, bassist, Robin Walker and saxophonist, Alan Vickers, were also there as well as people Graham had known from his schooldays and the Cubs. Some things had changed since the old days, the stage had moved from the right hand side to the right corner, but the large room seemed the same size. The gig was well attended and Graham sung his heart out going through a batch of Rainbow, MSG and Alcatrazz songs. Everyone was waiting for the Marbles' song; 'Only One Woman,' and Graham didn't disappoint and even played it with Trevor Gordon's guitar. It was nice to be part of such a special evening."*

The set list was 'Eyes Of The Word', 'All Night Long', 'S.O.S.', 'God Blessed Video', 'Will You Be Home Tonight', 'Night Games', 'Dancer', 'Love's No Friend', 'Desert Song', 'The Mirror Lies', 'The Witchwood', 'Only One Woman', 'Since You Been Gone', 'Assault Attack', and 'Lost In Hollywood' with 'Island In The Sun' and 'Suffer Me' being the encores. To keep everyone on their toes the songs were swopped around throughout the tour and on some nights 'Only One

Skegness • *A pensive moment while preparing for the homecoming show, 2016. Right :* **The Graham Bonnet Band 2016** • *L-r Mark Zonder, Graham, Beth-Ami Heavenstone, Conrado Pesinato.*

Woman' and 'Suffer Me' weren't played at all. The final gig took place in London at the O2 Academy 2 on February 20th with Russ Ballard, Doogie White and Kaplan Kaye and others there to support Graham. The band returned home to Los Angeles two days later.

After taking a breather for the remainder of February, more recording took place for their debut album during March, and Graham also managed to find time to add his vocals to the backing track for Elektric Zoo's version of 'Since You Been Gone' in 2004. (Two brand new songs were later recorded for the project titled 'Cest La Vie' and 'Guys From God'.) He then jetted off to the Czech Republic for gigs in Prague and Ostrava with John Lawton and Dan McCafferty on March 22nd and 24th as part of the 'Legends Of Rock' package. The set list was the same as when he played there back in May 2015, with the exception of 'All Shook Up', which the threesome did as the encore instead of 'With A Little Help From My Friends'.

The Graham Bonnet Band were scheduled to do an 8 date tour of Australasia (six in Australia and two in New Zealand) between April 6th to 16th, but this fell through so they spent the time doing some more recording. Prior to a short tour of Finland (with a gig in Italy tagged on) the band were scheduled to do a warm up show at Paladinos in Tarzana on April 14th, but after waiting for two and a half hours for the sound-man to turn up this was cancelled.

The Finnish tour began at Möysän Esso in Lahti on April 20th followed by the On The Rocks club in Helsinki the day after. Their third gig in three days saw them perform in the nightclub on board the MS Mariella (Viking Line), the ferry from Helsinki to Stockholm. The following day they made a record store appearance at Plugged Records in Gamla Stan in the city performing a 30 minute set in front of around 60 people, which was all the small shop could accommodate. Following this the band travelled to Italy for the Frontiers Rock Festival III at the Live Club in Milan, recorded for a CD DVD release. The set list for the tour was 'Eyes Of The World', 'All Night Long', 'S.O.S.', ('Stand In Line' added on 3rd and 4th shows), 'God Blessed Video', 'Will You Be Home Tonight', ('Jet To Jet' added on 3rd and 4th shows), 'Night Games', 'Suffer Me', 'Dancer', 'Love's No Friend', 'Desert Song', 'Island In The Sun', 'The Mirror Lies', 'Since You Been Gone', 'Assault Attack' and 'Lost In Hollywood'.

In-between the gigs, Rainbow's heavily bootlegged headlining appearance at the Donington Festival back in 1980 was officially released by Eagle Rock on April 22nd as a CD/DVD set. The UK and Europe were short changed yet again with a single CD, which didn't include 'Love's No Friend' and 'Man On The Silver Mountain'. The Japanese got a double CD that included an extra ten minutes from the show.

Graham also rekindled his friendship with ex-Alcatrazz and Blackthorne keyboard player Jimmy Waldo and this lead to him adding his parts to some of the new songs on the bands' album.

It was back to Scandinavia during early June for their debut appearance at the Sweden Rock Festival in Sölvesborg on June 8th in front of around 8000 people. The set list was the same as in Italy at the Frontiers Rock Festival, minus 'Love's No Friend' and 'The Mirror Lies'. Sweden Rock also saw Graham appear as part of the Michael Schenker Fest two days later where he sung 'Desert Song', 'Dancer' and 'Assault Attack'. The line-up featured MSG's original singer, Gary Barden and Robin McAuley, original bassist, Chris Glen and drummer, Ted McKenna, plus guitarist / keyboard player, Steve Mann. To make the trip worthwhile the Graham Bonnet Band played at Göta Källare on June 12th in Stockholm where 'The Witchwood'

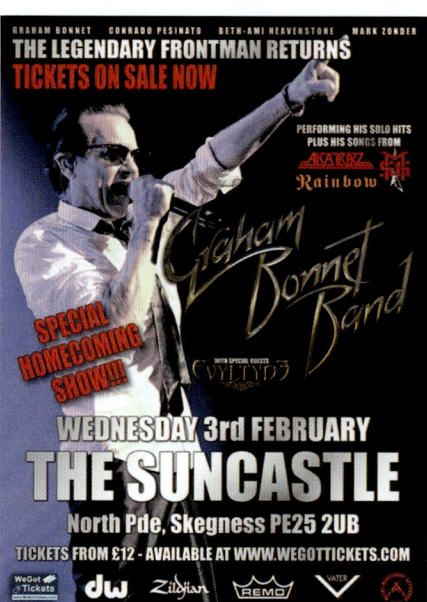

was added to the set. Towards the end of the month Graham ticked off another country with a solo appearance at the Voxbotn Festival in Tórshavn on the Faroe Islands on June 25th. The set list was 'All Night Long', 'God Blessed Video', 'Only One Woman', 'Lost In Hollywood' and 'Since You Been Gone'. Graham also joined in with Mickey Thomas of Starship on 'We Built This City' and Eagle-Eye Cherry on the song 'Save Tonight', along with Mickey too.

It was decided to title the bands' album 'The Book' after the song of the same name, which had begun life when the very last line-up of Alcatrazz rehearsed it as long ago as 1987. Graham finished his vocals for the album on July 20th after which the band left for shows at the Rock Of Ages Festival near Stuttgart on July 29th, and the Classic Rock Night Festival in Thalmässing the day after. Graham then appeared at the 'Voices Of Rainbow' open-air concert with Doogie White at Saarbrücken on August 5th. Later in the month, Graham joined the Michael Schenker Fest for a short three date tour of Japan. Graham sung 'Assault Attack', 'Desert Song' and 'Dancer' on the first two nights (with 'Broken Promises' added in Sapporo) and the first verse of 'Doctor Doctor' on each night, which was part of the encore.

September saw the release of the intended second Blackthorne album from 1994 by Hear No Evil Records, titled 'Don't Kill The Thrill'. It features the ten planned studio tracks, along with 'Wild Inside', an outtake from the 'Afterlife' sessions, plus a bonus CD of interviews from 1993 and live tracks from 1992, 1993 and 1994.

The Graham Bonnet Band took a break then began plans for a two week tour (thirteen shows over fifteen days) to support the new studio album issued on November 4th.

The Book was well received overall ("he sounds happier and more into the songs and music than he has in many, many years" wrote the Rocktopia reviewer) and the good reviews helped the band's profile, which also seemed to benefit from the determined approach to touring. Early copies even came with a bonus CD of re-recorded tracks from Rainbow and others.

Even more line-up changes failed to halt their progress; before the UK shows began, drummer Mark Zonder left the band. One of his final shows (from the

Prague, 2016 • l-r : John Lawton, Graham and Dan MacCafferty.

The Graham Bonnet Band • Leeds, 2016 UK tour. Left : The Graham Bonnet Band 2017 line-up. Above : The Graham Bonnet Set at Skegness 2017.

Below : Graham at home • with his children l-r Aaron, Tayla and Keeley, and grandchildren Shiloh and Asher.

2016 Frontiers Festival in Italy) appeared on CD and DVD in July 2017, "Live... Here Comes The Night", which included material from Rainbow, MSG, Alcatrazz, Impellitteri as well as new band numbers. Just a few weeks before this release it was also announced that Conrado Pesinato was leaving, and so as the band prepared for a British tour in July (to coincide with the live album) the line-up included Joey Tafolla on guitar and Mark Banquechea (who had joined for the 20216 U.K. tour) on drums. The publicity photo for this (above) was classic Bonnet, his bright pink suit (the top half of which has been seen on stage!) contrasting with the black leathers of the rest of the group.

2017 continued to be busy, with a new studio album, shows across Europe and a UK Schenkerfest spot in London. As he had a couple of U.K. festivals booked, Graham's manager put together a short tour around these at the end of July, including a return to The Sandcastle at Skegness, but even better Steve Hardy, Robin Walker and Rob Turner from Graham's original band appeared as special guests, ripping through Lucille.

It is now over 50 years since that original Graham Bonnet Set first trod the boards and he now has regained enough confidence to have his own name fronting a band. It has been a long journey and it's not over yet.

The future looks bright, but you've got to wear shades!

GRAHAM BONNET DISCOGRAPHY 1967-2016

Solo Singles (PS = picture or text sleeve)

Whisper In The Night / Rare Specimen (1972 : UK only)
Trying To Say Goodbye / Castles In The Air (1973 : UK only)
Back Row In The Stalls / Ghost Writer In My Eye (1974 : UK only)
Dreams (Out In The Forest) / We're Free (As Billy Beethoven. 1975 : UK only)
It's All Over Now Baby Blue / Heroes On My Picture Wall (1977 : UK)
  Holland (Mercury), Japan, New Zealand, Portugal, Germany, Yugoslavia (Pic Sleeves); Australia, Guatemala, Holland (Ring O), Ireland, Mexico, USA.
Danny / Rock Island Line (1977 : UK only. TS / PS on early copies)
Danny / Wino Song (1977 : Australia)
It's All Over Now Baby Blue / Danny (1977 : France)
Goodnight And Goodmorning (edited version) / Wino Song (1977 : UK)
  Holland (PS), New Zealand.
Rock Island Line / Soul Seeker (1978 : Australia)
Warm Ride (short version) / 10/12 Observation (1978 : UK)
  France, Holland, Ireland, New Zealand, Scandinavia, Germany (all PS). Australia, Zimbabwe.
Warm Ride (short version) / 10 / 12 Observation (1978 : UK only extended 12")
Only You Can Lift Me / Such A Shame (1978)
  Australia, New Zealand.
Can't Complain / High School Angel (1978)
  France, Germany, Holland (all PS).
Night Games / Out On The Water (1981 : UK PS)
  Bolivia, France, Holland, Japan, Portugal, Spain, Germany (all PS). Australia, New Zealand.
Liar / Bad Days Are Gone (1981 : UK PS)
  Holland (PS).
Bad Days Are Gone / Liar (1981 : Japan PS)
Liar / S.O.S. (1981 : France)
That's The Way That It Is / Don't Tell Me To Go (1981 : UK PS)
  Australia, New Zealand.
I'm A Lover / Don't Tell Me To Go (1981 : Finland PS)
Set Me Free / Be My Baby (1981 : Japan PS)
Anthony Boy / Don't Tell Me To Go (1981)
  Germany, Holland, Spain (1982) (all PS).

Solo Albums

Graham Bonnet (1977)
No Bad Habits (1978)
  Australia, New Zealand (with Warm Ride), Holland (without Warm Ride), Japan (1982, includes Bad Days Are Gone instead of Warm Ride).
Line Up (1981)
Here Comes The Night (1991)
Underground (1997 : Korea)
The Day I Went Mad (1999 : Japan)
Back Row In The Stalls (2016 : CD remaster)
  1974 unreleased album + Dont Drink The Water, Dreams (Out In The Forest), We're Free (from the soundtrack of Three For All), Whisper In The Night, Rare Specimen (1972 solo single), Trying To Say Goodbye, Castles In The Air (1973 solo single), Dog Song, Express Yourself (1973 single by Adrienne Posta, which features Graham).

Graham Bonnet / No Bad Habits (2016 : 2CD remaster)
  CD1 bonus tracks : Heroes On My Picture Wall (B-side), Goodnight And Goodmorning (single edit), I Who Am I (1977 demo for Lords Of The Universe), Do What You Gotta Do (demo), You've Lost That Lovin Feeling (demo), It Ain't Easy (demo), The Loving Touch (1976 demo with Victy Silva).
  CD2 bonus tracks : 10/12 Observation, Such A Shame (B-sides), Only You Can Lift Me (single edit), Warm Ride (long version), Warm Ride (long disco version).
Line Up (2016 : CD remaster)
  Album bonus tracks : Bad Days Are Gone, Don't Tell Me To Go (B-sides), Night Games, Out On The Water (single edits).

Compilation Albums

The Best Of Graham Bonnet (1979)
  New Zealand : songs from Graham's 1977 and 1978 solo albums.
Graham Bonnet (1980)
  Australia : Rock Legends series, tracks from Graham's 1977 and 1978 solo albums. Also issued in Holland.
Can't Complain (1980)
  Germany : songs from Grahams 1977 and 1978 solo albums.
Graham Bonnet The Rock Singers Anthology (1990 : CD)
  Australia : songs by the Marbles, Rainbow, and from Graham's 1977, 1978 and 1981 albums. Also released in Germany with a different sleeve.
A Collection (2015 : CD)
  Songs from Graham's 1977, 1978, 1997 and 1999 solo albums.
Anthology (2017 : 2CD)
  Includes some Elektric Zoo demos, rarities and a DVD of promos.

Interesting Solo Compilation Appearances

The Sounds Of DJM (1973 : promo LP features Dog Song by Adrienne Posta)
DJM Book Of Records (1974 : promo LP features: Back Row In The Stalls)
Three For All (1975 soundtrack LP)
  Features Don't Drink The Water, Dreams (Out In The Forest), Untitled (Here Comes The Rain), We're Free. All as Billy Beethoven.
Flexi-disc (1981 EP : features Night Games – long version)
  4 track orange flexi-disc given with Flexipop magazine.

Session Appearances – Singles

Trevor Gordon - Spend All The Money / Daytime (1970 : UK)
  Graham plays acoustic guitar and bass guitar on the tracks.
Trevor Gordon - Spend All The Money / Wounded Soldiers (1970 : Germany PS)
Adrienne Posta - Dog Song / Express Yourself (1973 : UK, 1974 : USA Crested Butte Records)
  Graham wrote Dog Song and provides acoustic guitar, bass, backing vocals. Acoustic guitar, bass on Express Yourself.

Session Appearances - Albums

Trevor Gordon - Alphabet (1970)
  Graham plays acoustic guitar, bass and sings backing vocals on some tracks.
Paul Gallico's The Snow Goose (1976)
  Graham hums on Walking By The Sea.
Arrested: Royal Philharmonic Orchestra & Friends Presents The Music Of The Police (1983)
  Graham vocals Truth Hits Everybody.

Pretty Maids - Future World (1987)
Graham backing vocals on We Came To Rock, Loud 'N' Proud.

Wind In The Willows (1992)
Graham vocals on Good Morning To You, The Badger, I'm Looking Forward To Tomorrow, Piper At The Gates Of Dawn, Why Can't We Go Home, Wayfarers All.

Iain Ashley Hersey - The Holy Grail (2005)
Graham vocals on Going Down, Walking The Talk, The Holy Grail.

Moonstone Project - Time To Take A Stand (2006)
Graham vocals on Not Dead Yet.

The Countdown Spectacular Live 2 (2007)
Graham vocals on It's All Over Now Baby Blue.

J21 - Yellow Mind : Blue Mind (2009)
Graham vocals on The Truth Behind The Veil, The Edge Of Now.

Lyraka - Lyraka Vol. 1 (2010)
Graham vocals on Coronation, Palace Guard, Erranda, Beyond The Palace.

Pushking - The World As We Love It (2011)
Graham vocals on God Made Us Free and is one of five singers on Kukaracha.

Sunset - Viaggio Libero (2012)
Graham vocals on Lunghezza d'onda.

Osmos Comos - Show (2012)
Graham vocals on Seven Years.

Tomorrow's Outlook - 34613 (2012)
Graham vocals on Red Rum and Glass Mountain.

Natasha Lea Jones - Soar (2013)
Graham vocals on Come To Call.

Don Airey - Keyed Up (2014)
Graham vocals on Mini Suite.

Stardust Reverie - Ancient Rites Of The Moon (2014)
Graham vocals on Conqueror Of Both.

A Classic Rock Salute To The Doors – Light My Fire (2014)
Graham vocals on The Soft Parade.

Axel Rudi Pell & Friends - Magic Moments – 25th Anniversary Special Show (2015)
Graham vocals on Since You Been Gone, Long Live Rock 'n Roll, Smoke On The Water.

Stardust Reverie - Proclamation Of Shadows (2015)
Graham vocals on Imagining Confucius.

Rough Rockers – A Safe Pair Of Hands EP (2015)
Graham vocals on Unleash The Beast.

Wishing Well - Chasing Rainbows (2016)
Graham vocals on Hippie Heart Gypsy Soul.

THE GRAHAM BONNET SET

A Love Like Yours / Devil In Her Heart (1967 : unissued acetate UK Banner Productions)

MARBLES Singles

Only One Woman / By The Light Of The Burning Candle (1968 : UK)
Austria, France, Holland, Italy, Japan, Scandinavia, Singapore, South Africa, Spain, Germany (all PS), Argentina, Australia, Lebanon, Turkey, New Zealand, USA.

The Walls Fell Down / Love You (1969 : UK)
Austria, France, Holland, Italy, Japan, Malaysia, Portugal, Scandinavia, South Africa, Spain, Germany (all PS), Australia, Lebanon, New Zealand and USA.

I Can't See Nobody / Little Boy (1969)
Austria, Chile, France, Germany, Holland, Italy, Japan, Norway, South Africa, Spain (all PS), Australia, New Zealand, USA.

Breaking Up Is Hard To Do / I Can't See Nobody (1970 : UK)
Denmark, Malaysia, Sweden (all PS).

Breaking Up Is Hard To Do / Daytime (1970)
Germany, Italy, Spain (all PS), Australia, New Zealand.

Breaking Up Is Hard To Do / A House Is Not A Home (1970 : Portugal PS)

Breaking Up Is Hard To Do / Little Laughing Girl (1970 : USA)

Bee Gee Hits (1970 - 4 track EP : New Zealand PS)
includes I Can't See Nobody, Only One Woman, To Love Somebody, The Walls Fell Down.

MARBLES Albums

The Marbles (1970)
Canada, Germany, Norway, South Africa, Spain, USA. Re-released in Germany 1981 as a club pressing.

The Marbles featuring Graham Bonnet (1980 : Australia Rock Legends series)

Marble – ized (1994 : CD Australia)

The Marbles (2003 : CD)
LP plus their 3 UK singles A and B sides in mono.

RAINBOW Singles

Since You Been Gone / Bad Girl (1979 : UK and worldwide PS)

Since You Been Gone / No Time To Lose (1979 : Germany / Italy PS)

Since You Been Gone / All Night Long (1979 : Scandinavia 12")

All Night Long / Weiss Heim (1980 UK and worldwide PS)

All Night Long / No Time To Lose (1980 : Holland PS)

All Night Long / Danger Zone (1980 : USA)

Bad Girl / Spotlight Kid (live in Tokyo 1984) - Man On The Silver Mountain (live in Atlanta 1978) (1986 : UK 12" PS issued to promote Finyl Vinyl compilation see below)

Bad Girl / Bad Girl (1986 : USA 12" promo)

RAINBOW Albums

Down To Earth (1979 : UK, 10,000 copies in clear vinyl)

Down To Earth Deluxe Edition (2011 : 2CD remaster)
includes Bad Girl, Weiss Hiem (B-sides), Spark Don't Mean A Fire, Ain't A Lot Of Love In The Heart Of Me (unissued).

Denver 1979 Down To Earth Tour (2015 : 2LP USA)
Holograph sleeve, red, green and blue vinyl 1000 copies per colour.

Down To Earth Tour 1979 (2015 : 3CD)
Live shows Denver 1979, Long Island 1979, Chicago 1979 taken from official radio broadcasts.

Monsters Of Rock Live At Donington 1980 (2016 : CD + DVD)
Japanese edition CD has extra 10 minutes of music.

RAINBOW Compilation Albums

Finyl Vinyl (1986)
Includes Since You Been Gone live from Donington 1980.

Anthology 1975 – 1986 (2009 : 2CD)
Includes Will You Love Me Tomorrow live from Donington 1980.

A Light In The Black 75-84 (2015 : 5 CD, 1 DVD box set)
Includes live versions of Over The Rainbow, Eyes Of The World, Love's No Friend, Ode To Joy from Calderone, New York 1979 on disc 3. DVD from Donington 1980.

RAINBOW Compilation Appearances

Monsters Of Rock (1980)
Includes Stargazer and All Night Long from Donington 1980.

MSG Singles

Dancer / Girl From Uptown (1982 : UK PS. Also 7" picture disc, a clear vinyl 7" PS, 12" single PS) *Japan (PS)*

MSG Albums

Assault Attack (1982 : UK also Ltd Ed pic disc)
Tales Of Rock N Roll - Twenty-Five Years Celebration (2006)
Graham vocals on Rock 'N' Roll, which also appears on the Revolution Mind 3 track EP.
Assault Attack (2009 : CD remaster)
Includes Girl From Uptown B-side.

ALCATRAZZ Singles

Island In The Sun / Hiroshima Mon Amour (1983)
USA, Japan (PS).
Island In The Sun / Hiroshima Mon Amour - Interview (1984)
USA Promotional 12" single + interview with band members.
Island In The Sun / General Hospital (1984 : UK 7" PS)
Spain (PS), Australia, New Zealand.
Island In The Sun / General Hospital - Suffer Me (1984 : UK 12" PS)
God Blessed Video / Wire And Wood (1985 : UK)
Sons And Lovers / God Blessed Video (1985 : Japan promo PS)
Will You Be Home Tonight edit / edit with intro (1985 : USA promo single)
Includes PSA (Against Drunk Driving) 30 seconds intro where Graham speaks.
It's My Life / It's My Life (1986 : USA 12" promo)
Undercover / Undercover (1986 : USA 12" promo)
Dangerous Games / Double Man (1986 : USA 12" promo)

ALCATRAZZ Albums

No Parole From Rock 'N' Roll (1983 : USA)
Japan (+ free poster). Released elsewhere in 1984.
Live Sentence (1984 : USA)
Japan (+ free poster).
Disturbing The Peace (1985)
Dangerous Games (1986 : USA also Ltd Ed pic disc)
Live 83 (2010 : USA LP / CD)
No Parole From Rock 'N Roll Tour (2010 : CD Japan)
Audio from the DVD of the band's January 28th 1984 show in Tokyo.
Disturbing The Peace Tour (2010 : Japan CD)
Audio from the DVD of the bands October 10th 1984 show in Tokyo.
No Parole From Rock N Roll (2016 : CD remaster)
Includes bonus instrumental demos of all the tracks.
Live Sentence (2016 : CD remaster + DVD)
Includes full concert of the Japan, January 28th 1984 show.
The Ultimate Fortress Rock Set (2016 : 5 CDs + 1 DVD Box set)
Includes all five albums (Live Sentence is the full show) plus bonus tracks. First time on CD for the 1983 Rocshire Records interview with Graham, Graham's spoken intro to Will You Be Home Tonight from 1985, and Escape From Alcatrazz 6-track EP from the Graham Bonnet Band. DVD extras include 3 tracks from the Rock Palace (early 1984), promo videos for Island In The Sun, Hiroshima Mon Amour, God Blessed Video, Feb 1984 interview with Graham from Japan.
Disturbing The Peace (2016 : CD remaster + DVD)
CD includes Will You Be Home Tonight (Anti-Drunk Driving PSA single edit), instrumental demos for God Blessed Video, Wire And Wood, Stripper, Painted Lover, Sons And Lovers, Skyfire and Breaking The Heart Of City, plus Steve Vai rehearsal. The DVD is from Tokyo in Oct 1984.
Dangerous Games (2016 : CD remaster)

Includes a live recording at Bayshore, Long Island, New York on November 29th 1986.

ALCATRAZZ Compilation Albums

The Best Of Alcatrazz (1998 : CD USA, reissued many times worldwide)

IMPELLITTERI Singles

Since You've Been Gone / Stand In Line (1988 : Japan 3" CD)

IMPELLITTERI Albums

Stand In Line (1988)
System X (2002 : Japan)

IMPELLITTERI Compilation Albums

The Very Best Of Impellitteri (2002 : Japan)
Graham vocals on non-album track Anti Social Disease.

FORCEFIELD

To Oz And Back (1989)
Let The Wild Run Free (1990)

BLACKTHORNE

Afterlife (1993)
Don't Kill The Thrill (Deluxe Edition) (2016 : 2CD)
Includes the intended 10 tracks for Blackthorne's second album in 1994, Wild Inside from the Afterlife sessions, interviews and live tracks from 1992, 1993 and 1994.
Afterlife Expanded (2016 : CD remaster)
Includes live acoustic tracks and a rehearsal from December 16th 1992 (sic).

The first MURDERERS ROW album contained all the demos for the the second Blackthorne album, but all trace of Graham's writing contributions was removed. The ten songs were 'Paralyzed' (retitled 'Raven's Eye'), 'Insanity' (retitled 'Suicide Saloon'), 'Man In The Black Hat' (same title and lyrics), 'Judgement Day' (retitled 'India'), 'Sanctuary' (re-titled 'Hangman's Moon' with different lyrics), 'Save Me' (retitled 'Overdrive'), 'Twist The Blade' (retitled 'Bad Side Of Love' with new lyrics), 'Dreaming In The Hideaway' (retitled 'Red Rain Falling'), 'Skeletons In The Closet' (same title) and 'Don't Kill The Thrill' (retitled 'Blood On Fire').

ANTHEM

Gypsy Ways (Win, Lose Or Draw) (2000 : Japan 3 track CD)
Featuring non-album track Love In Vain.
Heavy Metal Anthem (2000 : Japan)

ANTHEM Compilation Albums

Anthems 2000 - 2011 30th Anniversary (Best Of) (2015 : Japan 2CD + DVD)
Features Love In Vain, Hungry Soul on the DVD with Graham from June 2000 at On Air East in Tokyo.

TAZ TAYLOR BAND

Welcome To America (2006)

GRAHAM BONNET BAND

My Kingdom Come / The Mirror Lies (2015 : Download single)
Escape From Alcatrazz - Live In Japan (2015 : Download Mini-album)
Later available in the Alcatrazz 6-disc set, The Ultimate Fortress Rock Set.
The Book (2016 : 2CD)
New studio album plus 16 re-recordings.

APPENDIX ONE • Concert Diary 1959-2016

This gig diary covers the majority of live concerts played by Graham since he joined Rainbow in 1979 together with some documented shows from his early days and known venues. Information is limited but gives an idea of the types of show and venue Graham and his bandmates played in. I would welcome information on any shows not included.

GRAHAM BONNETT — 1950s - 62

Graham sang at various events for the Cubs during the mid to late Fifties, including a parents evening on March 20th 1959. He played guitar in the school orchestra which gave various performances in churches and other venues. Graham also sang and played guitar at The Embassy and at the Derbyshire Miners Welfare Club in Skegness in his early teens at various talent competitions.

THE SKYLINERS / THE PETER TOMLINSON BAND — 1963 / 64

Early 1963 - Spring 1964. Played numerous venues including The Parade Hotel and the North Shore Hotel in Skegness, The Bell in Burgh le March and village halls in Friskney, Wainfleet and Benington. Graham was paid £2.00 per show.

THE JIMMY ALDRED BAND — 1964

Spring. Butlins, Ingoldmells, Nr. Skegness.

THE JAN RAMSDEN BAND — 1964

Spring. Graham only played a couple of gigs with the band at the most, including Butlins, Ingoldmells, Nr. Skegness.

THE MISSING LINKS — 1964 / 65

Spring 1964 - May 1965. Played many local Skegness venues including The Chatta Box coffee bar, Brief Encounter and Sea View Hotel (Sunday lunch time), as well as at social clubs on caravan sites, and in village halls and youth clubs.

THE BLUESET / THE BLUESECT / THE BLUESECTE — 1965 / 66

May 1965 - Late Autumn 1966. The band played many venues in Skegness, often regularly, including Hildred's Hotel, Ex-Servicemen's Club, Sea View Hotel, Beachcomber Bar, The Chatta Box, The Ship, Derbyshire Miner's Welfare Club, The British Legion Club and the Imperial Café. They also played at The Bamboo coffee bar in Wainfleet, Stoke Roachford Hall in South Kesteven, Dungeon Club in Nottingham, 10-12 Club in Boston, Art College in Lincoln and the Girl's College in Peterborough.

THE GRAHAM BONNET SET — 1966 / 67

November and December 1966. The band played various youth clubs, village halls, hotels and social clubs in and around the Skegness area to begin with.

1967. For a time Graham kept note of their shows in his diary which give us a better idea of the band's workload and sometimes their fees.

Jan	6th	Friday	Parade Hotel, Skegness
	7th	Saturday	Blue Anchor, Ingoldmells
	8th	Sunday	Blue Anchor, Ingoldmells
	15th	Sunday	Blue Anchor, Ingoldmells
Feb	4th	Saturday	Parade Hotel, (Party), Skegness £12
	11th	Saturday	Grosseteste T.C. Lincoln £12
	16th	Thursday	Motor Club Dance, Sun Castle, Skegness £12
	18th	Saturday	Parade Hotel, Skegness £12
	25th	Saturday	Bardney Village Hall £12
Mar	4th	Saturday	Parade Hotel, Skegness £15
	16th	Thursday	Parade Liberals, Skegness £15
	17th	Friday	63 Club, Lincoln £10
	18th	Saturday	Mereham Le Fen £10
	20th	Monday	Grammar School, Skegness £10
	22nd	Wednesday	Practice
	23rd	Thursday	Charity Dance, Youth Club, Horncastle
	25th	Saturday	Happy Days, Car Park, Ingoldmells £10
April	1st	Saturday	Embassy Club, Skegness £12
	8th	Saturday	Imperial Hotel, Skegness £12
	10th	Monday	Golden Butterfly, Winthorpe
	14th	Friday	Parade Hotel, Skegness £15
	15th	Saturday	Embassy Club, Skegness £15
	21st	Friday	Parade Hotel, Skegness £15
	22nd	Saturday	Embassy Club, Skegness £15
May	5th	Friday	Grosseetete T.C. Lincoln (with Herman's Hermits)
	6th	Saturday	Parade Hotel, Skegness £15
	18th	Thursday	Boston Charity Ball
	19th	Friday	Butlins Staff Dance, Ingoldmells
	27th	Saturday	Parade Hotel, Skegness
June	2nd	Friday	Parade Hotel, Skegness
	3rd	Saturday	Festival Pavilion, Skegness
	10th	Saturday	Festival Pavilion, Skegness £15
	16th	Friday	Parade Hotel, Skegness
	17th	Saturday	Festival Pavilion, Skegness
	23rd	Friday	Parade Hotel, Skegness (cancelled - band in Sweden)

When the band returned from Sweden they started to broaden their scope and as well as the usual Skegness venues as before, along with the Derbyshire Miner's Welfare Club and The Arcadia, travelled to venues including Copper Kettle Club in Boston, The Scales in Doncaster, Penny Farthing in Leicester, Dial House in Sheffield, Firth Park in Rotherham, and the Golden Diamond Club in Sutton in Ashfield. After they turned professional they progressed to playing in Nightclubs such as The Butterfly Club in Skegness, Talk Of The Midlands in Nottingham, Clouds in Derby, Motown in Grimsby and the Golden Slipper in West Bridgeford, Nottinghamshire. They also played at various venues in Mansfield, Newark, Peterborough and some RAF bases in Lincolnshire.

Late Autumn - Winter. When Trevor Gordon joined the band they played mainly in the North-east including the Blue Star Club in Newcastle and the Sunnyside WMC in Sunderland.

1968 Late January - Early February. During their final days together they did two nights at the Revolution Club, London.

MARBLES — 1969

The Marbles didn't play many proper dates as reasons explained in the main text, but those known about are listed below.

March 22nd	West Berlin, West Germany	(Annual convention of Polydor Records)
April 13th	London, Empire Pool, Wembley	(The Daily Express Record Star Show)
May ?	Varity Club, Batley, West Yorkshire, England	
May 22nd	Stockton Fiesta, Stockton-on-Tees, England	
Late May / Early June		Scottish Tour
June	West German Tour	
August	Revolution Club, London	

SOUTHERN COMFORT — 1971

January - February. Venues and dates unknown. A handful of gigs at the very most around the London area only. Graham played bass guitar and did occasional backing vocals.

RONNIE HARWOOD BAND — 1976

Mid January - Mid March. Graham played a few pubs (including the Old Spotted Dog, Neasden, London) and clubs with the band, firstly as a guest then as a full time member on bass and doing occasional backing vocals.

VICTY SILVA and GRAHAM BONNET — 1976

Early Sept. Benvenute Hotel, Chapel St. Leonards, Lincolnshire

Victy and Graham made a guest appearance with Kenny Bray's band. Victy was on piano and Graham on bass guitar.

Sept. 21 - 23rd Maunkberry's Nightclub, London

Graham played bass guitar and did lead vocals on one song, three duets and some backing vocals.

GRAHAM BONNET — 1977

Apart from a one off show early in the year at Brown's Club, London, there were no more live shows until Graham joined Rainbow and his touring schedule took off.

RAINBOW   Down To Earth Tour — 1979

Supporting Blue Oyster Cult

Sept. 18th	Coliseum, New Haven, Connecticut	American Tour
19th	Civic Center, Glens Fall, New York	
20th	War Memorial Auditorium, Rochester, New York	
21st	Cobo Hall, Detroit, Michigan	
22nd	Civic Center, Lansing, Michigan	
23rd	Lakeview Arena, Marquette, Michigan	
26th	Broome County Veterans' Memorial Arena, Binghampton, New York	
27th	Erie County Field House, Erie, Pennsylvania	
28th	Memorial Auditorium, Utica, New York	
29th	Spectrum, Philadelphia, Pennsylvania	
30th	Civic Center, Baltimore, Maryland	
Oct. 2nd	Veterans Memorial Hall, Columbus, Ohio	
3rd	Wendler Arena, Saginaw, Michigan	
4th	War Memorial, Buffalo, New York	
5th	Civic Arena, Pittsburgh, Pennsylvania	
6th	Hara Arena, Dayton Ohio	
7th	Richfield Coliseum, Cleveland Ohio	
10th	Dane County Memorial Coliseum, Madison, Wisconsin	
11th	Brown County Veterans' Memorial Arena, Green Bay, Wisconsin	
12th	International Amphitheatre, Chicago, Illinois	
13th	Civic Auditorium, Omaha, Nebraska	
14th	Hammons Center, Springfield, Missouri (cancelled)	
16th	Wings Stadium, Kalamazoo, Michigan	
18th	Market Square Arena, Indianapolis, Indiana (cancelled)	
20th	Freedom Hall Civic Center, Johnson City, Tennessee	

Some sources say the gig was 19th, others that Rainbow didn't play

21st	Civic Center, Huntington, West Virginia	
24th	The Armory, Springfield, Illinois	
25th	Pauley Pavilion UCLA, Los Angeles, California	
26th	Met Center, Minneapolis, Minnesota (cancelled)	

Rainbow pulled a 12 date mostly German tour to extend the US visit as headliners.

Nov. 6th	Civic Auditorium, Santa Cruz, California	
7th	Civic Auditorium, Oakland, California	
9th	Swing Auditorium, San Bernardino, California	
10th	Fox Theater, San Diego, California	
11th	Long Beach Arena, Los Angeles, California	
13th	Warners Theater, Fresno, California	
16th	Rainbow Music Hall, Denver, Colarado	
?	Salt Palace, Salt Lake City, Utah	
?	Sports Arena, Toledo, Ohio	
20th	Music Hall, Royal Oak, Michigan	
21st	Music Hall, Royal Oak, Michigan	
?	Cobo Hall, Detroit, Michigan	
23rd	Beacon Theater, New York City, New York	
27th	War Memorial Auditorium, Worcester, Massachusetts	
28th	War Memorial Auditorium, Ucita, New York	
30th	Calderone Concert Hall, Hempstead, Long Island, New York	
Dec. 1st	Capitol Theater, Passaic, New Jersey	
2nd	Fairgrounds, Allentown, Pennsylvania	
4th	Stanley Theater, Pittsburgh, Pennsylvania	
5th	Cumberland County Civic Center, Portland, Maine	
6th	Manning Bowl, Lynn, Massachusetts	
7th	Ocean State Performing Arts Center, Providence, Rhode Island	
8th	Landmark Theater, Syracuse, New York	
9th	Palace Theater, Albany, New York	

1980

Jan. 17th	Scandinavium, Gothenburg, Sweden	Scandinavian and European Tour
18th	Johanneshov Isstadion, Stockholm, Sweden	
20th	Falkoner Teatret, Copenhagen, Denmark	
22nd	Eilenriedehalle, Hannover, Germany	
23rd	Festhalle, Frankfurt, Germany	
25th	Saarlandhalle, Saarbruken, Germany	
26th	Le Rhenus Hall, Strasbourg, France	
27th	Palais Des Grottes, Cambrai, France	
29th	Gruga-Halle, Essen, Germany	
30th	Stadthalle, Bremen, Germany	
Feb. 1st	Forest National, Brussels, Belgium	
2nd	Sportpeleis Ahoy, Rotterdam, Holland	
3rd	Rodahal, Kerkrade, Holland	
5th	Sporthalle, Cologne, Germany	
6th	Neunkirchen, Hemmerleinhalle, Nurnburg, Germany (cancelled)	
7th	Messehalle, Stuttgart Sindelfingen, Germany	
9th	Parc des Expositions Alexpo Hall, Grenoble, France	
10th	Eulachhalle, Winterthur, Switzerland	
12th	Porte De Pantin Pavillon, Paris, France	
14th	Munsterlandhalle, Munster, Germany	
15th	Eppelheim Rhein-Neckarhalle, Heidelberg, Germany	
16th	Olympianhalle, Munich, Germany	
19th	City Hall, Newcastle, England	
20th	City Hall, Newcastle, England	
22nd	Ingliston Exhibition Hall, Edinburgh, Scotland	
23rd	New Bingley Hall, Stafford, England	
24th	Hipperhome, Bristol, England (cancelled)	
24th	New Bingley Hall, Stafford, England	
26th	Apollo Theatre, Manchester, England	
27th	Deeside Leisure Centre, Chester, England	
29th	Wembley Arena, London, England	
March 1st	Wembley Arena, London, England	
3rd	Granby Halls, Leicester, England	
4th	Brighton Centre, Brighton, England	
5th	Sophia Gardens, Cardiff, Wales	
6th	Apollo Theatre, Manchester, England	
8th	Rainbow Theatre, London, England	
May 8th	Budokan Hall, Tokyo	Japanese Tour
9th	Budokan Hall, Tokyo	
12th	Budokan Hall, Tokyo	
13th	Festival Hall, Osaka	
14th	Festival Hall, Osaka	
15th	Festival Hall, Osaka	
Aug. 8th	Vejlby-Risskov Hallen, Aarhus, Denmark	Scandinavian Tour
9th	Folkets Park, Malmo, Sweden	
10th	Aalborg Hallen, Aalborg, Denmark	
16th	Monsters Of Rock Festival. Castle Donington, Donington Park, England	

Graham and Cozy's final show with the group

MSG — 1982

Aug. 27th	Polytechnic, Phoenix Hall, Sheffield, England

ALCATRAZZ No Parole From Rock 'N' Roll Tour — 1983

Oct. ?	Venue unknown, Bakersfield, California	American Tour
?	Venue unknown, Fresno, California	
31st	Country Club, Reseda, Los Angeles, California	
Nov. 18th	Old Waldorf, San Francisco, California (cancelled)	
19th	Wolfgang's, San Francisco, California (cancelled)	
Dec. 8th	Country Club, Reseda, Los Angeles, California (rescheduled from Nov. 24th)	
18th	Wolfgang's, San Francisco, California	
20th	Warners Star Theater, Fresno, California	
21st	Golden Bear Club, Huntington Beach, California	
26th	South Exhibit Hall, Milwaukee, Wisconsin	

Following five shows were Eddie Money / Saga / Alcatrazz triple bill.

27th	Coliseum, Columbus, Ohio

28th	Coliseum, Columbus, Ohio		20th	Civic Center, Savannah, Georgia
29th	Cobo Hall, Detroit, Michigan		22nd	Agora Ballroom, Hartford, Connecticut
30th	Kellog Arena, Battle Creek, Michigan		23rd	Civic Center, Springfield, Massachusetts
31st	Richfield Coliseum, Cleveland, Ohio		24th	Twilight Zone, Newhaven, Connecticut

ALCATRAZZ No Parole From Rock 'N' Roll Tour — 1984

Jan. 7th	Country Club, Reseda, Los Angeles, California	American Tour continued
11th	Venue unknown, San Francisco, California	
?	Rock Palace, Hollywood, Los Angeles, California (Live TV, three songs.)	
24th	Festival Hall, Osaka	Japanese Tour
26th	City Hall, Nagoya	
28th	Nakano Sun Plaza Hall, Tokyo	
29th	Nakano Sun Plaza Hall, Tokyo 3:00 pm and 6:30 pm shows	
Feb. 3rd	Campus Center Ballroom, Honolulu, Hawaii	American Tour continued
19th	Grand Central Station, Albuquerque, New Mexico	
24th	The Palladium, Hollywood, California	
26th	Rockefellers, Tuscan, Arizona	
27th	Graham Central Station, Phoenix, Arizona	
29th	Graham Central Station, Albuquerque, New Mexico	
Mar. 1st	The Rainbow, Denver, Colorado	
3rd	Roberto Clemente Coliseum, San Juan, Puerto Rico (supporting Loverboy)	
6th	Cardi's, Beaumont, Texas	
7th	Cardi's, Houston, Texas	
8th	Daddy's, San Antonio, Texas	
9th	Abbey Road, Lubbock, Texas	
10th	6th Street Live, Austin, Texas	
11th	Nick's Uptown, Dallas, Texas	
23rd, 24th	Paramount Theater, Seattle, Washington (supporting Heart)	
26th	Lawler Events Center, Reno, Nevada	
29th	Country Club, Reseda, California	
Early - mid Apr.	Six shows with Night Ranger.	
Dates, venues unknown, but included Fresno, Bakersfield, Sacramento, Cupertino		
Apr. 21st	Perkins Palace, Pasadena, California	
27th	Venue unknown, San Jose, California	
28th	Pomona Valley Auditorium, Pomona, California	
May 7th	Venue unknown, Pittsburg, Pennsylvania	
11th	Radio City, Anaheim, California	
12th	Kabuki Theatre, San Francisco, California	
13th	Sherwood Hall, Salinas, California	
May - June	Thirty one shows with Ted Nugent.	
18th	Brady Auditorium, Tulsa, Oklahoma	
19th	Music Hall, Omaha, Nebraska	
20th	Memorial Hall, Joplin, Missouri	
22nd	Sports Arena, Toledo, Ohio	
23rd	Richfield Coliseum, Richfield or The Agora Ballroom, Cleveland Ohio	
24th	Hara Arena, Dayton, Ohio	
26th	Cotton Carnival Music Festival, Memphis, Tennessee	
27th	Memorial Hall, Kansas, Missouri	
30th	Veteran's Memorial, Columbus, Ohio	
June 1st	Amphitheatre, Darien Lake, New York	
2nd	Mid Hudson Civic Center, Ploughkeepsie, New York	
3rd	Erie Civic Center, Erie, Pennsylvania	
4th	C.N.E. Toronto, Ontario, Canada	
5th	Dundas Arena, Dundas, Ontario, Canada	
7th	The Palace, Albany, New York	
8th	Six Flags Great Adventure Park, Jackson, New Jersey	
9th	One For The Sun, Nashville, Tennessee	
10th	The Dome, Virginia Beach, Virginia	
12th	Prairie Capitol Convention Center, Springfield, Illinois	
13th	Poplar Creek, Chicago, Illinois	
14th	Stanley Theatre, Pittsburg, Pennsylvania	
15th	Tower Theatre, Upper Darby, Philadelphia, Pennsylvania	
16th	Merriweather Post Pavilion, Columbia, Missouri	
19th	Municipal Auditorium, Columbus, Georgia	
26th	Cumberland County Civic Center, Portland, Maine	
27th	Club Casino, Hampton Beach, New Hampshire	
30th	Pier '84, New York, New York	
July 5th	Venue unknown, Pittsburg, Pennsylvania	
7th	Summer Festival, Milwaukee, Wisconsin (Yngwie's last gig.)	
13th	De Anza Theater, Riverside, California (Steve Vai's debut gig.)	
15th	Perkins Palace, Pasadena, California	
Sept. 29th	Country Club, Los Angeles, CA. Warm up show for Japanese tour.	
Oct. 3rd	Kinrou Kaikan, Nagoya	Japanese Tour
4th	Amagasaki Archaic Hall, Osaka	
8th	Shibuya Kokaido, Tokyo	
10th	Kosei Nenkin Hall, Tokyo	
11th	Nakano Sun Plaza Hall, Tokyo	

ALCATRAZZ Disturbing The Peace Tour — 1985

May 31st	Roberto Clemente Coliseum, San Juan, Puerto Rico (supporting Kerry Livgren)	
July 21st	Country Club, Reseda, California	American Tour
Aug. 6th	Golden Bear, Huntington Beach, California	
7th	The Mason Jar, Phoenix, Arizona	
9h	The Rainbow Theater, Denver, Colorado	
11th	Graham Central Station, Albuquerque, New Mexico	
14th	The Ritz, Dallas, Texas	
15th	Cardi's, Houston, Texas	
16th	Villa Royal, McAllen, Texas (supporting Helix)	
17th	Buckner Sunset Gardens, San Antonio, Texas (supporting Helix)	
18th	Opry House, Austin, Texas (supporting Helix)	

ALCATRAZZ Dangerous Games Tour — 1986

First seven shows supporting Starship.

Oct. 16th	U.T. Pavilion, Martin, Tennessee	American Tour
18th	U.M. Auditorium, Ann Arbor, Michigan	
21st	Lake View Arena, Marquette, Michigan	
22nd	La Crosse Center, Lacros, Wisconsin	
24th	Ahearn Fieldhouse, Kansas, Texas	
25th	G.M. Coliseum, Kansas, Texas	
26th	Ollign Coliseum Wichita Falls, Texas	

Rest of shows with Rough Cutt (except final date).

Nov. 4th	Jimmy's, New Orleans, Oklahoma
5th	Nightown, Destin, Florida
7th	Summers, Ft. Lauderdale, Florida
8th	Brassey's, Coco Beach, Florida
10th	Timothy John's, Atlanta, Georgia
11th	Kidnapper's, Charlotte, North Carolina
13th	Switch, Raleigh, North Carolina
14th	Boathouse, Norfolk, Virginia
15th	Network, Baltimore, Maryland
16th	Bayou, Washington, D.C.
17th	Mancini's Pittsburgh, Pennsylvania
18th	Penny Arcade, Rochester, New York
20th	Living Room, Providence, Rhode Island
21st	Freeze St Pub, Portland, Maine
22nd	The Agoura, Hartford, Connecticut
23rd	Lost Horizon, Syracuse, New York
25th	The Channel, Boston, Massachusetts
28th	Lamour East, Queens, New York
29th	Bayshore, Long Island, New York
30th	The Empire Room, Philadelphia, Pennsylvania
Dec. 1st	The Ritz, New York City, New York
2nd	Shadows, Cleveland, Ohio
3rd	The Metro, Chicago, Illinois

4th	Annie's, Cincinnati, Ohio	
5th	Harpo's, Detroit, Michigan	
6th	Hoosir Ballroom, Indianapolis, Indiana	
8th	Miss Night, St. Louis, Missouri	
10th	Uptown Theater, Kansas City, Missouri	
13th	The Metro, Phoenix, Arizona	
16th	The Roxy, Hollywood, California	
18th	Country Club, Reseda, California (headliners)	
19th	Coach House, San Juan Capistrano, California (headliners)	
20th	Fenders, Long Beach, California (headliners)	
21st	De Anza Theater, Riverside, California (headliners)	
26th	The Omni, Oakland, California	
31st	Civic Auditorium, San Jose, California (supporting Stryper)	

ALACTRAZZ — 1987

January 1st Santa Monica Civic, Santa Monica, California (supporting Stryper)

THE PARTY BOYS — 1988

January 8th Kitchener Park, Mona Vale, Sydney, Australia
? Selinas, Sydney, Australia
Graham is thought to have only played three shows with the band.

IMPELLITTERI — 1988

July 17th Nissin Power Station, Toyko, Japan
24th Tokyo Dome, Tokyo, Japan
Sept. 24th Civic Auditorium, San Jose, California, USA

GRAHAM BONNET — 1988

Nov. 13th Adelaide, Australia (Australian Grand Prix, Rock Of Ages Concert)
Dec. ? Colonnades Tavern, Port Noarlunga, Australia
Graham made a guest appearance with the Master Apprentices during the encore performing 'River Deep Mountain High' and 'All Night Long'.

GRAHAM BONNET — 1989

Jan. ? Cartoons, Adelaide, Australia. Graham made a guest appearance

GRAHAM BONNET Night Of The Shooting Star Tour — 1989

Feb. 16th	The Westlands Hotel, Whyalla	Australia Tour
17th	The Old Lion Hotel (Ballroom), Adelaide	
18th	The Bridgeway Hotel, Adelaide	
19th	The Tivoli, Adelaide	
23rd	Chasers, Melbourne	
24th	The Palace, Melbourne	
25th	Richmond Social Club, Melbourne	

GRAHAM BONNET

March 26th The Bridgeway Hotel, Adelaide
31st The Old Lion Hotel (Ballroom), Adelaide (Youth Arts Festival)
April 15th The Tivoli, Adelaide
May 6th The Bridgeway Hotel, Adelaide
June 9th Marion Hotel (front bar), Adelaide Graham was a guest
? Lennie's Tavern, Adelaide Graham was a guest
? 'Practice New Years Eve Party', SA FM David Day's Dance Club, Adelaide
Graham was a guest.

WIND IN THE WILLOWS — 1991

Jun. 14, 15th Freiburg Zeltfestival, Germany

BLACKTHORNE — 1992

June 30th	The Bacchanal, San Diego, California	American Tour
July ?	The Pelican's, Los Angeles, California	
?	Jezebel's, Corona, California,	
31st	Sound FX, San Francisco, California	

The band possibly played more shows during July, but dates are unknown.

Aug. 22nd	The Marquee, Anaheim, California
?	The FM Station, Los Angeles, California
?	The Pelican's, Los Angeles, California
?	The Omni, Oakland, California
29th	The Cadillac Club, Fresno, California

1993

Mar. 7th GB Rabbits, Shinjuku, Tokyo, Japan
  Short acoustic set consisting of at least two songs.

1994

Sept. 9th Foundations Forum, Burbank Hilton Hotel, Los Angeles, USA

AN EVENING WITH SIR GEORGE MARTIN — 1997

Summer ? Palace Theater, Los Angeles, USA

GRAHAM BONNET — 2000

May 12th Joxer Daley's Irish Pub, Culver City, California, USA

ANTHEM — 2000

July 11th	Heat Beat, Osaka	Japanese Tour
13th	On Air East, Tokyo	
14th	On Air East, Tokyo	

GRAHAM BONNET — 2000

Sept. 23rd Coconut Teaser, Los Angeles, USA

GRAHAM BONNET — 2001

July 14th Blues & Soul Festival, Great Gransden, England

GRAHAM BONNET & DON AIREY — 2001

July 19th	The Rock Garden, Easington Colliery	UK Tour
20th	Venue unknown, Carlisle	
26th	Rock Café 2000, Stourbridge	
27th	Guild Hall, Portsmouth	
Nov. 9th	Rock Café 2000, Stourbridge	UK Tour
10th	Rock Café 2000, Stourbridge	
11th	Coal Exchange, Cardiff (cancelled)	
13th	Cooperage, Plymouth	
14th	Forum, Birmingham	
16th	Cellar Bar, South Shields	
17th	Zaks, Milton Keynes	
18th	The Waterfront, Norwich	
20th	Witchwood, Manchester	
21st	Beachcomber, Cleethorpes	
22nd	Rock Garden, Easington	
24th	Village Hall, Wilbarston (cancelled)	
25th	Guildhall, Southampton (cancelled)	
26th	The Underworld, Camden, London (cancelled)	
28th	The Limelight Club, Crewe	
29th	Pennington's, Bradford	
30th	Chinnery's, Southend	
Dec. 1st	Bikini Club, Barcelona, Spain	

GRAHAM BONNET — 2003

Feb. 21st Paladinos, Tarzana, California, USA
July 12th Blues & Soul Festival, Great Gransden, England
26th Paladinos, Tarzana, California, USA

GRAHAM BONNET — 2004

March 11th Club Vodka, Hollywood, California, USA

Blackthorne • *San Diego, June 30th 1992.*

ELEKTRIC ZOO — 2004
Date	Venue	Tour
Apr. 17th	Vox Pub, Vittuone, Milan, Italy	European & UK Tour
19th	Orpheum, Graz, Austria	
29th	Sala Macumba, Madrid, Spain	
30th	Sala Razmatazz 2, Barcelona, Spain	
May 1st	Artsaia, Pamplona, Spain	
4th	Rock Café 2000, Stourbridge, England	
6th	Limelight, Crewe, England	
7th	Rio's, Bradford, England	
8th	West One Four, London, England	
10th	Café Drummonds, Aberdeen, Scotland	

GRAHAM BONNET — 2004
- July 16th — Blues & Soul Festival, Great Gransden, England
- Sept. 24th — Paladinos, Tarzana, California, USA

GRAHAM BONNET — 2005
Date	Venue	Tour
Feb. 22nd	B2 Club, Moscow	Russian Tour
25th	City Park, Kaliningrad	
27th	Forum Palace Galaxy, Vilnius, Lithuania	

IAIN ASHLEY HERSEY — 2005
March 26th — Paladinos, Tarzana, California, USA — Graham made a guest appearance.

GRAHAM BONNET — 2005
Date	Venue	Tour
May 6th	Tullikamarin Pakkahuone, Tampere, Finland	Scandinavian Tour
7th	Sokos Hotel Lappee, Lapeenranta, Finland	
8th	Rockcafe, Tallinn, Estonia	
9th	Tavastia Club, Helsinki, Finland	
10th	Prisma, Vasteras, Sweden	
Oct. 21st	Queens Hall, Nuneaton	UK Tour
22nd	Rock Café 2000, Stourbridge	
23rd	Rock Café 2000, Stourbridge	
25th	The Underworld, Camden, London	
26th	Princess Pavilion, Falmouth	
27th	The Half Moon, Paignton (cancelled)	
28th	Patti Pavilion, Swansea	
29th	Baths Hall, Scunthorpe	
30th	LA Rock Café, Cannock	
31st	The Limelight, Crewe	
Nov. 2nd	Trillions, Newcastle	

ULI JON ROTH SKY ACADEMY — 2006
May 26th — UCLA Ralph Freud Theater, Los Angeles, USA. Graham made a guest appearance.

GRAHAM BONNET — 2006
Date	Venue	Tour
July 1st	Blues & Soul Festival, Great Gransden, England	
Aug. 9th	Foxia, Oula	Finnish Tour
10th	Henry's Pub, Kuopio	
11th	Calle Night Club, Kokkola	
12th	Rock To The River Festival, Imatra	
16th	Klubi, Tampere	
17th	On The Rocks, Helsinki	
18th	Sokos Hotel Vaakuna/Night Vaakuna, Mikkeli	
19th	House Of Rock, Kouvola	

TAZ TAYLOR BAND — 2006
Nov. 3rd — Brick By Brick, San Diego, USA

GRAHAM BONNET — 2007
Mar. 23rd — Ahoy, Rotterdam, Holland 'Classics In Rock'

ALCATRAZZ FEATURING GRAHAM BONNET — 2007
May 25th — Paladinos, Tarzana, California, USA

ALCATRAZZ FEATURING GRAHAM BONNET vs JOE LYNN TURNER with Akira Kajiyama
May 30th	O-East, Tokyo	Japanese Tour
31st	O-East, Tokyo	
June 1st	Club Quattro, Osaka	
4th	Zepp Sapporo, Sapporo	

TAZ TAYLOR BAND — 2007
Date	Venue	Tour
Jun. 22, 23rd	Rock Café 2000, Stourbridge	UK Tour
24th	The Iron Works, Inverness	
25th	The Classic Grand, Glasgow	
27th	Riffs, Blackpool	
28th	The Boardwalk, Sheffield	
29th	The Dolls House, Abertillery, Gwent	
30th	The Royal Standard, Walthamstow, London	
July 1st	The Brook, Southampton	
3rd	The Waterfront, Norwich	
5th	The Diamond, Sutton in Ashfield	
6th	The Twist, Colchester	
7th	Riga Music Bar, Southend	
8th	The Stables, Milton Keynes	
10th	The 12 Bar, Swindon	
12th	Komedia, Brighton	
13th	The Nightowl, Cheltenham	
14th	Junction 7, Nottingham	
15th	LA Rock Café, Cannock (cancelled)	

GRAHAM BONNET and JOE LYNN TURNER — 2007
Aug. 8th	Klubi, Tampere	Finnish Tour
9th	Virgin Oil Co, Helsinki	
10th	Jurassic Rock Festival, Mikkeli	
11th	Rock To The River Festival, Imatra	

GRAHAM BONNET The Countdown Spectacular 2 Tour — 2007
Aug. 18th	Entertainment Centre, Newcastle	Australia Tour
21st	Entertainment Centre, Brisbane	
24th	Acer Arena, Sydney	
28th	Entertainment Centre, Hobart, Derwent	
30th	Rod Laver Arena, Melbourne	
Sept. 2nd	Entertainment Centre, Adelaide	
5th	Burswood Dome, Perth	
Dec. 5th	Niceto Club, Buenos Aires, Argentina	

ALCATRAZZ FEATURING GRAHAM BONNET — 2007
Dec. 31st — The Avalon, Santa Clara, California, USA (supporting Y & T)

TAZ TAYLOR BAND — 2008
Jan. 4th — Knitting Factory, Hollywood, California, USA

ALCATRAZZ FEATURING GRAHAM BONNET — 2008
- Jan. 18th — Loffler's, Anaheim, California, USA
- Feb. 29th — Paladinos, Tarzana, California, USA

TAZ TAYLOR BAND — 2008
Date	Venue	Tour
Apr. 4th	Gladhaus, Cottbus, Germany	European Tour
5th	Kato, Berlin, Germany	
6th	Logo, Hamburg, Germany	
7th	Nachtleben, Frankfurt, Germany	
9th	Zeche, Bochum, Germany	
10th	Spectrum, Augsburg, Germany	

Alcatrazz • *San Diego, June 11th 2011.*

11th	Rock City, Zurich, Switzerland	
13th	Rockfabrik, Bruschal, Germany	
15th	Hammerhalle, Citydome, Rosenheim, Germany	
16th	Planet, Vienna, Austria	
17th	Avalon, Budapest, Hungary	
18th	Retro Music, Prague, Czech Republic	

GRAHAM BONNET and JOE LYNN TURNER — 2008

June 4th	Teatria, Oulu	Finnish Tour
5th	Puijonsarvi, Kuopio	
6th	Ice Rink, Rauma	
8th	Sauna Open Air, Tempere	
11th	Tavastia Klubi, Helsinki	
12th	Klubi, Turku	
15th	Myötätuuli Rock, Vantaa	

GRAHAM BONNET — 2008

June 28th	BikeFest-2008, Maloyaroslavec	Russian Tour
29th	Club Grafit, Moscow	

ALCATRAZZ FEATURING GRAHAM BONNET — 2008

July 26th	BerkRock Festival 2008, Berkovitsa, Bulgaria

MARIO PARGA & SAVAGE PARADISE — 2009

Jan. 17th	NAMM Show, Anaheim, California, USA

ALCATRAZZ FEATURING GRAHAM BONNET — 2009

Feb. 13th	Paladinos, Tarzana, California, USA
27th	The Haunt, Yonkers, New York, USA
28th	Jaxx, Springfield, Virginia, USA

GRAHAM BONNET — 2009

July 2nd	SESC, Santos	Brazil Tour
10th	Araraquara Rock, Araraquara	
11th	Blackmore Rock Bar, Sao Paulo	
Aug. 26th	Osmo's Cosmos Bar, Imatra	Finnish Tour
27th	Wanha Satama, Kuopio	
28th	Sokos Hotel Night Club, Mikkeli	
29th	House of Rock, Kouvola	

ALCATRAZZ FEATURING GRAHAM BONNET — 2009

Sept. 12th	Arena Santa Lucia, Monterrey (supporting Testament)	Mexican Tour
13th	Salon Vive Cuervo, Mexico City (supporting Testament)	
Nov. 25th	Kult 8034, Germering, Germany	European Tour
26th	Zeche Carl, Essen, Germany	
27th	The Rock Temple, Kerkrade, Holland	
Dec. 2nd	Orpheum, Graz, Austria	
3rd	Szene, Vienna, Austria	
4th	Exit Chmelnice, Prague, Czech Republic	

ALCATRAZZ FEATURING GRAHAM BONNET — 2010

May 22nd	Paladinos, Tarzana, California, USA (warm-up gig for Russian Tour)	
27th	Jaggar Club, St. Petersburg	Russian Tour
28th	JIMI Club, Moscow	
31st	Rk Ogni Ufy, Ufa City	
June 3rd	News Pub, Volgograd City	

ALCATRAZZ FEATURING GRAHAM BONNET The Voices of Rainbow — 2010

Show featured sets by Graham Bonnet, Joe Lynn Turner and Doogie White.

27th	Big Cat, Osaka	Japanese Tour
29th	Bottom Line, Nagoya	
30th	Shibuya C.C. Lemon Hall, Tokyo	

GBS (Giardino / Bonnet / Smith) — 2010

Dec. 18th	Teatro Flores, Buenos Aires, Argentina.

ALCATRAZZ FEATURING GRAHAM BONNET — 2011

Jan. 20th	Ventura Theater, Ventura, California	
March 31st	Wolf Den in the Mohegan Sun Casino, Uncasville, Connecticut	
June 11th	4th & B, San Diego, California	
July 2nd	House of Blues, West Hollywood, Los Angeles, CA (supporting Hurricane)	
Nov. 28th	Spodek, Katowice, Poland (supporting Whitesnake)	European Tour
29th	Golum Club, Zlin, Czech Republic (headliners)	
Dec. 1st	7er Club, Mannheim, Germany (headliners)	
3rd	Rock Temple, Kerkrade, Netherlands (headliners)	

GRAHAM BONNET — 2011

Dec. 15th	Hard Rock Café, Hollywood, California, USA

Acoustic set with Howie Simon for the United Rockers 4U American Red Cross Benefit Concert for Disaster Relief.

ALCATRAZZ FEATURING GRAHAM BONNET — 2012

Feb. 10th	Marquee 15, Corona, California, USA

GRAHAM BONNET — 2012

Feb. 22nd	Music Town Club (Indoor Festival), Moscow, Russia	
March 14th	Klubi, Tampere	Finnish Tour
15th	Virgin Oil, Helsinki	
16th	House Of Rock, Kouvola	
17th	Osmo's Cosmos Bar, Imatra	
June 30th	Dubrava Hall, Sergiev Posad, Russia	

ALCATRAZZ FEATURING GRAHAM BONNET — 2012

Nov. 17th	Wolf Den in the Mohegan Sun Casino, Uncasville, Connecticut, USA

ROCKSTAR — 2012

Dec. 18th	Krysha Mira, Moscow	Russian Tour
19th	Venue Unknown, Moscow	
20th	Music Town Rock Club, Moscow	

ALCATRAZZ FEATURING GRAHAM BONNET — 2012

Dec. 28th	Studio Seven, Seattle, Washington, USA

ALCATRAZZ FEATURING GRAHAM BONNET The Voices of Rainbow — 2013

Show featured sets by Graham Bonnet, Joe Lynn Turner and Doogie White.

March 13th	Nakano Sun Plaza, Tokyo	Japanese Tour
13th	Bottom Line, Nagoya	
14th	Club Quatro, Osaka	
Mar. 16-20th	Monsters Of Rock Cruise, USA	

GRAHAM BONNET Legends - The Voices of Rock Tour — 2013

Show featured Graham Bonnet, Bill Champlin, Bobby Kimball and Steve Augeri.

April 17th	Istropolis, Bratislava, Slovakia	European Tour
18th	Szene Club, Vienna, Austria	
21st	Joy Eslava, Madrid, Spain	

HARDLY DANGEROUS — 2013

June 25th	Whiskey A Go Go, West Hollywood, LA. Graham made a guest appearance.

GRAHAM BONNET — 2013

29th	Blues & Soul Festival, Great Gransden, Cambridge, England

ALCATRAZZ FEATURNG GRAHAM BONNET — 2013

Sept. 1st	Carioca Club, San Paulo, Brazil

GRAHAM BONNET Legends - The Voices of Rock Tour — 2013

Show featured Graham Bonnet, Eric Martin and Bobby Kimball.

Oct. 18th	Hotell Lapland, Lycksele	Swedish Tour
19th	Hotell Lapland, Lycksele	
20th	Rock City, Nottingham, England (Firefest event)	
23rd	Konserthuset, Växjö	
24th	Konserthuset, Karlskrona	
25th	Konserthuset, Helsingborg	
26th	Teatern, Halmstad	
27th	Konserthuset, Kristianstad	
29th	Teatern, Ystad	
30th	Kalmarsalen, Kalmar	
31st	Konserthuset, Jönköping	
Nov 1st	Valhall, Skövde	
2nd	Hotel Tanumstrand, Grebbestad	

GRAHAM BONNET — 2014

March 16th	Fibbers, York	UK Tour
17th	The Robin 2, Bilston	
18th	Bierkeller, Bristol	
19th	The Garage, London	
20th	The River Rooms, Stourbridge	
21st	Warehouse 23, Wakefield	
22nd	Hard Rock Hell Festival, Pwllheli	
23rd	The Grape & Vine, Workington	
24th	The Liquid Rooms, Edinburgh	

BONNET — 2014

May 2nd — Carpenter Community Charter School, Studio City, Los Angeles, USA

GRAHAM BONNET — 2014

July 11th	Bang Your Head Festival, Messegelände, Balingen, Germany	
August 7th	Stopp Pressen, Oslo, Norway	Scandinavian Tour
8th	Restaurang, Vasterhus, Gothenburg, Sweden	

GRAHAM BONNET Anthems Of Rock

Featuring Graham Bonnet, Bobby Kimball and Nik Kershaw.

9th — Bonna Rock, Kopparberg, Sweden

BONNET — 2014

Sept. 20th — Whiskey A Go Go, West Hollywood, Los Angeles, USA

GRAHAM BONNET — 2014

Oct. 18th	Stormbringer Rock Club, Gjovik, Norway
19th	Sports Hall, Fauske, Norway

BONNET — 2014

Nov. 13th	Bikini Club, Barcelona, Spain	European and UK Tour
14th	Sala Caracol, Madrid, Spain	
15th	Backstage Club, Bilbao, Spain	
28th	The Patronaat, Haarlem, Holland	
Dec. 1st	O2 Academy 2, Islington, London	
2nd	O2 Academy 2, Sheffield	
3rd	O2 Academy 2, Liverpool	
4th	O2 ABC 2, Glasgow	
5th	Academy 2, Birmingham (shows in Newcastle and Southampton cancelled)	

GRAHAM BONNET — 2015

Mar. 11th — Lucky Strike, Hollywood, California, USA Graham made a guest appearance.

GRAHAM BONNET Living Legends of Rock Tour

Featuring sets by Graham Bonnet, John Lawton and Dan McCafferty.

May 7th — Velka Synagoga, Pilsen. Czech Republic

11th	Fesco Hall, Vladivostok, Russia
13th	Platinum Arena, Khabarovsk, Russia
17th	Andrey-Arena (Afips), Krasnodar, Russia
20th	Drama Theater, Rostov on Don, Russia
22nd	Festival Concert Hall, Sochi, Russia
24th	October Palace, Kiev, Ukraine

GRAHAM BONNET BAND — 2015

The band supported Micheal Schenker's Temple Of Rock and Graham sung 'Assault Attack' and 'Desert Song' with them every night.

June 14th	Zepp Namba, Osaka	Japanese Tour
15th	Diamond Hall, Nagoya	
17th	Nakano Sun Plaza, Tokyo	
18th	Nakano Sun Plaza, Tokyo	
19th	Nakano Sun Plaza, Tokyo	
July 22nd	Lucky Strike, Hollywood, California, USA The band made a guest appearance.	
25th	Whiskey A Go Go, Hollywood, Los Angeles, USA (Cruefest event)	

GRAHAM BONNET — 2015

August 1st — Rock Of Ages Festival, Seebronn / Rottenburg, near Stuttgart, Germany

Graham made a guest appearance with Michael Schenker's Temple Of Rock singing 'Assault Attack' and 'Desert Song'.

Nov. 12th — Count's Vamp'd, Las Vegas, USA

Graham was a special guest of the Sin City Sinners.

GRAHAM BONNET BAND — 2016

Jan. 22nd	Malone's, Santa Ana, California, USA This was part of the NAMM event.	
Jan. 29th	Butlins, Minehead ('Giants Of Rock' weekend)	UK Tour
30th	Level 3, Swindon	
Feb. 3rd	The Suncastle, Skegness	
4th	The Venue, Carlisle	
5th	O2 ABC 2, Glasgow	
6th	O2 Academy 2, Newcastle	
7th	O2 Academy 2, Sheffield	
9th	Brudenell Social Club, Leeds	
10th	Rebellion Bar, Manchester	
11th	O2 Academy 2, Liverpool	
12th	Slade Rooms, Wolverhampton	
13th	Waterfront, Norwich	
16th	The Haunt, Brighton	
17th	Sin City, Swansea	
18th	Talking Heads, Southampton	
19th	Bierkeller, Bristol	
20th	O2 Academy 2, Islington, London	

GRAHAM BONNET Legends of Rock Tour — 2016

Featuring Graham Bonnet, John Lawton and Dan McCafferty.

Mar. 22nd	Lucerna Velký sál, Prague. Czech Republic
24th	Multifunkční Centrum, Gong, Ostrava. Czech Republic

GRAHAM BONNET BAND — 2016

Apr 20th	Möysän Esso, Lahti, Finland	Scandinavian and European Tour
21st	On The Rocks, Helsinki, Finland	
22nd	Viking Line MS Mariella (Cruise - ferry from Helsinki to Stockholm)	
23rd	Plugged Records, Gamla Stan, Stockholm, Sweden (promo 30 mins set)	
24th	Live Club, Trezzo, Milan, Italy Part of the Frontiers Rock Festival III.	
June 8th	Sweden Rock Festival	

GRAHAM BONNET — 2016

June 10th — Sweden Rock Festival Graham sang three songs as part of the Michael Schenker Fest.

GRAHAM BONNET BAND — 2016

June 12th — Göta Källare, Stockholm, Sweden

GRAHAM BONNET		2016
June 25th	Voxbotn Festival, Tórshavn, Faroe Islands	

GRAHAM BONNET BAND		2016
July 29th	'Rock Of Ages' Festival, Seebronn / Rottenburg, near Stuttgart, Germany	
30th	'Classic Rock Night' Festival Brauereigutshof, Pyras, Thalmässing, Germany	

GRAHAM BONNET Voices Of Rainbow		2016
August 5th	Open-air show, Saarbrücken, Germany (with Doogie White)	

GRAHAM BONNET		
Aug. 23rd	Zepp Namba, Osaka	Japanese Tour
24th	International Hall A, Tokyo	
26th	Zepp Sapporo, Hokkaido	

Graham sang three songs at the first two shows and four on the last as part of the Michael Schenker Fest on this short Japanese tour. He also sung the first verse on 'Doctor Doctor' in the encore each night.

GRAHAM BONNET BAND		2016
Nov. 3rd	Sala Chango, Madrid	Spanish Tour
4th	Sala Totem, Pamplona	
5th	Sala Capitol, Santiago de Compstela	
8th	Boston Music Room, London	UK and Irish Tour
9th	River Rooms, Stourbridge	
10th	Warehouse 23, Wakefield	
11th	Hard Rock Hell Festival, Pwllheli	
12th	Club Academy, Manchester	
13th	Bannermans, Edinburgh	
15th	Diamond Live Lounge, Doncaster	
16th	Think Tank, Newcastle	
18th	Nerve Centre, Londonderry	
19th	Limelight 2 Belfast	
20th	Monroes, Galway	
21st	Voodoo Lounge, Dublin	
22nd	Fuel Rock Club, Cardiff	

Backstage • *Graham's manager Giles Lavery (left) with Graham being interviewed by journalist Jon Kirkman before the Manchester show Nov. 2016. Tasty looking kebab Jon.*

APPENDIX TWO • About the songs

A listing of Graham's song-writing with his recollections of the inspiration behind them.

MARBLES 1969

Little Laughing Girl (Graham Bonnet)

"This was a song for my niece Vicky, whom I babysat, along with her brother Vincent, most weeks when I was at home. It is about the sadness I felt when she got upset, as she was always having fun when we were together, but all little kids cry and it's sad that it happens. So small and young, but sadness effects all of us, even though we have had very short life experiences that would effect us in such a hard way."

GRAHAM BONNET 1972 - 1978

Rare Specimen (Graham Bonnet) Written in the mid 60s

"I made up this song after seeing a title in the Radio Times for a show about butterflies called Rare Specimen. So I applied that to a person."

Dog Song (Graham Bonnet) Released by Adrienne Posta

"It was a very simple song, but from the heart so to speak about our dog, Sachi. It was just a novelty song for my own amusement, but I'd had it around for a while."

Dreams (Out In The Forest) (Graham Bonnet)

"The song is just about a dream really!"

We're Free (Graham Bonnet)

"This is pretty self-explanatory. It is about gigging around the clubs for peanuts and wanting to become successful."

Back Row In The Stalls (Graham Bonnet)

"This is about schooldays and the weekend movie shows for kids on Saturday afternoons. There were cartoons and a series that you would follow week to week, like Superman, or some other superhero. It's in the words in the song."

Ghost Writer In My Eye (Graham Bonnet)

"This song is about someone who is telling lies about me so he can get my girl. The title was a play on an old pop/country song from the 50s, 'Ghost Riders In The Sky', which Burl Ives did. I first heard it when I was about 5 years old."

Untitled (Here Comes The Rain) (Graham Bonnet)

"This is about a straightforward break up. The 'Untitled' bit is because that was on the tape box for a while as I didn't have a title. So we always referred to it as untitled!"

Don't Drink The Water (Graham Bonnet)

"The words tell the story about a trip abroad. The water there is best drunk from the bottles. Everyone does it now, but back then it was unusual!"

Wino Song (Graham Bonnet)

"This was my observations of the winos in Hyde Park in London, where I walked my Old English sheep dog every day, seeing them and sort of getting to know them to say 'hi' to. There was a guy that used to lie in the park, on the tar paths, singing to the path kind of thing. They were always there, purple faced and very sad, but I could not ignore them, as people often do. They liked it when you spoke to them. Of course these people were homeless."

10/12 Observation (Graham Bonnet)

"This is about the question of UFO's. Are they real, and mysteries like why the dinosaurs died etc. Things like that. The title was the date we recorded it. So unexplained mysteries ... it's in the words."

High School Angel (Music Graham Bonnet / Words Peter Hutchins)

"It is my tune and his words. It is about the way school girls look so mature, and need to be more honest with their age kind of thing."

MSG 1982

Assault Attack (Schenker / Bonnet / Glen / McKenna)

"A regular break up between a girl and a boy. Also, the lies what people tell each other, 'Don't you want me? You did I know, why leave me, then go!' Quite silly and straight forward. Probably daft words, but sung with aggression and anger because of the woman's lies. Well, that was my intention!"

Rock You To The Ground (Music Michael Schenker / Words Graham Bonnet)

"This it is about drug taking and how we become unaware that this could maybe kill us. Police arresting users, but the user is immortal, so he thinks."

Dancer (Music Michael Schenker / Words Graham Bonnet)

"When I went to Los Angeles with Adrienne to do the 'Lampoon' show that was shelved in 1974, because of a law suit with the magazine of the same name, I met Toni Basil. She had her own dance group called The Lockers and had five guys she did routines with in parts of the show. Toni also told me her group had opened up for David Bowie on some of his shows, as well as warmed up the crowd for Muhammad Ali in the boxing ring, before his fights. Years later suddenly she is making a single and I saw her on TV, and she suddenly was a pop star in England. Then I read an article somewhere, about her shows and made the song up from the article I read. As I knew her, it was a real surprise she was suddenly a star! But I haven't seen her after our first meeting in LA, back in '74. I never had any phone numbers or addresses from that first trip."

Samurai (Schenker / Bonnet / Glen)

"Samurai is about a warrior fighting for peace so he can return to his lover, but even if he dies, no one can take his feelings away that he has for her."

Desert Song (Music Michael Schenker / Words Graham Bonnet)

"The ships of the desert are camels. That's what they are nicknamed. Sailing ships, hence riding camels. It's just a colourful way of saying something ordinary. 'Heat of a dusky lady, born of the sand' is a native Arabian woman who is hot for sex. You know the double meaning? 'Burning with desert fire, cooling the man' means wearing him out! 'Desert fire' is an energetic, native sexual maniac!"

Broken Promises (Schenker / Bonnet / Glen)

"Is just another story basically, right kind of woman, but you know something's not right, and she is keeping you hanging on. She says one thing and does the opposite. Not keeping to her word. So, you have to make a decision as whether to leave her or not, but deep down you want to stay with her."

Searching For A Reason (Music Michael Schenker / Words Graham Bonnet)

"It says what it means. No hidden message. Pretty straight forward. Everyone has a right to live, so what are we fighting for and why all the wars? Does anyone have an answer?"

Girl From Uptown (Music Michael Schenker / Words Graham Bonnet)

"This it is about a girl who is out of reach. Too good for me. So I would wait and watch her. I think that was the story. It sounds boring doesn't it?"

ALACTRAZZ 1983 - 1986

Island In The Sun (Bonnet / Malmsteen / Waldo)

"This was a tongue in cheek title, you know, the perfect place, but this wasn't. It was a place where people killed each other in a prison environment. Sarcastic, maybe that's what the title is. It was in fact a place of horror."

General Hospital (Bonnet / Malmsteen / Waldo)

"It's about my first epileptic seizure and when I went to Whittington hospital in London. The worst hospital you can imagine. I think it got closed down. It was creepy, and very old, with a bad reputation. This is when Ade and I were together in Highgate. They put me in the ward for terminally sick people, as that was the only space there. It was like a cattle shed."

Jet To Jet (Music Yngwie Malmsteen / Words Graham Bonnet)

"This is about drunken vacationers going to Africa. The words are the story. 'Jet', Black and 'Jet', the plane, so Jet To Jet."

Hiroshima Mon Amour (Music Yngwie Malmsteen / Words Graham Bonnet)

"It's about the bomb and named after the film, because it was something that moved me when I was a child. I just couldn't believe what happened and that people would do such things."

Kree Nakoorie (Bonnet / Malmsteen / Waldo)

"The Kree Nakoorie are a tribe of people who live in South America and who had never seen white people. They lived like this for thousands of years, without change. Their real name is Krenakarore. The song is about interrupting their lives. I saw a documentary on them on TV years before the song. People have actually emailed me to tell me they have found out about them by checking them out on google!"

Too Young To Die, Too Drunk To Live (Music Yngwie Malmsteen / Words Graham Bonnet)

"It is about high school kids with every day habits as it was, and still is. Then in the last verse I say, 'Years from now, look how they are', meaning they have changed etc. But the guy comes home from work and asks for a drink. So the addiction is still there, but more acceptable. Alcohol, instead of cocaine let's say. So they are still addicts."

Big Foot (Music Yngwie Malmsteen / Words Graham Bonnet)

"Big Foot is about the Yeti."

Starcarr Lane (Bonnet / Malmsteen / Waldo)

"It is where I used to spend my summer vacation as a child. I would go to my Granddad's on my Dad's side who lived in Wrawby, near Brigg. There was lots of open fields and farmland there."

Suffer Me (Music Yngwie Malmsteen / Words Graham Bonnet)

"This is about my Mum suffering. Also, my behaviour and disappointments."

God Blessed Video (Music Steve Vai / Words Graham Bonnet)

"Self explanatory. It was inspired by watching a Duran Duran video. Crappy song, but great video. So the words tell the story, which is about spending money on videos in exotic places ... so we went to Hawaii!"

Mercy (Vai / Bonnet / Waldo / Shea / Uvena)

"Mercy is about the cruel way the Tiger was killed for its skin and we should never have to kill animals for fashion, or as a showing of wealth. The stupidity of the merciless killing and the cruelty."

Will You Be Home Tonight (Vai / Bonnet / Waldo)

"This is about James Dean. The words explain the story. He loved to drive and it also tells a tale of we shouldn't drink and drive, but mainly it's about him."

Wire And Wood (Music Steve Vai / Words Graham Bonnet)

"This one is about the guitar, the rock and roll instrument of all rock songs. It's made of wood and wire, wire and wood. Guitar strings are wire … etc."

Desert Diamond (Music Steve Vai / Words Graham Bonnet)

"Desert Diamond is about the pyramids being diamond shaped and their mystery."

Stripper (Music Steve Vai / Words Graham Bonnet)

"This isn't about any particular person, just a stripper."

Painted Lover (Music Steve Vai / Words Graham Bonnet)

"The song tells the story that it's fun once in a while for some people to pay for a lay ...."

Sons And Lovers (Music Steve Vai / Words Graham Bonnet)

"As with all my tunes, the story is in the words. This is about life on the road."

Skyfire (Music Steve Vai / Words Graham Bonnet)

"This is about what I saw in the sky in 1982, outside my window, over towards Malibu was a large green object. It was sort of misty stuff that hung there for an hour or so. People were calling the TV stations to ask what it was. We were told it was the fuel burn from a rocket testing."

Breaking The Heart Of The City (Music Steve Vai / Words Graham Bonnet)

"This is the story of John Lennon and his killer."

Undercover (Johnson / Waldo / Bonnet)

"A girl spy who lies to her lover kind of thing. It explains itself I think."

That Ain't Nothing (Eime-Bonnet / Johnson / Shea / Waldo / Unvena)

"This is about being ripped off by managers and agents."

No Imagination (Josephine Eime-Bonnet)

"This song is about a woman who thinks she's really something sexually, but when it comes round to it she is kind of boring."

Ohayo Tokyo (Josephine Eime-Bonnet)

"The Tokyo song is about the experience of going to Japan. My first impressions. Lunacy back in the day. Good morning or good evening. It means one or the other … Ohayo."

Blue Boar (Eime-Bonnet / Johnson / Waldo)

"Blue Boar was the services on the M1 and other motorways in England. Lots of bands used to stop off there, as there was nowhere else much back then. It's very famous."

The Witchwood (Johnson / Eime-Bonnet / Waldo)

"This is about the woods. Highgate Woods where I would walk my dog at night sometimes in the early 70s, and so called witches did their games in there. Performing their rituals at certain times of the year."

Double Man (Shea / Eime-Bonnet / Johnson / Waldo / Unvena)

"This one is about seeing myself."

Night Of The Shooting Star (Josephine Eime-Bonnet)
"This is about Haley's comet. We will only see it once in a life time. It comes around every 100 years or something but, this song can relate also to a romantic love theme. A double meaning."

IMPELLITTERI 1988 (songs written in 1987)

Stand In Line (Music Chris Impellitteri / Words Graham Bonnet)
"This is about the good looking guy, who has all the girls wanting him, well, so he thinks. It's about his high self-esteem."

Secret Lover (Music Chris Impellitteri / Words Graham Bonnet)
"This song is about a drinker in secret, but the drink is the most important thing in the drinker's life. In the words it tells the story. It is the drinker's lover and nothing will kill their love."

Tonight I Fly (Music Chris Impellitteri / Words Graham Bonnet)
"This one is about the British actress, who jumped from the Hollywood sign!"

White And Perfect (Impellitteri / Bonnet / Wright / Torpey)
"Young, gifted and black. It's about being ashamed of being white. The English have done bad things. So I answered it with this."

Leviathan (Impellitteri / Bonnet / Wright / Torpey)
"It is about the Loch Ness Monster and is it really there."

Goodnight And Goodbye (Music Chris Impellitteri / Words Graham Bonnet)
"The lyrics are about the one night stand. Hello, goodbye type of thing."

FORCEFIELD 1990

Women On Wings (R. Fenwick / C. Powell / J. Eime)
"This is about flight attendants and their fake joy of being flying waiters and having to be so nice to all the demanding passengers etc."

Living By Numbers (R. Fenwick / C. Powell / J. Eime)
"Here, I talk about the outside world instructions on bottles V8 juice and 10CC for example. It's like painting by numbers. All the rules and info' we get is in measurements and numbers, age and everything."

GRAHAM BONNET 1991

Long Time Gone (Jo Eime)
"Live while you can. You will be a long time dead … Morbid huh?!!"

Look Don't Touch (Jo Eime)
"This is about telling guys to keep away from a girl I want back, but she is very vulnerable. So keep away."

Please Call Me (R. Fenwick / J. Eime)
"A broken hearted girl advertising in the newspaper for the perfect guy."

What She Says, You Hear It Means (R. Fenwick / J. Eime)
"When a woman tells you something, she says one thing. You hear that, but misunderstand what she really means. It's all misinterpreted. The things women say to men sometimes have different actual meanings. So leaves you in confusion as to actually what they are telling you."

BLACKTHORNE 1993 (songs written in 1992)

Cradle To The Grave (Bob Kulick / Jimmy Waldo / J. E. Bonnet / Steven Rosen)
"This one is about birth to death. Simple as that!"

Afterlife (J. E. Bonnet / Jimmy Waldo / Bob Kulick / Steven Rosen)
"This was one of the better songs we made up and it is about the rebirth of musicians who had been out of the spotlight for a while."

Sex Crime (J. E. Bonnet / Bob Kulick / Jimmy Waldo / Steve Plunkett)
"This song is about child abuse. Steve Plunkett made most of it up. It is a stupid song. This was virtually nothing to do with me. I just sang it."

Love From The Ashes (J. E. Bonnet / Jimmy Waldo / Bob Kulick / Steven Rosen)
"Rebirth of a dead love."

GRAHAM BONNET 1997 - 1999 (songs written between 1996 and 1998)

Underground (Eime / Johnson / Valentine / Regan)
"Danny wrote most of this song, with a couple of lines from me. It was mainly his."

Whiplash (Eime / Johnson) Originally written in 1988
"This is about naughty things that go on behind closed doors … you know … sex stuff!!!"

Breakaway (Eime)
"I think this one is about breaking away from a bad relationship."

Movin' On (Eime)
"Don't look back on what you have done in your life, but look forward to better things."

The Strange (Eime / Johnson / St. James / Regan)
"This is Danny's song. He wrote most of it and I possibly added some words and part of the melody."

Cajun Pink (Eime / Johnson / Valentine)
"This is about New Orleans. The Cajun women and the drink Hurricane, which is very strong! Cajun Pink being a hidden meaning of the naughty parts of the Cajun high yellow woman. High yellow being bi/racial, black with white parents and the rest is self explanatory. It's a great music place and Bourbon Street being the main area for that."

Winter Skin (Eime / Johnson)
"Winter Skin was fucked up by Pat Reagan. He mixed the vocals wrong. The falsetto was the lead and he thought it sounded too girly, or like Brian Wilson. The original mix we did was good. We recorded it live, vocal and all. It is about a ghost woman that I imagined that the guy in the song would see in hot summer days, but she never got darker skin. So she wasn't real. There were some Indian chants at the end, but again they were taken out and it spoiled the whole song. The low octave that became the lead (by Regan) was a very casual vocal and not spot-on as the higher one was. So a completely messed up track! The first mix I did with Kevin was rather good, a real shame."

The Day I Went Mad (Jo Eime)
"It is saying how horrible things we see and hear about can be entertaining like plane crashes and car accidents. People love to stop and look. Murder is fascinating and we all cheer when a cop kills a bad guy, but he is a murderer also. That kind of thing is all in there. We are all a little mad that's what I think when I am watching other people's misery."

Killer (Jo Eime / Kevin Valentine / Danny Johnson)
"This is about one of my heroes, Jerry Lee Lewis. I'm just saying don't ever say anything bad about him, as Elvis did and he threatened to go and shoot Elvis as he gave him some bad press."

Hey That's Me (Jo Eime)
"It is just me saying, wait a minute that's me over there."

This Day (Jo Eime)
"This one was inspired by my English teacher at school. He made a movie at school with that title. It is cherishing the moment we will always have this day and every day is a gift, or not sometimes. Blackbirds on the wires are like music notes making a melody on the power lines like when reading music."

Flying Not Falling (Jo Eime)
"My tribute to Cozy as he was always taking risks and looking for thrills, climbing up a radio tower was one thing he did and up the side of a hotel and through a window to someone's room. He was always the daredevil."

Lolita Crush (Jo Eime)
"It's about the older man lusting after a younger girl and basically stalking her as she leaves school every day, but he can't approach her as he knows it's wrong."

Model Inc (Jo Eime / Kevin Valentine / Danny Johnson / Pat Regan)
"Named after the TV show, it is about the needs to be a model, young, thin and of course beautiful, almost impossible."

Spiked! (Jo Eime / John Thomas)
"This is about being pierced and having tattoos beyond ridiculous. If there is some unmarked skin, it needs some decorating or piercing."

Greenwich Meantime (Jo Eime)
"This one's about the people of Greenwich village, San Francisco. The art community and how they are different from your regular guys … meanwhile back in Greenwich …"

IMPELLITTERI 2002 (songs written in 2001)

Perfect Crime (Music Chris Impellitteri / Words Jo Eime)
"This is about a guy who is driving his friends around … me … in Los Angeles and they get involved in a shooting and he doesn't realise that his friends are gang bangers. So they committed the prefect crime by hiding their true identity."

She's A Nighttime Lover (Music Chris Impellitteri / Words Jo Eime)
"This song has terrible words. I think Chris may have written some of them, but I'm not sure. It sounds like filler words from me playing on an old theme … like 'Painted Lover'. The song was mainly Chris' idea, but the melody was mine. Not my kind of words though or my title."

Slow Kill (Music Chris Impellitteri / Words Jo Eime)
"This is a true story of some people that kept their child under the stairs and I think she died. The ultimate in cruelty and they were her parents!"

Why Do They Do That (Music Chris Impellitteri / Words Jo Eime)
"It is about people's jealousy at other people's acquirements, wealth, cars and the anger it causes in some. Cozy inspired this song. He was in a store in England and some little jerk decided that his BMW should be keyed, and scratched it all along the side. Cozy saw that happen and rushed him and threw him across the hood of the car and made him pay for it … or die!"

Rock & Roll Heroes (Music Chris Impellitteri / Words Jo Eime)
"Basically, this is about being a band member, but the reality is about all the trappings. It's about all the merchandise you can move, and really the other side of music is all about how to make money and that can be more than the actual performance fee and the crowd no nothing about this. Well, they do now, but I'm talking years ago!"

Gotta Get Home (Music Chris Impellitteri / Words Jo Eime)
"This is about my trip to Tijuana and how horrible it was. It's just like Skegness, but dirtier and with a Spanish accent. Plus, the tourist crap for sale and painted animals. The cruelty of it all!"

What Kind Of Sanity (Music Chris Impellitteri / Words Jo Eime)
"I didn't write the words to this song as they are too flowery and nondescript, but I must have contributed something!"

IAIN ASHLEY HERSEY 2005

Although Graham is credited on two songs, Iain wrote the lyrics, as well as the music, as explained in the book: **Walking The Talk** (Hersey / Bonnet) and **The Holy Grail** (Hersey / Bonnet)

MSG 2006

Rock 'N' Roll (Music Michael Schenker / Words Graham Bonnet)
"It was originally called 'Tales Of Rock An' Roll' as he wanted me to write the title track, but it was changed for political reasons. So as not to make the other singers etc seem a lesser contributor. The song is basically real things that have happened to me within the bands that I have been with. They are all in there, especially the Rainbow guys."

TAZ TAYLOR BAND 2006

Fighter's Fist (Music Neil Taylor / Words Graham Bonnet)
"This is about a girl in a night club who doesn't fall for the corny come-ons that some guys say when trying to pick up girls. And how she had been told when growing up, don't be taken for a ride and have your own mind and strength. So, don't think trying to pick her up will be easy or she'll punch you out!"

Radio Luxembourg (Music Neil Taylor / Words Graham Bonnet)
"Here are my first memories of hearing rock and pop music. 7 o'clock in the evening or so was when the signal was best!"

Happy Hour (Music Neil Taylor / Words Graham Bonnet)
"Happy Hour is about AA meetings. It was a meeting I went to which lasted an hour and all American office workers etc look forward to that happy hour after work, 5-ish, when drinks are cheaper. So, two meetings for the happy hour, one for drinkers and those wanting to quit."

Haunted (Music Neil Taylor / Words Graham Bonnet)
"This is about a guy whose wife has died and he still loves her and feels her presence around him, in denial basically!"

Welcome To America (Music Neil Taylor / Words Graham Bonnet)
"This one is about Spanish people. Mail Order brides, so to speak. Who get in to the country by marrying Americans."

Wall Of Sound (Music Neil Taylor / Words Graham Bonnet)
"This tells the story of Phil Spector and his arrest on that day and how he crashed and burned in to the wall of sound, so to speak. It's in the words."

Silent Fall (Music Neil Taylor / Words Graham Bonnet)
"This is about the personal pain we all suffer sometimes. Does anyone know and does anyone care? That kind of vibe. It's a in the words and self explanatory."

TOMORROW'S OUTLOOK 2012 (song written in 2010)

Glass Mountain (Music Trond Nicolaisen & Andreas Stenseth / Words Graham Bonnet)
"The guys in the band wanted me to write about the story of Titanic and the idea about changing the iceberg to a glass mountain just came to me. Basically it describes the thing they thought would never go down and the horror of the unsinkable ship. Plus, the loss of lives was unbelievable."

APPENDIX THREE • "Our next song is…"

A list of songs that The Blueset, The Bluesect, The Bluesecte and The Graham Bonnet Set performed between 1965 and early 1968. I am indebted to Steve Hardy, the late Roger Sleath, Bob Turner and Graham himself for much of this information. Graham loved his time performing with his Skegness based bands: "There was no pressure on us at all and it was a wonderful time to play in a band. We played lots of different styles. We played a few Ledbelly songs in The Bluesect. That was an era when Bob Dylan, blues, and folk music all merged … the Mod days … it was fashionable to embrace all kinds of vintage music and new music."

SONGS PERFORMED BY: - THE BLUESET / THE BLUESECT / THE BLUESECTE

Chris Andrews 'I'm Her Yesterday Man'; The Beatles 'Day Tripper', 'I Feel Fine'; The Beatles' version of 'Boys' (Rog on vocals); Chuck Berry 'Johnny B Goode', 'Rock and Roll Music', 'Put On Your High Heel Sneakers', 'Shake', 'Anthony Boy', 'Reelin' And Rockin', 'Roll Over Beethoven'; Blind Blake 'Too Tight'; James Brown 'I'll Go Crazy'; Big Bill Broonzy 'In The Evening (When The Sun Goes Down)'; James Brown 'I Feel Good'; Sam Cooke 'Bring It On Home To Me' (later recorded by The Animals); Bobby Darin 'Up A Lazy River'; Bob Dylan 'Blowin' In The Wind', 'Mighty Quinn', 'Mr. Tambourine Man', 'Corina Corina', 'She Belongs To Me', 'Like A Rolling Stone'; Drifters 'Under the Boardwalk'; Richie Havens 'If I Had A Hammer'; The Kinks 'You Really Got Me'; Huddie (Leadbelly) Ledbetter 'Black Girl', 'Goodnight Irene', 'St. Louis Blues', 'Kansas City Blues', 'Rock Island Line', 'Where Did You Sleep Last Night'; Peggy Lee 'Fever'; Wilson Pickett 'Midnight Hour'; PJ Proby 'Hold Me'; The Rolling Stones 'Walking The Dog', 'Satisfaction'; The Searchers 'Goodbye My Love'; Sonny Boy Williamson 'Bring It On Home'; Stevie Wonder My Cherie Amour' plus 'Rare Specimen', 'Just To Get Her', 'Helen's Gone' written by Graham.

SONGS PERFORMED BY: - THE GRAHAM BONNET SET

The Animals 'Don't Let Me Be Misunderstood'; The Beach Boys 'Do You Wanna Dance'; The Beatles 'Eight Days A Week', 'When I'm Sixty Four', 'Lucy In The Sky With Diamonds', 'Michelle', 'Your Mother Should Know', 'Help', 'If I Fell', 'Got To Get You Into My Life'; The Beatles' version of 'Devil In Her Heart'; Arthur Conley 'Sweet Soul Music'; Lee Dorsey 'Working In A Coalmine'; Georgie Fame 'Yeh Yeh'; Chris Farlowe 'Out Of Time'; Procul Harum 'Whiter Shade Of Pale'; Wilson Pickett 'Midnight Hour', 'Mustang Sally'; The Ronettes 'Be My Baby', 'Baby I love You'; Percy Sledge 'When A Man Loves A Woman'; Spencer Davis Group 'Keep On Running', 'Somebody Help Me', 'I'm A Man'; Jimmy Smith 'Got My Mojo Working'; Tom Jones 'Green Green Grass Of Home'; Ike & Tina Turner 'A Love Like Yours'; The Turtles 'Happy Together', 'Some Girls'; Stevie Wonder 'Hold Me'; Brenton Wood 'Gimme Little Sign'; and The Young Rascals 'Groovin'.

GRAHAM BONNET CREDITS

easy on the eye books / Nethergate / Sheffield.   www.easyontheeyebooks.wordpress.com

Text copyright © Steve Wright / Easy On The Eye Books 2017
Designed by easy on the eye. copyright © Easy On The Eye Books 2017
First edition 2017. British Library Cataloguing in Publication Data. A catalogue record for this book is available from the British Library.
ISBN 978-0-9561439-6-9

All rights reserved. No part of this publication may be reproduced, stored in a retrieval system, or transmitted, in any form or by any means, electronic, mechanical, photocopying, recording or otherwise, without the prior permission of the publishers.

main book set in adobe garamond pro

IMAGE CREDITS • Front cover photograph Mario Parga. Back cover main photo Jeff Price. Other back photos Emili Muraki, Sue Hedley, Peter Dokus, Mercury Records and Graham Bonnet. Graham Bonnet memorabilia page 7, 8, 13, 22, 36, 79, 90 . Graham Bonnet photos page 5, 7, 9, 10, 12 top, 13, 21, 27, 38, 41, 42, 47, 66, 70, 81, 82, 83, 93, 97, 101. Steve Mann page 2. Vicky Bonnett page 6, 40, 68, memorabilia page 41 bottom left. Steve Wright page 12 top right, 113 top, bottom left, 119, 124, 126, 135 and all memorabilia unless credited otherwise. Steve Hardy page 12, 13 top, 16 top right and bottom, 22, 23, memorabilia page 14, 17, 20 (and MU card on inner cover.) Roger Sleath page 14, 15, 16 top left. Barry Plummer page 19, 29, 31. Bob Turner page 18, 20. 21. Christine Acred page 25. Reinhard Wenesch memorabilia page 28 right, 34, 37 left, 49 bottom right, 159 sleeve . Peter Foldy page 33, 34, 35 top. Rex page 38 top. Getty Images page 34 bottom, 41, 74, 75. Victy Silva page 44. Daffy memorabilia 48 top, 72 top right. Dmitry Epstein page 49, Mercury Records photo page 50. Polydor Records photo page 53. Steve Wunrow page 57. Alan Perry page 59, 60 (both), 61. Colin Hart page 64 all. Photoshot page 69. Rex page 72. Vertigo Records photo page 65, 72. Chris Walter page 86, 89. Gary Shea memorabilia page 87. Frank White page 91, 99. Capitol Records page 94, 98. Music For Nations photo page 102. Relativity Records photo page 104. Sue Hedley photos 107, 108, 109, 110. President Records photo page 111. Antonio Scettri photo 113 right. Markus Winterhalter memorabilia page 113 bottom. Peter Nikolic photo page 114. John Tucker photo page 117. Andrew Mon Hughes page 118, Jeff Price page 125, back cover. Dirk Krause photo page 131 left. Patrick Wright photo page 131 right. Val Trainor photo page 132 . Harri Hinkka page 138 below. Martin Motnik photos page 129, 138 top. Junko Ogawara memorabilia page 143 top right. Marko Syrjälä page 136, 137, 144, 145, 146. Emili Muraki page 1, 147, 148, 150, 153, 160, 175, inside front cover. Lenny Warren, 151. Hogne Høysæter page 149. Giles Lavery photos page 154, 155 bottom right. Alex Solca photo page 155 bottom left. Keeley Bonnet photo page 156. Michael Richards page 159 sleeve. Tom Wallace page 4, 115, 139, 143, 165, 167, 176. Simon Robinson, memorabilia page 49, 53, 54, 56, 57, 59, 60, 61, photos page 133, 156. Thanks to John Tucker, Tom Dixon, Alexi Kononov. Every attempt has been made to trace copyright owners, we will be happy to credit anyone we have missed in future editions.

www.facebook.com/grahambonnetmusic/   www.grahambonnetband.com

easyontheeyebooks

BIBLIOGRAPHY

Music magazines quoted from have been credited in the main text. The following titles and sleeve notes proved helpful during the writing of this book.

Melinda Bilyeu, Hector Cook and Andrew Môn Hughes — The Ultimate Biography Of The Bee Gees (Omnibus Press 2000). Deidre Cartwright, Julian Colbeck, Alastair Gavin, Chris Lent, Geoff Nicholls and Henry Thomas — Rockschool II The Book Of The Second BBC TV Series (Music Maker Books 1988)
Brent Currie - Notes in CD the booklet for 'Mable-ized' by the Marbles on Polydor Records in Australia (1994)
Franck Leenheer & Ed Dieckmann - The International Dark Horse & Ring O'Records Discography (Updated & extended edition) - (Self published 2004)
Dave Ling — Notes in the CD booklet for 'Assault Attack' by MSG on EMI / Chrysalis Records in the UK (2009)
Martin Popoff - UFO Shoot Out The Lights (Metal Blade 2005)
Martin Popoff - Rainbow English Castle Magic (Metal Blade 2005)
Martin Popoff - Notes in the CD booklet for 'Live '83' by Alcatrazz on Deadline Music in America (2010)
Guinness World Records British Hit Singles 15th Edition (Guinness World Records Ltd 2002)
Books LLC — The Party Boys Members (Books LLC 2010). Darker Than Blue magazine.

EASY ON THE EYE BOOKS

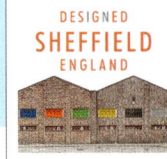
DESIGNED
SHEFFIELD
ENGLAND

OUT NOW

COVERED!
Classic Sleeves And Their Imitators
ISBN: 978-0-9561439-2-1
The title says it all. 1,000 different sleeves shown and annotated; funny, sharp, and subversive versions of well known sleeves by bands from around the globe.

DEEP PURPLE • WAIT FOR THE RICOCHET
The Story of Deep Purple In Rock, 1969 - 1970
ISBN : 978-0-9561439-6-9
A detailed look at one of the most famous and hard hitting rock albums of all time, profusely illustrated. First edition sold out, second edition 2017.

DUE IN 2018

DEEP PURPLE • FIRE IN THE SKY
The Story of Machine Head and Smoke On The Water
ISBN : 978-0-9561439-9-0
From the people who brough you the In Rock book, a detailed look at one of the most influential rock albums of all time, and the single which sold 12 million copies and contains one of the most famous rock riffs of all time.

STARSTRUCK
Art of Japanese Single Sleeve : Volume 1
ISBN: 978-0-9561439-0-7
Japan was one of the first countries to issue vinyl singles in sleeves, and were free to do their own covers. This book presents a stunning selection of 7" covers from the 60s to the 80s, around a thousand sleeves in colour.

WHEN COVER GIRLS RULED THE WORLD
The Story of the Top Of The Pops Albums
ISBN: 978-0-9561439-1-4
Anyone who went to a party in the Seventies will remember the Top Of The Pops albums, budget priced collections of hits with a difference - these were all cover versions! This book tells the story of how the albums came about, the heroic efforts of the session players and of course the famous cover girls.

BOOM BOOM BOOM BOOM • American Rhythm & Blues In England 1962 - 1966 • The photographs of Brian Smith
ISBN : 978-0-9561439-4-5
A stunning collection of mostly never seen before images taken in Manchester during the height of the blues boom.

More details at www.easyontheeyebooks.wordpress.com

We are always interested in hearing from collectors who may have ideas for future titles, contact us via the website. We would much urge customers to order from their local bookshop and support them. The big online retailers demand massive discounts which are especially damaging to small independent publishers, bookshops and specialist retailers.

Alcatrazz • San Diego, June 11th 2011.